The Great Ocean

The Great Ocean

Pacific Worlds from Captain Cook to the Gold Rush

DAVID IGLER

OXFORD
UNIVERSITY PRESS

OXFORD
UNIVERSITY PRESS

Oxford University Press is a department of the University of Oxford.
It furthers the University's objective of excellence in research,
scholarship, and education by publishing worldwide.

Oxford   New York

Auckland   Cape Town   Dar es Salaam   Hong Kong   Karachi
Kuala Lumpur   Madrid   Melbourne   Mexico City   Nairobi
New Delhi   Shanghai   Taipei   Toronto

With offices in

Argentina   Austria   Brazil   Chile   Czech Republic   France   Greece
Guatemala   Hungary   Italy   Japan   Poland   Portugal   Singapore
South Korea   Switzerland   Thailand   Turkey   Ukraine   Vietnam

Oxford is a registered trade mark of Oxford University Press
in the UK and certain other countries.

Published in the United States of America by
Oxford University Press
198 Madison Avenue, New York, NY 10016

Library of Congress Cataloging-in-Publication Data
Igler, David, 1964–
The great ocean : Pacific worlds from Captain Cook to the gold rush / David Igler.
pages cm
Includes bibliographical references and index.
ISBN 978-0-19-991495-1 (hardcover : alk. paper); 978-0-19-049875-7 (paperback : alk. paper)
1. Pacific Ocean—Discovery and exploration. 2. Culture diffusion—Pacific Area—History—
18th century. 3. Culture diffusion—Pacific Area—History—19th century. 4. Pacific Area—
Commerce—History—18th century. 5. Pacific Area—Commerce—History—19th century.
6. Indigenous peoples—Pacific Area—History—18th century. 7. Indigenous peoples—Pacific
Area—History—19th century. 8. Natural history—Pacific Area—History—18th century. 9.
Natural history—Pacific Area—History—19th century. 10. East and West. I. Title.
DU20.I45   2013
909'.09823081—dc23   2012038256

1 3 5 7 9 8 6 4 2

Printed in the United States of America
on acid-free paper

To Cindy, for everything significant and ordinary

CONTENTS

Acknowledgments   ix

Introduction: Ocean Worlds   3
1. Seas of Commerce   17
2. Disease, Sex, and Indigenous Depopulation   43
3. Hostages and Captives   73
4. The Great Hunt   99
5. Naturalists and Natives in the Great Ocean   129
6. Assembling the Pacific   155
Conclusion: When East Became West   181

Notes   187
Bibliography   225
Index   245

ACKNOWLEDGMENTS

The origins of this book, like so many others in the discipline of history, go back to a conversation with an obliging archivist. Possessing little more than a text-book knowledge of Pacific history in 2001, I approached the Bancroft Library's curator, Walter Brem, and asked him to recommend archival collections that could shed light on patterns of trade between the western Americas and other places around the Pacific Ocean. During his long career, Walter had developed a remarkable degree of good humor and civility for dealing with researchers like me who ask naive questions, and he could have simply told me to spend some additional time with the Bancroft's online catalogue. Instead, he graciously directed me to the shipping records assembled by the Berkeley historian, Adele Ogden, fifty years earlier. Then, with only a slight pause, Walter rattled off a long list of collections held by archives around the world that I would also need to consult. With this book now finished, Walter will have to forgive me for only making my way through part of his list.

Many friends and colleagues generously agreed to read large portions of this book in draft form. For this burdensome task, I am most grateful to Steven Hackel, Matt Matsuda, Ann Fabian, Bill Deverell, Jennifer Graham Staver, Anne Salmond, Ryan Jones, Seth Archer, Kariann Akemi Yokota, Dan Lewis, and Rainer Buschmann. I greatly appreciate their comments and criticisms, and I look forward to returning the favor.

Many other people in the profession offered their extensive knowledge and particular skills. Elliott West patiently listened to my lunchtime chatter about whale blubber (a slight obsession of mine, if truth be told); Josh Reid allowed me to read his unpublished work on Makah maritime communities; Laurie Dickmeyer labored through my jumbled footnotes and assembled a bibliography; Kenneth Owens shared his vast knowledge of far northern indigenous peoples; *American Historical Review* editor Michael Grossberg took a chance on my half-baked article submission to the journal; the inestimable editors

(Carl Abbott, David Johnson, and Susan Wladaver-Morgan) of the *Pacific Historical Review* once again schooled me in the rigors of manuscript revision; Bob Moeller went to the mat for me on numerous occasions; and Stephen Aron continues to offer his sage advice on matters professional and otherwise.

The Huntington Library, my home away from home, has provided an unparalleled scholarly community throughout the years in addition to various forms of support. I would especially like to thank Roy Ritchie, Alan Jutzi, Peter Mancall, Janet Fireman, Doug Smith, Philip Goff, Susi Krasnoo, and Steve Hindle. Western American Manuscripts Curator Peter Blodgett supplied an endless stream of archival leads; his ongoing recommendations are both a blessing and a reminder of how much research is left to accomplish.

My other academic community, members of the History Department at the University of California, Irvine, profoundly influenced this project with their diverse areas of expertise and collegiality. I am particularly indebted to our Americanist cohort and the World History crowd, including Alice Fahs, Emily Rosenberg, Sharon Block, Yong Chen, Jon Wiener, Vicki Ruiz, Sharon Salinger, Sarah Farmer, Laura Mitchell, Jeff Wasserstrom, Ken Pomeranz, Doug Haynes, Rachel O'Toole, Marc Baer, and Steve Topik. At UCI I have had the distinct pleasure of advising some of the very best doctoral students anyone could imagine. They are creative and rigorous young scholars, they bake superb pie, and they know enough to decide when not to follow my advice. In these troubling times for all doctoral students, my deep respect goes to Jana Remy, Karen Jenks, Angela Hawk, Eric Steiger, Robert Chase, Aubrey Adams, Erik Altenbernd, Jennifer Graham Staver, Laurie Dickmeyer, and Alex Jacoby.

A number of institutions and foundations have generously supported the completion of this project, including the National Endowment for the Humanities, the Andrew W. Mellon Foundation, the Frederick Burkhardt Residential Fellows Program of the American Council of Learned Societies, the Huntington Library, and the School of Humanities at UC Irvine. Many universities around the country invited me to present portions of this work at their seminars and symposia. My appreciation to Yale University's Howard R. Lamar Center, Harvard University's International and Global History Seminar, Stanford University's Bill Lane Center, the University of Texas at Austin's Institute for Historical Studies, UCLA's Department of History US Colloquium, California State University Northridge's W. P. Whitsett Annual Lecture, and the Huntington-USC Institute on California and the West. I've found myself humbled in most of these settings, but I also received tremendously constructive criticism. Thanks to my editor at Oxford University Press, Susan Ferber, as well as the helpful feedback of three anonymous reviewers.

The final words must go to my family. I would like to say (as many writers do) that my children helped with this book in countless ways, but that would merely be one more parental lie. More truthfully, I am grateful for all the time-consuming distractions and entertainment provided by Noah and Sam, who continue to enrich my life on a daily basis. Cindy, to her credit and my good fortune, has stuck with me since our junior year of college. She provided invaluable support as well as the most perceptive counsel throughout the years it took to complete this project. I love her dearly and dedicate the book to her.

The Great Ocean

Introduction

Ocean Worlds

We return to the Great Ocean, which has been called the Pacific Ocean
and the South Sea, two names which are both equally inappropriate.
—Adelbert von Chamisso, "Remarks of the Naturalist" (1821)

John Kendrick led a captivating life until a hail of grapeshot cut him down in his
fifty-fourth year. Born in Massachusetts well before revolutionary unrest wracked
the colony, Kendrick took to the sea at an early age and was captaining his own
coastal trade vessels by the early 1770s. Like many patriot seamen, he served in
the Continental Navy during the Revolution, commanding an eighteen-gun
sloop named *Fanny*. Kendrick and the *Fanny*'s crew disrupted British shipping in
the Atlantic Ocean and captured a few vessels, which garnered him wealth, ac-
claim, and enough dexterity to work as a maritime privateer in the coming years.

Kendrick's subsequent fame, however, derived from activities not in the
Atlantic but in the Pacific. In 1787, he captained the first privately financed US
circumnavigation of the globe on two vessels, the *Lady Washington* and *Columbia Rediviva*. With this voyage he helped establish a US commercial presence on
the northwest coast of North America and strengthened the young nation's
mounting interest in the China trade. Kendrick never returned to Boston from
this voyage. Instead, he and the *Lady Washington*'s crew continued trading in the
Pacific for the next six years while the second-in-command officer, Robert Gray,
completed the circumnavigation on the *Columbia Rediviva*.

From his service during the Revolution to his ventures in the Pacific, Kendrick's career linked the nation's colonial past to its commercial and expansionist
future. Even his 1794 death in Hawai'i echoed this sense of national history and
destiny: under a warm sun in Honolulu Bay, the *Lady Washington* prepared for a
ceremonial exchange of cannon fire with a British schooner, the *Jackall*. The
Lady Washington may have fired the first salute, immediately followed by the

3

thunderous roar of the *Jackall*'s guns.[1] One of those cannons was mysteriously filled with a load of grapeshot, which tore first through the side of Kendrick's ship and then through Kendrick himself. Sailors buried his bloody remains under a grove of palm trees.

Told in this fashion, John Kendrick's life resonates as a distinctly American story, down to the name of the ship upon which he was killed: the *Lady Washington*. His humble origins led to patriotic service during the Revolution, while his rising social status and wealth inspired even greater ambitions after the war. Those aspirations took Kendrick to the Pacific, where this middle-aged American could explore markets for the United States and privateer in the maritime trade—going so far as to hijack the *Lady Washington* from its Boston investors rather than returning home from Canton, per his orders. He never adequately explained this action other than to suggest he was in the hot pursuit of commercial profits and would soon present the ship's owners with "a proper statement of my affairs and transactions."[2] In the coming decades, hundreds upon hundreds of American ships would follow in Kendrick's wake on voyages of trade, exploration, whaling, and, ultimately, territorial conquest. From this vantage point, it might appear that Kendrick had entered an ocean largely unsullied by the rivalries, wars, and cultural complexities of the Atlantic. But the veteran sailor knew this was far from the truth.

The Pacific encountered by John Kendrick was not a single ocean world. Rather, it represented a vast waterscape where imperial and personal contests played out in isolated bays and coastlines, where indigenous communities sought to control the terms of exchange, and where maritime traders plied the waters for profitable commodities. The ocean's geography was bafflingly complex and varied, from its long continental shorelines to its twenty-five thousand islands.[3] By the time of his death in 1794, Kendrick's ship had shared the waters with a great many vessels from nations around the globe: England, France, Portugal, the Netherlands, Russia, China, and Spain. Territorial hostilities, imperial rivalries, and personal suspicion prevailed everywhere. Spanish officials in Alta California circulated orders to "secure [Kendrick's] vessel and all the people on board, with discretion, tact, cleverness, and caution," while Chinese traders and British East India Company officers in Canton also monitored his activities.[4]

Many acquaintances measured the character of this curious American trader. The Nuu-chah-nulth of Vancouver Island, whom he repeatedly supplied with guns in exchange for furs, may have viewed him as an easy mark if not an outright buffoon for his novel practice of securing furs with advance payment. British, Spanish, and American traders on the coast certainly shared this opinion to varying degrees. Some of them believed Kendrick had lost his mind; after all, he had failed to return the *Lady Washington* to its rightful owners in Boston, instead following his own circuitous trading route around the Pacific for more than seven years. The celebrated American trader Amasa Delano, however, considered Kendrick a model for his dealings with natives.[5] In the end, these conflicting views of

John Kendrick—alarm, suspicion, curiosity, ridicule, and respect—reflect larger tensions throughout the Pacific, a setting where competing agendas only multiplied as distinct groups encountered one another during the late eighteenth and early nineteenth centuries. Americans like Delano and Kendrick fashioned their own life stories as part of the nation's creation story, and yet Americans constituted only one group among many in the Pacific's turbulent waterscape.

Over the millennia the Pacific Ocean framed the worldviews and supported the lifeways of many indigenous groups.[6] The ocean offered material sustenance, the means to travel or migrate on seacraft, and a spiritual link to the earth's life force and what lay beyond. Pacific islanders considered themselves *kakai mei tahi* or "people from the sea," according to Tongan anthropologist and writer Epeli Hauʻofa.[7] Neither a barrier nor devoid of humanity, the ocean allowed passage between innumerable settled islands. Native communities of the western American coastline—or the eastern edge of the Pacific—shared elements of the islanders' worldview, especially in regards to the life-sustaining nature of the sea. These continental groups traveled the coastal waters for trade and hunted its marine creatures. Some of them inhabited the offshore islands of North America and had done so for more than ten thousand years.[8] They plied sea channels to forge unions with their neighbors and sometimes to conduct warfare against them. For all these Pacific peoples, the ocean represented a place of profound meaning and ancestral associations—in short, water deeply etched with history.

The Great Ocean examines interactions between different groups—indigenous "ocean peoples," mainland native communities, and a wide variety of foreign voyagers—who encountered one another through the pathways of the ocean during a period of rapid change. That period began with the three historic voyages of Captain James Cook (the first voyage commenced in 1768) and continued until the discovery of fabulously rich gold deposits in California (1848). Cook's voyages—quickly followed by the wide dissemination of his journals—brought global attention to the Pacific as well as sustained contact with native groups throughout the ocean. Those voyages also intensified European rivalries for scientific exploration, trade, and empire. Seven decades later, the California gold rush sparked a global convergence of workers and entrepreneurs to this one area of the eastern Pacific. The world not only rushed in to California, but in the process, ever larger populations now circulated around the Pacific due to new technologies, established ports, and circuits of knowledge generated during the previous seven decades. By this time, the Great Ocean's many shores were fully enmeshed in world markets and systems of knowledge. How did this happen?

A set of historical themes structure the transformations examined in *The Great Ocean*. A brief outline of these thematic chapters reads in the following manner: Prior to the 1770s, the eastern Pacific encompassed a disconnected set of indigenous homelands and contending European imperial ventures. In the coming decades, however, commerce quickly multiplied the range of

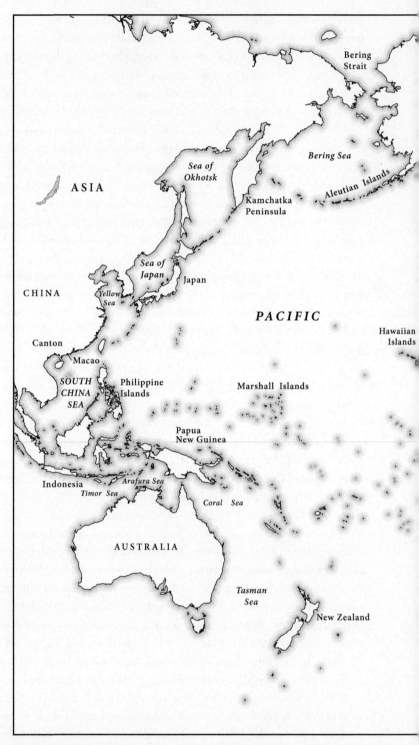

Figure 0.1 The Pacific Ocean with places identified in the text. Map by Pease Press Cartography.

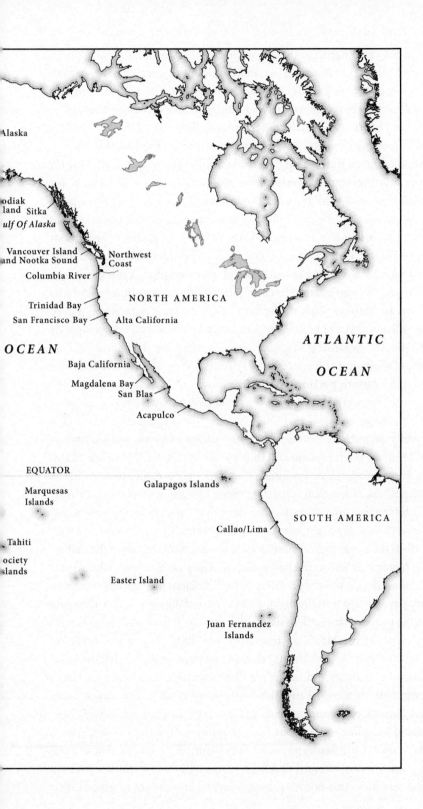

Alaska

odiak
land Sitka
ulf Of Alaska

Vancouver Island   Northwest
and Nootka Sound   Coast

Columbia River

NORTH AMERICA

Trinidad Bay

San Francisco Bay   Alta California

OCEAN

Baja California

Magdalena Bay

San Blas

Acapulco

ATLANTIC

OCEAN

EQUATOR

Marquesas   Galapagos Islands
Islands

SOUTH AMERICA

Callao/Lima

Tahiti

ociety
slands

Easter Island

Juan Fernandez
Islands

interactions between maritime traders and indigenous peoples. Native populations from Polynesia to Alaska experienced epidemiological chaos as exploratory and trading voyages introduced new diseases to indigenous communities.
Encounter scenarios between natives and foreigners played out on beaches, in
villages, and on board ships. Such contact frequently involved the swapping of
go-between hostages or the outright taking of captives. Expanded trade networks gradually linked the eastern Pacific to worldwide markets, especially for
certain specialty products harvested from the ocean. The "Great Hunt" for
marine mammals destroyed most of the ocean's otter, seal, and whale populations during this period. By the 1820s, an international cast of scientists, native and non-native laborers, traders, and beachcombers circulated throughout
the Pacific. Scientific investigations—conducted by naturalists on board most
government-sponsored voyages—combined ethnographic, ecological, and
geological research in an attempt to comprehend the Pacific's human and natural varieties. In all these ways, the eastern Pacific became known and placed
in a worldwide context of markets, imperial nation-states, and knowledge. By
the late 1840s, the expansion of global trade, consequent decades of indigenous depopulation, and the effects of US territorial conquests had radically
transformed the eastern portions of the Pacific.

The oceanic perspective offered by *The Great Ocean* may seem counterintui-
tive to some readers' sense of traditional historical and geographic space. The
"places" usually subjected to historical analysis—nations, regions, and localities—
have fixed borders enclosing land and thus constitute terrestrial history. Historians have far less experience imagining the ways that oceanic space connects
people and polities, rather than separating them. Oceans, it would seem, hardly
register on historians' "mental maps" of places that truly matter because we so
often imagine the sea as a flight *from* history and humanity.[9]

By contrast, the ocean figured prominently on the mental maps of the earliest
indigenous travelers as well as the European and American mariners who arrived
in large numbers during the early modern period. Ancient Polynesians set out on
exploratory voyages and read the night sky as a chart of the ocean's ever-changing
surface. In the process they settled islands as far east as Rapa Nui (Easter Island)
and as far north as the Hawaiian Islands, establishing history and tradition
(*mo'olelo*) in the Great Ocean (*Moana*) through ancestral lineages.[10] For the international cast of merchants and sailors a millennium later, the ocean provided a
venue for exploration, imperial ambition, and history making. This was certainly
the case for James Cook, Jean-François de Galaup de La Pérouse, Vitus Bering,
and Ferdinand Magellan—illustrious Pacific explorers who never returned from
their final voyages. Their deaths provide a fitting epitaph to the inherent dangers
of voyaging and imperial hubris. For others—especially those lesser-known individuals who feature in this book—personal and private ambitions guided their

experiences in the ocean. William Shaler sought wealth through the China trade. Mary Brewster longed for a cargo of whale oil and a safe voyage home. Timofei Tarakanov desired freedom from captivity. James Dwight Dana pursued a scientific understanding of the earth's origins. The Marshallese native named Kadu wanted to see more of the ocean and meet people far from his island home. Adelbert von Chamisso carefully compiled natural and ethnographic notes. And Lewis Coolidge merely hoped to survive the dreaded scurvy and receive his seaman's wages. Their stories, and those of many others like them, offer an appropriately kaleidoscopic perspective on the oceanic worlds of the eastern Pacific.

This so-called eastern Pacific—which includes the coastal Americas, its offshore islands, and the most proximate links in the island Pacific—is admittedly an unstable concept for a tremendously complex oceanic space. Therein may lie its conceptual utility: it describes a waterscape betwixt and between, a patchwork of disparate coastal areas connected to one another by maritime traffic. The eastern Pacific would have made little sense before the late 1700s. In the sixteenth century, the silver trade between Spanish-American ports and the Philippines initiated cross-Pacific commodity exchange, bringing the "Spanish Lake" into world markets. And, in the western Pacific, China and Southeast Asian polities had also formed strong economic connections with European traders long before 1800.[11] Thus, global commodity flows already transected the southern Pacific and Southeast Asia prior to 1800. But the economic integration of the entire Pacific Ocean and the emergence of something approximating a Pacific World would depend upon developments in the ocean's eastern and northern portions.[12] It was Cook's voyages in the 1770s and the subsequent convergence of British, Spanish, Russian, French, and US commercial ventures along the American coastline that linked these parts of the Pacific to the rest of the ocean and beyond.

A geographic concept like the eastern Pacific begins to make sense in light of developments that took place on the sea and the land. On the American coastline, indigenous and Spanish communities increasingly directed their trade westward to the maritime commercial system, rather than eastward to the continent's empires or former indigenous trading partners. A preponderance of coastal trade (operated by Atlantic-based vessels) emerged in the decades around 1800, running south from Russian Alaska to the shores of Chile and Peru. The Hawaiian Islands gradually became the center-point destination not only for trade, but also for sailors' libidinous desires, naturalists' investigations, and, by the 1820s, Protestant missionary activities.[13] These connections on the Pacific's eastern side mirrored other maritime systems in the western and southern portions of the Pacific.

The eastern Pacific's waterscape provided the primary connection between the disparate borderlands.[14] But many factors altered these oceanic connections by the late 1840s. Independent polities from Chile to Mexico broke free from the Spanish Empire, asserting their own sovereignty over borders and oceanic space. Russian Alaska (and the Russian-American Company) lost its raison d'être due to its own success in slaughtering marine mammals for the market. Meanwhile, indigenous depopulation undercut the vitality of once-powerful native communities. As much as any other set of factors, the US-Mexico War, the California gold rush, and US annexation of its initial Pacific Coast territories forever altered the oceanic connections and, in the process, reconfigured large portions of the coastal geography. For the expansionist United States, much of the *eastern* Pacific rapidly became the American *West*, while other areas around the ocean were now inextricably enmeshed in the broader world economy. These pivotal years in the late 1840s initiated a new phase of consolidations and connections in the Pacific.

Similar to the "eastern" qualifier used to demarcate this oceanic space, the Pacific World concept is also unstable and problematic, even if its shorthand utility makes it hard to resist. On the one hand, the term "Pacific World" acknowledges the social, economic, and environmental connections as not only real, but also ever more vital to Pacific polities and people—native and non-native alike.[15] As a conceptual tool, furthermore, the Pacific World offers similar analytical payoff to the term "Atlantic World", a descriptor that provides valuable insight to the interconnected histories of Africa, Europe, and the Americas following Columbus's voyages.[16] Numerous factors distinguish these two ocean worlds, not the least of which are timing (the Atlantic's "Columbian exchange" was in full swing by the mid-1600s); scale (the Pacific is far larger than the Atlantic and more difficult to imagine as *one* oceanic world); large demographic shifts (such as transatlantic migrations, the majority of which were comprised of enslaved Africans); contact with indigenous populations (most Pacific groups remained buffered from sustained contact until the late 1700s); and the nature of global commerce (market capitalism hit parts of the Pacific within decades of contact). Differences aside, the ocean world concept appears ripe for the Pacific, particularly because of its increasing interconnectedness with the Atlantic and Indian oceans.[17]

And yet numerous issues urge caution against embracing a concept like *the* Pacific World, beginning with the questions of *which* Pacific and *whose* Pacific history? The Pacific contains many distinct histories associated with different geographic spheres: Asia, the Subarctic, North and South America, Australia, and the twenty-five thousand islands that generally constituted the heart of Pacific history. Furthermore, each of these geographic areas reveals a multiplicity of seas and cultural systems, similar to Fernand Braudel's notion of the "Mediterranean World" containing a "complex of seas" and distinct "civilizations."[18] From this standpoint, the Pacific is far too large, diverse, and variegated to encompass one oceanic "world" or to generalize about its multitude of places. The Pacific is a "multilocal space," writes historian Matt Matsuda, and it demands "an oceanic history much more located in thinking outward from Islanders and local cultures."[19] Matsuda's point couples issues of scale with those of perspective: *whose* Pacific? This question reflects the extent to which European and American outsiders rationalized the ocean—as *one* Pacific Ocean—in a vain attempt to simplify its tremendous social and natural complexity. At its worst, the term "Pacific World" elides native histories and reifies imperial agendas.[20] To the extent that Pacific World works as a general concept, its value resides as a way to frame *history* itself: an oceanic rather than terrestrial approach, a peopled rather than vacant waterscape, a place of movement and transits, and a methodology that searches for the vital interplay between global, oceanic, and local scales of history.[21]

One of this book's aims is to connect events and processes set in motion on these three historical scales.[22] Global forces—including international trade, disease transmission, resource demands, and scientific inquiry—converged throughout the eastern Pacific following the 1760s. This age of imperial expansion and conflicts transpired around the world, and yet as historian Ann Stoler writes, "partial and ambiguous sovereignties over land, labor, and 'regimes of living'" may best characterize the role of most foreign empires in the eastern Pacific.[23] Thus, *The Great Ocean* is less concerned with the formal actions of global empires and more interested in the limits of empire, the negotiations of non-state actors, and the significance of places that defy easy categorization. This downplay of imperial politics also illustrates my own reading of specific historical moments and actors. For example, John Kendrick's venture in the Pacific *could* symbolize and presage the United States' ultimate desire for oceanic power and recognition among other global empires. But such an interpretation of Kendrick's Pacific meanderings reads history backward while also disregarding the fluid and contested oceanic world he encountered. In all likelihood, curiosity and personal greed guided his actions more than any geopolitical ambition.

The global forces connect with the oceanic scale of events and trends that resonated outward across the Pacific. For instance, the end of two different global wars—the Seven Years' War in 1763 and the Napoleonic Wars in 1815— held specific repercussions for the Pacific: a period of initial exploration throughout the ocean followed the first conflagration, and a resurgence of traffic and scientific investigations followed the second. During each period new transits of goods, germs, and people flowed across the ocean as well as along a north-south axis of the American-Pacific littoral. The oceanic scale was also a product of human cognition, by which people constructed the Pacific as a geographic entity. The naturalist Adelbert von Chamisso did this during his 1815–1818 voyage, and few did this more perceptively than the geologist James Dwight

Dana, who in the early 1840s found geological coherence across the Pacific's islands, continental edges, and the entire ocean basin.

Finally, the local setting of villages, communities, and vessels demonstrates the personal and ecological dynamics that triggered and responded to the global and oceanic trends. The events that took place in locales like Honolulu Bay, the Columbia River basin, or Baja California's Magdalena Bay were not simply matters of foreigners' demands or impositions. Instead, local community politics played an important role in all outcomes, such as King Kamehameha's concerted effort to consolidate his power across the Hawaiian Islands.[24] Local ecologies also influenced events, as in the subsistence crisis faced by the Nuu-chah-nulth Chief Maquinna in the 1790s, or in the case of Magdalena Bay, where the unique migratory route of Pacific gray whales led to a rapid slaughter of the species.[25] In the end, specific localities mattered in ways that shaped both oceanic and world history.

Certain geopolitical episodes and economic trends resonated sharply on the global, oceanic, and local scales, as the following chapters demonstrate. The crumbling of Spain's empire in the Americas during the 1810s had profound implications for global Europe, while its significance in the Pacific influenced trade patterns and the appearance of new nation-states, such as Mexico. Yet lesser-known events intrinsic to Pacific history presaged the revolutionary movements that tore apart New Spain. The Nootka Sound Crisis of 1789, for example, revealed the severe limitations of Spanish power on the Northwest Coast, a region it hoped to control. Nor did Spain—the once great European maritime power in the Pacific—listen to its navigators who best understood the ocean's political currents, such as commander Alejandro Malaspina, who circled the ocean and the globe in the early 1790s.[26] Malaspina's well-intentioned suggestions to the Crown regarding free trade and the need for imperial reforms earned him nothing but a cold prison cell in the San Antón fortress for the next six years.

Spain's collapse in the Americas coincided with the expansion of the United States as a continental power. The United States did not exist when James Cook departed on his first voyage in 1768, and the Revolution's outcome remained uncertain when Cook's third voyage returned to England in 1779. However, by the time California gold was discovered in 1848, the republic had won a second war against the British, repopulated the Ohio Valley with settlers, purchased the Louisiana Territory from France, and established a continental empire through indigenous dispossession and the US-Mexico War. Yet lost in this standard narrative of the nation's expansion is the fact that American mariners had continuously plied the Pacific and increasingly dominated certain parts of it since the late 1780s. To the extent that the Pacific (and its transits to Asia) figured into US continental expansion, it was a goal achieved decades earlier by private American maritime interests, who carried an abiding faith in a doctrine of free trade on the seas.

China also played an unmistakable role in the Pacific's great convergence with the world.[27] Chinese merchants in Canton showed a keen awareness for the transformations taking place around the Great Ocean. If the world "rushed in" to California after the momentous gold strikes, then for the previous three generations the Pacific maritime traders had been rushing to the open port of Canton. This began much earlier with Spanish sales of silver to Chinese merchants, and it continued in the late eighteenth century with Pacific traders searching for commodities (furs, opium, specie, sandalwood, and others) desired by Chinese merchants and consumers. The British Empire hoped to control and monopolize the China trade in the late 1700s through the East India Company, but Chinese merchants asserted their own rules of engagement with the many different groups of foreign traders in Canton. At least until the outbreak of the first Opium War in 1839, Chinese markets had profoundly influenced Pacific commerce and its connections to world trade.

Oceanic voyages provide a structuring and narrative device for the following chapters. *The Great Ocean* draws upon hundreds of documented voyages—some painstakingly recorded by participants, some only known by archeological remains or indigenous memory—as a window into the resulting commercial, cultural, and ecological transformations. Specific voyages and their chroniclers also provide entry points for different historical themes, beginning in the first chapter with the expansion of trade and the travels of William Shaler, captain of the American brig *Lelia Byrd*.

William Shaler crossed the Pacific Ocean between China and the American coastline four times between 1802 and 1806. His personal account of the voyage—published two years later in the *American Register*—illustrates the dynamics of early commerce in the ocean and the new linkages between isolated Pacific communities and global trade systems. The eastern Pacific in particular witnessed a surge of activity through its commercial networks and ports that connected Alta California, the Hawaiian Islands, the Northwest Coast, the Alaskan coastline, and Peru with the burgeoning marketplace of Canton. Two main themes converge in this analysis of commercial growth. First is the structural component of the new Pacific trade, including ports, cargos, social customs, and voyage routes. Second is the personal nature of interactions between traders like Shaler and their indigenous counterparts: narratives from both groups reveal ongoing tensions over "free" trade practices in this oceanic marketplace.

Commerce brought a hidden layer of global travelers to Pacific communities during this period: an influx of new germs responsible for ghastly deaths, reduced fertility for indigenous women, and demographic catastrophe for many native groups. The second chapter approaches these grim processes primarily through an examination of indigenous-foreigner sexual relations and the resulting spread of venereal syphilis. The story of Charles Clerke, second-in-command to Captain James Cook during his ill-fated third Pacific voyage, demonstrates the tragic ramifications of these encounters. Neither Cook nor Clerke survived the voyage, and yet more important than their widely mourned deaths was the disease burden transmitted to all native groups by European and American voyagers. This chapter follows disease vectors in Hawai'i, the Californias (Baja and Alta), Tahiti, and the Northwest Coast's Columbia River basin, charting the appalling human cost of maritime traffic and personal encounters in the Pacific.

Beyond diseases, outsiders and natives exchanged an assortment of things in their meetings, including goods, language, and systems of knowledge. Chapter 3 explores the particular exchange of people in their roles as captives and temporary hostages. The trading of hostages and taking of captives formed a common feature of interactions between groups throughout the Pacific Basin. In few places did this become more prevalent than along the Northwest Coast of North America, where a thriving fur trade prior to 1810 brought together myriad native groups with Russian, English, Spanish, and American traders. Timofei Tarakanov, a young employee of the Russian-American Company, understood the dangers and opportunities of this coastline, as well as the means of survival if events turned disastrous. His story of shipwreck and captivity—counterbalanced by the oral history passed down by his Indian captors—provides a startling glimpse into the various conditions of freedom and captivity in this turbulent part of the world.

The exchange of goods, diseases, and people all played a role in the new social relations of the eastern Pacific during the early nineteenth century. A primary motivator for all this human activity was a commodity of the nonhuman variety: marine mammals. Chapter 4 recounts "The Great Hunt," an unparalleled attack on the ocean's most valuable mammals carried out by foreign traders and indigenous hunters along the American coastline from Alaska in the north to Tierra del Fuego in the south. Sea otters and fur seals faced near extinction in the early 1800s due to this brutal assault. Decades later, the Pacific's unsurpassed population of whales encountered the rapidly expanding US whaling fleet. A tremendous slaughter commenced for the sake of whale oil, with American factories as the main beneficiary. The eyewitness narrative of Mary Brewster, whose husband captained the whaleship *Tiger*, describes the results. In the lagoons of Baja California, Mary Brewster watched a small whaling fleet attack the gray whales' isolated spawning grounds, and then Mary witnessed the whales fight back. In all, the Great Hunt unfolded over seven decades of slaughter, bloodshed, and greed.

The final two chapters explore the work of trained and amateur naturalists. Almost every government-sponsored voyage brought natural scientists to the Pacific, whose work pursued the dissemination of knowledge regarding this little-known ocean, its native cultures, and its ecologies. Chapter 5 focuses on a select group of naturalists employed by Russian, French, and British ventures during the two decades following the Napoleonic Wars. Some scientists, such as Adelbert von Chamisso, attempted to gain knowledge through meetings with indigenous people, like the Marshallese islander Kadu, who accompanied Chamisso for a portion of the voyage. Other naturalists viewed all Pacific natives as a dying race, such as the British physician Meredith Gairdner, who in the end turned to Indian grave-robbing to satisfy his scientific ambition.

In contrast to the limited worldviews of most naturalists, geologist James Dwight Dana developed a holistic and theoretical approach to the essential structures of the Pacific Ocean and its landmasses. Dana, who spent three years in the Pacific as one of seven "Scientifics" attached to the US Exploring Expedition (1838–1842), was the first geologist to study the eastern Pacific and theorize the underlying connections of the entire ocean basin. Like Charles Darwin before him, Dana's science was bold and experiential in the way he speculated about the Pacific's dramatic earth processes, including volcanoes, earthquakes, and coral reefs. During the early 1840s, he viewed the ocean and all lands joined to it as part of an interconnected Pacific world. However, by the early 1850s the nation's most prominent geologists found cause and profit in explicating a continental geology to match the nation's new continental boundaries—and Dana's new work celebrated this path of imperial consolidation.

Dreams of empire were far from John Kendrick's mind when he wrote to the *Lady Washington*'s owner, Joseph Barrell, in 1792. Kendrick and the vessel lay at anchor in Macao, China, while Barrell resided half a world away in Boston, where he could only speculate about Kendrick's long absence and questionable behavior during the previous four years. Kendrick's protracted voyage had not yet turned a profit. To the contrary, he informed Barrell, his current troubles included mounting debt, sailors lost to scurvy and drowning, a misplaced cargo of furs from the Northwest Coast, smuggling rather than honest trading in Canton, and a sea-worn *Lady Washington* in dire need of repairs before he could "prosecute the voyage or voyages to the end."[28] Joseph Barrell likely shook his head in dismay upon receiving this letter, the last such communication from Kendrick before his violent death in Honolulu Bay two years later. But Barrell would learn something from this voyage regarding Pacific commerce and the need for reliable captains. And, in the coming decades, many more foreigners would enter the Pacific on voyages of trade, scientific exploration, whaling, and imperial reckoning. They met people of diverse cultural heritages and encountered a multiplicity of seas. Some of them spread disease to native communities, while others like John Kendrick died in places hardly yet fixed on world maps. Following the routes of earlier explorers, these foreigners pursued an ocean of commerce.

1

Seas of Commerce

The Commerce of the World, especially as it is now carried on, is an unbounded Ocean of Business; Trackless and unknown, like the Seas it is managed upon; the Merchant is no more to be follow'd in his Adventures, than a Maze or Labyrinth is to be trac'd out without a Clue.
—Daniel Defoe, *A Plan of the English Commerce* (1728)

Lelia Byrd, 1803–1805

The *Lelia Byrd* traversed the Pacific three times over the course of two years. These crossings posed significant dangers to any sailing vessel, but it was even more perilous for a small and leaky ship. The 175-ton *Lelia Byrd* sailed from Canton to the Northwest Coast of America, returned back across the ocean to Canton, and charted a final course for North America before a slow, waterlogged journey to Hawai'i. The ship covered over twenty thousand miles of open ocean, not including its numerous journeys up and down the American coastline between the Columbia River and Guatemala. William Shaler and his twenty-five crewmembers sighted trading vessels every time they approached land. They saw European, American, and Asian vessels as they passed Macao and entered Canton's Pearl River Delta, indigenous canoes and Atlantic-based ships on the American coastline, and Hawaiian outriggers in the Sandwich Islands. Native seacraft in particular plied the coastal waters at almost every place the ocean touched shore. The opportunities for trade thrilled William Shaler, but some natives met the *Lelia Byrd*'s arrival with decidedly less enthusiasm.

On May 11, 1804, after the *Lelia Byrd*'s third Pacific crossing, Shaler moored the ocean-battered brig in Trinidad Bay, an inlet far north of the coastal swath of Alta California governed by Spain. The Yurok called this place Tsuräu, so named for the village located on the bay's shore. Shaler needed a foremast, water, and furs, and he planned to attain these necessities through aggressive trade with the local villagers.[1] The Yurok required nothing from this group, but they had learned from previous encounters to use caution with light-skinned foreigners. At the very least, the Yurok expected gifts for their tolerance and supplies.

During the first two days, the Yurok traded alongside the ship and openly resisted the foreigners' attempts to come ashore. On three occasions the Yurok stopped a shore landing party from the *Lelia Byrd* and, in one incident, they confiscated the water casks the crewmembers sought to fill. Breaking the casks, the Yurok made off with the most valuable part: the iron hoops. The Yurok would turn these hoops into daggers and other useful tools. Angered by the Yurok's resistance, Shaler ordered the firing of rifles from the *Lelia Byrd*'s launch on May 14, to which the natives responded with a "cloud of arrows."[2] Finally, the foreigners took four Yurok as hostages, forcing the villagers to allow Shaler's men on shore for wood and water. They entered the village of Tsuräu and managed to offend most everyone. They attempted to smell the villagers' bodies, lavished undue attention on a man with light skin, and, most appalling, made rude offers to the females, including the young girls. The ship and its offensive men departed several days later carrying the necessary supplies as well as some sea otter pelts acquired in trade. Shaler's journal noted all these incidents, but the meaning he drew from them derived from the opposite side of the beach than that inhabited by the Yurok. He considered them "savages"—tribal people "hardly emerged from a state of nature."[3] With that thought in mind, Shaler turned the ship south for the more "civilized" parts of Alta California.

The *Lelia Byrd* went on to spend many months along the coast of Alta California, during which time Shaler drew several conclusions regarding this province and its Spanish colonizers. The Spanish, he wrote, "at a great expence and considerable industry, [have] removed every obstacle out of the way of an invading enemy."[4] They had filled the country with livestock, "reduced" the coastal Indians, and failed to prevent their own colonists from conducting a furtive trade with foreign ships despite official policy against such commerce. "In a word, they have done every thing that could be done to render California an object worthy the attention of the great maritime powers: they have placed it in a situation to want nothing but a good government to rise rapidly to wealth and importance." Predating by four decades the sentiments of famed American sailor and diarist Richard Henry Dana, Shaler concluded: "The conquest of this country would be absolutely nothing; it would fall without an effort to the most inconsiderable force."[5]

Given the tenor of these comments, Shaler's journal (and the *Lelia Byrd*'s voyage) might be read as an early primer for US territorial expansion into the Pacific Ocean. Geopolitical objectives, however, remained far from Shaler's mind during the voyage. He mostly ignored the territorial, imperial, or national claims asserted throughout the Pacific Ocean: Spain's exclusionary trade policies on the Central and North American coast, England's assertion of domain on the

Northwest Coast, China's commercial regulations on the Pearl River Delta, Russia's presumptuous claim to the North Pacific fur trade, or the desire of native communities to set the terms of exchange for their trade items and natural resources. Shaler's repeated dismissal of these territorial claims occasionally led to violence, as evidenced by his encounter with the Yurok in 1804, as well as the *Lelia Byrd*'s hasty retreat from the Spanish port of San Diego in 1803, cannons blazing from ship and shore alike. Shaler was an American free trader specializing in furs destined for the Canton market, and the *Lelia Byrd* would continue to collect cargo so long as the crew kept it afloat.

By August 1805, keeping the brig afloat much longer seemed in doubt. Shaler had filled the *Lelia Byrd*'s cargo hold with furs, pelts, a team of horses, "hogs, sheep, &c.," and he turned the ship away from California's coast and toward the Hawaiian Islands. "We experienced nothing extraordinary in our passage [to Hawai'i], except a violent hurricane, which began on the night of the 8th of August, and lasted until the 10th at midnight." The leaking brig strained mightily under the force of wind and waves, forcing the crew to work two pumps around the clock. "Fortunately," Shaler wrote, "as the gale abated, she leaked less, and our prospects brightened again. At 2 o'clock at night, of the 19th, we, to our great joy, saw fires on the high lands of Owhyhee, and the next morning . . . we were, as usual, visited by great numbers of the natives, of both sexes, who brought us refreshments, &c."[6] Once ashore and refreshed, Shaler transferred his valuable cargo of pelts and furs to the New England frigates *Atahualpa* and *Huron* for shipment to Canton. He bartered the *Lelia Byrd* to King Kamehameha in exchange for a smaller, Hawaiian-built schooner, christened *Tamana*. Shaler accompanied his cargo west to Canton, while the *Tamana* sailed east for California under Shaler's agent, John Hudson.[7] Within a year Hudson had sold the *Tamana* to the Russian Captain Pavel Slobodchikov, who renamed the vessel *Sv. Nikolai* in honor of the Russian patron saint of sailors. Such fluidity defined this incipient ocean of commerce, as crews, captains, cargos, and vessels departed in new configurations and different transits around the ocean, all in pursuit of profit.

The events recorded by Shaler were neither commonplace nor extraordinary. Instead, they reveal emerging patterns of Pacific trade and social intercourse that deepened in the early nineteenth century and fundamentally reshaped the lives of Pacific people. Other accounts of the *Lelia Byrd*'s activities offset Shaler's many prejudices, but on the whole, his *Journal of a Voyage between China and the North-Western Coast of America* provides a compelling view of Pacific commerce. In particular, Shaler's account casts light on the primary components of this trade and how it functioned throughout the eastern Pacific Basin. Those components included the superimposition of new trade on existing indigenous and foreign patterns, the linkages between different Pacific ports and coastlines, the constant commerce between foreign and local populations, a reliance on indigenous trading partners and laborers, and a distinct entrepreneurialism alternatively defined as illegal, contraband, or free trade.

Shaler's voyage coincided with and reflected a period of tremendous transformation throughout the Pacific Ocean. As European, Asian, American, and native populations converged for trade during the years around 1800, they linked isolated Pacific communities to global trade systems. The eastern Pacific, in particular, encompassed an immense and largely unfamiliar waterscape where social and economic systems collided in specific ports and coastal borderlands—the most prominent being Alta California, the Northwest Coast, Sitka (Alaska), the Hawaiian Islands, Callao (Peru), San Blas and Acapulco (Mexico), and, on the Pacific's western rim, Canton (China).[8] Each of these places forged regional linkages based on commodities and trade routes, and those regional networks were increasingly tied to trade systems encircling the globe.

This chapter examines Pacific commerce as a set of dynamic relationships between peoples and markets, economic and sociopolitical systems, and contending perspectives on trade itself. It focuses specifically on Alta California as a hub through which to view the numerous sites of transoceanic and international trade in the decades between the 1770s and the 1840s. While not the most powerful center of commerce during these decades, Alta California nonetheless reveals important components of that trade as well as the linkages to the primary Pacific markets of Hawai'i and Canton. Yet, as William Shaler predicted in 1808, California's commercial status would rapidly change in the 1840s, and the reverberations echoed across the Pacific and around the world.

An Oceanscape of Trade prior to 1800

The Yurok who boarded the *Lelia Byrd* in 1804 knew all about bartering for goods by virtue of a long history of trade with neighbors: the Wiyot immediately to the south, the coastal Tolowa to the north, the Karok up the Klamath River, and the inland Hupa. Exchange networks also linked them to more distant communities, such as the central California Shasta and Wintu, or the coastal Pomo far south of Yurok territory. But this trade was either land- or river-based traffic; the Yurok did not venture into the coastal waters for long-distance trade simply because necessity never demanded it.[9] Other indigenous groups around the Pacific did venture into the ocean for trade, often traveling great distances in the process. Far from inaugurating maritime commerce in the Pacific, the international traders who arrived in the late 1700s superimposed new forms of exchange and longer routes on existing trade patterns.

Examples drawn from North America and Hawai'i confirm the long history of indigenous maritime trade. The southern California Chumash economy thrived on trade with interior and coastal neighbors, especially during the past one thousand years when plank canoes (*tiats*) enabled mainland-island trade between the island Chumash and the Tongva (or Gabrielino) on Catalina Island to the south.[10] In addition to customary handcraft items, the Chumash built one of the largest microlithic and shellworking industries in North America, due to their chert quarries on the coastal islands.[11] Similarly, Alaska's Aleut and Kodiak (*Alutiiq*) subsistence patterns owed greatly to its coastal waterscape and hunting culture; men and boys alike paddled kayaks (called *baidarkas* by Russian traders) great distances for hunting, travel, and trade. Some objects of the hunt—primarily seal and sea otter skins—traveled even longer distances to the annual Inuit trade fair at Sisualik on the Bering Strait and eventually crossed the frigid waters to Asia's Chukchi Peninsula.[12] Pre-contact Hawaiians also held regular market fairs—the largest may have taken place on the banks of the Big Island's Wailuku River—with vendors and consumers arriving from numerous islands. Plank and dugout canoes brought specialty goods from different islands, such as yams and *makaloa* mats from Ni'ihau, woven tapa cloth from O'ahu, dried fish from the Kona coast, and wood products (canoes, paddles, spears) from Kaua'i.[13]

Moving beyond the eastern Pacific, premodern trade circuits were most evident in Melanesia, western Polynesia, and coastal Southeast Asia. For instance, Samoan mats and Fijian canoes came to Tonga, at times in exchange for Tongan women. One highly developed regional trading network was the "Kula ring" across the Melanesian Islands. Basic Melanesian commodities and ceremonial items exchanged hands in this interisland system that reinforced social and kin relationships dating back centuries.[14] Archeological evidence also confirms the very long history of Pacific exchanges: discoveries of basalt adzes (stone tools) in Samoa and the southern Cook Islands confirm exchanges between these two places for many millennia.[15]

Throughout the Pacific, local trade between neighboring communities certainly predominated, but middle-distance trade (island-to-island, island-to-mainland) occurred wherever necessity encouraged it. Seacraft skills—including vessel construction and use—not only facilitated trade but also held significant cultural, political, and military meaning for Pacific populations. In this way, some Pacific groups were remarkably similar to the maritime nations and foreign traders that converged in the Pacific during the late eighteenth century. Natives, furthermore, had a great appreciation and tenacity for commodity exchange and distinct ways of dealing with known trading partners as well as outsiders. They sought to acquire items they could not easily produce, and they valued those items accordingly. If this last point seems all too obvious, it was not always understood by foreign traders who expressed amusement or anger over how natives valued simple iron objects or small mirrors.

Beginning in the 1500s, the commercial traffic of Asian and European nations in the southwestern Pacific distinguished itself by global commodity exchanges, long-distance voyages, and, with the Spanish galleon trade, transoceanic trade routes. China, as with many subsequent commercial affairs, propelled early oceanic trade in the Pacific. The Nanyang ("Southern Ocean") trade in the China Sea dated back to the eleventh century, with junks departing from Guangzhou (Canton) and other ports for an arc of polities from the Gulf of Siam to Burma, Sumatra, western Java, and Borneo.[16] Curtailed over the centuries by various rulers, the Nanyang trade reappeared in 1684 when the Kangxi emperor declared the south China coast open to commerce. Junks soon sailed the western Pacific Ocean from Japan to the South China Sea, a waterscape that historian Robert Marks termed "a Chinese-dominated lake."[17] Chinese trade in this region far outpaced that of the British or Dutch throughout the 1700s, although equally significant to tonnage or number of vessels was the fact that transpacific commercial voyages intersected with trade vessels from the Atlantic, Indian, and western Pacific Ocean. Maritime commerce from around the globe intermingled and competed in this quadrant of the Pacific Ocean.

Originating in the eastern Pacific, the Spanish galleon trade crossed the ocean and linked the vibrant commerce of the South Pacific and China to the Americas. Three places proved crucial to the Spanish: Manila, which Spain founded in 1571 and served as the "linchpin" connecting New World silver to Chinese silks and other commodities; China, which functioned as a suction pump for the world's silver supply; and central Mexico, the world's leading silver producer during the fifty-year heyday (1700–1750) of the galleon trade.[18] Between these places emerged the possibility of commerce involving the northern Pacific: to sail east back across the ocean, Spanish galleons had to first sail north toward Japan in order to catch the North Pacific current, which pulled vessels to the Americas. Thus, like William Shaler's Pacific crossing in 1804, Spanish galleons followed the easterly current from Japan to the North American coastline before turning south past California en route to Acapulco. Pacific winds and currents all but determined this clockwise circulation of traffic. Shaler's ship was not the first American vessel to ride that current to Alta California, but the *Lelia Byrd* was among the earliest to receive cannon fire once it arrived.

California's "Rise to Ease and Affluence"

By 1804 Spanish officials in Alta California viewed Shaler as something more than an unwelcome nuisance. The previous year Spanish authorities in Monterey had ordered four American fur trade ships (the *Alexander*, *Hazard*, *Lelia Byrd*, and the *O'Cain*) to leave California ports for violating commercial restrictions.

The *Lelia Byrd* represented the worst offender due to events that transpired on the night of March 22, 1803. On a deserted stretch of beach near the San Diego presidio, Commander Manuel Rodríguez had apprehended three crewmembers of the *Lelia Byrd* for attempting to purchase a pile of sea otter pelts from soldiers under his command. Outraged at this illegal behavior—or more likely his inability to profit from it—Rodríguez left the three Americans on the beach under armed guard and returned to the presidio. As dawn approached an armed party from the *Lelia Byrd* rowed ashore and forced the release of their fellow crewmembers; they returned to the ship and then disarmed the six Spanish soldiers whom Rodríguez had already stationed on it. Shaler gave orders to weigh anchor and the *Lelia Byrd* slowly sailed past the San Diego presidio, at which point the ship and presidio exchanged cannon fire. The vessel took at least one direct hit. But the presidio soon halted its fire: at close range its gunners could now see the six Spanish soldiers that Shaler had lashed to the near side of the *Lelia Byrd*. The American vessel left San Diego Bay with no further altercations, and Shaler placed the soldier-hostages safely on shore before turning the vessel south for San Quentín Bay, Baja California.[19] The episode demonstrates an emerging conflict between different expressions of power: the imperial regulations of a Spanish colony versus the early American belief in free trade, an ideology that helped rationalize the nation's continental empire in the mid-nineteenth century.

Conflicts between Alta California authorities and foreign traders rarely reached this level of hostilities. The event was so exceptional, according to diarist Richard Henry Dana, that "the story was yet current in San Diego and neighboring ports and missions" more than thirty years later.[20] But tensions repeatedly arose due to Spanish trade policies that formally excluded foreign trade ships from Spanish ports.[21] If commercial policy was highly restrictive, commercial practice played out quite differently and implicated everyone in California who hoped to partake in trade, which included most everyone. Thus, when Shaler returned to the California coast one year after the conflict in San Diego, he kept the *Lelia Byrd* away from the main ports and instead sought trade with people outside direct administrative control.[22]

Such trade posed little difficulty. Shaler trafficked along the Alta and Baja California coastline, trading for furs and pelts near San Luis Obispo, Refugio, Santa Catalina Island, the Channel Islands, Cedros Island, Guaymas, and what would soon become the well-known contraband port of San Pedro near Alta California's second pueblo, Los Angeles. Spanish officials at Guaymas dined on board the *Lelia Byrd* and "behaved with great civility, though rigid in their duty," Shaler sarcastically noted.[23] The padre of Mission San Luis Obispo reported to Spanish authorities that he received Shaler "with little amiability," though the meeting between these two men indicates that trade certainly took place.[24] Shaler bartered with Don Juan Ortega's family at Rancho Refugio (near Santa

Barbara) and the Tongva people ("our Indian friends") on Catalina Island.[25] Many other commercial exchanges transpired between Shaler and native or Spanish individuals—all of it deemed illegal under Spanish law.

Rather than a difficult trade environment, Shaler's account highlighted the ease of commerce in Alta and Baja California. "At present," he observed, "a person acquainted with the coast may always procure abundant supplies and provisions. All these circumstances prove, that, under a good government, the Californias would soon rise to ease and affluence."[26] Shaler's point deserves some emphasis, because it forecasted the commercial revolution that soon enveloped California and the Pacific Basin. He identified knowledge of "the coast" as crucial to a trader's success because indigenous Californians and Spaniards alike could safely trade most anywhere along the coast except the main ports. California's littoral zone—from ship to beach to shoreline dwellings—became the active mart where all participants paid little heed to Spain's trade restrictions. The "abundant supplies and provisions" procured by Shaler confirmed the lively trade with Franciscan missionaries, which he also noted in an 1804 letter to his partner, Richard Cleveland.[27] Finally, Shaler's prediction that "the Californias would soon rise to ease and affluence" refers to California as a place rather than to its inhabitants—an odd phrasing, but one that accurately measured the place in the context of the Pacific's commercial geography.

A quick glance forward in time shows Shaler to have been remarkably prophetic. In 1827—a year fairly representative in the growth of California's maritime commerce—thirty commercial vessels arrived in Alta California, now the northernmost province of Mexico. Almost half of these ships were American, while the other ships flew flags from England, Russia, France, Mexico, Hamburg, and Hawai'i. (The Hawaiian royal flag combined elements of the British and American flags in order to appease both American and British interests.) Many of these vessels exhibited a distinct fusion of international influences: a Peruvian-based partnership owned the British *Aurora*; the Alaska-based Russian-American Company owned the *Baikal*, *Golovnin*, and *Okhotsk*; the two Hawaiian ships were constructed in Atlantic shipyards; and the Hudson's Bay Company ship *Cadboro* also hailed from the Atlantic but spent most of its career in the Pacific Ocean. Taken as a whole, these thirty vessels stopped at all major North and South American ports in the Pacific, almost half dropped anchor in Hawai'i, and some voyaged across the Pacific to Canton or the Philippines. The ships carried supplies, luxury goods, and some unique items, such as the Santa Cruz mission bell transported by the British brig *Fulham* to Callao for recasting, or the sixteen hundred pounds of beaver pelts aboard the *Franklin* bound for Boston, courtesy of the legendary fur trapper Jedediah Smith.[28] The free trade desired by Shaler twenty years earlier now thrived in Alta California by virtue of its connections around the Pacific.

Much in and around California had changed since Shaler's time on the coast two decades earlier. With the end of the Napoleonic Wars in 1815, European and American vessels descended on the Pacific in numbers never before seen. Furthermore, it was Mexico rather than Spain that governed Alta California's "settled" coastal regions during the 1820s, and Mexican officials quickly suspended the trade restrictions against what a former Spanish official considered the "great danger . . . of free trade."[29] Mexico's import and export taxes continued to make clandestine coastal trade the most common form of commodity exchange for traders, missionaries, Californios, Indians, and officials alike. Governor José Darío Argüello best summed up the economic environment of the 1820s: "Necessity makes licit what is not licit by law."[30] Cattle hides and tallow constituted the largest export item, while the highly prized sea otters were virtually extinct on the California coastline due to a comprehensive slaughter by hunters (see chapter 4). Shaler could not have predicted these and the many other changes to the province, but his prophecy of California's role in the Pacific's bustling marketplace proved correct. An energetic trade now linked California's coastal waters to the surrounding ocean and world.

Counting Ships in Alta California

Trade steadily increased during the first half of the nineteenth century in most places around the Pacific, including Hawai'i, Canton, Sydney, the Northwest Coast, and Chile, a commercial upswing well tabulated and documented.[31] But Alta California's mounting trade has been an outlier to this maritime historiography, despite the fact that at least 953 vessels trafficked and traded along the coast prior to the gold rush—a far larger and more international maritime presence than previously acknowledged.[32] What parameters and characteristics defined this region's maritime commerce?

Of the 953 ships entering California waters, 6.8 percent arrived between 1786 and 1799, 5.7 percent in the decade after 1800, 7.6 percent in the 1810s, 24 percent in the 1820s, 22 percent in the 1830s, and 34 percent in the first eight years of the 1840s.[33] In short, trade gradually increased each decade until the 1820s, when it swelled due to events in California and throughout the Pacific, including Mexican independence, the termination of trade restrictions in many ports (especially Canton and previously Spanish-controlled ports), and the global spread of information about Pacific trading opportunities.[34] Yet international events also played a crucial role in Pacific trade, especially the close of the Napoleonic Wars and, for American shipping, the end of the War of 1812. Both private voyages and government-sponsored ventures took to the seas following these international conflagrations.

As the number of vessels on the California coast increased each decade—especially in the 1820s and 1840s—so grew the international cast of participants.[35] The largest share of ships entering California waters came from five nations: the United States (45 percent), England (13 percent), Spain (12 percent), Mexico (12 percent), and Russia (7 percent). But trading vessels from at least seventeen other Pacific and European polities also visited California in the first half of the nineteenth century.[36] Stated simply—and borrowing historian Karen Kupperman's characterization of eastern colonial America—California and coastal North America was "international before it became national."[37]

These statistics on ship national origins raise two important issues. First, while Spanish supply ships from Mexico made up the largest share of California traffic prior to 1800, US vessels soon surpassed all other trading nations by a large margin. US commercial interests in the Pacific therefore anticipated and ultimately influenced its geopolitical and military interests of the mid-nineteenth century, a process forecasted by William Shaler in 1808. Second, despite the strong position attained by US trading vessels in California and the eastern Pacific, at least 527 ships sailing under more than twenty different flags also entered California waters. Thus, when the American "Pathfinder" John Charles Frémont surveyed the California coastline aboard the *Sterling* in 1844–1845, he crossed paths with ships from England, France, Russia, Mexico, the United States, Germany, Sweden, Hamburg, Canada, and California, not to mention the truly international cast of sailors aboard those ships.[38] This pronounced internationalism in Alta California reflected the situation throughout the Pacific Basin.

To what extent did Alta California's traffic intersect with other places around the Pacific? The voyage routes of these 953 vessels provide a view of the interconnections as well as a strong indication of which ports rose or declined in prominence. Based on vessels entering California, the most frequently visited ports were Hawai'i (42 percent of ships), Callao (22 percent), San Blas (19 percent), Acapulco (18 percent), the Russian port at Sitka (12 percent), and Canton (7 percent). In addition, 13 percent of ships stopped somewhere along the Northwest Coast, conducting trade at established forts and coastal native communities. The island Pacific—beyond Hawai'i—also witnessed increased trade, with the Galápagos, Marquesas, Tahiti, and Philippine islands leading all others.[39] Over 50 percent of ships visiting California had also docked on a Pacific island, a figure that speaks to the volume of transoceanic trade and, as the next chapter argues, the exceedingly high rate of introduced diseases on Pacific islands. By the 1820s this group of major ports had begun to systematize commodity flows and market activity in the eastern Pacific.

Trading Places around the Pacific: Hawai'i

The Hawaiian Islands might seem exceedingly isolated in the vastness of the Pacific Ocean: a series of small dots surrounded by a waterscape covering one-third of the earth's surface. But that perspective derives from the mainland, from Atlantic-centered maps that relegate the islands to the far left margin, and from histories that prioritize continents and terrestrial environments rather than the oceans connecting those landmasses.[40] Hawai'i's presumed isolation only makes sense if the ocean is seen as a barrier. View the ocean as an expansive expressway and suddenly Hawai'i becomes the central point for exchange in the Pacific's commercial world. Ancient Polynesian navigators were able to reach Hawai'i throughout the millennia—Tahitian warriors accomplished this some eight hundred years ago on a mission of conquest and settlement—and early nineteenth-century navigators steered toward the islands for a variety of significant reasons. William Shaler's ambition was clear: his California trading had netted a small fortune in the currency of sea otter pelts, but he had to get those pelts to Canton's market. The *Lelia Byrd*—taking on water as fast as the crew could pump it overboard—would only stay afloat as far as the Hawaiian Islands.

Hawai'i received a steady annual supply of exploratory and commercial voyages prior to 1820. In the period between Cook's "discovery" of the Sandwich Islands in 1778 and the arrival of the first whalers (the American *Balena*) in late 1819, 131 vessels docked in Hawai'i. These vessels were primarily British and American, with a few Russian and French ships.[41] This total was nearly one-third fewer than the number of ships that trafficked along the California coast by this date. But Hawai'i's traffic multiplied almost exponentially after 1820. During the next thirty years the number of ship arrivals and departures almost defy the imagination: nearly one thousand commercial ships and upward of three thousand whaling vessels stopped over in Hawai'i between 1824 and 1849.[42] Even as rough approximations, such numbers confirm that Hawai'i—primarily the ports of Honolulu and Lahaina—ranked as the Pacific's busiest island port during this period, if not among the busiest in the world.

While native Hawaiians attacked some ships and discouraged certain forms of trade in the late 1700s, they also enabled the creation of a mid-Pacific stopover that soon attracted commercial fleets. The native and imported biota (including pigs, yams, taro, and fruits) that sustained large Hawaiian populations proved instrumental in provisioning ships on their multiyear voyages.[43] Scurvy-wracked shipping crews literally hungered for the fresh foods available on the islands, while healthy and unhealthy sailors alike also desired the sexual opportunities available in Hawai'i. The sheer abundance of Hawaiian supplies sustained a thriving trade, yet that trade would ultimately not benefit the average Hawaiian. The hierarchical nature of Hawaiian society allowed that Hawaiian hereditary

Figure 1.1 View from the shore of Honolulu Bay in 1817. Artist Louis Choris offered an indigenous perspective to this coastal scene by focusing on Hawaiians' dwellings, activities, and domesticated animals. European and American artists more typically drew coastlines and harbors from offshore with their own sailing vessels in the foreground. Courtesy of the Huntington Library.

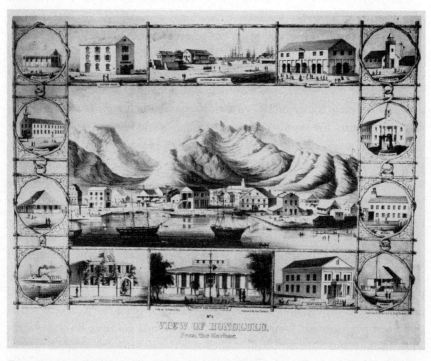

Figure 1.2 "View of Honolulu," 1853. Artist Paul Emmert depicts the midcentury commercial expansion of Honolulu, a product of foreign investment and trade during the previous three decades. Courtesy of the Huntington Library.

elites (*ali'i*), rather than commoners, largely benefited from trade. King Kamehameha I (an *ali'i akua* or "god-king") established this pattern by gradually consolidating power across the islands and assembling his own commercial fleet, sending ships to California on one side of the Pacific and Canton on the other side.[44] Following Kamehameha's death in 1819, Kamehameha II (Liholiho) forged strong alliances with American and British merchant houses and turned the Honolulu harbor into the ocean's Great Exchange. One French naturalist labeled Hawai'i "*un grand Caravanserai*" (the great caravansary)—a place of goods and entertainment in the watery desert.[45]

Basic geography may have trumped all these attractions. The islands constituted the central place of the Pacific Ocean—not only its physical location, but its intersection with the Pacific's dominant shipping routes. For instance, the English schooner *Columbia* ran a constant course between the North American coast, Hawai'i, and Canton between June 1814 and Christmas Day 1817.[46] The *Columbia* crossed the entire Pacific four times to sell North American furs and Hawaiian sandalwood in Canton: twice exchanging basic necessities for furs in New Archangel (Sitka), five times collecting furs and other goods near the Columbia River, and three times visiting the Alta California coast for hides and provisions. The *Columbia* anchored in Hawai'i four times during its three years of Pacific crossings—for repairs, goods, and new crewmembers. Finally, Captain Peter Corney sold the *Columbia*—ocean weary but still afloat—to King Kamehameha for two full cargo loads of sandalwood, which he transshipped to Canton's market on another vessel.

The *Columbia*'s crisscrossing of the Pacific superimposed at least three common trade routes, all of which involved Hawai'i: the "triangle" fur trade between New England, the Pacific Northwest, and Canton; the Russian trade connecting Sitka and California to Hawai'i; and the bilateral California-Hawai'i trade. Each of these "trades" used Hawai'i as a market for raw goods and imported luxury products. Not only Hawaiian goods, but island laborers also figured prominently in these trade routes, primarily as crewmembers to replace sailors. For example, in Macao the *Columbia* picked up sixteen Hawaiians who had been left behind by the English ship *Isaac Todd* and took them as crewmembers, though "several of [them] died shortly after," noted Captain Corney. At O'ahu the following year the *Columbia* "took on 60 natives for the Columbia River," a place that soon had a sizeable diasporic population of Hawaiian laborers.[47]

Hawai'i's most intense transformation into the Pacific's Great Exchange occurred during the 1820s and 1830s with the establishment of American and British merchant houses in Honolulu. These houses, including Bryant and Sturgis, Palmer, Wilson & Company, Hudson's Bay Company, and Marshall & Wildes, streamlined the purchase and sale of goods, the repair of vessels, and often the contracting of native laborers. By the end of the 1830s, at least two dozen merchant houses operated in Honolulu with a wide assortment of specialty items. An 1844 report by the Scotsman Robert C. Wyllie listed over two hundred types of common and extraordinary items imported from around the world, including bear skins, cigars, "German stuff for trousers," Italian brandy, salmon (847 barrels), and fifty-one French accordions.[48] Though they were island traders on one level, these merchants also held strong international connections. They carried on active correspondence with their counterparts in Canton, California, Callao, Boston, and London during the 1820s and 1830s—demanding cleaner hides from California, complaining of bloated warehouses, and inquiring of market prices everywhere in the Pacific and beyond.[49] As international trade flourished in Hawai'i, the material "gifts of civilization" spread primarily among the ruling elite while the epidemiological "gifts" infected all segments of Hawaiian society.[50]

Canton

If Hawai'i functioned as *"un grand Caravanserai"* in the heart of the Pacific, then Canton was the market that inspired commerce from the Pacific's western edge. Canton drew ships and commodities from the Pacific and beyond: silver from Mexico and South America, textiles from India and England (prior to the 1780s), sea otter pelts from the North American Coast (1780s–1830s), sandalwood from Hawai'i, and bêche-de-mer from Fiji (1810s–1840s), among many other commodities. Significantly, traffic to Canton from the Pacific, Atlantic, and Indian oceans was "layered on top" of a preexisting Chinese coastal trade, which far surpassed foreign trade until the late eighteenth century.[51] Canton served as the Pacific's luxury marketplace where traders exchanged specie and natural resources for Chinese tea, silks, porcelain, and other goods.

Between coastal North America and Canton stretched some seven thousand miles of open ocean, making trade between the Pacific's eastern and western shores an arduous task at best. California shipping records demonstrate the result: less than 10 percent of ships entering California waters crossed the entire Pacific to China. But this low figure is misleading. Many cargoes gathered in California and destined for Canton—such as William Shaler's goods aboard the *Lelia Byrd*—were reassembled in Hawai'i or elsewhere before shipment to China. Ships engaged in the Pacific Northwest fur trade crossed to Canton with much greater frequency: approximately one-half of these vessels trafficked in Canton.[52] Canton, though an ocean away, played a dynamic role in the eastern Pacific's commercial world.

The transformation of Canton's marketplace during the early 1800s exemplified the Pacific-wide trends of internationalism, unrestricted trade, and American

Figure 1.3 "The European Factories, Canton," 1806. British painter William Daniell foregrounds this view of Canton's foreign trading houses with the busy activity of Chinese waterfront workers. Courtesy of Yale Center for British Art, Paul Mellon Collection.

maritime ascendancy. The declining fortunes of the British East India Company (EIC) dramatize these changes. The EIC permanently established its Canton "factory" (or commercial house) in 1751 as one of dozens of such factories stretching from the Atlantic Ocean to the Indian Ocean and on to China. Through parliamentary action, the EIC restricted non-EIC British traders from entering Canton, and through alliance with Canton's powerful Hong merchants, it also sought restrictions on other foreign ships. Hong merchants established their own rules for foreign traders, which included high import/export taxes and mandatory oversight of ships entering Canton by customs superintendents (or "Hoppos").[53] East India Company representatives in Canton carefully monitored all business rivals, according to the EIC's Lord George Macartney, as part of a mission to "spread the use of British manufactures throughout every part of Asia."[54] Textile and other imports from England to Canton provided "sure profit" to the company during the early 1800s, counterbalancing the company's losses in India.[55] This global commercial system, carefully designed in London and protected by parliamentary initiative, worked quite well so long as foreign competition was kept at bay.

Yet the EIC system only worked for so long, in large part because Hong merchants, international traders, and Chinese pirates favored their own profitable strategies.[56] Significant international competitors to the EIC appeared as early as the 1780s. The maiden voyage of the *Empress of China*—a 360-ton American vessel that reached China in the summer of 1784 with a crew of thirty-four sailors and a cargo of pelts, cloth, and ginseng—initiated a steady trickle of US maritime trade that gained considerable strength by the 1790s. By 1814, no fewer than 618 American vessels had reached Macao or Canton, the large majority sailing around the Cape of Good Hope rather than attempting a Pacific crossing. The EIC's "Select Committee" in Canton closely watched this foreign traffic and reported pertinent information to the EIC's "Secret Committee" in London. While the increasing volume of all foreign trade certainly alarmed these officials, the EIC representatives in Canton appeared most troubled by the American traders. With small crews operating vessels one-half or one-quarter the size of EIC ships, the American ships in Canton stunned and occasionally outraged British officials.

Two American ships engaged in the eastern Pacific and China trade demonstrate this pattern. The *Eagle* and the *Clarion* each left Boston in 1817 and arrived in California the following year. The 149-ton *Clarion* sailed by way of the Cape of Good Hope to Tasmania, then across the Pacific to California after a stop in Hawai'i. The *Eagle* came to the Pacific from the opposite direction: around the Horn to Hawai'i, a short stop in Sitka for sea otter pelts, and back to Hawai'i before arriving on the California coast. Both captains found eager trading partners in California, exchanging cargo they had brought from Boston for goods they would sell in Canton. Captain Henry Gyzelaar of the *Clarion* was "able to purchase of the people on shore some furs very valuable in Canton, paying therefore everything they had on board, saving what was indispensable to the safe navigation of the vessel."[57] Captain William Heath Davis of the *Eagle* traded with Juan Ortega and Ignacio Martinez, both of Santa Barbara, and "realized about $25,000 profit in Spanish doubloons and sea otter skins, from sales in California, aside from profits in the Russian settlements."[58] Each ship sailed to Canton by way of Sitka and Hawai'i, arriving at the Pearl River Delta in 1820—and once there, the British EIC secretary N. H. C. Plowden noted each ship's vital information in the "Canton Diary for season 1820/21."[59]

Plowden showed all signs of a desperate man by the time the *Eagle* and *Clarion* arrived in Canton. Since the end of the War of 1812 (which had severely limited US shipping in the Pacific), Plowden had noted the rising number of American vessels in Canton, taking special care to meticulously list details on homeport, destination, cargo, tonnage, and arrival/departure dates. His report to the EIC "Secret Committee" in London for the year 1821 voiced special alarm: "The Honorable Company . . . this season is incurring a very serious loss [in textile] investment, in consequence of the large importations" by American vessels.[60] More than doubling the previous year's arrivals, forty-two American vessels were anchored near Canton carrying imports valued at

$7,413,096, while the "Honorable Company's" own imports for the season tallied $6,199,242.[61] For the first time in the EIC's history, another nation—a former colony, no less—imported more goods to a port the company considered its own. Panic soon filled the missives from Canton to the EIC's London headquarters: "Unless some measures can be devised to prevent the introduction of these goods into China . . . by any ships besides those employed by the Honorable Company, it is difficult to calculate upon the effects of such a ruinous competition."[62]

No such "measures" could be devised to prevent European or American goods from entering Canton outside EIC channels. By the early 1820s, Canton's Hong merchants actively encouraged the opening of foreign agency houses to create new buyers for Chinese products.[63] French, Portuguese, Spanish, and (non-EIC) British traders increasingly sought business in Canton during the 1820s, while merchants from New York and Boston established some of the most active agency houses, including Perkins & Co., Russel & Co., Augustine Heard & Co., and W. S. Wetmore & Co.[64] During the 1820s the once-dominant "Honorable Company" struggled for advantage in the new market environment. It failed to stem the tide of foreign trade in Canton and unsuccessfully defended its monopoly in Parliament for the China trade against non-EIC British traders.[65] Searching for a new means to profit in China's enormous market, EIC officials secretly plotted to expand its narco-trafficker trade in highly addictive Patna opium—hardly an honorable direction for maintaining company earnings and one that eventually sparked the Opium Wars.[66]

The Northwest Coast

The most valuable and sought-after commodities for European and American traders in the early 1800s derived from animals: the pelts and furs from sea otters, land otters, seals, beavers, and bears, and, by the 1830s, the hides of California cattle. The primary killing fields and trading grounds for these items ranged from coastal Baja California to the Aleutian Islands, with the most intense hunting of marine mammals located north of the Columbia River. European empires struggled for dominion over the landed territory: Russia, Spain, and England each established (and in the case of Spain, lost) control over beachhead settlements and colonial outposts, while companies such as the Russian-American Company, the Hudson's Bay Company, and John Jacob Astor's American Fur Company attempted to structure and profit from the lively coastal trade. Presumably, beads and trinkets swapped for furs on the coast could bring high prices in Canton and, subsequently, valuable outbound cargos destined for New York, Boston, London, or some other Atlantic port.

Such is the standard, historical treatment of the Northwest fur trade. It explains the commercial draw of the North Pacific and the geopolitical rivalries that pre-dated the ultimate outcome: US control of Alaska, Washington, Oregon, and California. In terms of the Pacific's commercial geography, however, this synopsis veils three significant aspects of trade on the Northwest coast. First, maritime trade exhibited an international character similar to California's and other Pacific commercial regions—an internationalism that extended beyond the known geo-political rivalries. Second, the "Northwest Coast" was also the Pacific's Northeast rim; and viewed through this alternate geographic orientation, the fur trade was more enmeshed in Pacific trade than in continental commerce. Finally, native groups exerted a great deal of power in this trade by manipulating competition, hard bargaining, and at times, committing violence against outsiders.

The fur trade's international character is best viewed from offshore of the known trade centers and outposts, which included the Hudson's Bay Company's string of "forts" between Fort Simpson and Fort Vancouver, Astor's Fort Astoria, and coastal native villages. Offshore, almost six hundred vessels engaged in trade during the years between 1785 and 1825.[67] After surveying this busy fur trade, one historian concluded: "At the outset the trade was heavily British; but from 1789 onward the American traders, principally from Boston, gradually absorbed it, until by about 1800 it had become the practical monopoly of the city of Bos-ton."[68] From this perspective, the Northwest Coast appeared to be a resource-rich suburb of Boston.

But other factors and actors were also in play. Besides British and American ships, vessels flying the flags of Russia, Portugal, France, Spain, Sweden, and Hawai'i also traded on the Northwest Coast. While only 10 percent of total traffic, these ships nonetheless illustrated an international awareness of the new com-mercial opportunities in the eastern Pacific. The French commander of *Le Borde-lais*, M. Camille de Roquefeuil, sighted mostly American, British, and Russian vessels during his fourteen months on the Northwest Coast in 1817 and 1818, although Indians in the Nootka Sound region informed him of trading the pre-vious season with an unmarked ship. The ship's only distinguishing characteristic was its captain, who had a *jambe de bois*, or wooden leg.[69] Roquefeuil traded on the coast and coastal islands with Indians of various nations, and he contracted a group of Aleut hunters to collect sea otters in southern Alaska. Elsewhere during his three-year voyage—which took *Le Bordelais* to Chile, Peru, California, Hawai'i, the Marquesas Islands, and China—Roquefeuil trafficked with a range of island nations and mainland groups, not to mention the European, American, and Asian traders he met along the way. Such diverse contacts typified all voyages to the coast. Thus, while American and English ships controlled the volume of trade once they reached the Northwest Coast, the voyage of any given ship was marked by international and intercultural encounters.

Viewing America's Northwest Coast as the Pacific's northeastern quadrant refocuses attention on a second crucial aspect of this trade: its deep involvement with other commercial opportunities in the Pacific. Even those "Boston men" (a Chinook term that distinguished American traders from English "King George's men"[70]) who dominated the fur trade did not simply sail to the coast and return home with cargos of furs and pelts. Instead, they trafficked the Pacific Ocean as a whole in pursuit of profitable exchanges. Approximately 15 percent of all ships to the Northwest Coast stopped in California and South America (either Chile or Peru), while more than one-third stopped in Hawai'i and more than one-half stopped in Canton or Macao.[71] Less common (but nonetheless evident) trading or provisioning stops included Australia, the Marquesas, Galápagos, or Society islands, and the Kamchatka Peninsula. From the Northeast rim to the western port of Canton, the Pacific held many options for those traders who could reorient themselves to the ocean's commercial opportunities.

A final significant aspect of the Pacific fur trade was the power of indigenous communities to negotiate the terms of exchange. Native people—rather than Hudson's Bay Company or Astoria functionaries—did the actual hunting and preparation of furs and pelts, and their power derived in part from this role as suppliers. Their strength also resulted from tight-knit kinship groups and well-established regional trading networks. European and American ship captains therefore faced some very organized indigenous trading partners who exerted power in various ways: playing traders off one another, demanding the highest-quality trade items, and extending the negotiating process—all to secure the best trade goods in return for their furs.[72] Some prominent tribal leaders along the coast wielded tremendous authority in trading with outsiders. Maquinna of Nootka Sound, Wickaninish of Clayoquot Sound, Cunneah and Kow of the Queen Charlotte Islands, and a succession of Tsimshian headmen named Legaic all sought to control commercial relations, gaining or losing prestige among their followers in the process. Indigenous fur traders grasped the profit motive all too well, the British captain John Meares concluded in 1790: "We found to our cost" that the Indians "possessed all the cunning necessary to gains of mercantile life."[73] Captain Cook discovered the same tenacity among natives when he attempted to acquire basic supplies on the Northwest coast: "I have no[where] met with Indians who had such high notions of every thing the Country produced being their exclusive property as these; the very wood and water we took on board they at first wanted us to pay for."[74]

Surrounding these trade relations—and assisting indigenous groups at times—was an omnipresent possibility of violent confrontation. Many volleys of shot and arrows flew between trading vessels and canoes; ship cannon fire occasionally targeted villages; and more notably for ship captains and diarists, Indians attacked trading ships with varying degrees of success (including the

Lady Washington in 1791, the *Cheerful* in 1799, the *Boston* in 1803, the *Otter* and the *Tonquin* in 1811, among others).[75] At least fifteen organized assaults on Northwest trading vessels took place between 1785 and 1805. Though usually unsuccessful, news of such attacks circulated widely among maritime traders and forced them to cautiously negotiate with native communities of the Northwest Coast.

Callao, San Blas, and Sitka

Three other ports functioned prominently in the eastern Pacific's commercial geography, especially in the context of the Alta California trade. The port of Callao, just north of Lima, was a natural stopover point for vessels sailing around the Horn en route to the northern Pacific. At least 20 percent of ships visiting California also docked in Callao. Peru, however, had a much longer history of transpacific activity than did California. Callao had served the Spanish silver trade since the early 1600s and remained "a stronghold of Spanish authority" until 1818, when the viceroy officially opened the port to British trade.[76] Yet similar to California, contraband trade had steadily increased in Callao since 1800. Numerous ships stopped each year in this Peruvian port for clandestine trade before sailing north along the American coastline for California. Callao was opened to all international traffic in 1820, a year when more than two hundred American ships and nearly an equal number of British trade vessels plied the Pacific.[77] British and American traders quickly established merchant houses in Callao to capitalize on the new commercial opportunities, and Callao or Lima merchants now owned many ships flying the British flag (almost two-thirds of British ships that stopped in California after 1820 had this distinction). Peruvian free traders and protectionists waged political warfare throughout the 1820s and the protectionists reigned supreme by 1828, but Pacific vessels continued to frequent Callao despite high import tariffs. Though Charles Darwin expressed grave doubts about the prospects of this port city during his 1835 visit—he especially noted the prevalence of diseases, "anarchy," and the "depraved . . . mixture" of various races—Callao and Lima teemed with international trade and by 1850 were South American centers for wheat, copper, and guano exports.[78]

In contrast to the Pacific's rising commercial centers (California, Canton, Hawai'i, the Northwest Coast, and Callao), San Blas and Sitka were the only significant ports that declined during the first half of the nineteenth century. San Blas, a naval base in the Gulf of California designed for Spain's expansion up the North American coast, was located in a mangrove swamp brimming with mosquitoes and malaria. San Blas's large population of twenty thousand residents by 1800 more than served the needs of the infrequent Spanish supply ships that ran the Pacific coast from Baja California to Nootka Sound. Prior to Mexican independence in 1821, one-half of the vessels visiting California had also stopped in San Blas (mostly ships of Spanish origin). But following independence, Mexican shipping quickly reverted back to the healthier climes of the old silver-trade port at Acapulco, and San Blas steadily declined as a center of trade.[79]

Sitka served a similar function for Russia as San Blas did for Spain. The Russian-American Company, chartered by Tsar Paul I in the 1790s, dominated the north Pacific fur trade based from its Sitka headquarters, where it ran supply ships to the Kamchatka Peninsula and other ships down the coast to Alta California. By the 1810s, however, the company's yearly harvest of sea otter pelts and other furs dropped precipitously, as did the population of Aleut and Kodiak contract hunters, who succumbed to smallpox, influenza, and other diseases.[80] The Russian-American Company had only thrived in the late eighteenth century by brutalizing natives and slaughtering Alaska's marine mammal population to near extinction; to survive the early nineteenth century the company required fresh killing fields farther south. Russian traders remained at Sitka through the mid-1800s, but Sitka's place in international trade steadily declined.

Advancing the Ideology of Free Trade

In what other ways had Pacific commerce changed between the 1780s and the 1840s? What characteristics and ideologies influenced the nature of Pacific trade? The most obvious change was the steadily increasing volume of trade. Return to the example of Alta California: only 64 ships visited the California coast in the fourteen years prior to 1800, while at least 443 ships visited that coast in the fourteen years prior to 1848. A similar rise in the number of trading vessels took place throughout the eastern Pacific and the ocean as a whole. Another characteristic involved the international nature of that trade. In California alone, vessels from more than twenty nations or principalities appeared during those six decades—and while only a few nations made up the majority of voyages and the volume of trade, all the other nations demonstrated an international awareness of Pacific trade opportunities. The byproducts of this trade for many indigenous communities bordered on the catastrophic. International commerce, in its many guises and structures, had permeated and transformed almost all Pacific indigenous communities by the 1840s. The same could hardly be said of those communities in the late 1700s.

By the 1820s Americans had assumed a dominant role in certain key places (such as Hawai'i's merchant houses) and various activities (whaling, sealing, transpacific trade to China). Their practices and ambitions, moreover, epitomized an ideology of free trade shared by some groups around the ocean. Since the time of the Spanish galleon trade, imperial powers and government-sponsored companies had attempted to monopolize and regulate specific regions, markets, goods, and Pacific trade routes. Such controls over trade are well exemplified by the histories of the Russian-American Company, the British East India Company, the Dutch East India Company, the Royal Philippine Company, and the restrictive policies of the Spanish Empire. Regulating access to trade worked with varying degrees of success prior to 1800, in large part because of the lack of foreign competition. But trade restrictions and monopolies ceased to function rationally in the more competitive and rapidly expanding commerce following the Napoleonic Wars. American sea captains were certainly not the only ones promoting the new commerce, but Americans were the most enthusiastic advocates and successful practitioners of what they construed to be free trade.

Abby Jane Morrell was one such vocal advocate. The wife of Captain Benjamin Morrell, twenty-year-old Abby Morrell (at the time of the ship's departure) scribed to "fellow countrywomen" her account of a Pacific trading venture conducted in 1829 and 1830.[81] Their ship, the *Antarctic*, crisscrossed much of the ocean before seeking a cargo of bêche-de-mer (dried sea slugs) in Fiji for transport to Manila.[82] But acquiring that cargo from Fijian suppliers proved disastrous: villagers stole some unguarded tools, which prompted Captain Morrell to take a local chief hostage. The villagers responded with an attack that killed fourteen crewmembers ("victims to savage barbarity!" wrote Abby Morrell).[83] The *Antarctic* departed for Manila, where Captain Morrell gathered a crew of eighty-five men (plus his wife) and equipped the ship with additional cannon and brass swivel guns. The *Antarctic* returned to "Massacre Island," and Abby Morrell watched from the ship deck as the crew opened fire from a fortified encampment, cutting down large numbers of Fijians with the swivel guns. "The enemy did not expect such a reception," Abby Morrell wrote, and soon the "ground was strewed with implements of war" and dead "savages." Captain Morrell described "the ground being covered with the crimson clotted blood of these obstinate, infuriated savages."[84] Abby Morrell commented:

> I saw all this without any sensation of fear, so easy is it for a woman to catch the spirit of those near her. . . . Still I could not but deplore the sacrifice of the poor, misguided, ignorant creatures, who wore the human form, and had souls to save. Must the ignorant always be taught civilization through blood?—situated as we were, no other course could be taken.[85]

Curiously, the meaning Abby Morrell derived from this violent episode was not about civilization and savagery; instead, she turned the story into a parable about the necessity of free trade.

In the days that followed, the crew returned to their original mission. "We now commenced collecting and curing biche-de-mer [*sic*], and should have succeeded to our wishes, if we had not been continually harassed by the natives as soon as we began our efforts," she wrote. The *Antarctic* departed two weeks later because the crew found "it impossible to make [the Fijians] understand our motives and intentions"—which in her mind entailed a simple matter of securing a cargo of bêche-de-mer. That the islanders opposed Captain Morrell's mission from the start was beyond her comprehension. That the islanders sought to control their own property as well as the terms of exchange flew in the face of her belief in the virtue of free trade. Reflecting on her experiences, Abby Morrell concluded: "It is not only injurious but degrading to say you must not buy here, or sell there, but under a thousand restrictions. The world should be open for all, on equal terms . . . and no particular set of men ought to enjoy extraordinary privileges, nor any nation be particularly favoured."[86] Americans, Morrell believed, should rightfully propagate and defend this ideology despite the wishes of other people.[87]

Other observers had noted this ideological position among US traders for decades and some people considered it a particularly American trait. After his voyage around the world between 1800 and 1804, the British trader John Turnbull commented: "Scarcely is there a part of the world, scarcely an inlet in [the Pacific's] most unknown seas, in which this [American] commercial hive has not penetrated. The East-Indies is open to them, and their flags are displayed in the seas of China. And it must be confessed, to their honour, that their success is well merited by their industry."[88] Their "industry," according to the Scottish Captain Alexander M'Konochie, derived from a strategy of continual "speculation" as well as the "circuitous and desultory manner" by which American traders navigated the seas.[89] "Each American vessel," M'Konochie wrote in 1818,

> leaves its own port on general speculation, carrying perhaps a cargo of provisions to Madeira, and embarking wine in lieu; or to the Isle of France, the English settlements in India or New South Wales . . . with an assorted cargo suited to these several destinations. Wherever they unload, they are ready and willing to embark in any speculation, whether of country or of foreign trade, and close with any promising offer, keeping Canton only remotely in their view as the port whence, after a lapse even of years, they propose to proceed home, when they shall have accumulated from these slender beginnings a capital sufficient to complete the cargo of tea with which they mean to return.

The wars of the early 1800s had briefly slowed the tide of American trade in Canton, M'Konochie observed, "but they are now again out . . . in greater numbers than ever, an active, busy band, sagacious to discover and eager to improve every promising opportunity."[90]

M'Konochie's "Summary View" of Pacific commerce insightfully captured the nature of trade at a crucial moment of change, warning the British commercial community of their own lost opportunities. He sought to "fix public attention on the Pacific Ocean . . . whose shores extend to every habitable degree of latitude in our globe, and teem with every valuable article of exchange, and which yet hitherto have been scarcely visited once in a season by a British merchant ship[.]"[91] Americans, he argued, had captured the transpacific trade to Canton, while Great Britain had neglected its growing importance in China. The transpacific trade—"almost exclusively in the hands of that [US] republic," he wrote—followed three routes into China: from "New Albion" (California and the Northwest Coast), Hawai'i, and the Spanish-American mainland. These routes were vastly important, M'Konochie believed, but British trade policies protecting EIC activities in Canton had severely disadvantaged Britain's independent traders in the larger ocean.[92]

No mere heckler of his countrymen, Captain M'Konochie proposed a plan. England needed to "establish a *central colony* within the limits of the Pacific, but also to constitute its port or ports *free to all and every traffic* within its horizon; and to make it thus not only an emporium whence our own exports will readily diverge to their several destinations, but also a conduit by which the whole speculations of these seas shall be conveyed to the European and other Atlantic markets."[93] Where should Great Britain locate this free trade "colony" and how should the Commonwealth go about its acquisition? M'Konochie avoided these details, but it could have hardly escaped notice that the Hawaiian Islands fit all of M'Konochie's criteria for a free British port.

Despite the lack of specifics, M'Konochie's plan made perfect sense because it mirrored concurrent developments in the Pacific's commercial world. At the time of his book's publication, international vessels already sailed unmolested in most parts of the Pacific Ocean. The illegal or contraband commerce championed by earlier traders like William Shaler—a trade that worked well for them despite its drawbacks—was on the wane while unrestricted trade was on the rise. The commerce described by M'Konochie as "speculations of these seas" continued to grow in volume even as the specific commodities changed over time; entrepreneurial traders moved around the Pacific "eager to improve every promising opportunity" for pelts and furs, timber, bêche de mer, precious minerals and metals, whale oil, Chinese silks, teas, and porcelain.[94]

More than the writings of people like Abby Morrell, William Shaler, or Alexander M'Konochie, it was commercial and political factors that transformed the Pacific into a free trade waterscape in the years around 1820. Illicit maritime trade in Spanish America became far more licit due to independence movements in places like Peru and Mexico. Across the Pacific in Canton, the British EIC lost its balance of trade to the Americans in 1820, mostly because the Chinese Hong merchants embraced the notion of competition between foreign trading houses as a means to profit. Hawaiians had welcomed almost all trade since 1800 under King Kamehameha's rule; his death in 1819 only accelerated the volume of trade due to Liholiho's alliances with American and British merchant houses. Honolulu's new status as the ocean's central marketplace developed from those alliances as well as the network of other ports that now spanned the Pacific, enticing maritime entrepreneurs from around the globe. The Pacific's unrestricted commercial environment manifested itself in numerous ways after 1820: open and burgeoning ports, entrepreneurial shipping ventures designed to exploit specific commodities, private traders who paid little attention to geopolitical boundaries, and the speed with which information about Pacific trade flowed around the world.

Conclusion: The "Shadow Trade" of Disease

William Shaler's voyages on the *Lelia Byrd* in the opening years of the 1800s showed many elements of the Pacific trade that continued to expand over the next four decades. One defining element was the constant contact and bartering with indigenous people. This intercourse held a devastating—though initially invisible—biological impact. Arriving in Hawai'i in 1805, Shaler took a moment to reflect on the appearance of the people. "The Sandwich islanders are a large, well made, robust race of people, and many of their women are perfectly beautiful," he wrote. "Fortunately the good constitutions and temperance of these islanders prevents their having often occasion for the skill of their physicians."[95] Shaler may have noted the Hawaiians' "good constitutions" with some relief, because the previous year of trading had acquainted him with the ravages of various diseases among native peoples of the Pacific coastline. Shaler, however, was mistaken in his estimation of the Hawaiians' good health. Tuberculosis had already arrived on the islands, as had typhoid fevers and venereal syphilis. Introduced diseases carried off untold numbers of Hawaiians by 1805, while endemic sickness rather than "good constitutions" defined the health status of many native Hawaiians.

Shaler should have been more observant—or reported his observations more truthfully—because the Hawaiians he met on this second visit to the islands had just witnessed a deadly scourge take the lives of thousands of men, women, and children. Accounts of the *okuu* vary widely, including such basic facts as when it appeared and how many people died. But according to the most detailed study, the *okuu* was a strain of typhoid fever that arrived in late 1803 and cut its fatal course through the island populations for the next twelve months.[96] Estimates of the dead range widely from 5,000 to 175,000 people, though a lower figure seems most likely based on the few existing contemporary accounts.[97] Apparently, the disease was called *okuu* "because the people *okuu wale aku no i ka uhane*," or "dismissed freely their souls and died."[98] The *okuu* arrived on a foreign vessel carrying contaminated water or food. Only three ships arrived in 1802 (the *Atahualpa, Margaret,* and *Ann*), and only one ship arrived in Hawai'i in 1803: the first visit of the *Lelia Byrd.* It stayed in Hawai'i for sixteen days, more than enough time to introduce all sorts of bacteria. Less than two years later, the *Lelia Byrd* returned to Hawai'i and William Shaler reported the people to be in good health. Accounts of this island epidemic remain far too vague to consider its original cause, but Shaler's silence on the matter was strangely uncharacteristic, given his detailed descriptions of disease prevalence along the coast of North America.

Shaler sold the *Lelia Byrd* to King Kamehameha and the vessel stayed in Hawai'i as part of the king's fleet. Once adequately refurbished, it carried sandalwood to Canton on a number of voyages. Time and salt water had their way with the *Lelia Byrd*'s hull, and it never returned to Hawai'i from its last run to China. Anchored in the Whampoa harbor outside Canton, the *Lelia Byrd* was retired from active duty and spent its remaining days as a receiving depot for opium fresh from India—a floating drug house for British and American traders.[99]

2

Disease, Sex, and Indigenous Depopulation

Lawe liʻiliʻi ka make a ka Hawaiʻi, lawe nui ka make a ka haole.
Death by Hawaiians takes a few at a time; death by foreigners takes many.

—Hawaiian Proverb

Discovery and *Resolution*, 1776–1779

The HMS *Discovery* and *Resolution* finally departed from the Hawaiian Islands on February 28, 1779, a long fortnight after the killing of Captain James Cook. Command of the voyage fell to Charles Clerke, a man who most observers agreed was not long for the world. Mourning Cook and dreading the months ahead in the icy North Pacific, Clerke lamented his "own unhappy state of Health" while the other officers sadly monitored his diminishing frame. First Lieutenant James Burney saw Clerke "reduced to almost an absolute skeleton," a mere apparition of the hearty man who had sailed on all three of Cook's Pacific voyages and circumnavigated the globe as a teenager on the HMS *Dolphin*.

Clerke stubbornly clung to life and command during the late winter. The two ships sailed to the Kamchatka Peninsula, went north through the frigid Bering Strait, and returned back to Kamchatka in August, where Clerke's tubercular lungs pulled one final breath. On August 22, Lieutenant James King sat at Clerke's bedside, held his hand, and watched him die. "Never was a decay, so melancholy & gradual," King noted in his private journal. Clerke was thirty-six years old.[1]

Mycobacterium tuberculosis had spread throughout his lungs for three years, since the time he was first "attacked" by the "disorder" in the "King's bench prison," as Clerke informed Sir Joseph Banks in a dictated deathbed letter.[2] This stay in London's notorious debtors' prison for his brother's obligations proved most costly. Clerke took command of the *Discovery* upon his release in August 1776 and immediately sailed from Plymouth. He appeared in fine health when

43

he met up with Captain Cook and the *Resolution* at the Cape of Good Hope, despite isolated cases of smallpox on the *Discovery* and more widespread complaints of the venereal "French Pox."[3] In the following months Clerke's "wasting sickness" began to take its toll. Poor nutrition, possibly including scurvy and quite likely a venereal disease, undermined Clerke's immune system, allowing the tuberculosis to wreak havoc on his lungs. By fall 1777, Clerke's illness kept him all but confined to the *Discovery* while his sailors pursued sexual opportunities with the islanders of Tahiti and Huahine.

Clerke's consumption spread to Cook's surgeon William Anderson and possibly to Cook himself; by the time they reached Hawai'i Clerke confessed "my state of health is such, as to render me totally incapable."[4] Anderson deteriorated even more rapidly, until August 3, 1778, when he died just south of the Bering Strait. Cook named an island for him "to perpetuate the Memory of the deseased [*sic*] for whom I have a very great regard." Clerke, who may have feared he infected Anderson, ruefully noted a "Void in the Voyage much to be regretted."[5] Clerke would die one year later, one of only seven crewmembers of the *Resolution* and *Discovery* to perish from ill health during the voyage, a rare accomplishment given eighteenth-century shipboard mortality rates.[6]

And yet despite the low mortality, the actual disease load carried by the *Discovery* and *Resolution*—in conjunction with Cook's two previous Pacific voyages—still beggars the imagination. Officers and crewmembers became ill from tuberculosis, assorted "fevers" including malaria and dengue, dysentery, dropsy, pneumonia, influenza, viral hepatitis, smallpox, and venereal diseases.[7] Of course, the true burden of disease must be measured not only by its impact on the ships' crews, but more significantly, on the indigenous people plagued by these introduced diseases. Severe, in some instances devastating, consequences followed in the wake of Cook's vessels. Native groups in Tahiti, New Zealand, Australia, Hawai'i, and the Northwest Coast all paid dearly for their direct exposure to individuals like Charles Clerke, a man who spewed lethal tubercular bacilli with each cough. While Cook's men were no more diseased than any other group of foreign Pacific voyagers, they nonetheless represent the tip of an epidemiological iceberg that ravaged and depopulated indigenous communities in the coming decades.

The rising level of trade throughout the Pacific translated to more ships, more foreigners, and more moments of contact during which a variety of diseases could be transmitted. Put another way, the disease transmission routes became far more efficient and widespread with each decade after 1800. Indigenous people, meanwhile, more frequently worked in close contact with foreigners, especially as laborers aboard ships. This proximity exacerbated disease transmission and induced high death rates for native sailors.

As much as any other factor in depopulation, sex between indigenous people and outsiders—the primary focus of this chapter—often proved devastating. These sexual relations, which involved varying degrees of coercion, failed to produce healthy offspring or reproduce viable populations. Rather, sex with foreign sailors disseminated venereal disorders and their hidden consequences of infertility, infant mortality, and brutal assaults on immune systems. Thus, while commercial ventures increasingly connected the eastern Pacific during the first half of the nineteenth century, those oceanic linkages stood in stark relief to the fracturing and reduction of local indigenous communities.

Framing Disease and History

Indigenous people in the Americas and the Pacific died in astonishing numbers through the introduction of diseases to which they had no prior exposure and against which they held vulnerable immune systems. Recent scholarship by historians, anthropologists, and epidemiologists has documented a deathly "horror" so pervasive as to reframe most previous explanations of contact relations, indigenous resistance, and the reasons for European imperial "success."[8] Waves of pathogens introduced by Europeans hit the West Indies and the Americas after 1492 and spread through various channels to geographically dispersed native communities. These same pathogens arrived in the Pacific with Spanish imperialism during the 1500s, although they initially remained isolated to the contours of the Manila galleons' gold and silver trade in Peru, Mexico, the Philippines, and China. In terms of global disease flows, the larger Pacific was a fairly delayed recipient of what one historian has termed the "common market of viruses and other bacilli."[9] Indeed, the Pacific's northeastern quadrant may constitute the *final* stage of this common market. But regardless of the timing, the maritime traffic that arrived in the Pacific during the late 1700s delivered pathogens that radically reduced native populations, in some places by as much as 90 percent over the course of a few generations.[10]

To comprehend the deadly processes at work—processes at once social, historical, and epidemiological—requires moving beyond simple renderings of "virgin soil epidemics."[11] In a model virgin soil epidemic, an introduced pathogen decimates nearly an entire community because that population possesses no immunity to the new disease; the few survivors have little ability to recover and reconstitute their population. Some infections in the Americas and elsewhere may have been this virulent as they moved from one community to the next. But this chapter explores the more frequent pattern and impact of disease spread along with their conditioning factors. These factors included a variety of disease types introduced through different channels, environmental conditions that exacerbated the impact of pathogens, and finally, introduced venereal disorders that significantly limited fertility and simultaneously weakened individual immune systems.[12] Such factors worked in lethal combinations throughout the Pacific, channeling "vectors of death" to previously healthy indigenous populations.[13]

Indigenous Pacific peoples quickly grasped the changes in health affecting their bodies, families, and communities. While pre-contact ailments and infections had certainly influenced the quality of health and life expectancy, the pathogens delivered by foreigners introduced new magnitudes of suffering and death. "*Lawe li'ili'i ka make a ka Hawai'i, lawe nui ka make a ka haole,*" observed Hawaiians in the early 1800s: "Death by Hawaiians takes a few at a time; death by foreigners takes many."[14] If neither natives nor foreign sailors understood the precise epidemiology or etiology of the new diseases, many people still recognized the connection between the arrival of trading vessels and disease outbreaks.[15] Indigenous people crafted their own expressions of this understanding. Cook islanders who fell ill developed the phrase *Kua paî au*, or "I am shippy," to describe both their misery as well as the presumed agent of their illnesses: the trading ships.[16] Yakutat Tlingit villagers blamed foreign "disease boats" for bringing the deadly maladies, while their shaman believed a "boat of sickness" carried away the dead.[17] Hawaiians, too, dated their epidemiological assault to the arrival of the first ships. Prior to those ships, according to the nineteenth-century Hawaiian writer Samuel Kamakau, "there were no fatal diseases (*luku*), no epidemics (*ahulau*), no contagious diseases (*ma'i lele*), no diseases that eat away the body (*ma'i 'a 'ai*), no venereal diseases (*ma'i pala a me ke kaokao*)."[18] Thus, in the absence of a "germ theory" that would afford even greater specificity to causes, natives rightly viewed foreign vessels as the carriers of their new afflictions.

Nineteenth-century medical researchers reached similar conclusions. The German physician and medical historian August Hirsch published one of the first worldwide studies of disease prevalence, and the Pacific especially intrigued him because of the recently introduced epidemics.[19] Hirsch cited case upon case of ships and Pacific locales unknown to most of his readers: influenza on board the *Monarch* off the Chilean coast, a scarlet fever pandemic from Tahiti to Tasmania, malarial fevers in the Sacramento Valley, typhoid in Sitka, a smallpox outbreak introduced to the Northwest Coast by the British brig *Lama*, and syphilis everywhere due to the increase of "active traffic with other countries."[20] He cheered scientific progress and wrote at the cusp of major medical breakthroughs, and yet he also knew the "gifts of civilization" offered by European traffic had already devastated many indigenous populations.[21]

Hirsch's three-volume study gives a mistaken impression of pathological randomness: smallpox here, influenza there, and measles someplace else. Recent studies attempt to counter this randomness by establishing patterns of cause and effect: the documented introduction of a particular disease, its dispersion route with conditioning factors, and, to the extent possible, the death toll.[22] Nonetheless, a certain inexplicability in disease introduction and spread persists. For instance, little more than happenstance led Cook's third voyage to stumble upon the unmapped Hawaiian island chain in 1778, at which point crewmembers introduced tuberculosis and venereal disease. Randomness also factored into the localized nature of many outbreaks.[23] Smallpox, for example, struck certain indigenous communities on the Northwest Coast during the late eighteenth century while nearby communities remained geographically and socially buffered from contagion. Local outbreaks held the potential to spread far and wide, but they could also remain quite localized.

Many people witnessed the resulting ill health, death, and dying. Indigenous people kept alive memories of the epidemics in their oral histories. A Chinookan-speaking elder named William Charley told the story of the "fever and ague" outbreak among his people on the Columbia River in 1830. "The Indians were settled thick up and down the river and all the streams," he remarked. "This sickness broke out and they did not know what it was, nor know what to do about it. . . . Everyone who took sick, never got over it. All died."[24] Foreign traders left numerous accounts of depopulated villages. "I have touched at [many] places in the course of my voyages . . . which are now solitary and desert[ed]," William Shaler wrote in 1808 regarding the Baja California coast. He described the reduction of one native community from seven thousand to fifty "souls," and he found it "difficult to imagine what [could] have been the cause of this extraordinary depopulation" if not for the "loathsome [venereal] disorder."[25] From these and countless other firsthand accounts, one can only conclude that knowledge of disease impact was widespread at the time. Native depopulation transpired before a gallery of witting observers.

Fantasies and Force: The Sex Trade

Charles Clerke had spent over half of his short life at sea before succumbing to tuberculosis in 1779. He served as an officer on four of Great Britain's most famous circumnavigations: the *Dolphin* under Captain John Byron (1764–1766) followed by all three of Cook's voyages. Few officers amassed such a distinguished résumé punctuated by moments of pluck and luck. Not yet twenty years old and sailing on the seventy-four-gun HMS *Bellona* during the Seven Years' War, Clerke straddled the top of the ship's mizzenmast as it was shot out from under him during an engagement with the French ship *Courageux*. Clerke survived the long fall into the water, and his telling of this story (including its phallic imagery) entertained friends for the rest of his life.

Fellow officers and crewmembers thoroughly enjoyed Clerke's company. He demonstrated little of the arrogance of the British officer class and, on his final voyage with Cook, harbored little bitterness from his term in debtors' prison. "Huzza my Boys heave away," he wrote to Banks upon boarding the *Discovery* three weeks after Cook had left England on the *Resolution*, "I shall get hold of [Cook] I fear not."[26] Despite his consumption, Clerke planned to partake in the Pacific's many pleasures as he had done thrice before. One friend confirmed his record in this regard: "Clerke is a right good officer. At drinking and whoring he is as good as the best of them."[27]

Whatever else happened on Pacific voyages—trade, exploration, conflict with villagers, surveying, and a lot of hard work—sexual attractions ranked high on most every sailor's agenda. Some journal writers made only oblique references to their activities with native women, while others wrote candidly about the "obliging" women they met.[28] American midshipman William Reynolds, en route from the South Pacific to Hawai'i on the *Vincennes* in 1839, lapsed into the realm of sexual fantasy when he became enchanted by a particular young girl. Spending a night in the village of Avenga Alofa on the Samoan island of Tutuila, Reynolds described a welcoming crowd of men, women, and children: "My eye was soon attracted by the extraordinary grace & beauty of a young girl who was standing rather apart from the rest. She was about 15 & was the very emblem of innocent girlhood." Reynolds called this girl "Emma" and noted she was the daughter of the local "Prince" Maneitoa. "There was a sweet fascination about my Princess that was irresistible. If I had been 5 years younger," wrote the twenty-three-year-old Reynolds, "I should have been in love with her to distraction."[29]

Reynolds kept company with Emma for a few days before returning to the *Vincennes,* during which time he likely posed a public threat to the Samoan system of *taupou,* which strongly encouraged virginity for adolescent girls.[30] Emma had an even younger "companion," he wrote, and one day, "with these two, hand in hand, I strolled thro' the village ... until we came to the Big House. Here I undid my bundle & made my two companions presents of the most *valuable* things I had with me." The precise nature of Reynolds's "bundle" and *"valuable* things"—the emphasis is his—remains unclear: Did he mean material presents or something more corporeal? Or did he mean one followed by the other? If his precise meaning is ambiguous, his subsequent daydream is obvious:

> I could not help thinking of a life in this Eden—a half wish came in to my head, that I could free myself from my Ship, & under the shade of the delicious groves, form the mind of sweet Emma—ripen the bud into the full bloom of maturity—cherish the flower, & wear it for ever! What a dream!—yet it was natural.[31]

Reynolds's fantasy of leaving the ship for this island "Eden" mirrored the experiences of countless beachcombers, from the *Bounty*'s mutineers in 1789 to Herman Melville's desertion on the Marquesas Islands in 1842. Yet beyond this realm of fantasy remained a darker reality of European men purchasing sex and dominating young women, some of whom were prepubescent and had no alternative but to "consent." "Do not call it silly," warned Reynolds, "until you have tried [it] yourself."[32]

And try they did. Officers and crewmembers on Pacific voyages eagerly embraced the opportunities for "recreation," or "refreshment and recruitment" with islander women.[33] Nearing Hawai'i on August 19, 1805, William Shaler sighted "great numbers of the natives, of both sexes" approaching the *Lelia Byrd*, and commented on how they "brought us refreshments, &c."[34] Shaler's thinly veiled reference to sexual opportunities represented the shared ambition of decades of Pacific voyagers going back to Cook's arrival in Hawai'i. Naked young women swam out to the *Resolution* and *Discovery* in 1778, while Cook—one of the few celibates on the voyage and fearing the spread of the "greatest plague"—attempted with little success to control the sexual contacts between his men and the islanders. Cook's surgeon David Samwell described "exceedingly beautiful" women who "used all their arts to entice our people . . . [and] they absolutely would take no denial."[35] William Ellis agreed: "There are no people in the world who indulge themselves more in their sexual appetites than these [young women]," some of whom, he remarked, "could not be more than ten years old."[36] Forty years later Edmond Le Netrel of the *Héros* depicted a nearly identical scene: his captain "allowed the crew to receive on board as many women as they wished but only after the work was done and on express condition that they not proceed past the main mast."[37] If a few accounts noted the level of coercion in this sex trade, most observers ignored the nature of power in these sexual dealings.

Tahiti symbolized the original island sexual paradise due to reports from the initial contacts by Samuel Wallis (1767), Louis Antoine de Bougainville (1768), and James Cook (1769). Recounting how young women flocked to his ships *La Boudeuse* and *Étoile*, Bougainville queried: "I ask you, how was one to keep four hundred young French sailors, who hadn't seen women in six months, at their work in the midst of such a spectacle?" Despite his claimed vigilance at keeping women off the ships, Bougainville described one "young girl" who snuck aboard and "negligently let fall her robe for all to see." Chaos naturally ensued above and below decks as men scrambled to leer at this "Venus." "We managed to restrain these bedeviled men, however, but it was no less difficult to control oneself," Bougainville admitted.[38] The very *availability* of sex delighted sailors to no end and few participants failed to depict the women as promiscuous instigators. La Pérouse explained the situation on Easter Island in this way: "Not a single

Frenchman made use of the barbarous right which was given him; [but] if there were some moments *dedicated to nature*, the desire and consent were mutual, and the women made the first advances."[39] In some instances, the women's apparent enthusiasm openly mocked what they had already witnessed: the sailors' awkward and hasty sexual performances. Europeans "could credit Tahitians with innocence, happiness and sensuality, but not with critical intelligence," writes one scholar. "They had no idea that mere savages might be satirists too."[40]

What drove the active sexual marketplace that resulted in widespread infection, infertility, and life-threatening illness for indigenous people? The answer is fairly self-evident from the perspective of European and American sailors, who spent years away from home and, as Bougainville explained, "hadn't seen women in six months."[41] They all desired sex; preferably the kind that they could imagine was consensual. But a simple payment in the form of trade goods usually translated to adequate "consent" regardless of who actually received the goods. The participation of indigenous women is far more complicated and reflects a spectrum of circumstances, ranging from willing engagement to coercion and rape.

European and American sailors *perceived* willing consorts across Polynesia—most notably on Hawai'i, Tahiti, and the Marquesas, where sailors openly fornicated with native women on ship deck and shore. Many scholars have examined cultural factors to explain this apparent willingness by some Polynesian women to engage in sex with outsiders, especially during the early contact period. In Hawai'i, Marshall Sahlins asserts, "Sex was everything: rank, power, wealth, land, and the security of all these. Happy society, perhaps, that could make the pursuit of all the good things in life so enjoyable in itself."[42] Caroline Ralston distinguishes between elite or "noble" Hawaiian women and their "ordinary" (or non-noble) counterparts, who "threw themselves into the embrace of foreign sailors in what was an enactment of their established cultural practices and beliefs."[43] This all may be so. Yet behind these cultural explanations was the young women's expectation of social advancement: increased *mana* (or spiritual power) taken from a stranger, performing one's duty under the watchful eyes of village elders, and increasingly, an "avenue to foreign goods" in exchange for sexual favors.[44] The incentive of trade goods was crucial and women found they could demand them. Cook's sailors desperately yanked long nails from the ships' deck to compensate their sexual partners. Decades later, midshipman William Reynolds was "delighted" by three of the "prettiest damsels I could Select," and, he added with a wink: "My trinkets went."[45]

Long nails, hooks, trinkets, and coins—a sexual marketplace developed in many places in the island Pacific. But what began with proffered gratuities during the early contact period became an open and structured system of forced prostitution in later years.[46] Even at the outset a level of coercion was unmistakable, while short of coercion it was quite likely that sexual partners were unable to communicate about proper conduct, purpose, or the material terms of the exchange.[47] Recall the scene described by Bougainville: the *La Boudeuse* and *Étoile* were surrounded by Tahitian dugout canoes "filled with women. . . . Most of these nymphs were naked, since the men and old women who accompanied them had taken off the nymphs' robes." The young women and girls, physically undressed by their elders, appear mute in these highly charged proceedings. "The [village] men," Bougainville continues, "urged us to choose a woman and to follow her to land, and their unequivocal gestures made it plain how we were to treat her."[48] Bougainville's lurid description elides the actual terms and level of consent characterized in these intimate encounters. Other observers and participants were far clearer about the power dynamics at work and the level of sexual violence. George Reinhold Forster, the naturalist on Cook's second voyage, recorded how Maori men "sell the favours of their females to those of our ship's company, who were irresistibly attracted by their charms; and often were these victims of brutality dragged by the fathers into the dark recesses of the ship, and there left to the beastly appetite of their paramours."[49] In Polynesia, the expanding market exchange of sex for trade goods brought death and declining health to countless native women and men.

If European and American sailors generally imagined the island Pacific as a sexual paradise, the eastern Pacific coastline presented a different cultural environment where the exertion of force and patriarchal authority were undeniable. From Alaska to Baja California, indigenous women were abused as hostages, openly bartered as sex slaves, and prostituted for commodities. The Russian traders who established beachhead settlements along the Aleutian Islands during the late eighteenth century forced the male hunters to gather sea otter pelts by taking Aleut women as hostages and sexual consorts. Spanish soldiers and sailors used barter and force for their amorous encounters with native women from Baja California up the coast to Nootka Sound.[50] Other Europeans capitalized on preexisting forms of enslavement by Pacific Northwest tribes and had sex with enslaved native women, whose masters saw easy profits in this trade.[51]

Though the prostitution of women—whether enslaved or not—varied by locale, it nonetheless appeared widespread along the North American coastline. At Nootka Sound in 1792, José Mariano Moziño reported on the actions of Nuu-chah-nulth *taises* (chiefs): "The *taises* themselves prostitute these [lower class] women, especially to foreigners, in order to take advantage of the profit earned from this business."[52] Other sources suggest these women were enslaved war captives, rather than merely of a "lower class," and that Nuu-chah-nulth men refused to barter women of their own communities to foreigners.[53] William Shaler's crewmen encountered this barrier to sexual access when they came ashore at a Yurok village. Their offers for sex with the "young girls" were sharply rebuffed by the Yurok men. The sailors proceeded to make advances on the older women, but the Yurok men, according to Shaler, "were very jealous of their women; and, whether it was from fear or chastity, the latter rejected all the offers made them by our sailors, though some must have been of immense value in their estimation."[54] Clearly, Shaler's prior experience on the coastline led him to believe that sex was easily procured. But like other outsiders, Shaler failed to distinguish between enslaved women who may have lacked the power to resist, and free women of the community who had no interest in sex with foreigners, regardless of the compensation.

What conclusions can be drawn from these sexual encounters in the Pacific? First, sexual relations permeated contact situations throughout the region; sex was part and parcel of the unequal material, cultural, and epidemiological exchanges that transformed the region in the late 1700s and early 1800s. Second, while these intimate relations ranged in nature from consensual affairs to mass rape, some level of coercion led young women to employ their bodies for the satisfaction of foreign men. The promise of material gain—for themselves, their elders, or in the case of enslaved women, their masters—increasingly structured sexual dealings with outsiders. Finally and most important, these sexual relations held consequences for women's reproductive functions in society and catastrophic costs for indigenous health.[55] Venereal diseases introduced to native women and men rapidly spread through families and communities. Fertility and birthrates plummeted, while disfigurement and chronic ill health became common. Infant mortality rates rose, as did adult mortality through combinations of other introduced diseases. What were the biological agents of this mayhem?

The Bacteria: *Treponema Pallidum* and *Neisseria Gonorrhoeae*

The bacterial microorganism *Treponema* causes venereal syphilis and is closely associated with three other treponematosis diseases: endemic syphilis, yaws, and pinta. These latter three are skin diseases generally spread by hand-to-hand contact, and they appeared in some Pacific populations prior to the eighteenth century. Neither deadly nor a threat to human reproduction, they instead produce unsightly lesions and papillomas that often resemble the manifestations of venereal syphilis.[56] Venereal syphilis (*Treponema pallidum*), by contrast, had devastating effects on the skin, nervous system, reproductive and internal organs, general health, and mental health of infected individuals. Highly contagious through sexual intercourse, venereal syphilis once contracted could also spread to a pregnant woman's developing fetus. Such congenital infections, most common during the first few years after a woman contracted venereal syphilis, might result in miscarriages, stillbirths, premature births, and high infant mortality rates. Individuals who carried the untreated disease for many years could anticipate syphilitic rashes, paresis of the muscular and skeletal system, and dementia. The gonorrhea bacteria (*Neisseria gonorrhoeae*) caused fewer of these maladies, but it was equally contagious through sex and frequently resulted in male and female infertility. The infection proved highly damaging to a woman's uterus, fallopian tubes, and ovaries—conditions diagnosed today as pelvic inflammatory disease and endometritis.[57]

The medical meaning and possible treatments for foreign sailors and indigenous populations were quite distinct. In the best of circumstances for infected European sailors—satisfactory food, no exposure to new diseases, and what passed for medical intervention prior to antibiotic drugs—they could weather these diseases and maintain relatively good health for decades.[58] In the circumstances faced by newly infected indigenous populations—chronic ill health due to introduced diseases, subsistence crises leading to malnutrition, and healing treatments that failed to counter these conditions—venereal diseases proved disastrous to individuals as well as the larger community. Traditional herbal remedies, such as Polynesian healers' use of *Gardenia taitensis* for inflammation of the urogenital tract and testicles, would have done little to stop the advance of venereal disorders.[59]

Scientific and historical debates continue over the origins and diffusion of *Treponematosis*, especially venereal syphilis. For over five centuries the issue has boiled down to whether or not New World populations syphilized the Old World: given the catastrophic disease load carried from Europe to the Americas, did Native Americans send back on Columbus's ships at least *one* microbial disease capable of spreading like wildfire across Europe in the decades after 1493? Venereal syphilis, furthermore, was not just *any* disease, but instead one that came with the cultural baggage of sexual depravity, filth, and possibly savage origins. Research increasingly casts doubt on an exclusively New World origin for venereal syphilis.[60]

Regardless of its origins, a particularly virulent and "most presumptuous pox" spread across Europe in the late 1400s and 1500s, at which time this apparently new pox also began a worldwide tour to Africa, Asia, and the Americas in the loins of European sailors and merchants.[61] Most parts of the Pacific remained isolated from European maritime traffic *and* the pox until the late eighteenth century, at which point it appeared in all its painful and debilitating manifestations from the South Pacific to Hawai'i to the North American coastline. The disorder wrought havoc among these newly infected populations precisely because they lacked previous exposure to venereal syphilis, causing a response similar to the first outbreaks among European populations.[62]

In the Pacific, the physical symptoms on indigenous bodies shocked even those European observers who had extensive expertise treating the disease, as evidenced by the French surgeon Claude-Nicolas Rollin's 1786 description of a venereal disease that "prevailed" among the inhabitants of Maui:

> These scourges, the most humiliating and most destructive with which the human race are afflicted, display themselves among these islanders by the following symptoms: buboes, and scars which result from their suppurating, warts, spreading ulcers with caries of the bones, nodes, exostoses, fistula, tumors of the lachrymal and salival ducts, scrofulous swellings, inveterate ophthalmiae, ichorous ulcerations of the tunica conjunctiva, atrophy of the eyes, blindness, inflamed prurient herpetic eruptions, indolent swellings of the extremities, and among children, scald head, or a malignant tinea, from which exudes a fetid and acrid matter. I remarked, that the greater part of these unhappy victims of sensuality, when arrived at the age of nine or ten, were feeble and languid, exhausted by marasmus, and affected with the rickets.[63]

Dr. Rollin knew well what he observed: untreated second- and possibly third-stage venereal syphilis and, among children, quite likely its congenital form. The sight was equally if not more shocking to the untrained spectator. Anchored off-shore the island of Hawai'i in 1788, James Colnett described the male visitors to his ship: "Observ'd many Men in a most frightful state with the Dry Pox. Discharging from all Parts of ye Body."[64]

Rollin and Colnett were among the first visitors to the Hawaiian Islands following a seven-year gap after Cook's historic "first" encounter. Both observers bore witness to three interrelated phenomena: the sexual marketplace initiated by Cook's crews, the introduction of a potent bacteria to the island community, and the effects of venereal diseases on Hawaiian bodies. Rollin and Colnett were not alone in their awareness of what Colnett called "the disease left by the first discoverers."[65] To the contrary, foreigners and natives also knew that it came from the ships' officers and crews with their libidinous appetites.

Hawai'i and the "Miserable Plague"

Charles Clerke held a fairly liberal attitude toward sexually transmitted diseases. He understood that most sailors carried them and he believed relatively simple treatments could pacify these maladies. Three months into what would be his final voyage and "moor'd alongside my Old Friend Capt Cook" at the Cape of Good Hope, Clerke penned a lively letter to Sir Joseph Banks—a man whose reputation for sexual escapades during a Pacific voyage far exceeded Clerke's own. "We had a little of the Small[pox] and abundance of the French Pox among us at our sailing," he informed Banks, "but all hands were fairly cleans'd and perfectly healthy at our Arrival here."[66] Clerke offered no details about the "cleansing" treatment, which could have involved any combination of mercury, arsenic, potassium iodide, or a thick concoction brewed from the wood of a West Indies guaiac tree, in addition to probing and scraping the offending member.[67] But this much is certain: none of it cured the disease. Whatever improvements Clerke observed in the sailors' health resulted from the diseases' own natural cycles of remission and progression, not the "cures" widely offered by London surgeons and snake-oil salesmen.

The crews' gonorrhea and syphilis reactivated in a fierce way due to sexual activity in Tahiti during the summer of 1777. "We have ½ our people ill with the fowl disease & 4 or 5 has had the Yellow jaundice," wrote Cook's astronomer William Bayly on October 13, 1777.[68] The crew was so debilitated by this point that there were "scarce hands enough able to do duty on board."[69] Any island population that next came into sexual contact with these men would pay dearly for the experience—a fact that Cook perfectly understood. When the *Resolution* and *Discovery* came across the Hawaiian Islands two months later, Cook feared the epidemiological impact his men would have on Hawaiian women. Due to the "venereal complaints" still suffered by his crew, he had his men inspected by surgeon David Samwell and "gave orders that no Women, on any account whatever were to be admited [*sic*] on board the Ships. . . . [I] also forbid all manner of connection with them, and ordered that none who had the venereal upon them should go out of the ships." But "connections" took place within a matter of days, forcing Cook to admit "the very thing happened that I had above all others wished to prevent."[70]

At this point the timing of events and Cook's observations become crucial. During this initial "discovery" of the Hawaiian Islands, the two ships spent less than two weeks at Kaua'i and Ni'ihau, the westernmost of the eight main islands. Cook, Clerke, and the other voyagers saw nothing of the larger and more populous islands to the east, but they certainly gained an awareness of those islands' existence. After two weeks the *Resolution* and *Discovery* departed for the North American coast and the Bering Strait. They returned to the Hawaiian Islands nine months later, this time striking the island of Maui at the *eastern* end of the archipelago, approximately 250 nautical miles from the previous landing. Despite this distance, Cook was already troubled by what he feared they would find.

On the morning of November 26, 1778, the crew of the *Resolution* sighted land (Maui) and within hours canoes approached the ship. Cook's description of this meeting leaves no question as to his immediate concern:

Seeing some Canoes coming off to us I brought to; as soon as they got a long side many of the people who conducted them came into the Ships without the least hesitation. They were of the same Nation as those of the leeward islands, and if we did not mistake them they knew of our being there. Indeed it appeared rather too evident as these people had got amongst [them] the Veneral distemper, and I as yet knew of no other way they could come by it.[71]

Rather than describing the customary greetings or the eagerly anticipated trade, Cook instead immediately verified that venereal disease had spread throughout the islands during his nine-month absence. This was a moment of great remorse for Cook ("the evil I meant to prevent," he wrote "had already got amongst them") and also of tremendous awareness of his historic role. The crew had unleashed a dreaded disease upon an unexposed people and Cook knew the consequences would be devastating.[72]

Hawaiians immediately bore witness to their condition. Contemporary indigenous accounts of the disease's rapid spread only appear through the written words of British officers. While highly filtered in this way, they nonetheless confirm that Hawaiians understood the island-to-island spread of the disease as well as the foreigners' role in its introduction. Two days after arriving at Maui, midshipman Edward Riou wrote: "We heard that many of the natives had been complaining yesterday onboard the Resolution of the Venereal disease—one or two of them were examined by the Surgeon who Confirmed it,—they were asked about it & said a great many men & women were afflicted with it on Shore, and spoke of the Isle Atowi [Kaua'i], as if we had left it at that place the Last year." Riou mentions the possibility that Spaniards could have arrived first and introduced it, but he concedes "in the end it will appear it has been we ourselves that has entailed on these poor, Unhappy people an everlasting and Miserable plague."[73] Charles Clerke heard a similar story on board the *Discovery*: "The first Man that came on Board told me he knew the Ship very well & had been on board her at A'towi . . . & related some Anecdotes, which convinced me of his Veracity." Clerke left aside the question of whether or not this man was infected with the "Miserable plague," but he confirmed the natives' knowledge of its introduction and virulence:

Here are many of these good Folks both Men and Women about the Ship miserably afflicted with the Venereal disease, which they accuse us of introducing among them during our last visit, they say it does not go away, that they have no Antidote for it, but that they grow worse and worse, explaining the different symptoms in the progress of the disorder till it totally destroys them.

Clearly uncomfortable with this accusation, Clerke attempted to blame Hawaiians for the epidemic. That it "rage[d] more violently" in Hawai'i than in other islands they had visited, Clerke stated without great conviction, "I suppose may be attributed . . . to the quantity of Salt these People make use of in their customary diet."[74] But Clerke could muster no evidence to support this rationale.

These accounts demonstrate that Hawaiians immediately and forcefully testified to their plight, the disease's origins, and its virulent nature. They understood the affliction was not a mere itch or sore, but instead a malady that could incapacitate the carrier within a matter of months. At the time of Cook's second visit, Hawaiians would not yet report on miscarriages, high infant mortality, and infertility, but visitors arriving in the next two decades offered reports on a declining population. They saw pervasive signs of venereal disease such as scarring, sores, unhealthy children and adults, and abandoned villages.[75]

Hawaiians undoubtedly searched for specific remedies as well as for broader cosmological reasons behind these radically changed conditions of health, reproduction, and society. One can only speculate about specific herbal medicines and healing practices they attempted, given the absence of relevant source material from this period. But Hawaiian scholars have suggested a strong "alienation" of the people from the land (*'āina*), as well as a questioning of the balanced relationships between the body (*kino*), the spirit (*wailua*), and the mind (*no'ono'o*) that brought health and stability to the people.[76] *Kahuna* healers must have struggled to explain the meaning of this crisis, and for the next hundred years many commoners and elite Hawaiians relied on their knowledge and treatments.[77]

Some Hawaiians blamed their ancestors' social and sexual mores, especially as Christianity spread among the population during the 1820s and 1830s. The writer David Malo (1793–1853), in a rare indigenous testimony on depopulation from the 1830s, argued that women became the conduits through which disease entered the islands after "the arrival of Capt. Cook" and "reduced [the Kingdom] to a skeleton." According to Malo,

> [One] cause of the diminution of the people of the islands is, the licentiousness existing between Hawaiian females, and certain foreigners . . . [who] have thus polluted with a filthy disease the females of Hawai'i. This disease has, moreover, become prevalent among the people, and even children, and all the people of the islands are miserably diseased.

While Malo clearly blamed Cook's men for introducing disease, he believed female "licentiousness" also played a role—a patriarchal reading of events that ignored the power of Hawaiian men in early sexual activities, but a reading that accorded well with Malo's Christian message. "For this cause God is angry," he concluded.[78] While some Christian missionaries also laid blame on Hawaiian women, it remains unclear to what extent Hawaiians shared Malo's patriarchal view.

Less evident in Malo's account were the new conditions of widespread infertility and high infant mortality rates discovered and tabulated by his Christian missionary peers during the 1830s.[79] According to the Reverend Artemas Bishop, venereal disease's "greatest influence has been to destroy the powers of procreation, thus writing childless a vast majority of Hawaiian families."[80] The mission census records for the islands of Maui, Oʻahu, Kauaʻi, and Hawaiʻi for the 1830s and 1840s document the same startling conclusions as Bishop: rising infant mortality rates, recorded deaths far outnumbering live births, and birthrates continuing to tumble as infertility spread.[81] Records from the 1850s show a native population in freefall, with one child born for every eleven women, according to one study. The survival rate for those infants and children was dismally low. A missionary from Kailua, Hawaiʻi, reported: "In this district rather more than one half of the children die before the period of first dentition closes. In the district of Hilo . . . a very little less than one half die during the same period."[82]

Historical demographers continue to debate Hawaiʻi's pre-contact population, ranging from David Stannard's figure of 800,000 Hawaiians to the lower figures (250,000 to 500,000) posited by many other scholars. Regardless, the fact of drastic population decline by disease remains, offering a gruesome image of post-contact life. Native Hawaiians certainly died as a direct result of introduced diseases like tuberculosis and typhoid fever, but it was the pervasiveness of venereal syphilis and gonorrhea that produced what were likely the leading causes of depopulation: infertility and chronic ill health. Contemporary accounts and recent demographic studies support this causative chain of events, which led from Cook's first landing to the social chaos and demographic collapse that resulted from sexual relations with foreigners.[83]

Pox California: Counting Births and Deaths

The pox arrived in Tahiti, New Zealand, Australia, and many other places in the South Pacific during the decade before it reached Hawaiʻi on Cook's third voyage. Tahitians, who called it *apa no pretane*, or the "English disease," lost population from introduced epidemics and low fertility at a rate even faster than Hawaiians; they experienced an estimated 95 percent decline in the hundred years after 1767.[84] A similar rate of decline transpired in the Marquesas Islands, where *Te Enata* (the People) called foreign sailors *papaa*—venereal disease.[85] Venereal diseases followed the Spanish empire's presence on the South and Central American coast in the late 1500s and 1600s, and the pox crossed the ocean to the Philippines on Spanish galleons in the 1570s.[86] In the North Pacific, Russian explorers left behind venereal diseases on the Kamchatka Peninsula en route to the Aleutian Islands where, according to one Russian priest, it was soon "raging" through villages. He observed: "At that time there were whole families which, from the first to the last member, were infected with this horrible disease."[87]

Coastal California shared this Pacific-wide history of introduced venereal diseases. Recent paleopathological studies conclude that a non-venereal form of treponemal disease existed among Baja and Alta California Indians for thousands of years.[88] Yet skeletal records show that California Indians did not have venereal syphilis or gonorrhea—at least, not until a very isolated case appears dating from the mid-1500s.[89] This evidence comes from the "Skull Gulch" site of Santa Rosa Island, thirty miles offshore of the primary Chumash population center (near present-day Santa Barbara), which contains two skulls exhibiting cranial lesions indicative of "modern untreated venereal syphilis."[90] Carbon dating of these skulls confirms the two individuals died around the time of Juan Rodriguez Cabrillo's visit to Alta California in 1542–1543, during which time his sailors wintered on the Channel Islands of Santa Rosa, San Miguel, and Santa Cruz. This skeletal evidence raises far more questions than it may answer, and ongoing studies of Skull Gulch and associated sites may change the story altogether. Among the questions posed by these two syphilitic skeletons is, simply, why only two? Why didn't venereal syphilis spread throughout Chumash communities and neighboring groups as it did in Hawai'i? One possibility is that syphilis did in fact spread beyond these two individuals, yet not widely enough to appear in other excavated burial sites.[91] The other possibility is that sexual contact between Cabrillo's men and Chumash individuals was fairly limited. If so, traditional Chumash social-sexual mores could have prevented those women or their partners from spreading the disease to other individuals.[92] For now, one can only speculate about the impact of the numerous meetings with foreigners prior to Spanish colonization, and some scholars debate the possibility that other new diseases arrived by land and sea prior to 1769.[93]

What happened in Baja California requires far less speculation. Beginning with a first settlement in Loreto in 1697, Jesuit missionaries established a string of missions throughout Baja until the Jesuit expulsion in 1768, at which time Franciscan and later Dominican missionaries continued their self-appointed work of saving Indian souls. By this time, however, far fewer souls remained for the missionaries' attention. The original indigenous population, estimated at between forty thousand and sixty thousand had fewer than seven thousand survivors by 1768. And those survivors, according to one notable French observer, "were either dying or hastening toward death."[94] One generation later the population had dropped again by half, a horrendous trend confirmed by the missionaries' own baptismal records showing many more deaths than baptisms.[95] Infant baptisms, furthermore, indicated nothing about the likelihood of an infant's survival to childhood.

Epidemic disease played the largest role in Baja California's depopulation, including repeated outbreaks of smallpox, dysentery, measles, typhus, and other deadly maladies given such labels as "peste," "Colera Morbus," and "grande enfermedad."[96] These diseases arrived by visiting ships, through soldiers and settlers attached to the pueblos, and by the mestizo pearl fishermen visiting from mainland Mexico. Facing multifold crises in their own communities, some desperate native groups approached the missions for supplies or, as the priests believed, salvation. When smallpox hit Mission San Ignacio in 1729, the year after its founding, one observer noted: "Shortly after the founding of the mission a group of island Indians from the coast came to San Ignacio to request baptism. Most of those who were baptized died of an epidemic and, terrified, the rest retreated to their islands."[97] The smallpox variola virus may have accompanied their retreat. Similar scenarios played out again and again in Baja California as new germs swept up and down the peninsula.

Venereal diseases played a secondary role in depopulating Baja California due to the comprehensive force of these early epidemics. Nonetheless, syphilis still prevented the survivors of disease outbreaks from repopulating their communities. No reports of syphilis exist for the decades prior to the 1730s, though it seems implausible that sexual contact had not already spread the disease within and beyond the missions. Following a series of insurrections by mission Indians in southern Baja from 1734 to 1737, a Jesuit missionary reported the "evil effects" of syphilis among the natives and ascribed the cause to "Divine retribution for the revolt."[98]

Two decades later, numerous accounts concluded that syphilis was not only pervasive and destructive, but that it also prevented population growth in the remaining native communities. Reporting on the dwindling population of Indians at the three southernmost missions in 1768, Royal Officer Joaquín Velázquez de León estimated that a "majority" had syphilis. "Many are entirely castrated [infertile] and others are contagious," he wrote. "In fact, even the children here are born infected."[99] Military expedition leader Pedro Fages agreed with this assessment: "The disease syphilis ravages both sexes and to such an extent that the mothers no longer conceive and if they do conceive the young are born with little hope of surviving."[100] In 1792 the naturalist and physician José Mariano Moziño described Baja's native population as "consumed by the raging syphilis which the sailors of our ships have spread among them."[101]

In Alta California, by contrast, missionaries and visitors alike described the prevalence of venereal diseases directly on the heels of the first Spanish settlements. The Franciscan missionaries astutely observed and recorded the advance of this "putrid and contagious disease"—and many of them conceded the infectious role played by Spanish expedition parties dating back to the 1770s.[102] The mestizo soldiers on these military expeditions generally deserve the blame for instigating the pox among Indian communities, although other groups also abetted its introduction over time, including settlers, coastal traders, and even a few missionaries.[103] By 1790 syphilis appeared so manifest among the mission population that a visiting naturalist, José Longinos Martínez, erroneously considered it an "endemic disease" for California Indians.[104]

Historian Steven Hackel's examination of Indian-Spanish relations and depopulation in Alta California represents the most incisive research to date, a measured account of human actions and choices during a period of horrific changes for native communities. Hackel describes how native Californians faced "dual revolutions" of environmental change and demographic collapse: the former undermined native subsistence practices and forced Indians from their villages into the neighboring missions, while the latter undercut the viability of individual families and community survival.[105] Mission populations expanded and peaked just prior to 1800, but this apparent efflorescence was spurred by the arrival of desperate refugees from neighboring villages, not healthy reproduction in the missions. Rather than a safe refuge, the missions had become "maelstroms of destruction" for Indians, leaving a few conscionable Franciscans like Mariano Payeras to watch the human misery in horror, aghast at the deadly fallout from their spiritual efforts.[106]

The Alta California mission Indian population plummeted in parallel time and fashion to that of Native Hawaiians, wrought by low fertility and high infant/child mortality rates in addition to adult deaths from other introduced diseases. Hackel's "reconstitution" of Indian births and deaths, based on mission baptismal, marriage, and burial records, shows a persistent effort by natives to produce children and families despite these horrific circumstances. Disease and ill health consistently undermined their efforts. At Mission San Carlos in Monterey, 11 percent of infants died in the first month of life while 37 percent of infants died before their first birthday. Even more telling was the high rate of childhood deaths: of those infants fortunate enough to survive their first year of life, 43 percent died before the age of five years.[107] First Lieutenant George Peard of the HMS *Blossom* confirmed this in 1826: "From some cause or other which I have not been able to discover, a great Mortality to which the children are particularly subject takes place amongst the Indians in the Missions."[108] Adult sterility also stalked the missions of Alta California. At the San Carlos mission, married couples without children rose from 46 percent in the 1770s to 67 percent thirty years later. The percentage of childless couples was even higher at the San Diego and San Gabriel missions: roughly three-quarters of couples at these missions bore no children in the 1820s.[109] Thus, despite the mission Indians' best efforts to sustain families for conversion, parenthood itself was a vanishing role in a very unstable world.

The majority of indigenous Californians lived beyond the reach of Spanish (and later Mexican) authorities prior to the 1840s. Did these inland and north-ern California groups fare better in terms of health and reproduction? While the demographic decline and epidemiological history of these communities remain sketchy compared to the detailed records kept on mission Indians, many factors suggest their distance from colonial settlements provided at best a temporary and porous buffer from disease.

Numerous agents and disease vectors allowed pathogens to spread through-out Alta California's "interior world."[110] First and perhaps foremost, Indians who fled the missions carried viral and bacterial baggage with them as they traveled into the Central Valley and north of San Francisco Bay. Second, those coastal groups that lived north of the missions had their own biological encounters with foreigners, and voyage journals like William Shaler's confirm those encounters included both sexual contact and other disease introductions.[111] Third, the Rus-sian settlement at Fort Ross, established in 1812, served as a permanent conduit between foreign traders, hunters, and the indigenous groups who labored at the Russian fort. Pomo and Miwok Indians who lived near Fort Ross maintained extensive trade and cultural ties throughout northern California; any exposure to disease at Fort Ross would have followed these social vectors to the interior.[112] Finally, some of the most virulent disease outbreaks coincided with the influx of fur trappers and traders during the 1830s and 1840s, some of whom carried malarial fevers, influenza, smallpox, and diphtheria with them, which all cut deadly paths through interior California. Thus, in the final two decades before US conquest and the subsequent genocidal violence against California Indians, those interior groups experienced a biological convergence of disease from all directions.[113] The fact that foreign settlers in California also died during these outbreaks only highlights the demographic endgame. Foreigners had a seem-ingly endless supply of recruits to take their place. Indians fell victim to disease during a reproductive crisis, and their numbers would not stabilize until the early twentieth century.

Maritime Vectors and Other Diseases

The approach of a foreign vessel could inspire great excitement, but also tremen-dous alarm from indigenous communities. Some natives sought to distance them-selves from the ships, at times warning off the vessels from approaching shore. This occurred with Cook's earliest Pacific voyage in 1769, and it continued to happen in the nineteenth century. The US Exploring Expedition was repeatedly warned off Pacific beaches in 1839 and 1840; approaching the island of Reao near Tahiti, Captain Charles Wilkes's landing party was met by a group of armed and "menacing" islanders who, according to Wilkes's Maori interpreter, shouted: "Go to your own lands. This belongs to us."[114] Many valid reasons explain this resistance, but certainly one factor was the awareness that foreign vessels brought ill health and death.

Numerous examples drawn from specific ships support such reasoning. The poorly named missionary ship *Messenger of Peace* unleashed an influenza outbreak in Samoa in 1830. The Hudson's Bay Company's brigantine *Lama* brought smallpox to the Northwest Coast in 1836. Andrew Cheyne's ship *Naiad* introduced influenza to the Yap people (Caroline Islands) in 1843, while the *Monarch* brought influenza to Valparaiso four years later.[115] In 1848 the American naval frigate *Independence* arrived in Hawai'i carrying soldiers, supplies, and the measles virus. One month later a ship outbound from California arrived in Hawai'i delivering news of the gold fields; it also carried the bacterium *Bordetella pertussis*, or whooping cough.[116] These and many other disease-bearing ships illustrate the deadly cost of increased traffic in the 1830s and 1840s.

The rising volume of trade during these decades was accompanied by a greater efficiency and speed of connections between different ports. This especially facilitated disease transmission for viruses that were most effectively passed along by live carriers, such as smallpox. Smallpox had an unstable history in the Pacific, given the exigencies of an active viral agent surviving on ship over the course of a long ocean voyage.[117] Certain regions, such as Alta California prior to 1830, avoided the variola virus by virtue of luck, distance, quarantine, and successful inoculations and vaccinations.[118] Native groups on the Northwest Coast were not so fortunate. When the "spirit of pestilence" (smallpox) arrived on the Pacific Northwest coast in the late 1770s, the virus circulated through the coastal and inland communities of Tlingit, Haida, Salish, Upper Chinookans, Nez Perce, Flathead, and Tillamooks, killing as much as one-third of the population.[119] These affected groups provided the perfect social environment for variola's diffusion: relatively high population densities, frequent community gatherings, special potlatch ceremonies often held within the confines of cedar longhouses, and networks of exchange with neighboring groups.[120]

Much like an indigenous longhouse, ships also provided a perfect close-quartered environment for variola's diffusion among crewmembers. While many shipboard workers were effectively inoculated (and later vaccinated) against smallpox by the early 1800s, variola became more of a factor by the 1830s due to commercial growth, previously unexposed crewmembers, and faster transport. As a result, smallpox outbreaks after the 1820s hit everywhere in the eastern Pacific from Alaska to Peru, Alta California to Hawai'i, and Tahiti.

The *Don Quixote*, captained by John Paty, was one such fast-sailing vessel moving between coastal North and South America and the island Pacific.[121] The New England-born Paty had first sailed to the Pacific in 1834; within the next two decades he completed over one hundred voyages between Hawai'i, California, and other Pacific ports, including the quickest passage to date between California and Honolulu in 1837. By 1840 Paty and his brother Henry were well-known and respected traders in all Pacific ports. The *Don Quixote* sailed around the eastern portions of the ocean in late 1840 and early 1841: California to O'ahu, Honolulu to Valparaiso, then to Tahiti and a hasty turnaround for Valparaiso. The Paty brothers were trading goods of all varieties and also transporting passengers on their ship crewed by seven Hawaiian islanders.

At Valparaiso in April 1841 they obtained "quite an amount of goods" bound for Tahiti from the trading house Alsop and Company. Some *body* also carried the smallpox virus on board the ship. John Paty recounted the incident that soon led to thousands of deaths, including that of his own brother:

> About one week before leaving [Valparaiso], one of our crew, an Hawaiian native, fell from the main top-sail yard and caught on the main yard; he was not seriously injured although bruised considerably. Three or four days after, I let him go on shore on liberty and it appears that while on shore he contracted the Smallpox, as after we had been out a few days, he was taken sick with it. We had at this time seven [Sandwich Island] natives on board, which I excluded from him as much as possible, but five of them took it and died; the other two had been vacinated [*sic*] the year previous; they were slightly effected with it.

An English crewmember came down sick, but due to a previous exposure he had the smallpox "slightly" and recovered. John Paty got sick and could hardly leave his cabin. The first mate, Eli Southworth, was only "slightly unwell" and took temporary command of the ship. Henry Paty, according to John Paty, was "quite unwell and finally became delirious. . . . Brother H. grew worse and in an unguarded moment [he] destroyed himself."[122] Standing before his stateroom mirror, Brother Henry slashed his throat with a razor.[123] He was the only non-native fatality.

The *Don Quixote* found its way to Tahiti with only a skeleton crew able to guide the ship. Paty remained mostly silent on the resulting smallpox outbreak in Tahiti and its spread to the neighboring island of Mo'orea. Instead, he recounted his efforts to quarantine and "fumigate" the ship with the help of a local physician. Paty left a sketchy account of who left the ship while it was anchored at the Tahitian ports of Matavai Bay and Papeete, but he does acknowledge hiring Tahitians to clean the *Don Quixote*, recalling that one of these men "was taken sick with [smallpox] the day after he went on shore and died, and also some 25 or 30 natives died with it."[124] Another witness recounted additional infected passengers and crewmembers going ashore, including Paty himself. In fact, reported Charles Wilson of the London Missionary Society, it was only at Paty's urging that Tahitian chiefs "consented to allow the vessel to come to anchor," and quarantine regulations were "not strictly observed and too soon abandoned" by the ship's officers.[125] Either Paty believed his ship posed no danger of infection to the island residents, or that eventuality did not concern him.

Smallpox devastated Tahitians. Hundreds of islanders died in the two main ports visited by the *Don Quixote*, despite vaccinations conducted by English physicians years earlier. The most recent study of this outbreak estimates a mortality rate of 10 percent at the center of infection and less mortality elsewhere on the island and the neighboring island of Mo'orea.[126] Amidst this outbreak the *Don Quixote* sailed for Hawai'i with a new crew, and Paty described "a fine passage" of eighteen days. Paty never returned to Tahiti, nor did he take any responsibility for the outbreak. His *Journal* clearly assigns blame to one Hawaiian crewmember for bringing smallpox onto the *Don Quixote* at Valparaiso, and he charges a Tahitian for transmitting the virus from his ship to the island. Natives and their diseased bodies brought on the disaster, Paty concluded.

Apart from the islanders who died once the virus reached Tahiti, five of the seven Hawaiian crewmembers also succumbed to smallpox after the *Don Quixote* left Valparaiso. These individuals represented a rapidly growing trend of indigenous crewmembers on board Pacific trading vessels and whaling ships. Some of them had been inoculated against smallpox but most had not.[127] Mostly "voluntary" workers according to historian David Chappell's study of "Oceanian voyagers," these islanders had very mixed fates. Almost one-quarter of the sample group studied by Chappell died on their first voyage and another one-third had an "unknown" outcome: "It seems clear that most *kanakas* literally cast their fates to the winds when they sailed off on foreign ships."[128] Disease was the leading cause of their deaths, as illustrated by those Hawaiians who perished from smallpox aboard the *Don Quixote*.

Disease Boats and Potent Environments

That some native groups employed the neologism "disease boats" to describe foreign vessels provides us with a snapshot of indigenous formulations linking trade to disease.[129] "Disease boats" exposes a reductionist logic: if exogenous diseases often arrived with trading vessels, then all such ships carried disease in one form or another. Of course, not all ships carried sailors infected with smallpox, measles, influenza, or other diseases. But enough ships *did* arrive bearing disease-causing agents that "disease boats" contained an internal truth for those communities struck by epidemics. Ships arrived and departed, and then people got sick. The connection seemed all too clear for many indigenous groups.

A case in point is the deadly malaria outbreak on the Northwest Coast in the early 1830s. Recent reconstructions of the "fever and ague" outbreak confirm the disease was malaria. The *Plasmodium* parasite (either *Plasmodium falciparum* or *Plasmodium vivax*) found its way to the Columbia River basin in the blood of an individual from an infected region such as the Mississippi Valley or the Mexican port of San Blas. Once malaria arrived, *Anopheles* mosquitoes transmitted it from person to person. Hudson's Bay Company (HBC) officials blamed unhealthy miasmas emanating from the Columbia basin's swampy areas: "It doubtless proceeds from miasmata pervading the atmosphere whose virulent qualities are elicited only by certain coincidences of local origin," wrote the Hudson's Bay Company official Peter Skene Ogden.[130] The Chinookan-speaking villagers of the lower Columbia, however, linked the outbreak to the activities of "two big black canoes"—known to whites as the Boston-based brig *Owyhee* and its consort, the *Convoy*.[131] Though medically incorrect, this belief speaks to the tensions and fears within these native communities.

The *Owyhee* and *Convoy* crossed the treacherous bar of the Columbia River in February 1829, following a five-month voyage from Boston.[132] Captain John Dominis of the *Owyhee* noted the next few months of constant bustle in his logbook: a steady supply of furs (including beaver, bear, muskrat, and raccoon) arrived from villagers up and down the Columbia; the famed American trapper Jedediah Smith paid a visit to Dominis and sold some pelts; five Hawaiians joined the ships' crews; and a disgruntled sailor named Henry Wilson deserted after spending a day confined in irons "for refusing to do duty."[133] The two ships departed in late April for the Strait of Juan de Fuca and sought furs as far north as southeastern Alaska, but by midsummer the *Owyhee* and *Convoy* returned to the Columbia River and anchored near the HBC headquarters, Fort Vancouver. Captain Dominis reported "plenty of mosquitoes" after a visit to Fort Vancouver in August, and two months later the captain's mate "Mr. Jones" was struck by a persistent fever that nearly ended his life. Dominis removed him to Fort Vancouver's infirmary, where he likely received a tonic derived from cinchona bark (containing quinine, which kills the malaria parasite).[134] The HBC maintained a supply of this bark to combat seasonal (non-malarial) fevers. The patient eventually returned to work on the *Owyhee*; no signs indicated a horrendous malaria outbreak would strike six months later.

On July 29, 1830, exactly one year after the *Owyhee* arrived on the Columbia River, the ship departed for Boston. The timing was fortuitous for those crewmembers' health. The "fever and ague" had just broke out during the previous week, according to the noted Scottish botanist David Douglas, and this especially virulent form of the summer fever quickly made its way through Indian and white populations alike. However, the outcome for these two groups was quite distinct. The Hudson's Bay Company people—half of whom were "laid up with it" in Fort Vancouver, wrote Dr. John McLoughlin—received "[cinchona] bark and other tonics," and most of them survived the malady.[135] By contrast, the malarial fever decimated the neighboring Chinookan villages, as Douglas described in a letter eleven weeks after the outbreak:

> A dreadfully fatal intermittent fever broke out in the lower parts of this river about eleven weeks ago, which has depopulated the country. Villages, which had afforded from one to two hundred effective warriors are totally gone; not a soul remains. The houses are empty and flocks of famished dogs are howling about, while the dead bodies lie strewn in every direction on the sands of the river. I am one of the very few persons among the Hudson Bay Company's people that have stood it, and sometimes I think even I have got a *shake*, and can hardly consider myself out of danger, as the weather is yet very hot.[136]

Other witnesses confirm Douglas's horrific depiction. Ogden described a macabre scene of "unburied [Indian] carcasses" and the "foul birds" that "gorged" on them. The HBC postmaster William McKay visited the Indian village of Cathlanaquiah on Sauvie Island (between the Columbia and Willamette rivers) and discovered only two infant survivors from a known population of 150.[137]

Malaria persisted between July and December of that year, at which time the parasite finally ended its seasonal course. But it remained in the blood of survivors, allowing for its transmission the following summer during the mosquito breeding season. The 1830 outbreak was confined to an area immediately surrounding Fort Vancouver on the lower Columbia River. But in 1831 the infection expanded east on the Columbia and south on the Willamette River, depopulating Indian villages everywhere it reached. The following summer an HBC trapping party led by John Work carried the parasite to California's Sacramento Valley, but they also carried a supply of tonics for their own use. During this third season, the disease traveled person to person (via the *Anopheles* host) over seven hundred miles from the lower Columbia epicenter, infecting new carriers along its path.

David Douglas returned to the Columbia River in 1832 and discovered a virtual absence of native people. He busied himself collecting animal bones for the president of the Glasgow Geological Society, remarking that "human heads are [also] now plentiful in the Columbia, a dreadful intermittent fever having depopulated the neighborhood of the river; not twelve grown-up persons remain of those whom we saw . . . in 1825." The following year Douglas reported that "fever still clings to the native tribes with great obstinacy" and yet "thank God, I never was in better health." Within months, however, Douglas lay "prostrated with fever," but he survived with medical treatment.[138] He recuperated in Hawai'i, only to die there in 1834 after falling into a pit trap designed to catch wild boars. By that summer, the Columbia River outbreak (possibly in conjunction with influenza) had reached the southern end of California's Central Valley, killing tens of thousands of California Indians. Anthropologist Robert Boyd concludes these epidemics "probably constituted the single most important epidemiological event in the recorded history of what would eventually become the state of Oregon."[139] The same may hold true for the non-missionized Indians of interior California.

Two factors—one environmental, one medical—explain malaria's disproportionate impact on indigenous people of the eastern Pacific. The *Anopheles* mosquito bred in the same river valleys densely populated by native communities. More distant native groups traveled to those river valleys during the summer months for trade and other social exchanges. Once the malarial parasite arrived in 1829 from an exogenous source, traditional practices and gatherings in these areas allowed for speedy transmission by the mosquito carrier.[140] Therefore, the specific environment to which Indian groups traveled during the summer months had become a pathogenic hot spot, and they succumbed in large numbers as the epidemiological crisis prevented even modest care for the ill. Foreigners—the HBC people, American traders, even the Hawaiian sailors— would have died from malaria in similar proportion to Indians had it not been for the quinine-based treatments regularly supplied to the Hudson's Bay Company. Company officials only supplied the surviving Indian villages with these treatments after the malarial season of 1832. But as the outbreaks raged during the previous three seasons, Indians relied on traditional practices, including sweat baths followed by plunging into a cool body of water. A Clackamas Indian, Victoria Howard, reflected on the outbreak and these healing methods years later: "Their village was a large one, but they all got the ague. In each and every house so many of the people were ill now. . . . When some of them were feverish, they would run to the river, they would go and swim in it, they would go ashore, they would drop right there, they would die."[141] Such a treatment could immediately induce shock, which helps to explain the numerous contemporary reports of Indian corpses along the rivers and streams.

None of these environmental or medical explanations account for the *origin* of the epidemic, especially from an indigenous perspective. While Western medicine locates the etiology of malaria in a certain parasite and describes its transmission through mosquitoes, the indigenous survivors offered a different explanation. Native oral histories depict the "fever and ague" originating from a ship (the *Owyhee*) or two ships (the *Owyhee* and *Convoy*), and this reflects a more widely held assumption among Northwest groups that "disease boats" introduced an entire host of deadly new illnesses. According to one story told by a Haida elder, "they say that Pestilence came in. His canoe was like a white man's vessel."[142] Similarly, an oral history by the Klikitat William Charley in 1910 shows the collective memory of the epidemic and the role played by the black-sided ships, the *Owyhee* and *Convoy*:

> They saw two big black canoes, the largest they had ever seen. . . . Runners were sent to the other villages and all the Indians came to see. . . . It was not long after this that the Indians took sick. Those Indians who were given beads first, took sick first. . . . They came to find out that this sickness was taken from the things given them by the people from the big boats. . . . Some tried to get away by going to the mountains, but many had already taken the disease and died far away in the wilderness. This was the only way to escape the death. My grandmother and her people heard about the sickness and went out into the mountains and escaped.[143]

Other Indian oral histories established more specific elements of the story, including threats by Captain Dominis that he could unleash disease among the Indians. In 1833 the HBC physician Dr. William Tolmie recounted what he had heard from a "Sinnamish hunter & chief" during their visit at Fort Nisqually. Two American ships had arrived at Cape Flattery and the captain "threaten[ed] to send disease amongst them if they [did] not trade beaver. It appears that an American Captain who lay for some time in the Columbia . . . is considered by the Indians to have left the malady in revenge for his not receiving skins."[144] In 1840 a Methodist missionary on the lower Columbia relayed a variation on this account: the "cold sick was brought by Capt. Dominis" who had become "very angry" because the Indians were only trading small beaver pelts to him, while reserving the large pelts for "King Georges people." Upon his departure from the river, Dominis "opened his phial and let out the 'cold sick'!"[145] Two other Methodist missionaries transcribed the same details in the early 1840s.

Did Captain John Dominis of the *Owyhee* actually threaten to unleash disease among the Indians? Such "disease in a bottle" threats formed a part of white-Indian tensions going back to earlier smallpox outbreaks.[146] Whether or not Dominis made such a pronouncement is uncertain, but what becomes clear in native accounts is the level of enmity between this ship captain and different Indian groups. Equally evident is the Indians' conviction that a particular black-sided foreign vessel (or vessels) introduced mass suffering and deaths—a conviction possibly encouraged by the HBC people given their competitive relationship with American traders. Indians had witnessed ships come and go for at least two generations and they had traded with "King Georges men" and "Boston men" for decades on the lower Columbia. They mostly understood the ways of these foreigners. They also knew that all ships did not carry disease or diseased sailors. But the *Owyhee* left the Columbia River at the precise moment of a devastating outbreak; in its wake untold numbers of people died. For indigenous groups whose communities were increasingly affected by Pacific maritime trade, the *Owyhee* functioned as cause, symbol, and omen of the events now shaping their lives.

Conclusion

New trade relations in the eastern Pacific entangled native communities with foreign—and exceedingly deadly—biological agents. More specifically, trading vessels provided the primary means for diseases to travel around the Pacific's vast waterscape, infect island populations, and strike various communities along the American coastline. Of course, some infections traveled to the Pacific by overland routes, and other diseases arrived on noncommercial voyages; missionary activities certainly spread germs, and Spanish conquests had dispersed deadly germs in parts of the Americas and Pacific prior to the late eighteenth century. Yet, for the period between the 1770s and the 1840s, trading vessels were the main agents of disease introduction and dissemination, extending the "microbian unification of the world" to all Pacific shores.[147] By 1850, the microbes of Europe, Asia, and Africa circulated in almost every Pacific population.

While some diseases (smallpox, malaria, influenza, and others) could lead to quick death and the rapid depopulation of indigenous communities, such an emphasis on the major killers of humankind has tended to obscure the insidious and equally powerful role played by venereal diseases that critically attacked human reproduction. Introduced venereal syphilis and gonorrhea held catastrophic consequences for indigenous women, men, and children, including lower birthrates, higher infant mortality, and chronic ill health that undermined immune resistance to other introduced pathogens. Populations plummeted as a result. The point is *not* that indigenous groups were immunologically weak in their responses to venereal disorders or other diseases; instead, their biological response mirrored that of most every other population when confronted with a new array of deadly germs. These diseases, however, struck during a period of profound social change, subsistence crisis, and violence—and indigenous recovery and repopulation would have to take place in a twentieth-century historical context characterized by Tongan scholar Epeli Hau'ofa as one of isolation, quarantine, and colonialism.[148]

The spread of disease and its grim impacts did not unfold in silence, darkness, or incomprehensibility, as demonstrated by an abundance of firsthand accounts. Rather, it took place in front of foreigners (and sometimes *to* foreigners) who knew well what they saw, frequently wrote about it, and held varying reactions to the morbidity and mortality. To state this is neither a broad indictment of all disease-carrying foreigners nor a suggestion that they understood the science of disease vectors and causes, but instead it recognizes that disease manifestations and depopulation were easily visible and well documented. Indigenous people testified to their conditions and the likely causes throughout this period; for them, the new ways to death were self-evident and did not necessitate Western medical explanation.

3

Hostages and Captives

In the long, long ago a ship, carrying cannon, was wrecked offshore
here during a terrible storm; and, though the Indians had never seen a
ship or white men before, they attempted to capture the people. . . .
These people the Indians called "ho'kwat" (wanderers) and by that
name they call the white people to this day.

—Ben Hobucket (*Quileute*) (1909)

Sv. Nikolai, 1808

The Russian schooner *Sv. Nikolai* sailed south from New Arkhangel (Sitka) just
as the subarctic winter approached—an interminably long season of bitter cold
and darkness in that already dreary Russian settlement. Navigator Nikolai Isaakovich Bulygin commanded the *Sv. Nikolai* and Timofei Tarakanov served as
prikashchik, or supercargo. The rest of the company included Bulygin's wife,
Anna Petrovna, eleven Russians, and seven indigenous men and women identified by Tarakanov as Kodiak and Aleut islanders. An Englishman named John
Williams also crewed the vessel; he had sailed with William Shaler on the *Lelia
Byrd* before transferring to the Hawaiian schooner *Tamana*, which the Russians
purchased in 1807 and renamed *Sv. Nikolai*. These twenty-two individuals may
have eagerly anticipated the warmer climes farther south down the coastline: the
Northwest Coast, the Columbia River, and their final destination, Alta California. Two weeks out they sighted the Cape of Juan de Fuca and cautiously traded
with "the natives [who] came out to us in their canoes." Though friendly, those
natives had armed themselves for the encounter, carrying iron-tipped spears,
knives, firearms, and whalebone spikes known as "slave killers." Four weeks out a
violent gale thrashed the *Sv. Nikolai* for three straight days. "It seemed to us that
the loss of the ship was inevitable, and we expected death at any moment," wrote
Timofei Tarakanov. "Then, through the grace of God, we received a northwest
wind which kept us away from the shore."[1]

Battered but still seaworthy, the *Sv. Nikolai* sailed south for one more day before high seas again pushed the ship into "the midst of dangerous shoals," at which point Commander Bulygin order four anchors dropped. In the complete darkness of night the crew listened to the howling winds and crashing waves; as dawn approached they heard the anchor cables begin to snap, one after another. "Finally," Tarakanov wrote, "at ten o'clock on the morning of November 1st, a swell cast us into the surf and then ashore at 47° 56'N. Latitude. Thus the brig met its fate."[2] Cresting waves pounded the *Sv. Nikolai* and the ship's hold quickly filled with water. In between swells the crew jumped overboard and waded to the relative safety of the wet beach, directly north of the Quillayute River. They salvaged the ship's arms and ammunition, one cannon, two tents, and other necessities. According to Tarakanov's account, their thoughts focused on captivity even before their feet touched the sand. "We had to save ourselves, and also to rescue our firearms, our only means to preserve our liberty," he recalled. "If captured, we would live out a miserable life as slaves of the savages, a consequence a hundred times more horrible than death."[3] Thus began a two-year odyssey for the *Sv. Nikolai*'s crew.

Why was captivity and slavery foremost on Tarakanov's mind? One answer is that his published narrative was based on a known outcome, which included captivity and enslavement by various indigenous communities. But even if Tarakanov had *not* known the outcome, the specter of captivity would have been a rational response to their predicament. As employees of the Russian-American Company, all of Tarakanov's fellow countrymen (as well as Anna Petrovna Bulygin) aboard the *Sv. Nikolai* were well acquainted with social positions of the *unfree*—a category ranging from indigenous contract laborers to outright slaves. After all, the company's origins and marginal profitability owed itself to the early captivity and ongoing oppression of Aleuts and Kodiaks (*Alutiiq*), seven of whom crossed that beach with Tarakanov in 1808.

Tarakonov understood the conventions of the coastline as well as any European alive. He had twice sailed south from New Arkhangel to Alta California on American ships carrying teams of Aleut sea otter hunters, and he certainly gathered information en route regarding the practices of coastal indigenous communities. The recent history of trade along this stretch of coastline included depredations of the worst sort, carried out by most everyone involved. Tarakanov undoubtedly knew this much. He had resided in Russian America for almost a decade, and during this time he had come into contact with Europeans from many nations and Pacific peoples from many *more* nations. He would have heard numerous captivity stories from these acquaintances. Tarakanov's experience taught him two lessons for meeting a new group: crossing an unknown beach should always be done with caution, and it was best done from a position of strength.

Tarakanov and the others crossed the beach on November 1, 1808, and they proceeded to erect two tents and build a fire for warmth. "We had hardly completed these first tasks," he recalled, "when a large number of the natives, who had seen us land, came close." One young man from a neighboring Hoh community identified himself as a *toyon* (chieftain), and Tarakanov attempted to persuade him of their "peaceableness." One can only imagine the awkwardness of this halting exchange: the Russian *promyshenniks* and their indigenous hunters all held firearms at the ready while the more numerous Hoh villagers grasped spears and large rocks. Tarakanov and the *toyon* continued their negotiation, but, he admitted, "since we did not understand each other very well, our conversation was prolonged."[4] It was at this point that all hell broke loose.

"Since we did not understand each other very well, our conversation was prolonged." Few Pacific voyage narrators have more accurately encapsulated a moment of halting negotiation between natives and outsiders. Though unintentional, Tarakanov's statement negates a range of possible assumptions about what happened when strangers met on the beaches throughout the Pacific: for instance, that each side understood the other; or that conversation would lead to peaceful relations; or that martial strength was easily assessed; or possibly most important, that such a moment of contact soon ended, followed by a more established relationship between the parties. The *Sv. Nikolai's* appearance on the beach presented an intriguing moment not because the Hoh and neighboring Quileute people had never met Europeans, nor because Tarakanov had never met Northwest coastal peoples. Each knew of the other in a generic way. Instead, the tension of this unscripted moment derived from the fact that neither group had any idea how the other group would act. Spontaneity would rule the day. Fortunately, two accounts of the subsequent drama survive, and these narratives—as shown in the latter half of this chapter—were produced by people who inhabited the two opposing sides of the beach.

First meetings in the Americas and elsewhere have attained an aura of mythic proportion because they appear shrouded in the virginal self-consciousness of discovery. Cook and the Hawaiians in 1778. The Tahitians and Wallis in 1767. Cabrillo in California in 1542. Columbus in San Salvador in 1492. Each of these—and countless other—first meetings established contact between groups previously unknown to each other, and through these meetings ideas were conveyed, negotiated, and, more often than not, misunderstood. These events actually initiated history itself for the discovered natives—or so believed many of the European "discoverers." Indigenous groups, for their part, typically incorporated those meetings with foreigners into their own sense of time, history, and cosmology.[5] Furthermore, contact (whether first or subsequent) was rarely a simple two-sided encounter between one homogenous group and another. Rather, it involved complex negotiations and rivalries between multiple parties and the contending perspectives of everyone involved. How the Hoh community responded to the *Sv. Nikolai's* survivors was decidedly shaped by previous meetings with foreigners, but of equal if not greater significance were the rivalries between neighboring indigenous communities. This fact was entirely lost on Tarakanov, but likely foremost in the minds of those villagers who witnessed the shipwreck and then pondered their options.

Viewed collectively as an ongoing process rather than a series of isolated moments, such meetings between foreigners and indigenous Pacific peoples unfolded everywhere—often for a well-rehearsed exchange of goods, sometimes when an unanticipated and unseaworthy ship (such as the *Sv. Nikolai*) washed ashore. A range of possible actions could take place: people on the shore welcomed or warned off ships, people exchanged goods or blows, some people spoke while others listened, and people fled, chased, hid, embraced, and fornicated. All of this and much more was possible. But certain actions transpired with such regularity that they appear almost commonplace. Among these conventions were the exchanging of hostages and the taking of captives.[6]

Hostage- and captive-taking occurred with surprising frequency around the Pacific, from Australia to Japan, from the Aleutian Islands to Tierra del Fuego.[7] Both indigenous communities and foreign voyagers shared in the practice. If a certain universality marked these practices of captive-taking, specific episodes of it shed light on the tensions created by the increasing volume of European and American traffic in the late eighteenth and early nineteenth centuries. In short, these episodes demonstrate shifting power dynamics, anger, ingenuity, and confusion—emotions that intermingled as trade and informal diplomacy proceeded throughout the Pacific. Furthermore, individual captives and hostages shed light on larger populations of unfree people living most places around the Pacific Basin. Certainly in existence prior to encounters with outsiders, the numbers and identities of unfree people grew in the wake of increased commercial traffic and imperial ventures.[8]

Who were the unfree—an awkward term at best—and why dwell on their existence? Ocean-going vessels carried enslaved Africans, conscripted seamen, captured beachcombers, indentured servants, stolen or purchased native women, island castoffs-turned-impressed laborers, and unreturned indigenous hostages, among other categories of unfree people. Even the most "free" sailor would quickly learn the limits of his autonomy if, for instance, he jumped ship for some unauthorized time on shore. Likewise, hierarchical and coercive indigenous societies abounded on the shore side of many Pacific beaches. The lower social rungs were comprised of war hostages and slaves, commoner girls prostituted to chiefs or outsiders, and other commoners who lacked individual autonomy. Imperial conquests in the Pacific only increased the range of unfree populations, most notably in Russian Alaska, the Franciscan missions of Alta

California, or certain Pacific island ports where "blackbirding" (conscripting or stealing) shore workers became common practice. Thus, not only was some portion of contact relations enacted by people who possessed limited degrees of freedom, but, more to the point, encounters were processes through which notions of freedom and captivity were constantly negotiated.

The Northwest Coast I: Entangled Captivities, 1789–1792

In June of 1791, the American captain Robert Gray took a local headman he called "Tootiscoosettle" hostage aboard the *Columbia* while anchored in Clayoquot Sound on the west coast of Vancouver Island. Gray was on his second voyage to the Northwest Coast and the Nuu-chah-nulth (or Nootka) tribal area in particular. His previous voyage on the *Columbia* (1787–1790) had inaugurated American interests in the maritime fur trade; Gray had completed the voyage, while his erstwhile captain John Kendrick (on the companion vessel *Lady Washington*) inexplicably continued trading in the Pacific until his 1794 death in Hawai'i.[9] Gray believed he knew exactly what he was doing by keeping Tootiscoosettle aboard the *Columbia*: forcing the return of a crewmember who had disappeared on shore the previous day. Tootiscoosettle, for his part, was deeply offended and possibly terrified by his captivity. He and his servant had only come aboard the *Columbia* after much pleading by Captain Gray; as a brother of Chief Wickaninish—who was among the most powerful of Nuu-chah-nulth chiefs—Tootiscoosettle understood his potential value to the foreigners. Gray informed Tootiscoosettle "he was his prisoner" and he would "carry him to sea" if the missing crewmember did not return to the ship.[10] Tootiscoosettle sent his servant ashore to locate the sailor and resolved the matter within hours: one missing sailor back on board the *Columbia*, one chief's brother (and his servant) safely ashore. But if this apparently isolated hostage exchange resolved the immediate situation, it also reveals a defining feature of hostage-taking on the Northwest Coast: any given captivity was usually entangled with other incidences of captivity.

The significance of this episode involves a wider net of relations that entwined these individuals. The thirty-six-year-old Gray was a demanding and determined captain prone to sudden decisions and aggression—whether that entailed taking a chief captive, destroying the well-built native village of Opitsat (which he did the following season), or driving his ship through the treacherous breakers at the mouth of the Columbia River in 1792. (The river was consequently named for his ship, the *Columbia*.) For Gray, contact relations were about confrontation, and violence often figured prominently in his repertoire. Gray had come to

Nootka and Clayoquot sounds to barter for as many furs as the Nuu-chah-nulth could provide him, and he gave little thought to the consequences of his actions for subsequent traders. Thus, Gray read the disappearance of his sailor on June 14, 1791, as an act of aggression by the natives, and according to the *Columbia*'s supercargo John Box Hoskins, "Captain Gray therefore determined to take the first Chief that came along."[11] Tootiscoosettle's appearance perfectly answered his need for a hostage.

Chief Wickaninish represented Gray's counterpart on shore. The most powerful chief around Clayoquot Sound, he carefully orchestrated the environment in which trade took place between outsiders and his Nuu-chah-nulth network of villages.[12] Gray would not acquire many furs or pelts without Wickaninish's permission. When Gray took Tootiscoosettle hostage in lieu of his sailor's return, Wickaninish likely directed the hostage exchange from his house in Opitsat village. The day following Tootiscoosettle's release, according to Hoskins, it was Wickaninish's *father* who came aboard the *Columbia* bearing two sea otter pelts as a good-faith gesture: "He was afraid to come on board, but after a little intreaty, and many professions of friendship, he came, soon traded, and went off in great haste."[13] Wickaninish quite rightly refused to trust Gray with his own safety—the chief would have proven an invaluable hostage—but he was more than willing to dispatch a series of emissaries, including his own father, to draw out the trading process and thereby continue Gray's engagement with his people rather than with his nearby rivals, such as Chief Maquinna to the north.[14]

Tootiscoosettle may have been of two minds about his brief captivity. On the one hand, he understood hostage-taking as an increasingly common convention of trade relations, having played the role before. In this instance, taking a hostage could resolve a dispute when neither side trusted the other.[15] But he also knew the possibility existed for violence and death in these scenarios. Fortunately, in this incident Tootiscoosettle knew where to find the missing sailor, and he dispatched his servant on the errand. According to fifth mate John Boit, a canoe "soon return'd with [the sailor] and ransom'd their Chief," at which point began a new set of proceedings.[16] Hoskins wrote: "It was now necessary, as an example to deter others, who should be guilty of the like in future, that [the sailor] should be punished . . . [and] the chief was ordered to be present at this punishment." While Tootiscoosettle witnessed the lashing of the sailor, Gray promised severe consequences for any native who captured crewmembers in the future, or harbored anyone who "ran away to his village."[17] The missing (and now returned) sailor went by the name of Atu.

Atu's departure from the *Columbia* had instigated these events, and his presence aboard the vessel further widens the net of interrelated captivities. Atu—known variously as Ottoo, Attoo, Jack Atu, and Jack—was a Native Hawaiian.

Captain Gray had signed him onto the *Columbia*'s crew during a brief stopover in Ni'ihau in November 1789.[18] All records indicate that Gray had not abducted Atu; instead the Hawaiian had willingly joined the *Columbia* on its way to China.[19] Atu remained on board the *Columbia* as it circumnavigated the globe (the first American ship to do so) to the voyage's end in Boston, where Gray reportedly escorted the "Hawaiian chief Attoo" through the streets costumed in a feathered helmet and "an exquisite cloak of the same yellow and scarlet plumage."[20] Atu had little more than a month to enjoy his local celebrity as Boston's first visiting "Hawaiian chief." When the *Columbia* left Boston on its second voyage to the Northwest Coast, Captain Gray listed "Jack Atoe" as "Cabin Boy"—a rank much closer to indentured servant than visiting island dignitary.[21] While certainly not a captive on board the ship, Atu learned the limits of his freedom when the ship dropped anchor in Clayoquot Sound on June 5, 1791.

Atu deserted the ship less than ten days later. "Ottoo, our Sandwich island boy," wrote Hoskins, "found means to leave the ship and go among the natives."[22] Neither Hoskins nor anyone else explained Atu's reasons for deserting—and he never left a written record—but it seems reasonable to assume he chafed under shipboard discipline as "Cabin Boy" and desired certain freedoms on shore among the Nuu-chah-nulth. His desertion quickly set events in motion: Gray would take a hostage, Wickaninish would direct the exchange of personnel, and Atu would pay for his temporary freedom with skin lashed from his backside. This incident casts light on the hazy boundary between freedom and captivity for all sailors, because neither Atu nor any other crewmembers possessed the autonomy to seek their own way among the Indians.

Atu had not joined the *Columbia*'s first voyage on his own in September 1789. Instead, he signed on with a young man named Opai from the island of Kaua'i. Opai (also known as Opie, Jack, Jack Opie, Kalehua, and Tarehooa, according to George Vancouver) and Atu sailed together to Boston, and once there, Atu remained in the service of Captain Gray while Opai served the interests of second officer Joseph Ingraham. Opai again shipped out for the Pacific with Ingraham (now captain of the brig *Hope*) two weeks before Atu left Boston on the *Columbia*, and Opai left the *Hope* when it arrived in Kealakekua Bay in May 1791. "Altho I took Opye as a servant, I always treated him more like a friend," wrote Ingraham, leaving him with clothes, a musket, and some shipboard edification on "the most favorable ideas of our nation."[23] Ingraham sailed for the Northwest Coast, where little more than a year later he would again see Opai, this time as a crewmember on George Vancouver's *Discovery*, fresh from Hawai'i. Ingraham and Opai had a happy reunion, except for one fact: Opai desperately wanted to leave the *Discovery* but Vancouver would not let him go. Ingraham described the situation:

[Opai] was very glad to see me and wished to return on board the *Hope*. I desired him to ask Captain Vancouver's leave, and if he was willing to part with him, it was quite agreeable to me to take him again. Not being able to get off with honor from the *Discovery*—as Captain Vancouver refused to discharge him till his return to Owhyhee—Opye made a new proposal, which was to meet me outside the harbor in an Indian canoe on the day we sailed. But this I could not think of agreeing to, for, in the first place, I was in no want of him, having plenty of men, and in the next place, Opye could assign no reason for his wishing to leave the *Discovery*. On the contrary, he said everyone treated him well, especially the captain.[24]

Why did Vancouver hold Opai aboard the *Discovery*, and why did Opai desire his leave? Opai, like Atu before him, had likely grown tired of British shipboard discipline and the lack of personal freedom. More important, the very nature of his employ by Vancouver had changed the moment the *Discovery* left the Hawaiian Islands. Opai's language skills had proven an "utmost utility" to Vancouver as he outfitted the ship in Hawai'i; Vancouver even "promoted [Opai] to the office of interpreter" during this time.[25] But Opai's bilingualism no longer mattered once the *Discovery* sailed for the Northwest Coast—that is, until the vessel returned to Hawai'i and Vancouver could once again employ Opai's linguistic talents for trading purposes. So Vancouver kept him, not explicitly a captive aboard the *Discovery*, but neither was he free to leave.

Vancouver was also motivated by the presence of two other captives—now *former* captives—on the *Discovery*. The 1792 trading season on the Northwest Coast was the busiest to date, including twenty-one vessels from five different nations, and Vancouver conducted business with many of them.[26] The British *Jenny* out of Bristol was quite ordinary in both its trading mission and itinerary, having stopped in Hawai'i for supplies en route to Nootka Sound before its departure for England. But the *Jenny* was somewhat peculiar in that its crew had kidnapped two young Hawaiian women from the island of Ni'ihau—and now the *Jenny*'s captain, James Baker, desired their return to Hawai'i before his homebound voyage. Vancouver agreed to take them, he noted in his journal on October 13, 1792:

I received on board two young women for the purpose of returning them to their native country, the Sandwich islands; which they had quitted in a vessel that arrived at Nootka ... called the Jenny[.] Mr. Baker her commander very earnestly requested, that I would permit these two unfortunate girls to take a passage in the Discovery to Onehow, the island of their birth and residence; from whence it seems they had been

brought, not only very contrary to their wishes and inclinations, but totally without the knowledge or consent of their friends or relations[.]

Once safely on the *Discovery*, according to clerk James Bell, these "two poor girls . . .
found themselves happy and satisfied not only with the pleasing idea of getting
soon home . . . but [also] having a companion on board"—namely Opai.[27] Vancouver had few qualms about taking natives hostage, but in this instance, he seemed
equally pleased with the opportunity to return captives to their island home, especially with Opai securely on board to serve as interpreter.

In fact, Vancouver seemed thoroughly enraptured by his new shipboard companions, named Raheina and Tymarow (who he estimated were ages fifteen and
twenty, respectively). "The elegance of Raheina's figure," he wrote, "the regularity
and softness of her features, and the delicacy which she naturally possessed . . . in
addition to which, her sensibility and turn of mind, her sweetness of temper and
complacency of manners, were beyond any thing that could have been expected
from her birth, or native education[.]" Vancouver directly criticized Captain Baker's
kidnapping of the two ("their seduction and detention on board Mr. Baker's vessel
were inexcusable," he wrote), but he also parried any suggestion of sexual abuse by
Baker and his crew with the claim "that they had been treated with every kindness
and attention whilst under his protection."[28] Were Raheina and Tymarow captive
sex slaves or detained stowaways? Their captivity aboard the British trade vessel
Jenny suggests the former, while Vancouver's very public and published recounting
of this incident rejected the charge. Vancouver's extensive treatment of the situation revealed his pressing need to clarify one point: British captains may frequently take male hostages for a variety of reasons, but the British did not
condone the "seduction and detention" of indigenous girls and women. Such an
accusation—recently circulated in the American press—Vancouver considered
absurd.[29]

Captain Ingraham's *Hope* traded on the Northwest Coast during the
summers of 1791 and 1792. He refused to harbor Opai as a runaway from
the *Discovery* because he did not need Opai's labor, but he also understood the
symbolic challenge of runaways for shipboard discipline. When Ingraham's
own cook Nicholas—a "Negro man whom I took from the Island of St. Jagos"—
jumped ship and hid in a village just north of Nootka Sound, Ingraham forced
the man's return by rewarding the local chief. Ingraham briefly considered
"detaining the chief" instead, but feared such an act would "put an end to all
traffic for the present." Yet in another instance Ingraham "detained two natives
as hostages" with no evident thought to later consequences, likely because no
trade was currently taking place between his ship and the natives.[30] Hostage-
taking therefore functioned as one of many possible tools for resolving the di-
lemmas surrounding trade relations and maintaining viable crews.

Within this narrative arc originating from the detention of one man, Tootiscoo-settle, at least nine other people experienced some form of captivity: Tootiscoo-settle's servant, Atu, Captain James Colnett, Opai, Raheina and Tymarow, Nicholas, and the "two natives" Ingraham detained on board the *Hope*. Given that eighteen other ships (apart from the *Columbia*, *Hope*, *Discovery*, and *Jenny*) trafficked on the Northwest Coast in 1792, it is safe to assume that dozens more hostage incidences highlighted that trading season.

How did the Nuu-chah-nulth view this ongoing capture and exchange of per-sonnel? Beyond the fear of their own detention or violent death resulting from these activities, they likely viewed it as existing within a range of fairly normal behaviors. The peoples of western Vancouver Island actively engaged in their own versions of slave trading and war captivities, as well as the more incidental exchanging of hostages. (Indeed, Tootiscoosettle's "servant" was probably cap-tured in a previous campaign led by Chief Wickaninish.) They frequently har-bored runaways such as Atu or Nicholas and they also bartered enslaved women to European and American men. The actions of Captains Gray, Ingraham, Baker, and Vancouver offered nothing new in the range of captive-related events, but these foreigners certainly stoked tensions between indigenous communities already accustomed to their own captive-taking practices.

The Cookbook for Taking Hostages

Captain James Cook's three Pacific voyages included countless variations on hostage-taking: he held islanders in lieu of pilfered equipment, he took hostages to force the return of runaway sailors, and he detained villagers for the purpose of intelligence gathering or purely as a preemptive measure against suspected hostilities. These and other motives encouraged Cook to seize natives, begin-ning with his first visit to Tahiti in 1769. But Cook hardly invented the practice of Europeans taking captives in the Pacific.

Two hundred and twenty-seven years earlier and thousands of miles to the northeast, Juan Rodriguez Cabrillo explored California's coastline as far north as present-day Oregon, taking temporary custody of numerous native inhabitants along the way. In the third-person voyage narrative penned by Bartolomé Fer-relo and Juan Paez, Cabrillo's men "captured" their first native Californian on August 22, 1542; two days later they "brought to the ship a boy and two women, gave them clothing and presents, and let them go"; the following day "brought [five Indians] to the ships"; in late September they "brought two boys" on board "who understood nothing by signs"; and near present-day San Pedro Bay in October they "held a colloquy with some Indians whom they captured in a canoe." Over four months passed before the next mention of seizing Indians: on

March 9, 1543, "they secured four Indians" with no explanation given, and finally, two days later they "secured two boys to take to New Spain as interpreters."[31] In all these incidences—except the final capture of two boys as interpreters—local information appeared to be the primary motive: Where is your food supply? Do you have any gold? Is there, by any chance, a Northwest Passage in the vicinity? While some California Indians willingly boarded Cabrillo's *San Salvador* and the support ship *Victoria*, those taken against their will must have been terrified by the creaking vessels and scurvy-ridden crew. The two boys taken away on the *San Salvador*'s departure certainly experienced a greater level of terror.

Between Cabrillo's and Cook's time, captivities repeatedly took place during Pacific voyages.[32] Cook, however, wrote the most widely circulated accounts of encounters with Pacific peoples, and subsequent voyagers employed his journals as veritable travel guides for exploration and interaction. They could hardly help but follow his example, including his taking of captives:[33]

- May 2, 1769: Tahitian nobles Purea and Tutaha held hostage for return of two deserting sailors; it "struck general Terror through the island & the Prisoners ('tho very well Treated) was inconsoleable"; Surgeon William Monkhouse and a corporal detained by villagers in response.[34]
- First contact with Maori in Turanganui (Poverty Bay): three boys forcibly taken from their canoes and held overnight on the *Endeavour*.
- At Ra'iatea (Society Islands), September 1773: Ta and lesser chief held hostage in lieu of stolen items.
- Matavai Bay, May 1774: John Marra (a gunner's mate) confined in irons for two weeks on charges of desertion.
- Huahine, May 1774: two chiefs held hostage in exchange for two sailors detained on shore.
- Tonga, May 1777: village chief confined for theft of iron bolt, ransomed for one large hog.
- Tonga, May 1777: Chief Tapa's son placed in irons for theft of *Discovery*'s two cats.
- Days later: two Tongans detained for theft; chief flogged to deter future thefts.
- Tonga, June 1777: chiefs Paulaho and Finau held hostage on *Resolution* for return of two stolen turkey cocks.
- Mo'orea, October 1777: Tahitian man placed in irons to force return of missing goats.
- Ra'iatea, November 1777: at least three sailors desert from ships: John Harrison given twenty-four lashes for desertion; chief Orio and pregnant daughter Poetua taken hostage, leading village women to "howl" from shore and cut their bodies with sharks' teeth.

- Kealakekua Bay, Hawaiʻi, February 11, 1779: Cook attempts to take chief Kalaniʻopuʻu hostage for return of *Discovery*'s cutter. Cook killed on the beach during this action.

These instances represent only a sample of the hostage situations during Cook's three Pacific voyages. As such, they show how Cook primarily took hostages as a form of leverage or retribution: he wanted the return of stolen items or deserters, or in the case of the three Maori boys pulled from their canoes, he likely desired information on the new surroundings. Maintaining "advantage" over the natives was pivotal in every situation. As Lieutenant James King noted in his journal just prior to his captain's death, Cook "expressd his sorrow" when "the Indians would at last oblige him to use force," but "they must not . . . imagine they have *gaind an advantage* over us."[35]

The islanders and mainlanders who encountered Cook and his crew immediately grasped one fact that all but ensured conflict: these strange men wanted things that the natives controlled. One telling episode illustrates this point. After releasing from captivity the three Maori boys in Turanganui Bay in 1769, Cook turned the *Endeavour* north and soon entered Whitianga harbor. A young boy named Horeta Te Taniwha watched the ship arrive. His account constitutes a rare glimpse of a first meeting from an indigenous perspective. "We lived at Whitianga," Te Taniwha recalled many decades later:

> and a vessel came there, and when our old men saw the ship they said it was an atua, a god, and the people on board were tupua, strange beings or "goblins." . . . When these goblins came on shore we (the children and women) took notice of them, but we ran away from them into the forest, and the warriors alone stayed in the presence of those goblins; but, as the goblins stayed some time, and did not do any evil to our braves, we came back one by one, and gazed at them.[36]

Te Taniwha recorded his peoples' reaction to these strange men during their twelve-day stay, and he realized their behavior, while mystifying at times, reflected human rather than supernatural origins. For example, the strangers wanted material things belonging to Te Taniwha's community: oysters, fish, roots and grasses, rocks, wood, and drinking water. Cook's people usually took these items without asking. Other times they did ask the natives to supply them with necessities, especially in the case of information about their surroundings.

In one incident Te Taniwha joined a group of villagers who visited the *Endeavour*, and Cook (the "supreme man" who spoke with a "hissing sound") made a speech "that was not understood by us in the least."

[Then he] took some charcoal and made marks on the deck of the ship, and pointed to the shore and looked at our warriors. One of our aged men said to our people, "He is asking for an outline of this land"; and that old man stood up, took the charcoal, and marked the outline of the Ika-a-maui (the North Island of New Zealand).[37]

Such information could prove invaluable to Cook as he circumnavigated New Zealand, and the "warriors" had the ability to offer or withhold the desired intelligence. In this case they granted Cook the information he sought. But other villagers would not be so generous, and conflict—often in the form of hostage-taking—resulted.

Cook's use of hostages generally led to the desired results—the return of stolen items, runaways, or detained sailors. But the significance of this practice lies in the way Cook influenced subsequent explorers and captain-traders alike. George Vancouver and Nathaniel Portlock, both of whom sailed on Cook's final voyage when so much hostage activity occurred, followed his example when leading their own expeditions in subsequent years. Alejandro Malaspina, Jean-François de Galaup de La Pérouse, Vasily Golovnin, and Charles Wilkes (each of whom commanded the premier Spanish, French, Russian, and American voyages, respectively) admired Cook as a navigator and enlightened individual, consumed his voyage accounts, and to varying degrees utilized his methods for gaining "advantage" over indigenous populations. The point here is not merely about hero-worship and Cook's considerable impact on later voyagers. It is also about the legacy of Cook's journals and the way his successors from different nations mined those writings for ways to act when communication with natives broke down.

Te Taniwha recalled that Cook's speech "was not understood by us in the least."[38] Cook came to agree with this assessment of communication with natives, telling the eminent diarist James Boswell that "he and his [crew] who visited the South Sea Island could not be certain of any information they got, or supposed they got . . . [because] their knowledge of the language was so imperfect they required the aid of their senses, and anything which they learnt about religion, government, or traditions might be quite erroneous."[39] Hostilities frequently ensued when verbal communication failed.

The Northwest Coast II: The Strange Career of Captive John Jewitt, 1803–1805

Fur trading along the Northwest Coast remained profitable from the 1780s to the 1810s. But the successful trade in furs depended entirely on the locale. Some parts of the coast, such as Nootka Sound and Clayoquot Sound, witnessed a complete collapse of the sea otter population after only a decade of intense hunting. As a result, some indigenous communities in this region faced a trade deficit and social disorder.[40] It was in this context that a young Englishman named John Jewitt found himself enslaved by Chief Maquinna—and Jewitt was the fortunate son from his ship.[41]

Jewitt's vessel, the *Boston*, anchored just north of Friendly Cove (named by Cook in 1778) on March 12, 1803, after a six-month voyage from Boston to England and around Cape Horn, en route to "Vancouver's Island." Jewitt, a nineteen-year-old Lincolnshire blacksmith, joined the ship's crew as an armorer in England. He weathered the long voyage with little difficulty and recalled the crew's well-being upon arrival. "All in good health," he subsequently noted, possibly a dark-humored allusion to the tragedy that ensued ten days later. The Mowachaht chief Maquinna and Captain John Salter exchanged pleasantries, news, and gifts; of special note was the double-barrel musket Salter gave Maquinna on March 15. Maquinna returned four days later bearing "nine pair" of ducks for the captain, but he also accused Salter of gifting him a faulty musket. Salter, according to Jewitt, "was very angry, called him a liar, took the musket and threw it down into the cabin and called for me to know whether I could repair it, I told him it could be done."[42] On May 22 Maquinna returned to the *Boston* with a large entourage of villagers. He informed Salter of the plentiful salmon run in Friendly Cove and the captain soon dispatched ten men on a fishing expedition. With fifteen crewmembers left on deck—Jewitt and the sailmaker John Thompson were working below deck—Maquinna's group attacked. Jewitt made a feeble attempt to climb up from the steerage, but he was struck with an axe and he fell back down the stairs. Maquinna secured the hatch with Jewitt below. Four hours later Maquinna called Jewitt from the steerage to witness a ghastly sight: a line of twenty-five heads arranged on the quarterdeck. Maquinna would spare his life (and the life of sailmaker Thompson), wrote Jewitt, but "he told me I must be his slave and work for him . . . to which I of course assented."[43] Thus began Jewitt's and Thompson's two years in captivity.

Jewitt's own account of their time in captivity—drawn from a diary he kept—contains the details of daily life and provides an ample summary of key events. Maquinna immediately claimed Jewitt as his slave due to his blacksmithing skills, though the master-slave relationship evolved in curious ways during the following months. Jewitt spent the majority of his time observing and participating in certain aspects of community life: gathering foodstuffs, trading with neighboring groups, crafting tools and weapons, and searching for sustenance beyond the customary diet of whale blubber and "train" (whale) oil. Jewitt's mental state alternated between despair ("I now beg[a]n to give up all hopes of ever seeing a Christian country,") and contentment ("We lived very well during the last week . . ."), often on the same day.[44] He took a wife, or

Figure 3.1 John Jewitt and John Thompson survived this orchestrated attack on the trading vessel *Boston* led by the Mowachaht chief Maquinna. The remaining twenty-five crewmembers and officers did not survive the assault. Jewitt and Carpenter became Maquinna's captives for two years. Courtesy of the Huntington Library.

Maquinna "bought" him a wife, or he "abducted" a young bride—the details vary by different accounts—named Eu-stochee-exqua, the daughter of the Ahousaht chief, Upquesta. The marriage may have briefly improved Jewitt's circumstances: "We [Jewitt and Thompson] live a great deal better since I got married, for my wife's father is always fishing. I leave the reader to judge of my feelings at being forced to take an Indian for a wife."[45] Six months later the two divorced.[46] In one of the more curious incidences, Jewitt may have participated in a bloody assault on the village of Ayshart and taken four slaves of his own. No evidence of this episode appears in his *Journal*, but his 1815 *Narrative* (ghostwritten by a Connecticut journalist) places Jewitt in the thick of the fighting.[47] Thus, the possibility remains that the captive Jewitt came to hold captives of his own.

Jewitt plotted his rescue throughout the two years in captivity. Visiting chiefs frequently offered to purchase Jewitt for his blacksmithing skills, but Maquinna always refused to sell his most valuable captive. Jewitt occasionally secreted letters to these chiefs for delivery to any trading vessel. On August 22, 1804, Jewitt handed two letters to the visiting Makah "chief called Makye . . . hoping they would fall into the hand of some christians." Jewitt identifies this important Makah chief (who later figured prominently in Tarakanov's captivity) as Machee Ulatilla and notes his "skin almost as fair as that of an European" as well as his friendly conversation in English.[48] Almost a year passed before the *Lydia* from Boston approached Friendly Cove, quite likely alerted by Jewitt's letter to the captives held there by Maquinna. Apparently without much difficulty, Jewitt

convinced Maquinna to board the ship at which point Captain Samuel Hill took
him hostage "until the two white men came on board." Captain Hill released
Maquinna shortly after Jewitt and Thompson boarded the vessel, thereby ending
their two-plus years in captivity.[49]

This brief recitation of events raises a number of questions about conditions
at Nootka Sound and the escalation of violence. Why did Maquinna and his
Mowachaht villagers attack the *Boston* in 1803? Why did Maquinna spare Jewitt and Thompson as captives? How did this captivity scenario reflect other
hostile encounters around the Pacific? Maquinna's power, exceedingly strong
during Nootka Sound's heyday in the sea otter trade between 1785 and 1795,
had seriously diminished by 1803.[50] Maquinna had turned to raiding and
trading with communities to the north and east, always hoping for new fur supplies to exchange with the few vessels that now visited Nootka Sound. Social
prestige within his community, rather than material wealth, was his primary
aim.[51] Jewitt the armorer (and to a lesser extent Thompson the sailmaker) supported these goals: the armorer crafted iron goods for trade and weapons for
warfare, helping to prop up Maquinna's waning power. On a deeper level, however, Maquinna's community faced an ecological crisis of survival. Native over-
hunting of sea otters along Vancouver Island's west coast had all but extinguished
this valuable commodity, while Maquinna's focus on the maritime trade had
severely disrupted his community's traditional subsistence patterns. Jewitt's
diary repeatedly mentioned the desperate search for food; he and Thompson
were intermittently starving, and Maquinna himself felt the pressure as well.
"Last night," Jewitt wrote on April 11, 1804, "our chief informed me he was
concerned for his life, because there were no fish to be caught; he told me that
his own people were going to kill him."[52]

These material and ecological explanations provide the backdrop to Maquinna's attack on the *Boston*, but they lack the specificity to explain the ghastly
scene on the ship's quarterdeck that met Jewitt on March 22, 1803. As in many
other meetings that turned violent, language and communication proved to be
key factors. Maquinna most likely made his decision to attack the ship a few
days prior, when he returned the broken double-barrel musket Captain Salter
had gifted him. "It was *peshak* (bad)," Maquinna told Salter. "Capt. Salter was
very much offended at this observation," Jewitt wrote, and in a clear display of
social power, the captain insulted Maquinna in front of his lesser chiefs.[53] Salter's error—for which he literally paid with his head—was his failure to recognize Maquinna's grasp of the English language. Maquinna had communicated
with English-speaking traders since the time he met Cook in 1778, and he certainly understood more English than he acknowledged to Captain Salter, an obvious trading strategy.[54] Not only did he understand Salter's insults, but Salter
delivered them in such a way that Maquinna's accompanying lesser chiefs also

understood them. The insults personally and specifically challenged Maquinna's prestige at a time of severe crisis for his leadership. Salter had left him few options to save face. However, the power of language and communication worked against Maquinna two years later when he boarded the *Lydia* bearing a note of introduction penned by Jewitt. Maquinna's linguistic skills—as impressive as they were—did not include literacy, and thus he was excluded from the communication that made him a temporary hostage and freed his most valuable captive, John Jewitt.

These material, ecological, and personal tensions influenced the outcome of events in the locality of Nootka Sound, and they also relate to the larger geographies of the eastern Pacific and beyond. In the same year that Maquinna massacred the *Boston* crew and took Jewitt captive, the general manager of the Russian-American Company sealed a deal with the Boston trader Joseph O'Cain (captain of the ship *O'Cain*) to hunt sea otters as far down the coast as Baja California.[55] Transported indigenous hunters and local native communities would play pivotal roles in this expansion of the fur trade, as the following chapter demonstrates. Jewitt's captivity crystallized the meaning of these larger events: sea otter depletion in certain locales sparked rising tensions in a trade that now linked Russian and American interests with Chinese markets. On the *O'Cain*'s voyage in 1803 sailed two Russian hunt supervisors. One of them was Timofei Tarakanov.

The Northwest Coast III: The *Sv. Nikolai's* Survivors Cross the Beach, 1808–1810

Five years later Tarakanov, now aboard the *Sv. Nikolai*, wrecked on a beach one hundred miles to the south of Maquinna's "Friendly Cove." Tarakanov, Captain Bulygin, his wife Anna Petrovna, and the others straggled ashore and there encountered the Hoh Indians. Once again the lines of communication were muddled, as Tarakanov later recalled: "Since we did not understand each other very well, our conversation was prolonged."[56] With deadly weapons in hand and neither side understanding the other, a peaceful outcome seemed remote at best. Two accounts survive of the resulting violence and multiple captivities, one authored by Tarakanov, the other told by a Quileute elder named Ben Hobucket.

Ben Hobucket was not near the beach on November 1, 1808; in fact, he would not be born for another three decades. But his grandfather certainly knew the villagers who stood on the beach facing the shipwrecked Russians and Aleuts. Hobucket recited the history passed down by his parents and grandparents:

> In the long, long ago a ship, carrying cannon, was wrecked offshore
> here during a terrible storm; and, though the Indians had never seen a
> ship or white men before, they attempted to capture the people. . . .
> These people the Indians called "ho'kwat" (wanderers) and by that
> name they call the white people to this day.[57]

Hobucket's version of the events contains a remarkable level of detail, much of which coincides with Tarakanov's account. Hobucket tells of the strangers making their way to the Queets River, twenty-five miles south of the main Quileute village. Once there, some Hoh villagers offered to ferry the strangers across the river. But the Hohs "had treachery in their brains" and attacked the people, taking a few captives in the process. "There was no rest for the strangers," Hobucket conceded, with the Hoh attacking from one side and "our people," the Quileute, harassing from the other side.[58]

Some time thereafter—Hobucket's chronology is not entirely linear—the strangers built a "stockade" for protection but soon "starvation took possession of the place." Tarakanov's people constructed a rough boat from logs and some of them attempted a run down the river to the ocean where "an unfriendly sea met them." The beach itself offered no respite—it was "alive with savages" (Hobucket meant the Hohs, not his own Quileute people). Hobucket describes in great detail how the waves pummeled the boat, several people were lost, and the stragglers made it to shore in small groups. While many of the strangers were taken captive by the "frenzied Hohs," a few escaped and staggered off into the woods. At this point, time compresses in Hobucket's account and his people lost track of the strangers for weeks, months, even a year. "At last," he continues,

> they [the strangers] came in sight of the chimney blaze of the Quileute
> fireplaces; and hunger overcoming fear they surrendered themselves to
> our people. . . . The men were made slaves, and the woman given to one
> of the subchiefs for his wife; and they were forced to do the drudgery
> for the tribe. But as the years passed they were given more and more
> freedom.[59]

Finally, one morning the captives were found to be missing, having successfully made their escape.

Ben Hobucket's account reads in a dreamlike fashion: linear time progresses in fits and starts while certain salient issues (at least those prominent in Tarakanov's version) evaporate as immaterial. Some elements only make sense for their narrative power rather than factual basis, such as Hobucket's claim that "the Indians had never seen a ship or white men before." And yet this narrative is an astonishing indigenous account of a long-ago event precisely because it prioritizes

Quileute meanings and local history rather than those meanings established by Tarakanov—and, by extension, European narrators as a whole.

For instance, the shipwreck, the Russian and Aleut deaths, the taking of captives as slaves, and the captives' eventual escape held only marginal meaning for Hobucket. What held far more meaning was the way these events intervened on local politics and relationships. Hobucket's Quileute community had been at odds with the neighboring Hoh community for some time—that much is clear from his narrative. The Quileutes and Hohs also frequently clashed with the Makah villagers directly to the north. All three groups safeguarded their territory against threats from one another. Both the Quileute and the Hoh desired to make captives of these strangers who possessed firearms, novel skills, and able bodies capable of doing "drudgery for the tribe." But Hobucket demonizes the enemy Hoh rather than the strangers: the Hoh "had treachery in their brains"; they were "savages" and "frenzied" in their attempts to capture the foreigners (who were portrayed as "wanderers," a form of derision that echoed other terms used by indigenous groups around the Pacific).[60] By contrast, Hobucket contends, his community ultimately offered sanctuary to the starving survivors, who were drawn to the "chimney blaze of the Quileute fireplaces" and "surrendered themselves to our people."[61] Thus captives and slaves they became, but this result seems almost peripheral to Hobucket's historical narrative. The *Sv. Nikolai* had wrecked on a beach near villages with their own tensions and ancestral animosities—in short, their own histories—and the Russian and Aleut survivors unwittingly staggered into this indigenous history.

Timofei Tarakanov scribed his own version of these events. Unlike Hobucket's account, Tarakanov's story—once refashioned by Russian naval captain Vasilii M. Golovnin—received widespread publication. Russian variations appeared in 1822, 1853, 1874, 1884, and 1949, a German edition was released in 1822, and English translations appeared in 1826, 1853, 1973, and 2000. The proliferation of this publication is hardly surprising; like John Jewitt's narrative a few years earlier, Tarakanov's story piqued the lurid imaginations, sexual fantasies, and racialist fears of many audiences.[62]

From the outset Tarakanov's story promised adventure among hostile savages in the American wilderness—also the Russian empire's far eastern frontier. After the brief skirmish on the beach with the *Koliuzhi* (Indians), Tarakanov recounts fleeing inland only to find their path blocked by the Queets River. Conflict with another group of Indians resulted in the capture of two Aleuts and two Russians (including the captain's wife, Anna Petrovna Bulygin). The rest of the party fled farther inland and spent a long winter foraging, trading with different Indian parties, meeting natives in various states of captivity, and raiding Indian camps when the opportunity presented itself. Tarakanov rarely distinguishes one indigenous group from another, and the bitter animosities between Quileute and Hoh villages are clearly lost on the Russian. His is a battle for survival against the Indians: "The natives had driven us to the last stage of human misery. Consequently we had every right not only to take from their countrymen by force what we needed for our lives, but also to take vengeance upon them."[63]

The following spring the Russian party learned that a Makah village now held some of their captured comrades, including Anna Petrovna Bulygin, and so they took a Makah hostage of their own to facilitate a prisoner exchange. But to Captain Bulygin's "horror, distress, and anger," his captive wife Anna Petrovna refused to leave her captors because she "was satisfied with her condition."[64] Tarakanov decided to end his resistance: he and four others surrendered themselves to Anna Petrovna's captors—and received kind treatment—while the remaining Russians were soon captured by members of a different community. After a year of captivity, Tarakanov's master made contact with an American ship captain (Captain Thomas Brown of the *Lydia* from Boston) and orchestrated the sale of all available captives. Thirteen of them returned to Sitka. Captain Bulygin and Anna Petrovna, though reunited, had died in the meantime.

This entire sequence of events makes only partial sense as rendered by Tarakanov or Hobucket. The most significant inconsistencies result from the inexplicable actions and identities of three primary actors who decidedly influenced both the course of events as well as the potential meanings derived from them.

The first was Anna Petrovna, who by Tarakanov's account, decided to remain with the Indians rather than agree to a hostage exchange. This action shocked and horrified her fellow Russians: it "struck us like a clap of thunder," wrote Tarakanov. "To Bulygin, who loved his wife passionately, I did not know what to say concerning her answer and her intentions."[65] After all, here was a Russian woman (the captain's wife no less!) intentionally crossing the cultural and racial divide from European to native, civilized to savage people—and deciding to cast her lot with the latter. She chose to "go native" and desired to remain with the family of her captor, a man identified as Yutramaki.[66] But her decision to stay in the Indian community only supports this interpretation if we fix her social identity (like Tarakanov did) as a white European woman. The record suggests otherwise. The only extant source on Anna Petrovna states she was "probably a Creole, of Sitka," meaning her mother was an Aleut or Kodiak native.[67] This Creole identity does not entirely clarify her choice to remain in the Makah community, but it goes a long way toward explaining her presence in Sitka (a place few Russian women ever visited), her adjustment to life among the Makah, and her apparent allegiance to Yutramaki. Thus, while Tarakanov stabilized her identity as a white Russian woman, her actions revealed a more adept and flexible social character.

The second main actor was Yutramaki. It was only through Anna Petrovna's urging that Tarakanov and four others surrendered themselves to Yutramaki, who had purchased her from the Hoh during the previous year. They all became

Yutramaki's slaves, captives, dependents, or family members—depending on one's perspective—and significantly, it would be Yutramaki who orchestrated their rescue and sale to Captain Brown of the *Lydia* within a year. Who was this Makah man who figured so prominently in these affairs (and possibly also in the freedom of John Jewitt)? Tarakanov's reference to him as Yutramaki appears to combine his real name, Machee Ulatilla or Utillah, and that of his likely father— an Irish surgeon named John McKay left behind by the ship *Captain Cook* in 1786.[68] Yutramaki's mixed parentage (like Anna Petrovna's) appeared to not concern his Makah community, who respected his matrilineal line of descent. Recall Jewitt's description: he spoke "tolerable English" and "had much more the appearance of a civilized man than any of the savages that I saw."[69] Though little more is known about him, his actions suggest he relished his role as a cultural go-between for his people, neighboring Indian groups, and white outsiders. He certainly profited from the sale of his Russian captives: Captain Brown ultimately paid "five patterned blankets, five *sazhens* [about thirty-five feet] of woolen cloth, a locksmith's file, two steel knives, one mirror, five packets of gunpowder, and the same quantity of small shot" for *each* captive.[70] But the fact that Yutramaki benefited from the sale of human beings should not discount the possibility of more sympathetic motives; he quite possibly viewed these people as lost wanderers in a foreign land and he sought to help them.

The third significant actor was Tarakanov, about whom one additional piece of information is significant, which he excludes from his narrative. Tarakanov was a serf. Born into serfdom in Kursk, Russia, he remained a serf throughout his service to the Russian-American Company.[71] Tarakanov therefore had to persevere for his freedom in two senses: first from his status at birth, and second from the Indians who held him decades later. The social boundary between free and unfree must have been rather murky for this otherwise accomplished Russian, and one could argue that his two years in flight and captivity on the Northwest Coast may have represented his greatest freedom to date. It was Tarakanov, after all, who took command of the *Sv. Nikolai*'s survivors once Captain Bulygin proved incapable of the challenge. And it was also Tarakanov who correctly read Anna Petrovna's endorsement of Yutramaki as a fair master and their best chance for eventual freedom. Tarakanov would survive his captivity in fine form and return to work for the Russian-American Company. He eventually attained his official manumission seven years later in a most unusual place, the Hawaiian Islands, where he was stationed during the Russian-American Company's ill-fated attempt at colonization.[72] He returned to Sitka in 1817, married a Koniag woman, and fell out of favor with the company's new governor. Tarakanov and his family made their way to Russia in the early 1830s.[73]

Tarakanov's life story, like those of many people who came to inhabit the eastern Pacific, was entangled in a mixed and heterogeneous world. Cultural binaries such as "European" and "indigenous" shed only dim light on the complex politics and negotiations that influenced all parties involved in these meetings. Even Ben Hobucket failed to acknowledge the social heterogeneity of those who washed up on his shore in 1808. Instead, he remarked, "the Indians called [them] *ho'kwat* (wanderers) and by that name they call the white people to this day."[74] Wanderers: the term describes a people in flight and a people of profound cultural difference. In Hobucket's telling, the Quileute saw a Russian ship driven ashore, and the survivors wandered desperately through the country searching for food and shelter. But barring their desperate predicament, those people were not unlike past groups that sometimes traded on the Quileute shore. They generally had light skin (darker skinned crewmembers would not be involved in the official trade) and covered their skin with elaborate costumes. They had few, if any, women aboard their vessels, but they frequently sought out sexual contact with women on shore. They attempted to trade for furs and pelts year after year, but they were little inclined to seek exchanges beyond the material kind. They came and they left, and those who followed only reenacted the previous group's solitary efforts. The Quileute understood quite well *why* these people came to their shores; they understood the profit motive, the drive to accumulate commodities, and possibly even the market on the other side of the ocean. But these foreign people—these "wanderers"—appeared to live outside social communities and beyond cultural practices that gave meaning to life. Their rootlessness and single-minded purpose was both pathetic and deeply disturbing: they seemed like wandering apparitions without souls.[75]

Enslaved Women and Pandering Men

Men have comprised the majority of people thus far described as hostages or captives. A number of reasons account for this gender imbalance. European and American ships carried very few women apart from the occasional captain's wife (such as Abby Morrell aboard the *Antarctic*, Anna Petrovna on the *Sv. Nikolai*, or Mary Brewster of the whaleship *Tiger*), a crewmember's indigenous partner (such as the "Otaheite girl" named Harriet on the *Lelia Byrd*, a "wife" of the carpenter's mate), or captives like the young Hawaiian women Raheina and Tymarow held on the *Jenny*. With few women aboard these ships—except those already in some form of captivity—it was highly unlikely that European women in general would be taken captive by indigenous groups. It was far more likely that indigenous women would find themselves taken captive by European or American mariners, such as in the previously cited example of Aleut women and children held by Russian *promyshlenniki* in exchange for sea otter pelts. Nonetheless, this apparent gender imbalance in captivities ignores one group of people involved in encounters on the Northwest Coast and throughout the Pacific: indigenous women forced into sexual roles with outsiders. Sex in this context—as examined in the previous chapter—ranged from consensual affairs to prostitution and rape.[76]

The Northwest Coast's most common form of sexual assault involved enslaved indigenous women. These women, generally taken by indigenous groups as war captives and treated as unfree individuals (if not chattel), were remarkably pervasive on the Northwest Coast. Female slaves constituted an important and growing part of indigenous trade networks even before contact with outsiders in the eighteenth century. Maritime commerce, however, altered a primary function and valuation of female slaves in their newly defined roles as prostitutes.[77] The visit to the Northwest Coast by Captain Cook's ships in 1778 offered ample instruction to indigenous slaveholders about the value of their female captives. In Nootka Sound that spring, the *Discovery*'s surgeon David Samwell wrote: "Hitherto we had seen none of their young Women tho' we had often given the men to understand how agreeable their Company would be to us & how profitable to themselves, in consequence of which they about this time brought two or three Girls to the Ships." In exchange for the price of a "Pewter plate well scoured," Samwell continued, the girls "were prevailed upon to sleep on board the Ships, or rather forced to it by their Fathers or other Relations who brought them on board."[78] But Samwell either misunderstood or obfuscated these girls' relationship to the men who bartered their bodies. The surgeon's second mate, William Ellis, observed more correctly: "The women brought . . . were not of their own tribe, but belonging to some other which they had overcome in battle." Ellis described the women as "mute," "quite dejected, and totally under the command of those who brought them."[79] Clearly enslaved women, their captivity experience would now include rape by foreign sailors.

More than a decade after Cook's voyage and farther north up the coastline, Alejandro Malaspina feigned confusion in writing about the enslaved women offered by the Yakutat Tlingit of Port Mulgrave. Within a day of their arrival on June 27, 1791, Malaspina noted "repeated signs that had been made to us, beginning the previous day, to allow us the use of the women while in port, although fairly clear, still seemed ambiguous and perhaps wrongly interpreted, considering the few visits made to these parts by European ships and the strangeness of the offer."[80] Malaspina's "ambiguity" was convenient cover for discussing the morality of prostitution and slavery in his official journal. Although Malaspina had never visited the Northwest Coast, he knew well about the European use of enslaved women from both Spanish accounts as well as his thorough study of Cook's journals. He could hardly claim naïveté on the subject.

Given the official nature of his journal, Malaspina also desired to establish his authority to adjudicate and control sexual meetings. Hoping "not to cloud a friendly relationship" with the Tlingit, he forbade his crew's "lower ranks" from "any contact with the women and children in their huts." Malaspina next sought to discover whether or not the proffered women "were a genuine offer." He writes:

> Guided, therefore, by two young natives who, with an air of mystery, repeated the well-understood word *Jhoüt* [woman], I approached some trees by the huts, where all my doubts vanished at once. Indeed, at the foot of a tree were four or five women, partially clad in seal skins and, of course, obedient to the will of almost the entire tribe, which seemed unanimous in its intention of prostituting them. If neither morality nor example had sufficed to discourage any such thoughts, it would certainly be achieved by their ugly appearance and the quantity of grease and filth that covers them, giving off a smell so unpleasant that it can hardly be described.

Though Malaspina concluded that these women were "obedient to the will of almost the entire tribe," his journal curiously elides a clear mention of their slave status.[81] (He does clarify their enslavement [*"esclavas"*] in a different report, *Viaje político-científico alrededor del mundo por las Corbetas Descubierta y Atrevida*.)[82] He also maintains that his men did not have sex with these enslaved women, despite the community's "insistent offering" of them.[83]

The astonishing aspect of this account is hardly the question of whether sex took place. Instead, most revealing about this situation is the timing: within one day of contact between the Yakutat Tlingit and this Spanish expedition, Malaspina could report on the entire spectrum of hostage-taking and captivity. Entering Port Mulgrave the previous day, three canoes approached the *Atrevida*, and Malaspina watched as an old man gave "commands and warnings" to his people and the foreigners alike. "At first [we] preceded on both sides by easily-misunderstood signs of social contact," Malaspina writes, "in which each gesture and expression was interpreted . . . by the dictates of imagination rather than reason." Malaspina desired some Tlingit to come on board the vessel so that "misunderstood signs" could yield to actual communication, but neither side trusted the other. What to do? Malaspina explains: "[We] acced[ed] to their requests that an equal number of our crew should get into their canoes as hostages as their men came on board. In this way they were soon convinced of our peaceful intentions."[84] These willing and temporary hostages served their purpose; no unwilling hostages or captives on either side would be necessary. But Malaspina encountered permanent captives during the next twenty-four hours—women offered to his men as items of trade and also trophies of masculine power. The enslavement and abuse of these women by prostitution represented the extreme condition of what was otherwise a fairly ordinary convention of contact relations: namely, some form of captivity.

Conclusion

European and American outsiders did not initiate the practices of taking captives or exchanging hostages on the Northwest Coast or elsewhere in the Pacific. Native societies—like many people around the world—had been doing these things for millennia as an ongoing set of social power dynamics. Those dynamics were fairly similar around the Pacific Ocean for all groups involved in contact situations: how to assert authority in moments when power relations appeared unequal. Far from representing aberrant behavior, taking or exchanging personnel revealed a rational response to local contingencies and politics. But the rapidly expanding numbers of newcomers who arrived in the Pacific during the late eighteenth century wanted ever more services and goods of material value. And sometimes they also made demands for the indigenous workers who could harvest or hunt those goods, as demonstrated in the next chapter. The captivities that seemed so customary—coincident with disease introductions and the establishment of beachhead settlements by foreigners—culminated in greater violence and eventually the colonial practices of indigenous containment.

Tarakanov, Tootiscoosettle, Raheina and Tymarow, Yutramaki, Jewitt, and Maquinna—none of these people anticipated or desired the entangled captivities in which they found themselves. Yet they lived in a place and time fraught by rapid change in local communities as well as the broader oceanic setting. Social worlds expanded and intermingled through ongoing contacts, while mistrust and miscommunication all but predicted the violence that ensued. Timofei Tarakanov, standing on a windswept beach, tried to convince Ben Hobucket's Hoh ancestors of his "peaceableness," but the long rifle Tarakanov clutched in his hands belied his words. The Aleut and Kodiak hunters who stood behind Tarakanov indicated the coming course of events for Hobucket's people; they now faced a period of conflict, resistance, and accommodation to new foreign groups on the Northwest Coast.

4

The Great Hunt

Tiger, 1845–1848

Like many whaling voyages, this one involved a fair measure of human blood-shed and an enormous amount of blubber. The profitable cargo at the journey's end delighted Captain William E. Brewster, but his wife, Mary, expressed no particular sentiment as the *Tiger* entered the harbor of Stonington, Connecticut, on March 8, 1848. "We went in so quickly and so still—We soon left our old home [the *Tiger*] and found our friends all well—and glad to see us," she wrote in her journal.[1] Mary Brewster had certainly anticipated this homecoming for well over two years. She was now a seasoned voyager, a "sister sailor" who experienced the extremes of oceanic conditions and witnessed the gruesome business of whaling as well as the depravity of masculine behavior aboard ship. Very little could now startle this twenty-five-year-old woman, and perhaps this explains her lack of sentiment. It had been a long voyage.

Two years earlier the *Tiger* entered the Pacific with a typical complement of experienced officers, skilled tradesmen and harpooners, and novice crewmen who signed on with varying degrees of willingness. Headed for the Northwest Coast of North America and planning to hunt sperm whales on the way up the South American coast, the *Tiger*'s crew was notably unsuccessful through the spring of 1846. Some crewmembers quietly spoke of deserting the ship at the first opportunity. There was "not very good feeling between the officers and boatsteerers," noted John Perkins, a Yale College dropout and twenty-year-old green-hand sailor. Mary Brewster only made matters worse: a woman's mere presence on the ship, Perkins alleged, turned "every danger double."[2] The *Tiger*'s whaleboats chased numerous whales in the southeast Pacific but came up empty, forcing the captain to report "clean"—the whalemen's term for "no oil"—during a stopover in Hawai'i.[3]

Figure 4.1 Mary Brewster kept one of the most detailed journals of whaling in the Pacific during her six years aboard the *Tiger*, a ship captained by her husband William Brewster. Courtesy of Mystic Seaport Museum.

John Perkins had the best time of his short life in the port of Hilo: "Never have I met with any people who pleased me so much as the Kanakers." He considered deserting the ship at Hilo and even "wished for [a gale] to 'stove her up,'" or wreck the *Tiger*. But Perkins remained on the *Tiger* when it left Hawai'i, only to perish weeks later from a different sort of "stoving." His journal abruptly ends with a quick entry on June 5, 1846: "Good breeze. Seven months out, no oil yet, all discouraged, no strings for the fiddle."[4] Days later, Perkins pulled hard on the oars of one of the ship's whaleboats in pursuit of a finback whale. The harpooner struck the sixty-foot-long creature with two irons, at which point the whale turned and lashed the boat with its tail. Perkins's body took the brunt of the blow. What was left of John Perkins and the small boat disappeared in a bloody froth. Mary Brewster watched this horrid scene from the relative safety of the *Tiger*'s deck. She described how the whale "struck the boat and stove it," killing Perkins "instantly" before "the waves clos[ed] over him forever concealing his form from our view." Mary retreated to her cabin and, with Bible in hand, inscribed words to her journal from the Book of Matthew: "*Be ye also ready*."[5]

The *Tiger* sailed on for the "nor'west," though Brewster observed that "not a smile is to be seen and scarcely a loud word." Perkins was soon forgotten in the busy summer of 1846. The *Tiger*'s crew killed more than two dozen whales, amounting to fifteen hundred barrels of oil. At times the fire heating the ship's tryworks (the large pots used for rendering the blubber into oil) blazed day and night, covering the deck in greasy gore. Mary gaped at whales in their death flurry "spouting thick blood," and she would later watch the tryworks spewing forth smoke, "the smell [of] which I abominate." These summer months flew by in a "murderous spectacle," and the voyage, at long last, turned profitable.[6] As autumn arrived and the cold winds closed in on the northern ocean, Captain Brewster sailed for warmer climes.

Bahía Magdalena, Lower California. The *Tiger* arrived at this secluded Baja bay on November 18, 1846. During the previous season two whaleships, the *Hibernia* and the *United States*, had discovered this calving ground for the eastern Pacific's population of gray whales. Whalemen called them "Devilfish" for their manner of viciously attacking whale boats; true to form, the *United States* lost two crewmembers in stoving accidents on the very first day of hunting the previous winter. Mary Brewster knew nothing of the impending danger, but her husband quickly learned of the gray's reputation from Captain James Smith of the *Hibernia*, an experienced sea captain later caricatured by Mark Twain as "contemplating the world from over the back of a gnarled crag of a nose."[7] Mary enjoyed a quiet month at Magdalena Bay before the whales arrived at this southern destination of their annual migration. She took long walks on the deserted beach. She read books from Captain Smith's impressive library, including Charles Wilkes's recently published narrative of the US Exploring Expedition in the Pacific. And she watched as a few other whaleships arrived to join their small flotilla in the quiet bay. On the last day of 1846, the New London ship *Catherine* appeared, captained by Richard Smith, a man widely regarded as the toughest bare-knuckle fighter in the American whaling fleet.[8] But it would be the gray Devilfish, rather than the whaling men of Magdalena Bay, that tested Smith's pugilistic reputation.

Mary Brewster carefully noted the arrival of gray whales in the latter half of December. A distant spout one day, followed the next day by a pair of whales sighted near the *Tiger*. She described with cool detachment the method by which the crew would capture and kill the grays:

WHALING SCENE IN THE CALIFORNIA LAGOONS.

Figure 4.2 Captain, artist, and writer Charles Scammon depicts the opportunities and dangers of hunting gray whales in Magdalena Bay. Courtesy of the Huntington Library.

These whales frequent this bay once a year to calve and can only be taken when they have a young one which [the harpooners] fasten to and by this means secure the mother who will never forsake it till dead but try every way to shield it from danger by taking it on her back and endeavor to help them along.[9]

To put it more bluntly, the whalers used the newborn calf as live bait to capture the mother. More and more whales arrived every day in Magdalena Bay—more than a thousand of them by the first weeks of 1847—and the cows gave birth to calves as they had done since time immemorial. Captain Brewster readied the *Tiger's* four whaleboats and sharpened the various harpoons, hand-lances, cutting spades, and other instruments of death. And then the slaughter commenced.

The world's greatest hunt for marine mammals began in the North Pacific during the mid-eighteenth century and continued throughout the eastern Pacific for the next hundred years. A brutal campaign of extermination, the hunt shifted by geography and species according to market value, technological innovation, and remaining—yet killable—animal populations.[10] The great hunt culminated in the near-annihilation of three marine mammals that held distinct historical meanings for the eastern Pacific. The sea otter (*Enhydra lutris*) commanded the world's highest fur prices and therefore served as the initial attraction for Russian, American, and British traders. Fur seals (including *Callorhinus ursinus, Arctocephalus townsendi,* and *Arctocephalus philippii*) existed in extraordinarily large numbers from the Aleutian Islands to the Juan Fernández Islands off the coast of Chile; the manual slaughter of these lesser-value marine mammals utilized the brute force of proto-industrial production rather than the skilled techniques and rituals of indigenous sea otter hunters. Finally, the taking of gray whales (*Eschrichtius robustus*) in their Baja California calving bays shows how European and American demand for whale oil led to a worldwide peak of whaling activity in the Pacific by the mid-nineteenth century. American whalers were not simply a variant on the maritime fur trade. Given the tremendous size of the US whaling fleet, they represented an advance maritime guard for US imperial goals in the Pacific. The fleet's brutal work also provided American textile factories with the crucial industrial lubricant of whale oil, which in turn drew upon expanded cotton production in the slave South. In this sense, whaling in the distant Pacific Ocean was inextricably connected to the major territorial and industrial ambitions of mid-century America.

The great hunt for marine mammals was both a function and byproduct of the expanding commerce that transformed the eastern Pacific, as examined in chapter 1. But here the commercial focus shifts to the involvement of specific groups—the hunters and the prey. Similar to the land-based fur trades of North America and Siberia, the killing of marine mammals appropriated and in some instances demanded indigenous skills. This was clearly evident during the early period of the hunt for the taking of sea otters, and it remained true to a lesser extent in fur seal hunting and whaling.[11] The targets of the hunt carried very different economic values, and, ironically, the smallest of them (an individual sea otter pelt) could bring more profit than the largest (the gray whale, rendered to

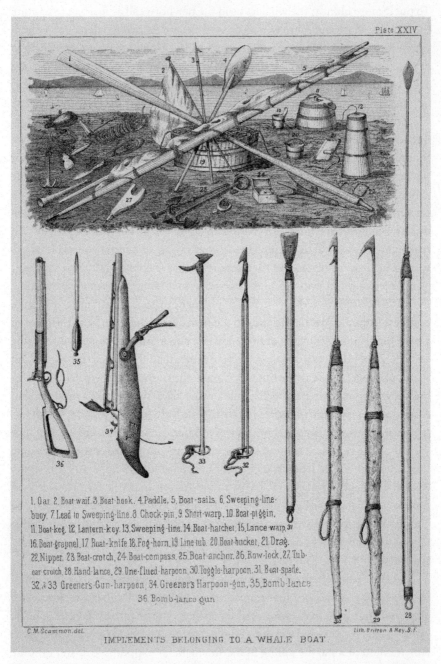

1. Oar. 2. Boat-waif. 3. Boat-hook. 4. Paddle, 5. Boat-sails. 6. Sweeping-line-buoy. 7. Lead to Sweeping-line. 8. Chock-pin. 9. Short-warp. 10. Boat-piggin. 11. Boat-keg. 12. Lantern-key. 13. Sweeping-line. 14. Boat-hatchet, 15. Lance-warp. 16. Boat-grapnel. 17. Boat-knife. 18. Fog-horn. 19. Line-tub. 20. Boat-bucket. 21. Drag. 22. Nipper. 23. Boat-crotch. 24. Boat-compass. 25. Boat-anchor. 26. Row-lock. 27. Tub-oar-crotch. 28. Hand-lance. 29. One-flued-harpoon. 30. Toggle-harpoon. 31. Boat-spade. 32. & 33. Greener's-Gun-harpoon. 34. Greener's Harpoon-gun. 35. Bomb-lance. 36. Bomb-lance gun.

C.M.Scammon.del.   Lith. Britton & Rey, S.F.

IMPLEMENTS BELONGING TO A WHALE BOAT.

Figure 4.3 By the late 1840s most whale ships would carry an extensive arsenal of killing instruments, including the newly invented "Greener's Harpoon-gun" and "Bomb-lance gun." Charles Scammon illustrated the array of weapons in his 1874 publication, *The Marine Mammals of the Northwestern Coast of North America*. Courtesy of the Huntington Library.

oil). Regardless of the prey's size, the hunters had to track them to certain locales where they gathered in large numbers, reproduced, and birthed their young. These sites were typically very isolated, even by the standards of the mostly uncharted eastern Pacific coastline.

What transpired in these remote localities illuminates something concealed by larger scales of history: the great hunt contained a level of violence and carnage that was thoroughly veiled by the worldwide marketplace. Furs, skins, or oil represented valuable and bloodless commodities for individual and industrial consumers who were likely grateful for the "obscured connections" back to the natural species from whence they came.[12] Yet, the moments when those mammals became lifeless carcasses on distant beaches or bays involved tremendous—and largely thoughtless—brutality.

Sea Otters: A Short History of Extirpation

The *Tiger's* journey down the North American coastline in the fall of 1846 traversed some of the most productive sea otter hunting grounds: Vancouver Island, San Francisco and Monterey bays, the Channel Islands, and at the southern end of the sea otter range, Baja California. Mary Brewster mused expansively in her journal about this southbound journey once the *Tiger* arrived in Magdalena Bay. However, she never once mentioned the "soft gold" of sea otter pelts for a simple reason: hunters had reduced the species to near-extinction by the 1840s. A few remnant otter colonies survived farther to the north, but Baja's lonely coastline—described by a previous visitor as "the most obscure corner of the World"—contained none.[13]

Baja's coastline would be one place to uncover the work of the sea otter trade, but an equally obscure starting place would be the trading posts of Kiakhta and Mai-mai-ch'eng on the Russian-Chinese border, just south of Lake Baikal. The coastline from Baja to the Siberian port of Okhotsk aligned with the historic range of the sea otter, and it was from Okhotsk that Russian traders began transporting the pelts inland to Kiakhta following Vitus Bering's voyage to the Aleutian Islands in 1741. Bering never returned from this voyage, and yet those sailors who survived the scurvy and other maladies brought back some exceedingly beautiful otter pelts described by the voyage naturalist Georg Steller: "The gloss of their hair surpasses the blackest velvet."[14] Well before Canton's ascendance as the Pacific's primary fur market, Kiakhta and Mai-mai-ch'eng flourished in the otter trade, linking the brutal expansion of Russian *promyshlenniki* across the Aleutian Islands with the consumer demands of the Chinese luxury fur market.

The bulk of the Russian sea otter harvest passed through these two remote trade towns prior to the 1790s; estimates vary from one-quarter to one-half million pelts sold, ranging in value from $10 (Spanish dollars) to well over $50 a piece.[15] This was a veritable fortune in soft gold, each pelt stripped from the carcass and transported thousands of miles for sale at staggering prices. No other sea or land mammal pelt came close to the value of sea otters. Prime silver fox pelts were the second most valuable, at one-quarter to one-third the price of sea otter pelts.[16] Russia's eastern expansion into the North Pacific spelled disaster for two populations: the sea otters of the North Pacific, and the indigenous Aleut and Kodiak hunters who were forced into "a state of abject slavery," according to one sympathetic chronicler.[17]

The hunt for sea otters in the Pacific and the fur market's global reach should not mask an essential truth about the otters themselves: they lived exceedingly local lives. *Enhydra lutris* never ranged far from its island or mainland tidewater home. Sea otters neither migrated nor found cause to travel any great distance from their "raft" (a term for the otter's colony, which describes the manner of linking together their floating bodies). Despite some explorers' optimistic reports that sea otters were as numerous as seals, the original population was quite small, numbering under four hundred thousand across the wide geographic arc from Baja California to the Sea of Okhotsk. Sex and reproduction patterns help explain this limited population size.[18] Females produced at most one pup a year, and the annual reproduction rate for the entire population was below a meager 15 percent. Furthermore, males and females typically lived in sex-segregated rafts, and the females exerted constant control over reproductive behavior: eager males approached and attempted awkward foreplay (rubbing, nuzzling, and sniffing the female body) while the female pondered her level of interest. "If the female is unreceptive," wrote one close observer, she "pushes him away with her flippers and paws, or snaps at him. Before departing [the male] may snatch whatever food items she has on her chest."[19] No small wonder the females chose to segregate themselves with their pups.

Though amphibious, sea otters spend most of their time in the water, which, especially in the frigid waters of the North Pacific, accounts for the unique splendor of their fur. This smallest of marine mammals compensates for its lack of body fat by wearing the densest coat in the animal kingdom: 650,000 hairs per square inch, glossy black and silky to the touch when dry. The American fur trader William Sturgis once extolled the sea otter's beauty in this way: it was "more pleasure to look at a splendid sea-otter skin, than to examine half the pictures that are stuck up [in museums] for exhibition." Except for a "beautiful woman and a lovely infant," Sturgis continued, sea otter pelts were "the most attractive natural objects" to be found.[20] Sturgis knew of what he spoke; he had transported well over ten thousand pelts across the Pacific to China during the twenty years following his first voyage in 1798.

Even Sturgis had arrived late to the sea otter hunt, at least so far as the majority of the species in Russian Alaska were concerned. The Russian hunt—conducted by Russian *promyshlenniki* and their conscripted indigenous hunters—cleaned out sea otters to such an extent that by 1792, according to naturalist Martin Sauer, "Sea otters are almost forgotten here . . . [due to the] havoc made among them by the hunters."[21] Jean François de Galaup de La Pérouse arrived in the North Pacific just as this first stage of the hunt waned and new participants plotted the next stage. La Pérouse heard of the *promyshlenniki*'s brutal relations with their conscripted native hunters, and through his meeting with Tlingit at Latuya Bay, he learned of the diminished number of sea otters in Russian-held territory. The Tlingit still had furs to exchange with La Pérouse, but this was only by virtue of their violent opposition to Russian incursion.[22] In Alta California, La Pérouse caught wind of Spain's own plan for a lucrative trade through a Crown-sponsored "Philippine Company" headed by Vicente Vasadre y Vega. "It is practically certain that the new Company will try to capture this trade, and this is the best thing that could happen to the Russians, because it is in the nature of monopolies to bring death or at least sluggishness to everything associated with them," La Pérouse commented.[23]

La Pérouse's assessment of the situation proved partially correct. The Russians *did* "bring death" to the northern sea otter colonies and rapid depopulation to Aleut hunters (mostly from disease and violent encounters), while Vasadre delivered thousands of otter furs harvested from the Alta California coast to Canton between 1786 and 1790.[24] But the Spanish plan to capture the coastal trade failed for reasons La Pérouse could not have foreseen. Spaniards in Alta California lacked trained indigenous hunters who could pursue otters in the offshore waters, while a temporarily glutted fur market diminished Vasadre's profits due to simultaneous English, American, Russian, and French fur shipments from the Northwest Coast. Intense competition for sea otter pelts suddenly materialized on the Northwest Coast during the late 1780s and 1790s, especially due to the influx of American traders.[25] By the 1800 season "Boston men" dominated the exchange of furs with indigenous hunters. As the otter hunt moved down the coastline during the next few seasons, the circumstances for California's sea otters turned bleak.

The most significant period of the sea otter hunt in terms of international connections and collaborations transpired between 1803 and 1812. Coordinated action brought together the contract labor system of the Russian-American Company with the maritime prowess of American traders to solve a specific problem: how to hunt sea otters in California given the absence of skilled indigenous hunters? Native Californians had proven themselves adept at killing only small numbers of sea otters during the 1780s and 1790s—primarily at the behest of Spanish authorities, and mostly by means of capture (and bludgeoning) on

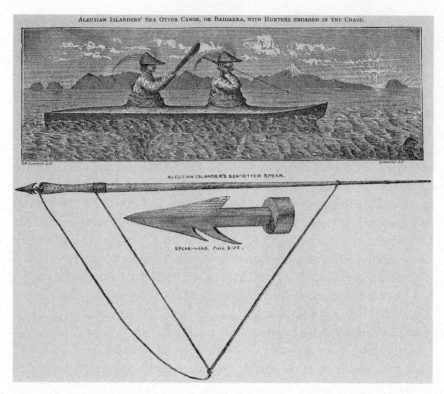

Figure 4.4 The Great Hunt for marine mammals in the eastern Pacific began with the wholesale slaughter of sea otters in the late eighteenth century. Russian and American traders conscripted the most skillful hunters, Aleutian and Kodiak islanders, to conduct the work along the North American coastline from Baja California to the Arctic Ocean. Courtesy of the Huntington Library.

the seashore. Yet hunting sea otters was in no way a traditional practice for them as it was for Northwest or Alaska natives. The answer to the California hunting problem was the importation of Aleut and Kodiak hunters along with their entire hunting complex (weaponry, *baidarkas*, Russian overseers, and in some instances female skinners) to California's coastal shores, bays, and islands.

The American captain Joseph O'Cain sailed to Alaska in 1803 and proposed this plan to Aleksandr Andreevich Baranov, governor of the Russian-American Company (RAC). Baranov's reputation for brutality was only surpassed by his determination to continue company rule over the North Pacific fur trade. O'Cain found Baranov in the company town of Three Saints Bay on Kodiak Island, where indigenous hunters and Russian traders had met each fall since 1784 to exchange furs for trade goods. Their agreement established a formula adopted by other American traders during the next nine years. Baranov supplied equipped hunters and Russian overseers (known as *baidarshchiks*) while O'Cain provided the transport to Alta California because, as one Russian navy lieutenant freely admitted in 1804, the existing RAC ships lacked "everything necessary for proper and safe sailing."[26] The two parties would split the take of furs. In agreeing to O'Cain's proposal, Baranov hoped to rejuvenate the company's finances by continuing its access to the most valuable fur in the Pacific. However, he was also following recent "Secret Instructions" from RAC officials in Irkutsk "to extend our claims" down the Northwest Coast—a coast that, if followed far enough, led to California.[27] In this plan lay the dream of a Russian colony in Alta California.

Aleut hunters proved instrumental to the temporary American-Russian business alliance. Despite their position of "abject slavery" during the early decades of Russian expansion, Aleuts had nonetheless displayed persistent resistance to submission and also irreplaceable skills in the hunting of the *promyshlenniki*'s most desired commodity. Even with the Aleut's ongoing population decline, they remained the most successful sea otter hunters, killing them to the point of near extinction.[28] By 1803, when O'Cain and Baranov agreed to terms for the California hunt, the Aleuts likely viewed their involvement as the best option among markedly diminished choices: colonialism had led to community crisis and even "forced resettlement" by the RAC, while the hunt offered a means to survive.[29]

Two months after meeting with Baranov, O'Cain sailed south with twenty double-hatched *baidarkas*, forty hunters, their provisions (including dried fish and "train," or whale oil), and at least two Russian *baidarshchiks*. One of those *baidarshchiks* was Timofei Tarakanov, the young indentured employee who would struggle for survival as a captive on the Northwest Coast five years later. Tarakanov had gained the respect of Aleut hunters by protecting their interests, weaponry, and especially their lightweight *baidarkas*. Handcrafted from driftwood, whalebone, and sealskin by an Aleut hunter over a period of many months, *baidarkas* were built with an almost mystical precision, such that "not even a mathematician could add very much or scarcely anything to the perfection of its nautical qualities," wrote the Russian Orthodox priest Ivan Veniaminov.[30] Tarakanov had never traveled so far south, and he watched the unfolding of California's coastline with amazement. The Spanish authorities warned the *O'Cain* out of San Diego harbor in December 1803, so the captain sailed almost two hundred miles farther south to a tiny Baja port with suitably lax governance, San Quintín.

Captain O'Cain fabricated a story of necessary ship repairs for the Spanish authorities in San Quintín—and likely offered generous bribes—while Tarakanov prepared and set loose the Aleuts in their two-man *baidarkas*. They disappeared north and south of the small bay in pursuit of sea otter rafts, working in teams described by one of the ship's officers, Jonathan Winship:

> The moment an otter was seen floating on the water the alert Indians fixed their eyes upon it, and trembled like the eager dog at the sight of

game! Swiftly but very silently the canoes approached from the wind-
ward. When within shooting distance, while the man at the stern guided
the boat, the nearest bowman raised his dart, and with sure aim threw
his pronged bone spear with incredible accuracy. For twenty minutes or
so the otter submerged, his course being marked by a bladder attached
to a long cord. When the animal arose to the surface for air a screaming
hunter was on hand to finish him.[31]

Apart from the racialized caricature of semi-wild natives hunting their prey,
Winship's celebration of Aleut skill, patience, and determination echoes numerous other descriptions of their unique talent. No other hunters could take
sea otters with such quiet and precise resolve. Within two months the hunt had
produced over one thousand furs, certainly enough to satisfy O'Cain and
Baranov on this first joint venture.

One Spanish authority reported the illegal hunting to his superior and noted
his inability to do anything about it. "There is not an otter left from Mission Rosa-
rio to Santo Domingo," wrote José Joaquín Arrillaga on March 4, 1804. Furthermore, he confessed, "there is no other way to prevent them except to tell them not
to hunt and to this they pay no attention."[32] The well-armed Tarakanov ensured
against any Spanish interference with their quick business. The Spanish authorities and missionaries likely carried on active trade with the American captain,
despite Arrillaga's claims to the contrary. By May the ship was under sail for Kodiak
Island, where Captain O'Cain delivered half the furs to Governor Baranov, while
the Aleut hunters received wages in the form of food, trade goods, and tobacco.

More than a dozen American-Russian joint voyages headed south from
Kodiak Island or Sitka in the next eight years on Boston ships, including the *Mercury, Isabella, Peacock, Derby, Eclipse,* and the *Albatross.* Aleut and Kodiak Island
hunters came south in increasing numbers accompanied by *baidarshchiks* like
Timofei Tarakanov, who also spent his time recruiting hunters for the ongoing
ventures. The need for hunters quickly expanded: in 1806 four Boston vessels—
the *O'Cain, Peacock, Derby,* and *Eclipse*—jointly carried well over two hundred
hunters and their *baidarkas* to the Alta and Baja California coast. The ship captains also complemented their labor force with Aleut women and children, who
would skin the otters, cook, and generally serve as a mobile support staff.

O'Cain and the other American captains targeted Alta California's otter herds,
which they could accomplish so long as the ships avoided the formidable Spanish garrisons of San Diego, San Francisco, and Monterey. The *O'Cain* landed at
Trinidad Bay (well north of Spanish settlements) and set up a temporary onshore
camp, but because of pressure from Yurok villagers "it was necessary to land the
field pieces [loaded with grape shot] to protect the camp." The Yurok traded
their own small supply of pelts with the foreigners, while they simultaneously

sought to prevent the Aleut hunters from pursuing otters in their coastal waters. The *O'Cain* continued far down the coast past San Quintín to Cedros Island, Baja California. Once there, the ship began depositing groups of hunters at different islands and coastal inlets, essentially blanketing the Baja coast with outfits of hunters, *baidarkas*, and female skinners.[33] The three other American vessels operated on the Alta California coast. The *Peacock* established a base at Bodega Bay and sent dozens of hunters immediately south into San Francisco Bay where "the valuable sea-otter was swimming in numbers about the bay, nearly unheeded," according to Georg Heinrich von Langsdorff's account.[34] The ship returned to Sitka after six months with over twelve hundred otter pelts, including more than five hundred yearlings and pups (whose slaughter held obvious repercussions for the population's decline).[35] Captain William Heath Davis of the *Mercury* followed a different strategy altogether, buying furs from Alta California missionaries (who likely secreted away otter pelts in hopes of trading for valuable supplies) while dispatching small groups of Aleut hunters in the vicinity of the more remote missions. The *Mercury* left California in August 1806, with a cargo of almost three thousand otter pelts.[36] The *O'Cain* departed for Russian Alaska with over "200 souls" on board, pelts valued at $136,310 in Canton, and two pregnant Aleut women who gave birth during the voyage north.[37]

The profits derived in Canton from these American-Russian ventures remained high for the years between 1803 and 1812, averaging over $25 per sea otter pelt, a veritable fortune for those traders fortunate enough to cash in. The cost to California's sea otter population was higher still. Though not completely destroyed, the main herds of Baja and Alta California were reduced to mere remnants struggling for survival. And the hunt staggered on well after 1812. By the late 1820s the hunt resembled a desperate contest to bag the final fur. The American fur trapper George Nidever teamed up with Allen Light (an African American hunter nicknamed "Black Steward") and "one Kanak" in 1835; together they scoured the once-plentiful otter grounds of the Santa Barbara channel. They used long rifles and bagged a couple dozen sea otters. Nidever noted with incredulity the "early times" when sea otters must have been "so abundant that the Indians killed them with spears."[38] What a waste of this valuable commodity, he intimates with envy.

Miraculously, *Enhydra lutris* survived as a species. It survived the protohistoric hunting by indigenous groups who wore sea otter pelts to weather the North Pacific's long winters, and the species survived the hunt conducted at the behest of profit-driven Russian, American, and British traders. A few sea otters even endured the mid-1830s assault by shoreline sharpshooters—highly trained riflemen who roved the coast and picked them off one by one. They survived, living in a handful of small and isolated colonies removed from human reach until the International Fur Seal Treaty in 1911 banned the hunting of sea otters, ending a decade when sea otter pelts could sell at auction for over $1,000 apiece.[39]

Fur Seals: "A Club Is Commonly Used"

The slaughter of sea otters represented but the tip of an iceberg. The hunt for all furs and pelts—both land and sea mammals—reached epic proportions in the eastern Pacific during the decades around 1800. This was especially true in Alaska, where the RAC's survival depended on the export of furs. Virtually everyone employed by the RAC recognized this economic imperative, and Baranov's successor Leontii Gagemeister articulated it to company overseers: "Advantage and profit of the company depends vitally on increasing the hunting of furbearing animals, and not on the increase in land."[40] Animal furs, in this way, became the raison d'être in Russian America, a strategy that eventually led to the empire's withdrawal from America due to the near-extinction of those mammals.

The Russians quantified their hunting success on a yearly basis and occasionally tabulated the cumulative kill. The RAC's first published history, *A Chronological History of the Discovery of the Aleutian Islands, or, The Exploits of Russian Merchants* (1823), authored by the Russian naval lieutenant Vasiliĭ Nikolaevich Berkh, offered a crude summary of Russian fur exports for the years 1743 to 1823:[41]

Animal	# Exported
Fur seals	2,324,364
Sea otters	200,839
Sea otter tails	143,689
Blue foxes	108,865
Red foxes	57,638
River beavers	58,729
Cross foxes	44,904
Black and black-brown foxes	30,158
River otters	22,807
Sables	18,121
Mink	5,349
White foxes	5,130
Bears	2,650
Lynx	1,819
Wolverine	1,234

Despite the seeming precision of Berkh's numbers, one can only guess at the real number of animals actually killed by the company's hunters. The number of sea otter pelts listed, for instance, appears to be short by almost half according to most scholars.[42] Far more remarkable in Berkh's table was the sheer variety of species slaughtered during the fur trade: sea- and land-based mammals, seals and foxes and bears and wolverines—it was a truly wide-ranging assault on any animal unfortunate enough to carry a marketable fur.

Berkh's accounting for Russian Alaska illustrates a fact that applies elsewhere in the eastern Pacific: the great hunt cut broadly across the animal kingdom, and it cut deeply into certain species because of their value or the relative ease of hunting them. If the sea otter represented the high-value fur, difficult kill, and limited original population, then fur seals were the opposite in each way. Furthermore, the method of taking fur seals in the decades around 1800 reveals a brutality masked by both the commodity market and Berkh's statistics. The taking of fur seals closely resembled an industrial slaughterhouse—gruesome in practice, workers knee-deep in gore.

Few people described it better than the American captain Amasa Delano, who participated in the initial carnage on Más Afuera Island, one of the Juan Fernández Islands located four hundred miles off the coast of Chile:

> When [we] came to this place, about the year 1797, and began to make a business of killing seals, there is no doubt but there were two or three millions of them on the island. . . . The method practiced to take them was, to get between them and the water, and make a lane of men, two abreast, forming three or four couples, and then drive the seals through this lane; each man furnished with a club, between five and six feet long; and as they passed, he knocked down such of them as he chose; which are commonly the half grown, or what are called young seals. This is easily done, as a very small blow on the nose effects it. When stunned, knives are taken to cut or rip them down on the breast, from the under jaw to the tail, giving a stab in the breast that will kill them. After this, all hands go to skinning. I have seen [one man who] would skin sixty in an hour. They take off all the fat, and some of the lean with the skin, as the more weight there is to the skin the easier it will [hang]. This is performed in the same manner in which curriers flesh their skins; after which it is stretched and pegged on the ground to dry. It is necessary to keep it two days in pegs, in fair weather, to make it keep its shape. After this they are taken out of pegs, and stacked in the manner of salted dried cod fish.[43]

Delano certainly exaggerated the speed with which workers could strip the skins from fur seals—"sixty in an hour" is unimaginable even for a skilled butcher wielding a razor-sharp blade—but he nonetheless captured the ease of rounding up, killing, and skinning this unwary and awkward mammal. The work process called for maximum efficiency and endurance, given the seemingly endless supply of fur seals that populated the offshore islands of North and South

America. Somewhere around ten *million* fur seals were killed in the Pacific in the decades around 1800.[44]

Unlike the sea otter's limited variety (one genus and species: *Enhydra lutris*), the marine mammals called "fur seals" came in great diversity across an extensive geographic area. The northern fur seals (*Callorhinus ursinus*) blanketed the islands of the North Pacific from the Alaskan Pribilof Islands to Baja California, while the southern cousins in the *Arctocephalus* genus came in seven different species and ranged from Antarctica to the Galápagos Islands. Five other genera exist elsewhere in the Pacific and Atlantic Oceans. From the standpoint of hunters all these varieties shared two essential characteristics: a dense underfur that gave them value in the marketplace, and a primordial calling to gather on the same rocky islands year after year for mating and birthing. Add to these characteristics their sluggish mobility, and the fur seals of the eastern Pacific became easy prey.[45]

In the North Pacific, Russian *promyshlenniki* began hunting fur seals on the Commander Islands (directly east of the Kamchatka Peninsula) in the 1740s and 1750s. By the 1780s the Russians discovered the fur seal rookeries on the Pribilof Islands containing animals too many to count, certainly in the millions, and therefore profitable by their sheer abundance. The *promyshlenniki* "harvested" over forty thousand seals on the Pribilofs during an initial season in 1786, using "clubs" wielded "at the discretion of the hunter," according to one Russian account.[46] The number of harvested furs grew every year thereafter, especially in the late 1790s when the Russians imported hundreds of Aleuts to carry out the gruesome work. In the span of a quarter century and despite their initial "unfathomable abundance," the Pribilof seals had "decrease[d] to the point that their future survival was in doubt," according to historian Ryan Jones.[47]

Fur seal hunting in the North Pacific peaked just before 1800, nearly simultaneous to the attack on the southern herds off the coast of Chile. Amasa Delano's account from Más Afuera Island of clubbing, skinning, and drying the skins depicted something that had gone on there since the early 1700s, though these earliest European hunters had taken fur seals numbering in the hundreds, rather than hundreds of thousands. William Dampier, the English three-time world circumnavigator, had never seen anything like the volume of seals blanketing the island called Más a Tierra when he approached it in 1686: "Seals swarm as thick about this Island, as if they had no other place in the World to live in; for there is not a Bay nor Rock that one can get ashore on, but is full of them. . . . Large ships might here load themselves with seal-skins[.]"[48] Dampier's prediction of "large ships" loading up with fur seals proved correct by the late 1790s. Sealing on these four islands easily challenged the scale of hunting on the Pribilofs in the North Pacific.[49]

British, French, and Spanish vessels all conducted sealing operations on the Juan Fernández Islands during the 1790s, but American ships out of New England quickly dominated the business. They made remarkably quick work of the seal population. Dozens of New England vessels landed hunting parties, who went about their sealing business for months at a time while the seals attempted their own business of mating and birthing. The Boston ship *Jefferson* took a relatively light load of thirteen thousand skins in 1793, the same year that the *Eliza* filled its cargo hold with thirty-eight thousand skins en route to Canton.[50] Captain Edmund Fanning of the *Betsey* described his crew's work on Más Afuera in 1800 as so productive that "even after the [ship's] hold was stowed so as not to have room for any more, then the cabin, and finally the forecastle, were filled, leaving just space enough for the accommodation of the ship's company."[51] More than a dozen other ships shared in the carnage on Más Afuera during that season, each taking away tens of thousands of skins. The Juan Fernández Islands were covered with rotting carcasses, an abominable stench, and insects so thick "as Sure as you open your mouth you will Catch it full of flies[,]" wrote the captain of the *Minerva*.[52]

American hunting parties pursued the hunt on the Juan Fernández Islands for about ten years, transporting hundreds of thousands of seal skins each year. Some voyages secured complete cargoes and earned high returns in Canton, but others did not. It took the *Minerva*'s crew almost three years of shuttling between islands, awaiting the seasonal appearance of the surviving fur seals, to claim a cargo of thirty thousand skins. The utterly predictable had happened: "Seals was scarce," wrote the *Minerva*'s captain in 1802.[53] So scarce, in fact, that within a few years sealing voyages would bypass the Juan Fernández Islands altogether. "We pass'd Juan Fernandez between the hours of ten and eleven oclock in the evening [close to] the Lee Shore," wrote Lewis Coolidge on February 15, 1807. Ten years earlier Coolidge would have heard the nearly deafening roar from a multitude of fur seals, but now he only heard "the noise of the Sea, breaking on the beach[.]"[54] The silence reflected a staggering change for the Juan Fernández Islands: the killing of some three million seals in little more than a decade.

Lewis Coolidge participated in the next stage of the hunt as it moved north up the American coastline. A twenty-three-year-old senior crewman aboard the Boston sealer *Amethyst*, Coolidge was headed to the one place in the eastern Pacific that still held substantial rookeries: the coastal islands of Baja and Alta California. Fifty-two men left Boston aboard the *Amethyst* in September 1806. Twenty of these men, according to Coolidge, "were afflicted With the Venereal in Various Stages, Some of them very bad." Other maladies soon appeared. A "Northwest Indian" cabin boy, enlisted during the previous voyage to the Northwest Coast, showed signs of ill health ("Strange uncommon fits") a month out of Boston.[55] He died within a year, as did numerous other crewmembers who succumbed to scurvy and other ailments. Coolidge remained healthy, but he had to watch help-lessly while many coworkers died around him on the islands off Baja California. Those healthy enough worked feverishly to kill more than thirty-five thousand Guadalupe fur seals (*Arctocephalus townsendi*).[56]

Coolidge's journal, which he maintained intermittently during the four-year undertaking, reveals the extraordinarily strange nature of sealing as a venture. First was the isolation: before even reaching the Pacific, the *Amethyst* dropped off a small party of men "to prosicute [*sic*] the business of the Voyage" on Gough Island, an uninhabited spot of land in the southern Atlantic Ocean.[57] Leaving enough supplies for the sealing party to survive in addition to his pledge to return sometime in the near future (it would be eighteen months), Captain Seth Smith sailed the *Amethyst* into the Pacific bound for Baja California. In the spring of 1807—six months into the voyage—the *Amethyst* reached a group of Baja islands, including San Benito, Guadalupe, Cedros, and Natividad. The captain left a small sealing party on each island. Coolidge watched from the shore of San Benito Island as the *Amethyst* set sail, knowing it would be gone for a year. He worried about the island's lack of fresh water and noted the readily apparent symptoms of scurvy among some men. To ward off loneliness, he began tran-scribing words in his journal from the Scottish poet James Beattie: "Rocks pill'd on Rocks, as if by magic spell[.]"[58]

At least a dozen other skinners from the *Amethyst* hunkered down with Coolidge on San Benito and the nearby Isla Cedros. Four or five Hawaiians joined them, men whom Captain Smith had contracted from a passing ship. Illness soon took its toll, with seven of the men (both Americans and Hawai-ians) dying from scurvy and various other maladies. Somehow—and his jour-nal offers no suitable explanation—Coolidge and a few others maintained decent health despite the lack of clean water and dietary needs.[59] Equally odd is Coolidge's lack of comment on the sealing work they finally conducted once the seals arrived on the island. For a period of five weeks the men (only those "being pretty well recover'd from the scurvey") went about the business of clubbing and skinning. Presumably the gory nature of this business had little emotional effect on Coolidge, or, if it did, he distracted himself by jotting down snippets of poetry in his journal (he quoted Addison: "On this first friendly Bank, we threw ourselves down").[60] They took "about 8500 skins" on San Benito and an additional three thousand on Cedros Island—busy work for a handful of malnourished men who had witnessed many human deaths during the previous months.

Half-starved, sun-baked, and wearing moccasins cut from sealskin, Coolidge's crew must have presented a wretched sight when the *Amethyst* finally returned on May 16, 1808. It had been gone for almost a year. Once again, Coolidge's journal is silent about what one might expect to hear: a report to Captain Smith about the loss of human life on San Benito or the captain's assessment of this tragic situation, for which the captain bore some responsibility given the lack of antiscorbutic provisions. Instead, Coolidge recounts the big take of skins by all the *Amethyst's* sealing parties. The sealing venture had now turned profitable based on these men's work, and the products of their labor would end up in the bustling market of Canton.[61]

By the time the *Amethyst* arrived at Canton in 1809, American voyages to this port had reached a high for the twenty-year period prior to the War of 1812, which would severely curtail American shipping. A total of 154 American ships traded in Canton between 1804 and 1809; approximately one-third of these vessels crossed the Pacific Ocean, and sealskins were easily the most common trade item carried by these Pacific trade ships.[62] But the seal harvest grew thinner each year due to the ongoing hunt in the North Pacific, the Juan Fernández Islands, Baja and Alta California. And yet, "hunt" is far too dignified a term to describe what transpired along this coastline. More accurately, millions of seals were bludgeoned to death and stripped of their furs by their American, Russian, and indigenous pursuers. Brute force rather than hunting prowess ruled the day.

In sum, the killing of fur seals left a perceptible void in the eastern Pacific's coastline and offshore islands, to say nothing of the ecological consequence of near extinction (the Guadalupe fur seal still remains a listed endangered species after a nadir population possibly in the dozens).[63] The change was remarkable: in the late 1700s fur seals had blanketed the coastal islands in deafening rookeries, but those rookeries were eerily silent three decades later. The product of this great hunt, namely millions and millions of sealskins stacked in the holds of ships and transported to distant commodity markets, masked the degree of violence required to secure it. Lewis Coolidge seemed to cope well with the odd juxtaposition of slaughtering thousands of fur seals by hand and the "lovely and Sublime" desert island surroundings of San Benito. "My hut was so situated as to command an extensive view," he wrote of the beautiful outlook from his small shelter. Then, without any mention of the surrounding carnage, he scrawled a line from the British Gothic novelist Ann Ward Radcliffe: "'Beauty sleeping in the lap of horror.'"[64]

Return to Magdalena Bay: The *Tiger* versus the Gray Whales

Mary Brewster observed a similar horror from the deck of the whaleship *Tiger* four decades later and farther south down the Baja coastline. During January and February of 1847 she witnessed whaling as it had rarely been practiced anywhere in the world. In the confines of Magdalena Bay, the crews of seven vessels pursued over a thousand female grays that were busily birthing and nursing—and simultaneously forced to protect their calves and themselves from the harpooners' strikes. It could hardly be considered a fair fight given the whales' "motherly affection" to safeguard their young, nor did this practice of slaughtering nursing cows square very well with the masculine image of man versus whale on the open sea.[65] *Moby-Dick* this was not. Instead, Mary Brewster and the crew of the *Tiger* participated in the zenith of the world's whaling industry, which coincided with the crucial decades of US territorial and industrial expansion. Those whaleships pursued Leviathan from the open ocean to the coastal bays where cows birthed the future of the species.

The factory-like ships of the American whaling fleet provided the nation's nascent industrial factories with two vital products: fuel for illumination and lubricants for fast-moving machinery. Household and urban uses for whale and sperm oil certainly gained the most public attention. As early as 1785 John Adams boasted to John Jay in London that sperm oil "gives the clearest and most beautiful flame of any substance that is known in nature, and we are all surprised that you [in London] prefer darkness, and consequent robberies, burglaries, and murders in your streets."[66] England, of course, did not prefer darkness and murders in its cities and towns; instead, the country carefully prioritized the sperm and whale oil produced by its own whaling industry for use in the textile factories where it was most needed. When its whaling industry declined in the early 1800s, US exports filled the ever-increasing demand.[67]

American use of sperm and whale oil was also concentrated in New England's textile mills by the 1830s, soon followed by more widespread applications in urban workshops-turned-factories and railroad engines. Sperm oil, the cleanest and most expensive oil rendered from sperm whales, lubricated delicate and costly machinery, while whale oil greased the moving parts of heavy machinery. The supply of sperm oil began a steady decline in the mid-1840s due to the success of the whalers' kill in the Pacific. Prices rose quickly and many factories had to make due with the lesser-quality but widely abundant whale oil.[68] By the time the seamen on the *Tiger* were slaughtering gray whales in Magdalena Bay, even the inferior gray oil was in great demand.

Whaling peaked as a worldwide phenomenon between 1835 and 1855, and by this time US whalers had far surpassed their European counterparts in tonnage and yearly kill, especially in the Pacific. By 1850, some seven hundred US ships in the Pacific comprised over three-quarters of the world's whaling fleet.[69] The Pacific Ocean had fundamentally transformed the whaling industry. According to the most comprehensive study, the Pacific contained over 1.8 million whales prior to extensive hunting. The Atlantic and Indian Ocean populations paled by comparison, with 346,000 and 544,000 whales, respectively.[70] The scale, scope, and character of the industry changed in order to meet the challenge of

Pacific whaling, including the duration of voyages (generally ranging from thirty to fifty months), the cost of outfitting a ship (approximately $20,000, excluding labor and the value of the ship), the diversity of the workforce (Hawaiians and Maoris became the most numerous recruits), and technological advances (such as swivel-mounted harpoon guns). Alongside these changes emerged a print media devoted to whaling, such as the weekly *Whalemens' Shipping List* (New Bedford) and the *Friend* (Honolulu), both of which Captain Brewster received from passing vessels during the *Tiger's* voyage.

The first week of whaling in Magdalena Bay proved dramatic for everyone involved. The *Tiger* sent out four boats, Mary Brewster noted, taking "all on board save [her] brother James who is both cooper and carpenter, the cook and Steward and cabin boy." Captain Brewster also stayed on board the *Tiger* and conveyed to Mary the strategy he had most likely learned from Captain Smith of the *Hibernia*: to use the newborn calf as bait to capture the mother. Braced with this knowledge, Mary began listing the killing of whales by the *Tiger's* different boats ("Larboard Boat, 35-barrel whale," "Waist Boat, 30-barrel whale," and so on), but she stopped these notations once the novelty of counting whale carcasses wore off.[71] A different list soon appeared in her journal: that of wrecked whaleboats and human casualties. "Bow boat badly stoven," Brewster wrote on January 8, 1847, though the boat's crew avoided injury.[72] From this day forward the ship's carpenter—Mary's brother, James—was kept constantly busy with the repair of shattered boats.

The Devilfish attacked the whaleboats and crews every day. The first serious injury involved the third mate of the *Hibernia*, "who got his leg broken" when a fifty-foot gray splintered the boat with her tail. Days later a seventeen-year-old green-hand sailor from the *Trescott* named Ledger Wilkinson was killed by a whale that had multiple irons stuck fast. Mary Brewster memorialized the "melancholy" episode in her journal: "A young man belonging to the *Trescott* was killed this morning by a whale which stove the boat and hit him, the boat upset and he sunk before they could reach him."[73] A quick search for Ledger Wilkinson's body proved futile. Two weeks later his remains washed ashore and Mary remarked on his final resting place: "He was buried . . . a little ways back [from shore] where 5 which were killed last season were laid desolate and alone."[74] The makeshift Magdalena Bay graveyard gained more residents in early February after a gray attacked one of the *Catherine's* boats. Two young men did not survive this stoving and one of their bodies never resurfaced. William Henry Hassell of the *America* never made it to the graveyard either: "Drowned," reported the *Friend* of Honolulu, two months later.[75] "Thus ends the life of many a young man with the Ocean for his grave," wrote Mary Brewster in early February.[76]

Despite the daily wreckage of whaleboats and battering of men, the 1846–1847 season at Magdalena Bay chronicled by Brewster contained fewer deaths than the previous season. That inaugural year of whaling in the bay was little short of a disaster if measured by the loss of human life—and certainly a disaster for the California gray whale as a species if one considers the explicit strategy of killing cows and leaving the calves to starve, since their bodies contained little blubber. Only two ships participated in this first season at Magdalena Bay, the *Hibernia* (New London) and the *United States* (Stonington). Of these two ships, the *Hibernia*'s success contrasts sharply with the ill fate of the *United States*, a ship that may have lost as many as five men in Magdalena Bay and returned home only partially filled with whale oil. Furthermore, a sperm whale took revenge on the *United States* two years later near Tonga, stoving the ship (now converted to a passenger vessel) with such force that it sank in minutes. The crew and nine passengers made it safely into the boats; four children went down with the ship.[77]

The *Hibernia* and *United States* had entered Magdalena Bay in late 1845 prob-ably on a lark. Neither ship had acquired much oil after more than a year of chasing whales across the Pacific Ocean, and both captains could surely sense the anxious grumblings of their crews. Information had only recently begun to circulate about the gray whale population and its annual migration: "10,000 California whale in sight," according to one exaggerated account from the whales' summer feeding grounds in the Bering Sea, while the winter "nurseries" for cows and calves (in-cluding Magdalena and two other Baja bays) were only made known a few years earlier by French and British survey parties.[78] From the Bering Sea to Baja was a long migration—perhaps *the* longest for any mammal in the world—and the gray whales, upon reaching their Baja calving grounds, had absolutely crucial business to conduct.[79] The grays' life cycle as well as the species' survival depended on it. Captain James Smith of the *Hibernia* and Captain Joshua Stevens of the *United States* knew little in advance about the gray whale's behavior in the Baja lagoons, but nicknames such as Devilfish and "Hardhead" already coined for grays by whalers in the North Pacific certainly gave the two captains some cause for alarm.[80]

The ample depth of Magdalena Bay allowed the whales to "sound" far below the surface and then "peak" like an "animated torpedo," according to one ob-server. "Every seat in the boat [was] an anxious seat," he continued, "very much like being over a powder-magazine about to explode."[81] The boat commanded by the *United States*'s second officer, "Mr. Nichols," exploded in just this fashion when upended by an enraged whale. Nichols, who likely stood at the bow grasping a ready harpoon, took the full force of the blow. A nearby whaleboat quickly recovered all hands from the water, including the broken body of Nich-ols, who died three days later. The ship's first officer also received the wrath of an angry whale that day when his boat was stoven and all men aboard flew into the water. The man's body must have been horribly mangled; Captain Stevens could only report that the first officer "would probably recover" when the ship arrived in Maui two months later.[82] Such stoving accidents contributed to a pronounced gallows humor among whaling crews, with one young man writing: "This being knocked 15 feet into the air and comeing down alongside of his jaw by a whale's rooting is not what it is cracked up to be."[83]

An awareness of the gray whale's destructive potential quickly dawned on the two ships' captains and crews. As the harpooner L. H. Vermilyea confided years later, "they are probably the worst whale to fight in the world."[84] Vermilyea's account shows one new strategy adopted by the *Hibernia* and *United States*: the whaleboats would chase the cows with their calves into the shallow waters of the shoreline where the whales had less maneuverability and the calves could easily get stranded. This tactic showed signs of success, especially for the *Hibernia*, which captured whale after whale close to the shore. The whaleboats tried to stay as far away as possible from the "she-whales," occasionally using an already hooked calf as bait to lure the mother into the shallows. Charles M. Scammon, the most successful whaling captain in the Baja bays during the 1850s, described the procedure of "run[ning] a line to the shore and hauling the calf into as shallow water as would float the [calf]." The distraught mother would attempt to stay near "her troubled young one," offering the harpooner "a good chance for a shot with his bomb-gun from the beach."[85]

The "bomb-gun" mentioned by Scammon may account for the different outcomes of these two ships in Magdalena Bay. This newly invented weapon (also known as a "bomb lance" or "harpoon gun") allowed the harpooner to strike the whale's "vital parts" at a relatively safe distance, while the explosive charge at the tip of the iron could accomplish some of the bloody finishing work otherwise done by the harpooner wielding a long "hand lance." The bomb-gun was first used in Magdalena Bay in 1846, according to Scammon, and it was surely the *Hibernia*'s harpooners who employed this new technology.[86] The *Hibernia* captured almost two dozen whales in less than two months of constant work, enough to fill over one thousand barrels with "fine clear oil." The *United States*, by contrast, took only ten gray whales in the same period and arrived in Maui with a deeply shaken crew who mourned the loss of four or five men.[87]

The promising yet cautionary reports of gray whaling in Magdalena Bay brought to Hawai'i by the *Hibernia* and *United States* caused at least a handful of ship captains to take interest, including Captain William Brewster of the *Tiger*. He decided he would try his luck in Magdalena Bay the following season. Mary and everyone else aboard the ship would not have had a vote in the matter. Mary relished the months spent in the bay; she read from Captain Smith's collection of books, ate fresh oysters and lobsters on many warm nights, and prayed for the safety of the *Tiger*'s crew. But she also witnessed the darker sides of a whaling voyage: the broken bones, the drownings, and what she considered the shameful immorality of sailors: "I see I am not the only female in the bay," she angrily noted after hearing of three young women "kept on board" another vessel for sexual purposes. She offered no details about their condition or origins—prostitutes or captives, local to Baja or imported on a ship—but she did spot one of the women "in a boat passing our ship bound to a neigh-boring one with the skipper by her side." From this incident, Mary could only conclude: "Oh shame, shame is not felt here, if actions which are so public is what we must judge from, and they speak louder than words."[88]

Clearly, Mary Brewster drew moral boundaries for men and their social rela-tions, and she appeared deeply affected by transgressions of those boundaries. And yet she remained strangely unaffected by whaling as a violent encounter between humans and marine mammals: the lancing, the dismemberment, the boiling pots, and the way her shipmates specifically targeted and slaughtered female gray whales with their young. She remarked:

> A plenty of boats stove every day and they all say these are the worst whale to strike they ever saw. The only way they can get fast [or harpoon a female whale] is to chase the calf till it gets tired out then they fasten to it and the whale will remain by its side and is then fastened too. Brother James has been in the boats a few times. [H]e said he saw a calf fastened to and the whale came up to it and *tried to get the iron out with her fin* and when she could not she took it on her back and endeavored to get it away. [F]requently the iron will kill them. [W]hen this is the case the whale ... finding her young dead will turn and fight the boats.[89]

The idea of a whale trying desperately to free her calf from a harpoon appeared to not bother Brewster in the least. Nor did the "cutting in" and "trying out" process trouble her by this late stage of the voyage. In fact, dismembering each whale and boiling down the blubber translated to more filled barrels, bringing the *Tiger* closer to its return voyage. The sight of the blubber-filled trypots blazing at night struck Brewster as almost majestic. "The moon is nearly full," she wrote one night from her cabin. "5 ships boiling ... and it seems to me they were trying to see who would make the greatest light. At times the blaze is so high the ships look as though they were all blazing."[90]

Here, Brewster touched on the central event described by all sailors who kept a diary or subsequently published a personal account of their experi-ences: the Herculean task of capturing, killing, and "cutting-in" a mammal larger and more powerful than a steam locomotive. Only twelve years old and a passenger on board the whaleship *William Lee* in 1839, Sereno Edwards Bishop described the roping in and dismembering of a sixty-foot whale.[91] "She was an enormous creature," he wrote, "[but] they made her fast to ship by passing a slip knot on her tail and leading the rope over the bow." Bishop closely followed the tricky procedure: the sailors fastened large tackle blocks to the mainmast and ran two-and-a-half-inch-wide ropes around the whale; one man "then went down on the whale with a rope round his waist and set a large hook" deep inside the carcass, and he next made large cuts with a spade in order to unwind the blubber.[92] This "operation," wrote another narrator, "somewhat resembled the unwinding of a lot of tape from a long bobbin."[93] The men "hoisted up" massive strips of blubber with rope pulleys and this process "gradually rolled the whale over" against the ship's starboard side. "It took two hours to roll the whale over once," Bishop observed, at which point "they cut off the head" and fastened it to the ship for rendering the next day.[94] Bishop ended his description at this point; perhaps he found the "cutting in" and rendering process too dreary. But other people found it fascinating.

The first time Mary Brewster witnessed this procedure she "seated [her]self in a boat [on the deck] and spent the whole afternoon in looking on. . . . All hands looked happy and greasy." She described the various positions of men on the deck, some of whom sliced the blubber into manageable strips before placing it in the boiling trypots. One man, she continued, "keeps constantly on the [try] works to mind the fire and to keep the oil from burning by constantly stirring and to dip it into the coolers when the pots get full. [The] Cooper was busy in fixing casks" for the oil once it was set in copper coolers.[95] The entire production was conducted with factory-like orchestration, according to crewman Thomas Atkinson. Men cut the massive "blanket pieces" into arm-length "horse pieces," and these were spliced into narrow strips by the "mincers" for placement in the sixty-four-gallon iron boilers (or trypots).[96] Life-threatening dangers accompanied every stage of this process. Even the blubber itself could kill, as evidenced by the case of Captain Edward Copping of the whaleship *Aladdin*, who met his end when an enormous dangling slab of blubber dropped from an overhead "fluke chain" and crushed him to death.[97] An odd way to die, for sure, but other accidents involving blubber were quite common, including limbs severed by razor-sharp cutting spades, sharks attacking the men who cut into the shipside whale carcass, and countless harpoon injuries. And yet these men were undoubtedly "happy," according to Mary Brewster, because each pot of rendered blubber translated into more pay (or "lays").[98]

In late February 1847 the *Tiger*'s crew readied the ship for departure. The oil was "coopered" in barrels, the lances and harpoons safely stowed, and the men's gore-encrusted clothes soaked in pots filled with their own collected urine (the high ammonia content cut the grease). Mary watched these preparations and quickly scribbled letters to her friends for dispatch on those ships "homeward bound" to Connecticut. "We poor souls to stop out a year longer," she wrote about the *Tiger*'s continuing voyage.[99] The *Tiger* had filled more than five hundred barrels with whale oil during January and February, while the six other ships from New England fared equally well. This small fleet killed upward of 150 full-grown female gray whales in two months; a similar number of gray whale calves were either harpooned or died from starvation. The calves represented collateral damage—no blubber to "flense" (or strip) from the carcass. A few men had been lost, and yet the gray whale had lost the security of one primary calving lagoon. The species as a whole now entered a downward spiral threatening extinction.

Magdalena Bay's calving population would have easily recovered from these two seasons of hunting if no ships had returned in 1847–1848. But this was not the nature of the great hunt for marine mammals in the eastern Pacific. Instead, somewhere between two and three dozen vessels descended on the bay during this third season for what Charles Scammon described as an "aquatic battle-scene" against the whales.[100] Somewhere in the neighborhood of five hundred gray whales and their newborn calves never left Magdalena Bay at season's end for their annual migration up the coastline, and only a small population returned the following year.[101]

The larger outside world intervened in this remote bay just as the ship captains readied their vessels for departure after this third season, in late March 1848. From California—now firmly in the hands of the US military—came news of a rich gold strike. Sailors quickly pondered their options and the most adventurous or disgruntled among them decided to jump ship. In late March seven sailors from the *Bowditch* slipped away at night in a whaleboat.[102] Other deserters followed this poorly conceived strategy for getting to California, likely with tragic results. The more patient crew of the *Bramin* waited until their vessel reached Honolulu; when their captain went ashore the crew immediately commandeered the entire ship for a quick sail to San Francisco Bay.[103] Working on a whale ship never led to riches, but fleeing to a gold rush just might.

Conquest and American Industry

These events in Magdalena Bay spotlight one locality that, by most common metrics, existed far off the beaten track of important historical places and trends. And yet, this isolated lagoon on the Baja coast—where men slaughtered whales and whales attacked boats in a macabre performance—offers an important vantage point on the convergence of three of the most significant historical developments in North America with immediate repercussions for the eastern Pacific: US conquest through territorial expansion, emergent industrialization with its natural resource needs, and the heyday of New England's whaling industry.

Regarding expansionism, the *Tiger's* 1845–1848 voyage perfectly overlapped with the central event of the nation's imperial drive: the US-Mexico War. The *Tiger* sailed in the fall of 1845 just as news of Texas's annexation by the United

States reverberated across New England's maritime industry. When the US officially declared war on Mexico in May 1846, the *Tiger* had days earlier departed from Hawai'i (a future American possession) for the Northwest Coast. Weeks later, Mary Brewster watched in horror while a whale killed young Thomas Perkins, one day after a motley crew of American settlers misguidedly announced an independent "Bear Flag" republic in California. As the whale men sharpened their lances at Magdalena Bay in December 1846, Mary recorded the exchange of optimistic "War news" between the seven whale ships, which came to fruition when US troops occupied Los Angeles in January and General Winfield Scott prepared his landing army for a siege of Veracruz.[104] Mary Brewster had tea with the proud officers of the US warship *Cyane* in O'ahu just days before the Battle of Mexico City, and the *Tiger* arrived in Connecticut two days before the US Senate ratified the Treaty of Guadalupe Hidalgo, ending the US-Mexico War.[105] Thus, the United States seized its continental empire during the thirty-month period that it took the *Tiger* to harvest three thousand barrels of whale oil.

Imperial expansion and whaling went hand in hand, if viewed from a Pacific standpoint. Consider two different perspectives on the Mexican territory eventually claimed by the United States through this war of conquest. Americans—and more specifically, expansionists—saw these far western lands as part of a continental destiny, a vast swath of underutilized real estate that bordered the Pacific and could open the "road to Asia."[106] Expansion could fulfill this destiny for western land and, in a still inchoate sense, incorporate the sea beyond it. By contrast, American maritime interests in the Pacific—of which New England whalers constituted the largest sector by the 1830s—viewed expansionism through a different logic. For them, the Pacific's natural resources and trade opportunities were already a given rather than a possibility; whalers knew this from their decades of activity in the ocean. Acting through their own private initiative, they had beaten the nation to what some people perceived as the end objective. The nation's empire moving west would meet New England's hardy whalers in the eastern Pacific.

Even some of the nation's foremost opponents of territorial expansion lauded the Pacific whaling fleet as an advance guard of economic and political imperialism. The Massachusetts Whig senator Daniel Webster strongly opposed the US-Mexico War and, from the Senate floor, he savagely dismantled President James K. Polk's justifications for the conflict and its likely territorial gains.[107] And yet he consistently lobbied for New England's maritime role in the Pacific, strongly supported the US Exploring Expedition (1838–1842) on behalf of the whaling industry, and authored the Tyler Doctrine (1842), which declared an American sphere of influence over large portions of the Pacific, especially the Hawaiian Islands. In 1842 Webster even asked for Congress to purchase San Francisco Bay and the Strait of Juan de Fuca from Mexico and England, respectively. The day after Congress issued its war declaration against Mexico, Webster implored the president he loathed to view "our large whaling fleet" as a "vital" wartime asset. He suggested in a letter to Polk that the US naval commander should "make such preparation for [the whaling fleet's] defence . . . and that the masters should be advised to continue their business through the present season," at which time the fleet should "rendezvous" in Hawai'i. Expansionism aside, Webster argued that the business of this "736-ship" fleet valued at "thirty millions of Dollars" was vital to the nation's industrializing economy.[108]

Meanwhile, other opponents of expansion questioned any role whatsoever for the nation in the Pacific Ocean. The South Carolina senator George McDuffie, a noted duelist and pro-slavery firebrand, railed against territorial expansion and the need for Pacific coast ports. "The wealth of the Indies would be insufficient" rationale for territorial expansion, he insisted from the Senate floor. "I would not give a pinch of snuff for the whole territory."[109] But McDuffie and his snuff-packed cheek were on the wrong side of history. Whalers and other American maritime traders had already revealed the Pacific's "wealth" to the nation—as well as the necessity of supplying whale oil to the northern textile industry, upon which Senator McDuffie's southern slave system completely depended. Indeed, the spindle rooms in Massachusetts's textile factories linked one resource from the slave south with another resource harvested by whale ships in the Pacific. The nation's economy thrived on the dynamic interaction of these three seemingly disparate production systems.[110]

Demand for whale oil only increased with its multifold uses. But it also filled a temporary industrial niche: between earlier types of greasy lubricants and the petroleum supplies that came on line in the 1860s, whale oil served the important needs of a rapidly advancing consumer economy. Factories and towns, streetlights and tabletop candles, lighthouses and steam locomotives—they all utilized the oil rendered from whale blubber harvested half a world away. Yet all these uses came at a deadly price, Captain Ahab cautioned his listeners: "For God's sake, be economical with your lamps and candles! Not a gallon you burn, but at least one drop of man's blood was spilled for it."[111] The US industry produced over 8 million gallons of whale oil and more than 3.6 million gallons of sperm oil in 1848, the year the *Tiger* returned to Connecticut.[112] The industry did not keep records on the annual amount of "spilled" human blood.

Conclusion: The Final Gray Whales of Baja California

Upon the *Tiger*'s return to Connecticut, Mary Brewster spent exactly three months and nineteen days "very happily" with friends. Then she and her captain-husband boarded the *Tiger* once again for a three-year whaling voyage in the Pacific.[113] The *Tiger* did not return to Magdalena Bay or the other Baja calving bays on its second voyage. In fact, only a handful of ship captains hunted whales along this coastline during the next five or six years. The reasons are fairly apparent. The *Tiger*, like most of the seven hundred ships in the American whaling fleet, headed for the North Pacific during the summer months and slaughtered bowhead, sperm, and right whales in tremendous numbers, sending whale oil production to a historic peak in 1849 (sperm oil had peaked a few years earlier). In these halcyon years of whaling, oil processors desired the cleanest oil they could secure, not the cloudy grayish stuff rendered from gray whales. But within five years of this historic peak, oil production entered a slippery decline (almost 25 percent in ten years), forcing oil processors to discriminate less about quality.[114] On the eve of the petroleum revolution sparked by an oil well in Titusville, Pennsylvania, in 1859, the whaling industry targeted any killable whale in the Pacific Ocean, including the grays of Baja California. Captain Charles Scammon led the charge.

For a man who devoted his later life to the study and preservation of marine mammals, Scammon's efficient work as captain of numerous whaleships (including the *Leonore, Boston,* and *Ocean Bird*) did everything possible to create the need for his latter-day preservationism. During the late 1850s, he hunted gray whales in their winter calving bays of Magdalena, Ojo de Liebre ("Scammon's Lagoon"), and San Ignacio (Ballenas Lagoon). A purely quantitative approach to the gray whale's annihilation suggests that nearly 90 percent of the remaining females were killed in less than a decade of Scammon's arrival on the *Leonore* in 1855.[115] The newborn calves of the female grays would perish from starvation, except for a small minority who received protection and nourishment from another cow. The biological endgame was apparent by the mid-1860s: approximately one thousand adult females survived, far fewer calves stayed alive, and the remaining adult males were picked off one by one during their annual migration along the North American coast. In the final years of the hunt, Scammon tabulated the number of whales killed, quantified the barrels of oil, and then pondered "whether this mammal will not be numbered among the extinct species of the Pacific."[116]

The gray whale population reached a historic low of less than 10 percent its original level before rising again, ever so slowly, in the twentieth century. Other fuels and lubricants took the place that whale oil once held in the American industrial workplace. The size of the US whaling fleet declined rapidly in the 1860s; by the late 1880s, well under one hundred vessels comprised the US fleet and virtually no market remained for whale oil (though sperm oil still found buyers). Other nations—especially Norway, Russia, and Japan—continued to hunt grays and other whales in the North Pacific into the twentieth century. One Russian ship, the prophetically named *Aleut,* killed 623 gray whales in the Arctic and North Pacific Oceans between 1932 and 1946.[117] Nearly two hundred years had passed since the Russian *promyshlenniki* had first conscripted the Aleut people to hunt a much smaller but more valuable prey, the sea otter. In the end, size did not rank in the profit-driven metrics of the great hunt for marine mammals. A three-foot-long sea otter in the eighteenth century carried greater value than a full-grown gray whale in the twentieth century.

The great hunt for marine mammals transpired in some very obscure, one might even say *small*, places. These localities included windswept coastal islands and remote lagoons: Isla Cedros, the Farallon and Juan Fernández islands, the Pribilof Islands in the Bering Sea, and Magdalena Bay, where Mary Brewster kept her journal during the warm winter months of 1846–1847 while the *Tiger's* crew assailed gray whales. Of course, these places were only small and obscure in comparison to the surrounding world's interconnected markets and production networks that ultimately commodified the furs, skins, and blubber—the disembodied matter of the great hunt. And for a brief period of years, depending on the time to near-extinction for each species, these remote places took center stage in the maritime trade connecting Asia, Europe, the Pacific islands, and the Americas.

|| 5 ||

Naturalists and Natives in the Great Ocean

Rurik, 1815–1818

Kadu climbed aboard the *Rurik* one sunny day at Aur, a small atoll in the Ratak chain of the Marshall Islands, and he insisted he would remain on the Russian ship for its expedition around the Great Ocean. This young man was a voyager at heart. He was born on Woleai atoll approximately two thousand miles west of Aur, and a voyage gone awry had brought him to the Ratak chain four years earlier. Only a handful of European ships had previously sighted this isolated island chain and even fewer meetings had taken place between the islanders and the *dri-belle*—a Marshallese term for foreigners with clothes and material wealth.[1] Neither the sea nor the ship's *dri-belle* frightened Kadu as he decided to join the expedition. Kadu knew the voyage would be a long one and he might never return; the *dri-belle* had emphasized this fact through every possible means of communication. Kadu's friends implored him to leave the ship, but when the *Rurik* finally departed for what one officer described as the "gloomy north" of the Bering Strait in March 1817, Kadu remained on board.[2]

Over the next nine months Kadu became a respected member of the ship's company. The thirty-two officers and sailors delighted in his good humor and curiosity, while the handful of officers welcomed Kadu at their table. The *Rurik*'s three "gentlemen of science" prodded him for information; one naturalist in particular, Adelbert von Chamisso, queried Kadu constantly about botany, religion, customs, the Marshallese language (*kajin Majol*), and his knowledge of the world beyond the Marshall Islands. Chamisso closely observed Kadu's reactions to the places and people they encountered: the frigid climes of the Bering Sea, the native inhabitants of Unalaska, and the Hawaiian islanders with whom Kadu "learned to make himself understood."[3] Chamisso loved Kadu as a

Figure 5.1 Kadu, a native of the Marshall Islands, accompanied the Russian expedition led by Otto von Kotzebue on the *Rurik* around the North Pacific in 1817. Courtesy of the Huntington Library.

friend by the time they returned to the Ratak Islands, but the naturalist also feared what "civilization" would bring to these island people. Chamisso had even begun to question his own markings of civilization, and he now desired a tattoo in the "Radakian" fashion. The islanders refused his request for spiritual reasons.[4]

What did Kadu make of Chamisso, this man who asked so many questions, took measurements of the sea and sky, collected plants and other objects from the ground, and continually wrote notes in a journal? He may have been amused by Chamisso's constant, almost frenetic activity. Kadu was not the only indigenous Pacific person to encounter foreign scientists, most of whom shared Chamisso's penchant for wandering far from shore, collecting specimens, and questioning the native inhabitants. Horeta Te Taniwha, a Maori youth who watched Captain James Cook's two naturalists, Sir Joseph Banks and Daniel Solander, gather specimens near Whitianga harbor in 1769, recalled: "They collected grasses from the cliffs, and kept knocking at the stones on the beach, and we said, 'Why are these acts done by these goblins?'"[5]

Naturalists were still conducting such "acts" five decades after Cook's first voyage, and at the time of Chamisso's journey these scientists came in greater

Figure 5.2 Sailing on the 1815–1818 voyage of the Russian ship *Rurik*, the French-Prussian naturalist Adelbert von Chamisso offered a bird's-eye description of what he termed the "Great Ocean." He also feared the impact on indigenous populations of ongoing European ventures in the Pacific.

numbers than ever before. They peered into Hawaiian volcanoes and counted whales off the coast of Chile. They observed Indians hunting rabbits near San Diego, and they collected rock samples in the high Arctic zone. The best among them posed genuine questions to the local villagers in order to gain knowledge, while the worst viewed those villagers as savages who therefore had no information worth collecting. A few naturalists gathered skulls in order to estimate how much knowledge could fit inside.

Chamisso's 1815–1818 voyage into the Pacific marked a new phase of exploration and naturalist activity. During the previous decade, the Napoleonic Wars had effectively curtailed major European expeditions into the Pacific. But in the following two decades ever larger numbers of European and American vessels ventured into the Great Ocean for exploration and trade. Many of these voyages carried "gentlemen of science."[6] While the nature of their work remained similar to the studies of previous naturalists—they still collected natural objects, studied natives in their environments, and took a variety of readings at sea and on land—the social, political, and economic context of that work had shifted. Independence movements in Mexico, Peru, Chile, and elsewhere severed most of Spanish America from Spain by 1821, which further opened the western American coastline to Pacific traffic and natural investigations. Adelbert von Chamisso, for instance, encountered Spanish restrictions on his freedom to wander the countryside in Chile and Alta California, but by the mid-1820s the naturalists aboard the French ship *Héros* faced no such limits in what was now *Mexican* Alta California. Both the *Héros* and *Rurik* expeditions demonstrate another change to the naturalists' work environment: voyages and their scientific travelers were often funded by private sponsors in conjunction with the imperial states. As a result of private sponsorship, the naturalists during this period were frequently not citizens of the country under whose flag they sailed, a status that gave them a degree of freedom to critique imperial goals. Such was the case with Chamisso, a French-born and Prussian-educated gentleman who heaped a fair amount of scorn on European imperial projects, despite his own complicity in what amounted to a major enterprise for the Russian Empire.

Finally, naturalists in the post-Napoleonic decades observed Pacific indigenous communities living in quite different conditions from those groups encountered fifty years earlier by Joseph Banks, Alejandro Malaspina, or Georg Steller. In this later period, naturalists witnessed native groups not at a moment of early contact, but instead two or more generations after the epidemics, community fragmentation, and instruments of colonialism had severely altered the lives and physical conditions of native populations. None of the three naturalists primarily examined in this chapter—Adelbert von Chamisso, Auguste Duhaut-Cilly, and Meredith Gairdner—arrived in the Pacific with any particular ethnographic interest or training. And yet, each of them gravitated toward the ethnographic side of science, which demonstrates the breadth of "natural history" as a field and also their desire to study natives during this period of severe social disruption. In the end, they expressed diverse reactions to the dire circumstances of indigenous groups, ranging from sincere awareness and sympathy on the one hand, to contempt and ghastly acts of grave robbing on the other.

The "Scientifics": Imperial Science and Individual Desires

Some early modern naturalists remain fairly well known two hundred years later: Sir Joseph Banks, Charles Darwin, Philibert Commerson, Georg Steller, Johann and George Forster, Archibald Menzies, James Dwight Dana, and Charles Pickering, among others. But the names of most naturalists are only recognizable to specialists in the field of scientific exploration. Naturalists sailed on almost every government-sponsored voyage and many privately funded expeditions as well, complementing the officer corps with their learned manners and training in natural history. Many people at the time simply called them naturalists, but they also received such titles as physician, natural historian, scientist, botanist, gentleman of science, scientific traveler, and, according to the vernacular of one skeptical commander who grudgingly maintained an entire faculty of naturalists under his charge, "the Scientifics."

Midshipman William Reynolds, who served under that skeptical commander, Lieutenant Charles Wilkes, wrote one of the liveliest descriptions of their shipboard activities:

> The Scientifics cut up & dissect and overhaul, and use a magnifying power the better to see, and make drawings & paintings, and search their books, and write down learned descriptions, and invent unpronounceable terms, and tell *us* all about the mysteries of organization, &c., &c. And they have dead & living lizards, and fish floating in alcohol, and shark jaws, & stuffed turtles, and veterbrata and animalculæ frisking in jars of salt water, and old shells, and many other equally interesting pieces of furniture hanging about their beds & around their state rooms—such sweet looking objects as doubtless glad scientific eyes to behold. Catch any of them in my *room*—no, no!—I'll *visit*, when I have curiosity in that way.

Captains frequently cursed the naturalists for their bulky accoutrements and constant desire for shore leave to collect ever more objects, while some common sailors resented their overeducated airs. For his part, William Reynolds found them a fascinating diversion from the daily toil of life at sea: "It is part of my day's amusement, to look over the labours of the Scientifics, and I learn much that I would not otherwise have known."[7]

This brief excerpt from Reynolds's diary, written in 1838 while on board the United States sloop *Vincennes*, provides a glimpse into the work that naturalists had been conducting on Pacific vessels during the preceding decades. They collected, dissected, and classified specimens; they drew, painted, and charted landscapes; they packaged and preserved things that could not survive the voyage, while carefully nurturing the living species that might endure the journey; they took readings and measurements at sea while waiting—often months on end—for the opportunity to climb mountains, botanize coastal plains, and shoot just about anything that moved. They studied and compared indigenous people through overlapping sentiments of curiosity, fear, and racial superiority. A few naturalists pondered very large questions about the Pacific Basin as an entire geographic space, but more of them were content to collect and decipher nature's minutiae and classify their discoveries within a Linnaean taxonomy. Laboratory scientists while at sea, once back home they sought to publish their discoveries in the most prestigious scientific journals.

A robust literature examines the work of European and American naturalists in the Pacific for the period between Cook's voyages and the mid-nineteenth century.[8] Beyond analyzing the discoveries and intellectual discourses of particular naturalists or expeditions, scholars have increasingly focused on the intentions of this "imperial science." To what extent did scientific exploration serve the economic and geopolitical goals of empire as well as intellectual rationalizations of Western superiority? Scholars parse the priority of these objectives, but they generally concur that science served a general imperial agenda, including commercial, geopolitical, and scientific goals. At the same time, naturalists frequently served more immediate interests, such as the expectations of wealthy patrons who financed their activities or their own professional desires for scientific recognition. These various goals were evident in the initial Pacific explorations of the late 1760s and 1770s, which followed closely on the heels of the Seven Years' War, a truly global competition between European powers.[9]

Scientific exploration played a prominent role in the post–Seven Years' War competition between England, France, Spain, and other nations. Science factored into the quest for maritime power: naturalists studied Pacific currents, winds, dangerous reefs, and the coordinate systems of longitude and latitude at the request of government sponsors.[10] Science also merged with the competitive drive for new geographic discoveries: Could anyone find the elusive Northwest Passage? Did a Southern continent exist and, if so, did it contain valuable resources? Where lay the next undiscovered island chain similar to the Hawaiian Islands? Such questions certainly inspired navigators during the late eighteenth century, and yet naturalists were also invested in these discoveries for their own professional reputations in the intersecting fields of botany, geography, and anthropology. In the aftermath of the Seven Years' War, European rivalries—especially for commercial markets and global exploration—expanded into the Pacific Ocean, and science took part in the contest.

Naturalists' activities were particularly significant in the commercial competition between imperial powers in the Pacific.[11] "Scientifics" amassed specimens and catalogued natural resources; in turn, many of those items manifested themselves as valuable commodities to sell in Canton, London, and Honolulu. Georg Steller, the naturalist on Vitus Bering's expedition in the North Pacific in 1741, reported on the "countless" fur seals and sea otters inhabiting certain islands, and within a decade Russian *promyshlenniki* initiated their brutal hunt for marketable furs.[12] William Ellis, a surgeon-naturalist employed on Cook's third voyage, was among the first Europeans to see Hawaiian sandalwood trees and publish a report on the islands' natural abundance. A thriving trade for the valuable sandalwood soon followed.[13] Naturalists also charted the locations of whale populations, observed the preparation of bêche-de-mer in Fiji, sketched the guano-covered islands near Chile and Peru, and answered government inquiries for details on vital maritime infrastructure, such as "Roads, Bays, Ports or Harbours."[14] Each of these areas of interest, ranging from whale oil to deepwater ports, contained real value to the expanding commerce of the late eighteenth century. The overlapping objectives of commerce, science, and imperial exploration remained every bit as vital for the *next* generation of naturalists who entered the Pacific at the close of the Napoleonic Wars.

Russian Dreams of Discovery on the *Rurik*, 1815–1818

James Cook never found the Northwest Passage; neither did Vitus Bering, Jean-François Galaup de La Pérouse, George Vancouver, nor Adam Johann von Krusenstern, to say nothing of explorers such as Henry Hudson who searched for the passage from the Atlantic side of North America.[15] Alejandro Malaspina held some cautious optimism for the discovery when he sailed up Yakutat Bay in the early summer of 1791. On the morning of July 2, Malaspina and a few crewmembers paddled the *Descrubita*'s (*Discovery*) small boats up the bay's long channel, wound their way through numerous ice floes, turned a final bend, and found the answer to their question. They discovered not a waterway to the Atlantic, but instead a towering wall of "ice covered rock." Malaspina named this terminus Bahia del Desengaño, or Disenchantment Bay. Always the pragmatist, Malaspina reasoned he had far more practical goals in the Pacific than searching for a fabled passage that even his hero, James Cook, could not locate.

Twenty-five years later in Saint Petersburg, Count Nikolai Petrovich Rumiantsev shared Malaspina's pragmatic nature, and yet he also held lofty ambitions for Russian maritime exploration despite the navy's decrepit condition following the Napoleonic Wars. What better way to assert Russia's place among nations

than to finally discover the Northwest Passage? Rumiantsev, a respected states-
man and wealthy philanthropist, financed the construction of the *Rurik* in 1814
and funded the entire voyage, complete with his own Russian imprint on it.[16] He
carefully chose the small crew from the Royal Navy and picked a scientifically
engaged naval lieutenant named Otto von Kotzebue to lead the expedition. As a
teenager, Kotzebue had sailed on the first Russian circumnavigation of the globe
(the Krusenstern voyage of 1803–1806). Rumiantsev's instructions to Kotzebue reflected Russia's special geographic concerns for the North Pacific: the
Rurik was ordered to "penetrate farther north from Beering's Straits than Cook
and Clerke have done," examine the northernmost "coast of America" for promising shallow inlets, and discover a route of "connection between the two seas
[the Pacific and Atlantic]." Finally, Rumiantsev directed Kotzebue to cross the
"South Sea twice, in quite different directions" for "knowledge of this great
ocean," its "island inhabitants," and to gather a "rich harvest of objects of natural
history" destined for his own Saint Petersburg collection. To this end, according
to Lieutenant Kotzebue, "the count had appointed an able naturalist to accom-
pany the expedition."[17]

The *Rurik* sailed with not one, but three individuals devoted to natural history, in addition to Otto von Kotzebue, an amateur naturalist himself. Louis
Choris, a twenty-year-old draughtsman educated in Prussia, produced what are
arguably the most significant drawings and paintings of Pacific landscapes and
native peoples in the early nineteenth century. His close attention to ethnographic detail rejected both the romanticism and the overt racialism of some
European artists who accompanied Pacific expeditions.[18] The *Rurik*'s physician,
Johann Friedrich Eschscholtz, was well educated in zoology, botany, and ento-
mology. He published the first scientific article on Alta California flora ("Descrip-
tiones Plantarum Novae Californiae") shortly before dying from work-related
exhaustion at the age of thirty-eight.[19] Finally, the "able naturalist" appointed by
Count Rumiantsev was Adelbert von Chamisso, a French-born exile educated in
natural science at the University of Berlin. A successful poet best known as the
author of *Peter Schlemihls wundersame Geschichte* (a bestselling fairy tale about a
man who sold his shadow to the devil), Chamisso was certainly not Rumiantsev's first choice for naturalist.[20] Chamisso received the post through family connections after other naturalists had rejected the offer. This thirty-four-year-old
exile-nobleman-poet-naturalist had never been to sea when he stepped on board
the *Rurik* in August 1815.

If scientific exploration set the agenda for this voyage, a quick overview of the
Rurik's journey and published accounts shows that "science" referred to diverse
investigations in politics, commerce, geography, ethnography, and nature. The
expedition's route included two counterclockwise circuits around the Pacific
Ocean with primary investigations at Chile, the Marshall Islands, the Kamchatka

Peninsula, the Bering Strait, Unalaska, Alta California, and the Hawaiian Islands. Kotzebue's own report on the voyage—translated and published in London three years after the *Rurik*'s return—is dry and faintly apologetic for his failure to discover the Northwest Passage. Yet almost half of the three-volume account is comprised of "Remarks and Opinions of the Naturalist of the Expedition," a beautifully crafted discourse by Chamisso that surveys the Pacific Ocean in its entirety as well as the people and locations visited. A decade later he published a second account (*A Voyage around the World with the Romanzov Exploring Expedition*), this time with a clear focus on his encounters with native peoples.

Chamisso's "Remarks and Opinions" opens with a global perspective on the surrounding continents and seas before focusing on the "Great Ocean, which has been called the Pacific Ocean and the South Sea, two names which are both equally inappropriate." He argues that the former term ("Pacific") elides its true character: the turbulent seas, the "burning volcanoes" that seem to "rise everywhere" on islands and continental shores, and the "monsoons and storms" that threaten all mariners, including the ancient indigenous "seamen" in their "distant voyages" across the sea.[21] Hardly "pacific" at all, Chamisso contends, the Great Ocean is a complex and riotous waterscape filled with life and history. Meanwhile, the latter term—the "South Sea"—cleverly conceals the bulk of the ocean, especially Russia's northern area of dominion and its many geographic mysteries.[22] Chamisso's bird's-eye view of the Pacific continues with expansive commentary on marine life, flora and fauna, native peoples, their languages and ancient migration patterns. He looks everywhere for comparisons and confluences between different places and Pacific communities, also suggesting possible theories for the ancient peopling of the Americas.[23]

The significance of Chamisso's bird's-eye view resided in its holistic approach to the ocean's natural history, even if it contained few original contributions to the knowledge accumulated by previous Pacific naturalists. But the rest of "Remarks and Opinions" continued on for another three hundred pages, offering two important contributions: an assessment of imperial practices in the eastern Pacific, and a guarded critique of their quest for a Northwest Passage.

Chamisso disparaged the institutions and representatives of European empires almost everywhere the *Rurik* touched land. At Chile's Conception Bay in 1816, he faulted Spain for the "political crisis in which this country is engaged." Spanish Royalists oppressed the "Patriots" while the country's "immense" wealth "languishe[d] in fetters, without navigation, commerce, or industry." Spanish officials forbade Chamisso and the other naturalists to venture outside the port city (he wanted to view the "unmixed" Indians who desired "liberty"), to which he could only conclude that "all the nations of Europe regard with undissembled favour the struggle of the Spanish colonies, . . . The separation from the mother-country is to be foreseen."[24] Chamisso made similar remarks

while visiting Alta California, where he noted Spain's "avaricious thirst for possession" resulted in a colony "without industry, trade and navigation, desert[ed]
and unpeopled." (Indeed, only a handful of ships visited the California coast
during the year of the *Rurik*'s visit.) Both Chamisso and Kotzebue ridiculed
New Spain's policies that stifled trade. Few Spanish settlers had arrived—in this
sense the land was "unpeopled"—and one health "disorder" in particular (venereal disease) "carrie[d] off [Indian] victims." Finally, he described the primary
instruments of the empire, the Franciscan missions, as "injudiciously begun
and ill-executed."[25] For European nations looking hopefully into the future
from the disastrous years of the Napoleonic Wars, Chamisso concluded,
Spain's example in the Pacific exemplified a decrepit and reactionary empire
not long for the world.

Chamisso reacted more cautiously to Russia's imperial venture in the North
Pacific, given his role on a Russian ship and the official nature of his "Remarks
and Opinions." As a result, he directed his ire at the Russian-American Company
rather than the empire itself, and he reiterated previous criticisms about the oppression of Aleuts and other northern peoples. The native people of the Kamchatka Peninsula, he wrote, are "almost entirely extinct under its new foreign
[Russian] yoke," while the "Russian American Company" had turned the Aleuts
into "wretched slaves" who "will soon be extinct."[26] In general, Chamisso viewed
the Russian colonial effort as antiquated and unenlightened, a view likely shared
by Kotzebue and even Count Rumiantsev, both of whom promoted a new
"enlightened" brand of Russian exploration based on science and discovery.[27]
Chamisso feared the impact that even the most "enlightened" exploration would
have among native groups, especially as he anticipated increased traffic in the
coming years. "May [God] keep Europeans away for a while from your bleak
reefs, which offer them no temptations," Chamisso remarked, referring specifically to his friend Kadu from the isolated Ratak Islands.[28]

And what did Chamisso make of the expedition's ostensible purpose, the
search for the Northwest Passage? In the *Rurik*'s official and published narrative
(1821), both Chamisso and Kotzebue were remarkably evasive about the effort
to answer this "last question" of global geography. The *Rurik*'s crew twice sailed
far north in the Bering Sea. During the summer of 1816, they passed through the
Bering Strait into the Chukchi Sea, where the captain named Kotzebue Sound
and Chamisso Island. The following summer the *Rurik* only made it as far north
as Saint Lawrence Island (directly south of the strait) before Kotzebue turned
the ship around. A decade after the voyage, Chamisso considered it a severe
blunder "to set all of the hopes of the enterprise" upon such a specious objective.
But he also disparaged Kotzebue's decision to turn back from the Bering Strait
once the ship encountered a seemingly impenetrable wall of ice during their second season in the far north.[29] Much about this portion of the voyage remains

ambiguous, beginning with the fundamental question of whether they were searching for a North*west* Passage through North America or a North*east* Passage through Northern Asia (as indicated by the subtitle of Kotzebue's voyage account: "*. . . for the Purpose of Exploring a North-East Passage . . .*"). Count Rumiantsev's orders to Kotzebue were equally vague on this matter, allowing the captain to conclude that either passage would constitute a sufficient discovery for the glory of Russia.[30]

The fact that no passage was discovered—through Asia, North America, or any other landmass—should not detract from Rumiantsev's compelling ambitions for the venture. Rumiantsev recognized that finding the passage could revolutionize trade across the world's oceans and provide tremendous strategic value to any nation fortunate enough to make the discovery. European empires, still reeling from more than ten years of Napoleonic Wars prior to 1815, had every desire to regenerate themselves at home and assert national power through exploration abroad. Russia's costly experience during the wars solidified this belief in the minds of Rumiantsev and Kotzebue, and many European leaders shared their opinions. Tellingly, the *Rurik* was only the first of more than a dozen scientific expeditions to set out for the Great Ocean between 1816 and 1830, representing more scientific voyages than in any other period since the 1760s.[31] And while some people like Chamisso expressed grave concern about the impact of ongoing investigations on native peoples, his was a minority opinion.

Kadu and Chamisso

For almost a decade Chamisso reflected on his experiences in the Great Ocean. Then, late in life, he decided to retell the story of the voyage.[32] Still resonating in Chamisso's mind was not the marine life or geology of the Great Ocean, nor the extensive botanical and insect specimens collected by his colleague Dr. Johann Friedrich Eschscholtz. Instead, Chamisso remained preoccupied with his Radakian friend Kadu. It was primarily through his relationship with Kadu that Chamisso offered his final account of the voyage—and Pacific ethnography, rather than other concerns, figured most prominently.

The *Rurik*'s naturalists indeed found something rare in the Ratak Islands in 1817: native communities that had *extremely* limited contact with Europeans. Perhaps a handful of European ships had passed by these small atolls, while even fewer person-to-person contacts had taken place.[33] The setting was pristine enough that Chamisso could imagine it even more so, despite the fact that Radakians knew far more about *dri-belle* than Chamisso understood. He vaguely refers to the *Rurik*'s arrival as a "first encounter" for the islanders, and he depicts the Ratak chain as an unsullied island paradise. "Nowhere is the sky fairer, the temperature more uniform, than on the low islands," he wrote. "You dive into the dark blue [water] to cool off when you are overheated from the sun directly overhead; and you dive into it to warm up when you feel the cool of the morning after a night spent outside." Such a beneficent environment demanded little technology, according to Chamisso, who counted only "a few pieces of iron" possessed by the islanders. Even these items, he imagined, were "found in the wreckage of ships" rather than acquired through trade. Chamisso, an avid reader of the European romanticists Johann Gottfried von Herder and Jean-Jacques Rousseau, could hardly believe his good fortune in finding this place that existed in stark contrast to "overcivilized" Europe. And what did he make of Kadu? With "pure" and "uncorrupted customs," Chamisso wrote, "my friend Kadu . . . [was] one of the finest characters I have met in my life, one of the people I have loved the most."[34] At least in Chamisso's mind, a deep affection developed between these two men during the nine months they spent together in the close confines of the *Rurik*.

Chamisso studied Kadu's quiet demeanor and closely observed his reactions to new environments throughout the voyage. "In Unalaska and everywhere that we landed Kadu saw us pay attention to all the products of nature, investigate them, and collect them," he wrote. Kadu took part in these investigations while assembling his own collections.[35] Kadu gathered objects with use-value, such as nails, discarded iron, and whetstones for sharpening tools, later presenting these items to friends upon his return to Ratak. Chamisso applauded his friend's generosity, though he may have misunderstood Kadu's goal in purposefully gifting items as a means to bolster his own status in the community hierarchy.

Chamisso, Eschscholtz, and Choris were particularly curious to see Kadu's reaction to one of their collections: three human skulls the naturalists had "found" during the previous season in the North Pacific. Chamisso unearthed one skull in a mound of gravel at "the height" of Saint Lawrence Island (most likely a burial ground), and he furtively "concealed" it in case he met any natives on his way back to the ship. The other two skulls were taken from graves on other islands—at least one of them from an "old gravesite," according to Chamisso, as if "old" justified the action of stealing human remains. One can hardly imagine Kadu's mental process when the naturalists confronted him with these three skulls shortly after the *Rurik* set sail from his home island. Chamisso recounted Kadu's stunned question: "What is this?" And then, according to Chamisso, Kadu cautiously offered "of his own volition to procure a skull from his tribe in Radak for me."[36] Of course Kadu never fulfilled this offer, since it would have violated all Radakian customs of burial and respect for the dead.

While Chamisso was unlikely to grasp the extent of Kadu's thoughts, their relationship decidedly influenced the naturalist's view of the indigenous communities they encountered. In the harbor of Honolulu, Chamisso was stunned by "the propositions shouted at us by all the women round about and by all the men in the name of all the women." He contrasted this sex trade in Hawai'i to the purity of Kadu's own people. He condemned the Hawaiians' "adulterous customs," but also viewed it as a byproduct of European colonialism: "We have grafted greed and avarice onto [the Hawaiians] and stripped the bark of shame off of them."[37] He watched with trepidation as Kadu "disappeared among the [Hawaiian] natives," fearing their "customs" would contaminate him. Kadu seemed to enjoy himself immensely. He "easily learned how to communicate with the Hawaiians" and likely enjoyed female companionship. Chamisso intimates as much but provides no details.[38] Hawai'i, for Chamisso, represented the fall from grace, a paradise corrupted by the same European influences he feared would soon reach Kadu's people.

The Indians of Alta California provided Chamisso with perhaps the starkest contrast to the unblemished island society he imagined existing in Ratak. Unlike Kadu's people, the California natives lived "in a subjugated condition" under the "yoke" of Spanish colonialism and, more specifically, under the command of Franciscan missionaries whom Chamisso likened to "masters of slaves." He clearly pitied the Indians he met—a very select group attached to Mission San Francisco de Asís—but such sympathy did not prevent him from ranking Native Californians on a racial hierarchy with other indigenous people. He assigned them a position "far below those on the north coast and the interior of America," and much further below the unsullied people of the Ratak Islands.[39] His companionship with Kadu certainly influenced this prejudice, since Kadu's personal freedom and individuality all but mocked the unfree condition of California's mission Indians.

Yet Chamisso also perceived something else in Alta California: a "demand" for "liberty" by the native inhabitants, a defiant undercurrent witnessed most closely by the *Rurik's* officers during the Feast of Saint Francis on October 9, 1816. Conducted in and around Mission San Francisco de Asís shortly after the *Rurik's* arrival, this festival included a Catholic mass and procession for the faithful. Chamisso and his artist-colleague Louis Choris focused their attention on the indigenous ceremony that also took place that day directly in front of the mission. Choris captured it in one of his most stunning sketches, *Danse des habitans de Californie al la mission de st. Francisco*. Choris portrayed Indians engaged in many activities: dancing, chanting, clapping, and gaming, while others sat on the ground striking percussion instruments. Two Franciscan priests stand in the entrance to the mission church, an imposing structure built with the forced labor of those now demonstrating before it. The priests are potentially defenseless against the gathered celebrants. Choris's rendering shows not a subjugated native population, but instead a large population that retained elements of its indigenous culture and also possessed the vigor for violent rebellion. Spanish

Figure 5.3 Dance of the Inhabitants of California at Mission San Francisco, 1816. The German-Russian artist Louis Choris, who also sailed on the *Rurik*, produced some of the most striking depictions of indigenous Pacific people during the early nineteenth century. Indians attached to Mission San Francisco de Asís conducted this dance as part of the Saint Francis festival on October 9, 1816. Courtesy of the Huntington Library.

soldiers are nowhere to be seen, although they were certainly present and well armed for this large gathering of Indians.

If Choris's *Danse des habitans* depicts one perspective on Mission Indians, then a second sketch by the artist offers quite a different story. *The Presidio of San Francisco* shows mounted Spanish soldiers driving forward at least two groups of Indians. The neophytes carry bundles on their backs as they hurry in tight formation in front of the mounted soldiers. The Indians appear enslaved, or at best, they function as conscripted laborers for the Spanish presidio that looms in the background. Rather than contradictory depictions, Choris's *Danse* and *Presidio* illustrate a tragic tension in Alta California under Spanish rule: Mission Indians could only enact their freedom at certain moments, while soldiers and priests governed their everyday lives through the force of violence.

These sketches, which Chamisso considered part of "an estimable series of portraits," help explain the naturalist's ethnography. At the Ratak Islands, Chamisso believed he had seen the beauty and virtue of an uncontaminated native society. Kadu served to interpret that society for him, while Kadu's presence on the voyage also provided a way for the naturalist to interpret other societies around the Great Ocean. Inevitably, those other societies paled by comparison due to what Chamisso considered the fallout of colonial settlement, including violence, disease, and servitude.

Figure 5.4 "View of the Presidio San Francisco," 1816. In contrast to the momentary freedom expressed by Indians dancing at the St. Francis festival, Louis Choris also depicted native Californians as forced laborers under the control of Spanish soldiers. Courtesy of the Huntington Library.

Yet Chamisso's ethnography did not end there. Similar to Choris's portrayal of the indigenous dancers, Chamisso saw dignity and perseverance in the bearing of indigenous people he met in many communities around the eastern Pacific. He frequently romanticized their indigeneity while also denigrating certain racial characteristics; racial difference both attracted and repelled this highly educated, enlightened writer. Choris's sketches—drawn with Chamisso standing by his side—encapsulated their ambivalent reactions to the subjugation and decline of "des habitans" while also illustrating the natives' strong masculinity and potential to revolt.

Auguste Duhaut-Cilly and the *Héros*, 1826–1829

The French ship *Héros* arrived in Alta California eleven years after the *Rurik's* departure. Much had changed during the previous decade. Mexican independence in Alta California (1821) was only one of the independence movements stretching down the Pacific coast from Alta California to Chile. Maritime commerce rapidly increased in the former Spanish colonies as the new governments revoked restrictions on trade. Ships hailing from many Atlantic and Pacific ports now entered California waters for trade and reconnaissance—and many of them carried scientific travelers who could roam more freely along the coast and inland valleys than Chamisso was allowed to in 1816.

The French voyage captained by Auguste Duhaut-Cilly has received slight notice by scholars of Pacific natural exploration despite its fortuitous timing for ethnographic study and the various reports penned by expedition members. Duhaut-Cilly, of noble ancestry and extensive command experience in the Atlantic and Pacific oceans, wrote a detailed account of the *Héros*'s three-year-long *voyage autour du monde*, filled with natural history. A talented artist too, Duhaut-Cilly's meticulous line drawings reveal a captain's attention to coastal approaches and littoral landscapes. His own observations were complemented by the avid fauna collecting of Paulo Emilio Botta, the Italian-born naturalist aboard the *Héros*. In later years Botta gained world renown for his Assyrian archeological discoveries, but he made no such notable discovery on this voyage. Instead, his researches reflected a young man's fascination with travel and the natural abundance he found in California. Second mate Edmond Le Netrel kept his own record of botanical and ethnographic observations when he was not accompanying the much-despised "Mr. R___" on shore for the purpose of trade.[40]

"Mr. R___" referred to Jean-Baptiste Rives, a French-born beachcomber who arrived in the Hawaiian Islands around 1810 and eventually served as translator for King Liholiho (Kamehameha II) following his succession to the throne in 1819. Rives accompanied Liholiho and Queen Kamāmalu on an ill-advised royal visit to London in 1824, where the two royals promptly died after contracting measles.[41] Ever the opportunist, Rives immediately made the rounds among French financiers with a story of Liholiho granting him "great privileges" for trade rights in the Hawaiian Islands—surely a tall tale for such a diminutive man (Duhaut-Cilly described Rives's "monkey head surmounting a meager body of four feet eight").[42] By hook or crook, Rives successfully convinced a group of bankers in Paris and Le Havre to support a commercial voyage to the coast of the Americas, the Hawaiian Islands, and China, with Rives in the role of supercargo on the *Héros*. The promoters attached a small "scientific corps" to the voyage, including Botta, Le Netrel, and the commander Duhaut-Cilly, with the charge to "seize every opportunity for making observations on hydrographic and other special matter."[43] Given such vague orders and a clear priority of commerce over science, the "scientific corps" generally followed their own desires in the pursuit of knowledge.

The Duhaut-Cilly voyage took just over three years to circumnavigate the globe, conducting trade in Lima, Mazatlan, California, the Hawaiian Islands, and Canton. The commercial proceeds certainly disappointed the French backers, and Rives's assertion of "great privileges" in Hawai'i were never tested because he failed to make it that far in the voyage, having departed from the California coast on another ship under suspicious circumstances.[44] Though a commercial failure, the scientific dimension of the *Héros* expedition was unique in one way: the ship spent almost two years trading on the California coast from the Russian

Fort Ross to the tip of Baja California, allowing these naturalists the most sustained opportunity to study the coastline and its native inhabitants.

Arriving outside San Francisco Bay on the fifteenth day of 1827, Duhaut-Cilly described the sense of optimism shared by all on board the *Héros*. "For it is truly on board ship that all are united by a common concern, at least in relation to the dangers or successes of the voyage. Each feels that his lot is linked to that of his fellows," he wrote.[45] Their shared "lot" in California would have to wait, for an impenetrable fog immediately descended on the ship, and kept the *Héros* from entering the bay for more than a week. Once moored in the bay, the *Héros*'s captain met and explained his business with the presidio's *commandante*, Don Ignacio Martinez, while Botta slipped away to initiate his researches. With rifle in hand, according to Duhaut-Cilly, Botta was intent on "spreading terror and death among the not very wild hosts of air and water."[46]

Botta's guns were rarely silent for the next year and a half. He targeted every bird within range, including shore birds, hawks, magpies, blackbirds, sparrows, geese, quail, partridge, and great blue herons. Botta was especially fascinated by hummingbirds, and he catalogued the different variations despite his frustration with the small target they offered.[47] In Monterey Bay, Duhaut-Cilly admired the diversity of avian life "ambling peacefully under the galleries of verdure," and yet "the scene might not be like this if Dr. Botta were to repeat often his work of collecting bird skins from California. In the two days he spent in Santa Cruz he did much to disturb the habits of these poor creatures, and in justice I must admit that I took part in this cruel aggression."[48] The two men, often with Le Netrel in tow, hunted not only birds but also wild game at every chance when the *Héros* touched land. Bears, in particular, seemed to appear with great frequency in their report on California wildlife, though none of the "scientific corps" actually shot one.[49]

North of San Diego at Point Loma they found the wildlife so abundant that Duhaut-Cilly feared his readers would "accuse [him] of exaggeration." "*Le vrai peut quelquefois n'être pas vraisemblable,*" he wrote in his journal, quoting the French poet Nicolas Boileau, "The truth is not always believable."[50] In this case the "truth" included a multitude of rabbits—great "bands" of "hares and rabbits moved . . . across the fragrant and flowering fields," wrote Duhaut-Cilly, "and several times it happened that we killed two with one shot." He gave a rare account of an Indian "rabbit drive" at Point Loma:

> Two or three times a year those [Indians] from Mission San Diego obtain permission from the padres for expeditions there. The hunters, to the number of two or three hundred, form themselves into a line of battle stretching from the steep face of the mountain to the shore of the bay, and they move forward abreast, driving before them the long-eared

band. The Indians are armed with *macanas*, curved and polished sticks that they throw with great skill. As they advance the number of fugitives, added to at each step, grows larger and brings on the excited cries of the hunters. . . . Having come to a narrow place, where the slope of the hill ends in a cliff, the hares, seeing themselves cut off on the left by the precipice, on the right by the unscalable escarpment of La Loma, and in front by impenetrable thickets, begin to recognize the imminence of danger. They are panic-stricken, and in their terror they dart here and there to find a way out. . . . There is a general massacre, a veritable Saint Bartholomew, in which many perish before the others can cross the battle line, opened up at last, by the Indians.[51]

Duhaut-Cilly's praise for the Indians' "great skill" at killing rabbits held a secondary message: the plentitude of rabbits, darting back and forth in almost unimaginable numbers, demonstrated the sheer abundance of wildlife on this Pacific shore.

For Botta, Duhaut-Cilly, and to a lesser degree Le Netrel, *abundance* was the central meaning of their encounter with California's nature. The lowly rabbit multiplied to astonishing numbers while the grand bear appeared with startling frequency. Flocks of birds blackened the sky and passed overhead "with a noise like a hurricane." Fish filled the easily accessible coastal bays: "It would be impossible to find a bay with more fish," Le Netrel reported during his stopover in Monterey, echoing Duhaut-Cilly's wonder at the hardly believable "truth" of nature's bounty.[52] The coastline's flora also stunned these visitors, especially the thick forests north of San Francisco Bay. While Botta hunted his way through the understory of the forests near the Russian-held Fort Ross, Duhaut-Cilly marveled at the towering trees overhead. The *palo colorado* (redwood, or *Sequoia sempervirens*), he reckoned, was "the largest tree that I have ever seen." He measured a recently felled redwood (20 feet in diameter and 230 feet high) and then pondered "what a huge quantity of boards [could] be obtained from a tree of this size." Then he translated the size of those trees into something more tangible: "I would like to have transformed the forest into a huge fleet, whose masts I could now see, still bearing their foliage, waving on the nearby mountains."[53]

Plentitude, variety, size, and abundance—nature's bounty in Alta California stunned the *Héros*'s naturalists, and they each translated that bounty into objects of their own imaginations.[54] At times they viewed the natural resources as marketable commodities, such as Duhaut-Cilly's estimate of board feet from a redwood tree. Other times the abundance held practical meanings for their survival on the long voyage ahead. For instance, Edmund Le Netrel stockpiled salted fish in barrels before the *Héros* departed Alta California for Hawai'i, measuring the plentiful fish through a metric of labor and mass: "Three men can load an ordinary boat [with fish] in less than three hours."[55] Alta California, as depicted in their accounts, was a timeless and unexploited coast of plenty.

Of course, this coastal region was neither timeless nor unexploited. The abundance witnessed by Duhaut-Cilly's cohort was due to the specific historical moment, and especially the demographic collapse of indigenous communities of this period. This was certainly a primary factor in the abundance of wild game they hunted along the coast. Prior to Spanish colonization, Native Californians had hunted throughout the coastal stretches and interior valleys with a variety of weapons, including intentional fires and the boomerang-like *macana* described by Duhaut-Cilly. Indians carefully "tended the wild" and lived well from the products of hunting and gathering.[56] However, Spanish colonization had altered this hunter-prey dynamic, especially around the coastal missions where Indian populations plummeted due to introduced diseases. The non-native population of Californios (established landowners, settlers, and soldiers) remained small during this period. Duhaut-Cilly and Le Netrel both noted the Californios' indifference to hunting wild game, explaining this indifference to "indolence" and "laziness."[57] Thus, the abundance described by the *Héros* naturalists in 1826 and 1827 represented a peculiar artifact of the moment: a proliferation of wild game on the coastal land due to declining hunting pressure, a direct result of the native depopulation.

While none of the *Héros*'s naturalists drew this conclusion, they each described the Indians' deplorable condition and explained that decline through distinct ethnographies. Edmond Le Netrel characterized the Indians living at Mission Santa Clara as "stupid beings" who only approached a level of "civilization" due to the "patience and perseverance" of Franciscan missionaries. Le Netrel's own scientific "curiosity" compelled him to investigate further; in the shadow of one mission building he peered inside an Indian brush hut and found "four or five Indians lying next to a big fire." He continued: "One cannot imagine anything dirtier or more revolting than what I saw in that little space. As I came in the inhabitants were occupied in hunting and eating their lice." Le Netrel offered no explanation for their apparent poverty or behavior, nor did scientific interest encourage him to question his initial impressions of Indian life. Indeed, his field of vision rarely extended beyond his own expectations. Approaching the coastline surrounding Fort Ross in June, 1828, Le Netrel had the opportunity to observe a well-populated native area, including Indians connected to the Russian settlement and other groups that lived quite apart from it. Yet Le Netrel failed to notice much of anything in particular. "This part of the country is not inhabited," he wrote. "There are only a few Indians living in very miserable huts on the seashore. . . . These Indians are usually very dirty. The earth was covered with Strawberries which were delicious."[58]

Duhaut-Cilly provided more careful and sympathetic observations of Indian life while also recognizing the limits of his perspective. Well-educated and sensitive to the plight of what he called "primitive people," the captain gathered data from missionaries on the Indians' declining numbers and desired much greater knowledge of "free Indians"—by which he meant "native Indians who have not yet suffered an admixture" with Spaniards or "creole" Mexicans.[59] Duhaut-Cilly found the "creole" settlers to be a "dull mosaic without life or character," a degenerate "confusion of Spanish, English, Mexican, and Indian" who literally embodied the adverse consequences of colonialism. "It is only the work of the Indian that supports [the creole population]," he wrote in regard to Indian productive labor. He applauded certain Franciscan missionaries (such as Father Antonio Ripoll of Santa Barbara, who learned a Chumash dialect) while strongly criticizing others "without talent or energy" to sustain their missions.[60]

Unlike Le Netrel, Duhaut-Cilly praised what he considered the Indians' "spirit of liberty," whose "desire for freedom may be stifled . . . but cannot be extinguished."[61] He supported this Enlightenment sentiment with a range of examples drawn from observation and recent events: the 1824 Chumash uprising, the frequent flight of coastal mission Indians to the interior *tulares*, the "revenge and reprisal" raids carried out by interior native groups against Mexican settlements, the martyrdom of mission deserters such as Pomponio and Valerio, and even such a momentary event as a young Indian girl's glance of "malicious mirth" noticed by Duhaut-Cilly in Santa Barbara.[62]

Botta shared none of Duhaut-Cilly's sentiment for indigenous Californians. Rather, his "Observations sur les habitans de la Californie" (1831) reads like a hallucinatory caricature of *les savage*, perhaps due to the lifelong habit of smoking opium he acquired during the *Héros*'s visit to Canton. (Botta's 1830 doctoral thesis, "The Uses of Smoking Opium," celebrated the narcotic for its medicinal and creative powers.[63]) In Botta's mind, Indians had malapportioned bodies, especially the women who seemed to lack "clear-cut features." The Mission Indians were "inclined to every sort of vice" while it was "impossible to obtain any specific data concerning the . . . wild Indians of the land." Impossible or not, Botta still cobbled together enough "data" to decide that "wild Indians" were "crueler and more savage" than their mission counterparts, altogether giving "the appearance of terrifying monsters."[64] The fact that Botta published his account three years into an opium habit may have influenced his "observations."

These assessments by Le Netrel, Duhaut-Cilly, and Botta fit into recognizable ethnographies of California Indians and other indigenous Pacific groups. Botta and Le Netrel viewed them as primitive specimens, pathetic and impoverished beings whose very bodies made them ill-equipped for civilization. Botta, for instance, opened his "Observations" with remarks on Indians' body parts:

"hands . . . so small that they do not fit with the rest of the body" and noses "like that of the Negroes."[65] These two observers echoed many previous ethnographic accounts that linked racial inferiority with poverty and presumed indolence.

Duhaut-Cilly fit into an ethnographic tradition similar to Adelbert von Chamisso. Both men often idealized natives' pre-contact "state of nature" and lamented the racial "admixture" resulting from contact and colonization, and yet at the same time they recognized indigenous desires for autonomy.[66] Their sympathy for natives' declining health, subjugation, and apparent poverty echoed some naturalists from the earlier period, including George Forster (from Cook's second voyage) and Martin Sauer (from Russia's Billings expedition).[67] Duhaut-Cilly, for his part, came closest to understanding California Indians' plight as related to the specific historical moment: fifty years of Spanish rule had come to an end, and the new Mexican landowners were unlikely to improve the lot of the native inhabitants. To the contrary, the rising volume of maritime commerce and the Californios' need for a tractable labor force would prolong the exploitation of Indians.

Dr. Meredith Gairdner: Scottish Physician-Turned-Grave Robber

Dr. Meredith Gairdner sailed into the Pacific on the *Ganymede* three years after Duhaut-Cilly left on the *Héros*. The two men were opposites in most ways. Duhaut-Cilly carried himself with the bearing of a disciplined naval officer but appeared humble to all around him, while Gairdner wore the "haughty airs of superiority" despite his meager twenty-two years at the time of the *Ganymede*'s departure from Gravesend, England, in 1832.[68] The Frenchman excelled at drawing and writing, while Gairdner viewed the world through a singularly scientific prism. He took a medical degree from the University of Edinburgh, completed postgraduate study in Germany, and immediately published his 420-page dissertation, "An Essay on the Natural History, Origin, Composition, and Medicinal Effects of Mineral and Thermal Springs." Duhaut-Cilly enjoyed fine health late into life, while Gairdner carried an early stage of *Mycobacterium tuberculosis* with him to Fort Vancouver. His own contagious disease certainly did not benefit the untold number of English and indigenous patients he treated during a two-year tenure as physician to the Hudson's Bay Company. Yet both men shared a deep interest in natural history, which for them included the study of plants, animals, Indian ethnography, and, in the case of Dr. Gairdner, a single foray into grave-robbing and skull-taking.

For most Pacific naturalists, the oceanic voyage and its various opportunities for collecting specimens on land was the purpose and extent of their employment.

They sailed into the Pacific, collected flora and fauna, sailed home and then—depending on their level of professional ambition—published their findings. Gairdner, by contrast, sailed to the Pacific in order to take a regular job. The Hudson's Bay Company desperately needed a physician at Fort Vancouver because the previous physician, John Frederick Kennedy, had nearly died during the "intermittent fever" season of 1831. Kennedy accepted a transfer to the HBC's Fort Simpson, situated well north and inland from the coastal "fever zone," and Gairdner assumed his post with a salary of £100 per annum.[69] (He arrived with a second Scottish physician, William Fraser Tolmie, who assumed medical duties at the nearby Fort Nisqually.) However, from the beginning of his tenure Gairdner held much grander aspirations than healing the sick of Fort Vancouver; he was a scientific naturalist and his interests had few boundaries.

Indeed, he initiated research and drafted a journal article before the *Ganymede* even touched shore at the mouth of the Columbia River. His "Observations during a Voyage from England to Fort Vancouver, on the North-West Coast of America," published in the *Edinburgh New Philosophical Journal*, was part of a long letter Gairdner sent to his mentor in natural history at the University of Edinburgh, Professor Robert Jameson. To Jameson and the *Journal*'s readers, Gairdner reported on the technical aspect of the voyage: barometric and astronomic measures, the "habits and structure of the different aërial and aquatic animals which fell in our way," ocean temperature differentials (by latitude) between the Atlantic and Pacific, and, among many other items, his calculations for the heights of Hawai'i's Mauna Loa and Mauna Kea. "In sailing along the north side of Owhyhee," he dryly wrote, "I embraced the opportunity to take a few angles for the trigonometric determination of [the volcanoes'] elevation."[70] Maritime adventure story, this certainly was not. Nor did Gairdner comment on his sudden immersion in the hybrid culture of the Northwest Coast, which began immediately upon the *Ganymede*'s arrival at the Columbia River on May 1, 1833. Within hours of embarkation, according to Gairdner's colleague William Fraser Tolmie, the two men departed on a forty-eight-hour journey upriver to Fort Vancouver, lying prone in a canoe manned by five Indians, a Hawaiian islander, and an HBC interpreter. Gairdner's only comment regarding these circumstances was typically sober: "I find my situation here very different from what I was led to expect on leaving Scotland."[71]

The "situation" was also quite different in terms of his medical practice at Fort Vancouver, the westernmost outpost of the Hudson's Bay Company string of habitations across British North America. Gairdner faced a seemingly endless line of patients—native and HBC employees alike—suffering from the seasonal outbreak of malarial fevers (see chapter 2). He treated 650 such cases in little more than a year, Gairdner complained, which allowed precious little time for his "scientific researches."[72] But somehow Gairdner found the time to pursue these interests. He sent rock and mineral "specimens" to Professor Jameson, followed by an adult male *Dryocopus lineatus* (lineated woodpecker) that, years later, John James Audubon would attribute to Gairdner. He also gradually developed a scientific interest in the Native Americans he treated, some of whom managed to survive the "fever and ague."[73]

Gairdner's diary for the first half of 1835 displays a remarkably integrative approach to natural history, ranging from geography and botany to detailed Indian ethnography (excerpts from this diary became his final posthumous article, published in the *Journal of the Royal Geographical Society of London*).[74] He wrote detailed descriptions of the coastline's main river systems, giving particular credit to information gathered from Indian sources about waterways and landmarks hundreds of miles away. This reliance on native informants was standard practice for HBC officials and fur traders, whose knowledge and survival was all but dependent on Indians. Yet Gairdner, a scientist-physician initially distinguished by his "haughty airs" and disaffection for the daily job, soon became absorbed by native culture and natives' physical surroundings. He sought greater knowledge of the interior country and native groups—as well as respite for his consumptive lungs—and in May 1835 received permission to travel more than 250 miles up the Columbia River to Fort Walla Walla. Gairdner's account of this ten-week episode reveals a naturalist discovering his true element, with lengthy notes on the waterways, varied topography, geology, thermal springs, and the diversity of flora high atop summit peaks.[75]

Gairdner closely studied the native groups along the Columbia, Snake, Salmon, and Grande Ronde rivers. On one day he observed the way that women peeled the inner bark from pine trees; the next day he described "Indian women digging Kamoss [camas]" roots in a swampy area. "It is a very laborious work," he wrote, "each woman, before midday, having dug up two large bags, of more than a bushel each." Gairdner's small party arrived at a gathering of Cayuse and Walla-Walla Indians on the third day of June, and he described their long "mat-lodges," an immense herd of horses, and "Indians galloping to and fro." Feeling welcomed, "we pitched our camp alongside of the Indians."[76] Confessing his own "ignorance of the language," Gairdner used an interpreter with these groups to assemble a detailed list of the region's "different nations." He noted the two different branches of the Nez-Perce, the Palouses, Blackfeet, Flathead, Cayuse, Walla-Walla, Blood, and Piegans. He included some general remarks about marriage practices, tensions between groups, and population sizes—information that could have only come from native informants. The Cayuse, he remarked, "have a dignity in their gait, and a gravity in their demeanour, not possessed by the [Walla-Walla]."[77] To these ethnographic comments Gairdner amended a list of some thirty-three native villages stretching down the Columbia River and along the Pacific coastline. For a Scottish physician whose scientific training did not extend much beyond thermal springs, Gairdner now displayed a genuine curiosity about native affairs.

And then Gairdner's curiosity took him to a realm of science generally reserved for phrenologists and ghouls. The object of this inquiry was a dead man named Concomly. One would be hard-pressed to find a more renowned and powerful headman along the Northwest Coast than Concomly. Born in the 1760s, he grew up to be a chief among the many Chinookan communities along the Columbia River and made his home at Qwatsa'mts, a village located near Cape Disappointment at the mouth of the Columbia River.[78] Concomly was known by whites for his river navigational skills, his trading acumen, and his single eye. Meriwether Lewis had met "Com com mo ly" near Qwatsa'mts in November 1805 and gave him a medal, but Concomly saw little reason to reciprocate with a visit to the Corps of Discovery's dreary encampment called Fort Clatsop. Years later, it was likely with diplomacy in mind that Concomly encouraged his daughter, Raven, to marry a Scottish fur trader temporarily attached to Fort Astoria, and later to wed a second Scotsman who worked for the Hudson's Bay Company.[79] Concomly's influence remained strong even when the fur trade began to wane in the 1820s, but even this most powerful headman could not outlast the malarial fever that struck his village in 1830. Surviving relatives interred his body in a bark canoe and, following Chinook custom, kept it raised on a platform for a period of two years. Then they buried his remains at Point Ellice, which afforded a nice view of the Columbia River's entrance to the Pacific Ocean.

Gairdner's decision to dig up the great Chinook leader seems to have been a hasty one, and certain knowledge played a role in it. Gairdner knew of Concomly's reputation for intelligence and widespread influence. He also knew that Concomly's great mind was encased in a flattened head, according to the Chinook tradition of "binding" an infant's head with boards in order to reshape the skull. This feature fascinated Gairdner, as he later wrote to Richardson: "When the phrenologists look at this frontal development what will they say to this?!"[80] A famous Indian with a flattened skull; such a unique trophy proved too tempting for the young doctor and naturalist. Finally, Gairdner knew his own time might be running out. He had experienced minor hemorrhages from his lungs during his first year at Fort Vancouver. Seeking relief from the "consumption," Gairdner regularly drew blood from his arms in hopes of lowering his blood pressure.[81] But by the time he returned from Fort Walla Walla in June 1835, Gairdner knew he could no longer perform his medical duties for another season's victims of malarial fevers, nor would he survive very long in this wet climate. Gairdner determined to take leave from the Hudson's Bay Company and seek out the dry climate on the west side of Hawai'i.

But just prior to his departure in September, Gairdner decided to take a trophy for science. Alone, he walked to Concomly's burial place at Point Ellice. The chief's relatives had inconspicuously marked the spot. Gairdner began exca-vating the grave under the cover of darkness, for surely he knew the act of grave-robbing was a vicious crime against the Chinookan people as a whole. "I assure you," he later confessed in a letter to his naturalist friend Dr. John Richardson, "no small resurrectionary labour was necessary to get at Comcomly's [body]." In the midst of his heavy exertion, Gairdner experienced what he described as a "severe paroxysm of haemoptysis"—in laymen's terms, he was spewing blood and lung tissue over the grave as he worked desperately to sever the chief's head from his body.

Did the doctor of medicine feel conflicted during this night of corporeal des-ecration? Apparently not, and perhaps at that very moment he was primarily concerned about surviving his own "severe paroxysm" and not getting caught in the act of grave-robbing. The prize itself thrilled Gairdner; he proudly noted that Comcomly's head had reached "a state of the most perfect exsiccation," or drying out.[82] The doctor bundled up the head, returned to Fort Vancouver, and sailed for Hawai'i within days. Gairdner's disease-wracked body "gradually wast[ed] away," and he died in Hawai'i sixteen months later.

The Chinook would have quickly connected Gairdner's sudden departure to the desecration of Comcomly's body. They had familiarity with grave robbers, having previously complained to HBC officials about such ghoulish acts carried out against their buried ancestors. They also learned of Gairdner's death and, according to one source, "they felt that the one deserved the other, and that the Great Spirit had acted rightly in imposing the punishment which they them-selves were unable to impose."[83] This may have been the only consolation to the surviving relatives of Comcomly, whose head Gairdner had packed off to Dr. Richardson, a physician at the Royal Naval Hospital near Portsmouth, England. The Chinook would not set eyes on Comcomly's skull until 1972, when the Smithsonian Institution returned it, having held the partial remains since 1946, after the Royal Naval Hospital no longer desired a collection of pilfered skulls.

Conclusion

In the end, had Dr. Meredith Gairdner done anything out of the ordinary for naturalists in the Pacific? It should be noted that the vast majority of European and American naturalists did not rob graves or decapitate bodies in the interests of science. Most would have been repulsed by such an act, or, at the very least, feared being caught in the act. However, on another level—that of collecting artifacts—Gairdner's actions drew on a long tradition of natural history with undetermined boundaries governing "scientific" methods and ethics. Skull gath-ering, in particular, filled the needs of collector-craniologists who measured the size, shape, and internal capacity of skulls. Those who gathered or collected skulls contributed to the ongoing "'science' of racial difference," according to historian Ann Fabian, a science that would only gain adherents during the nineteenth century.[84] Gairdner never fully articulated his reasons for taking Concomly's head, other than his rhetorical question to Richardson: "What will [phrenologists] say to this [flattened skull]?!"[85] But elsewhere Gairdner clearly stated a desire to transport natural objects to Britain, where they could be properly investigated by the greatest scientific minds. "How often have I wished," he wrote on one occasion, "when viewing . . . Mount Hood, which towers up within 40 miles of Fort Vancouver, that it were transported to Britain, within reach of so many men illustrious in the annals of physical research."[86] It was certainly an odd wish to move a mountain halfway around the world for the sake of research. And just like Concomly's head, it was surely better to leave Mount Hood where it rested.

Naturalists had been collecting objects and transporting them home since the 1760s. For many, their collections defined a sense of professional purpose: to gather, compare, and augment the Linnaean taxonomy of plants, animals, and minerals. Imperial science blossomed due to their efforts in the late eighteenth and early nineteenth centuries, and many naturalists were well rewarded for their efforts by scientific sponsors such as Sir Joseph Banks and Count Nikolai Petrovich Rumiantsev.

Naturalists also classified, compared, and ranked indigenous people. Banks did so everywhere the *Endeavour* touched land in 1769 and 1770: Did the people demonstrate signs of previous contact? Did their skin color indicate intelligence? Did they show skill in the traffic of goods? Did their bodies have lice? Two generations later, many of the questions and concerns had changed for the naturalists of the *Rurik, Héros,* and *Ganymede.* Adelbert von Chamisso was the only one who encountered a relatively healthy indigenous population—the Radakians—and his relationship with Kadu encouraged his sense of alarm and compassion for all native communities around the Pacific. Auguste Duhaut-Cilly displayed a similar compassion for the people of Alta California and Hawai'i, an attitude hardly shared by the *Héros's* two other naturalists, who viewed native decline as natural if not providence. Meredith Gairdner, like Chamisso and Duhaut-Cilly, did not come to the eastern Pacific to investigate indigenous groups. But in this period of the 1820s and 1830s, as a dreadful epidemic reduced Northwest coastal villages to fragments of their former strength, Gairdner's scientific curiosity drew him into the study of the people. Facing his own death and desiring a scientific trophy that would outlast him, Gairdner took the best head he could find.

‖ 6 ‖

Assembling the Pacific

Science, while it penetrates deeply the system of things about us, sees
everywhere, in the dim limits of vision, the word mystery.
—James Dwight Dana, *Corals and Coral Islands* (1872)

The United States Exploring Expedition, 1838–1842

Most European maritime nations sponsored scientific voyages into the Pacific
Ocean well before 1800 and increased the number of these exploratory ventures
after the Napoleonic Wars. The United States did not see fit to do so until 1838,
when the US Exploring Expedition struck out with not one or two vessels, but a
squadron of six ships carrying hundreds of sailors and seven naturalists. Optimism prevailed as the fleet set sail from the naval base at Hampton Roads, Virginia, in August 1838. "And behold!" Midshipman William Reynolds penned in
his diary, "now a nation, which but a short time ago was a discovery itself and a
wilderness, is taking its place among the enlightened of the world, and endeav-
ouring to contribute its mite in the cause of knowledge and research. For this
seems the age in which all men's minds are bent to learn all about the secrets of
the world which they inhabit."[1]

Reynolds would not step foot again on North American soil for three long
years. When he did, it was on the continent's western edge where the Columbia
River flowed into the Pacific Ocean. He stood on the beach as "the surf rolled its
foam close to our feet" and stared at the dead trees strewn around him: "Mam-
moths of the forest and of an age tha[t] one could hardly grasp at . . . mouldering
away by the hundreds." Bald eagles circled overhead while sea birds scavenged
for food on the shoreline. Reynolds gazed down "the white line of breakers" to
the place where, days earlier, he had looked on helplessly as one of the squadron's ships, the "poor old" *Peacock*, "found her grave" at the mouth of the Columbia. He pondered the Great Ocean that had consumed his life during the past
three years, and then his gaze returned to his North American surroundings.
"The whole scene was wild & strange to our eyes, after so long a stay among the

soft Isles of the South."[2] The untamed nature around him was bewildering and foreign—hardly the North America he remembered from the Eastern Seaboard.

The US Exploring Expedition (US Ex. Ex.) returned home via the Cape of Good Hope. Everyone, it appeared, looked forward to the homecoming. The scientists anticipated the coming years of organizing their collections and preparing their various researches for publication. The expedition's commander, Lieutenant Charles Wilkes, hoped for glory and naval advancement. But he soon stood trial before a court-martial tribunal for mistreatment of his sailors. William Reynolds longed for home and the end of the interminable voyage:

> I look upon the hardships, dangers & servitude that we have undergone in this Expedition as parallel in their extent to the worst years of the Revolutionary War, & if its operations had been protracted for 48 months longer, every one of us would have been *expended* from a *wearing out* of the system, if from no other causes.[3]

The voyage had taken its toll on William Reynolds, both physically and psychologically, and he most wanted to see family when his ship, the *Porpoise*, sailed into New York harbor on July 1, 1842. Three days later, amidst the July Fourth celebrations, Reynolds's older brother Sam boarded the *Porpoise* in search of William. He surveyed the grizzled and sunbaked sailors gathered before him and asked: "Which of you is it?"[4]

William Reynolds left the *Porpoise* and became a minor footnote in history, while one of his acquaintances, James Dwight Dana, disembarked in New York harbor and soon became one of the nation's leading geologists. Dana had spent the previous four years contemplating the geological origins, structure, and meaning of the Pacific Ocean and its landmasses. Like Adelbert von Chamisso before him, Dana's initial writings proposed an underlying coherence to the Pacific as a whole. But while Chamisso had gone little beyond description in his rendering of the Great Ocean, Dana's publications would theorize and provide compelling support for the geological structure and interconnectedness of the ocean basin. The four-year voyage had deeply influenced this young naturalist— the fiery volcanoes, beautiful coral reefs, and deep coastal valleys all presented him with geological questions to ponder. Upon his return to the United States, Dana now attempted to make sense of it all.

Like many of the indigenous people he met during the Pacific voyage, Dana viewed the Pacific's landforms with an unabashed wonder—even bewilderment— for nature's holism and power. "There is no part of the world where the sublime and picturesque mingle in stranger combinations," he wrote in *Geology* (1849), the 735-page volume he produced as part of the US Exploring Expedition's publications. The "agencies" creating these strange combinations fascinated

Figure 6.1 James Dwight Dana emerged as one of the world's leading geologists due to his extensive and diverse research conducted on the US Exploring Expedition between 1838 and 1842. Courtesy of Yale University Library.

Dana: "that through every part [of the Pacific Basin] there has been the volcano to build up mountains, and to shatter again its structures; a vast ocean to surge against exposed shores; rapid declivities to give force to descending torrents; besides a climate to favour the coral shrubbery of the ocean, and bury in foliage the most craggy steeps."[5] Nature's animate power—from towering volcanoes to small living coral—thrilled the young scientist. In studying Pacific islands and the surrounding continental edges, Dana came to realize essential characteristics of the ocean basin. Furthermore, he wrote, the "importance is not limited even by the Pacific Ocean . . . for it has an evident connexion with a system that pervades the world."[6] As Dana studied the

Pacific Ocean, he came to believe that the Pacific shed light on the entire earth's structure.

This chapter examines the US Ex. Ex., and especially Dana's research, to offer a number of overlapping arguments about the Pacific in the 1840s. First, while previous naturalists had studied discrete localities and populations around the ocean, Dana was the first to grapple systematically with the forces shaping the Pacific as a whole. He theorized in terms of holistic relationships and geological systems: an integrating Humboldtian approach (which emphasized nature's "chain of connection") that could have only resulted from his prolonged encounter with the Pacific's islands, volcanoes, and continental landmasses. Second, Dana viewed the ocean and all lands joined to it as part of an interconnected Pacific Basin; even his inland "tour" from the Columbia River to San Francisco Bay in 1841 convinced Dana that western North America was an integral component of the Pacific Basin. Significant here is the spatial understanding as well as its timing: on the eve of US conquest and consolidation, Dana construed the continent's Far West as part of the Pacific in extra-continental terms, not simply as the staging area for the expanding nation's "road" to Asia.[7] Finally, Dana would sustain neither his holistic and global geological perspective nor this spatial reading of the Far West's connection to the Pacific for long. By the early 1850s, the nation's most prominent geologists found cause and profit in explicating a continental geology to match the new continental boundaries of the United States—and Dana's science celebrated this path of imperial consolidation.

Seven Scientifics, Six Ships, One Brutish Captain

The US Exploring Expedition took government-sponsored scientific study of the Pacific beyond most previous endeavors.[8] While prior European voyages held specific scientific goals and enlisted highly esteemed naturalists, the US Exploring Expedition carried seven "Scientifics" trained in particular fields of study, including Dana (geologist), Horatio Hale (philologist), Titian R. Peale (naturalist), Charles Pickering (naturalist), William D. Brackenridge (botanist), William Rich (botanist), and Joseph P. Couthouy (conchologist).[9] Indeed, the US Congress and Navy designed this "global excursion" in part to highlight the distinctiveness of scientific fields and the maturity of the nation's scientific community.[10] The US Ex. Ex. maintained two other goals as well: first, to assist the expansion of American maritime commerce in the Pacific with detailed charting of coastlines and whaling grounds; and second, to make a clear statement of US naval power in an ocean covering one-third of the earth's surface. Thus, the Pacific Ocean represented a staging area for the nation's ability to merge exploration, science, commerce, and expansionist desires. The future American Far

West (and the continental empire it implied) figured large in these designs. But rather than explore the Far West from an overland route, as John C. Frémont accomplished in the early to mid-1840s, this expedition arrived from the ocean, a fact that decidedly influenced the geographic context through which scientists like Dana viewed the continent's western edge. While Frémont *presumed* a continental nation stretching to the Pacific shore—fulfilling his sponsor and father-in-law's vision of a path to the Far East—Dana's mental and scientific framework remained the ocean itself and its interrelated geological forms.

The voyage produced an astonishing scientific output in terms of publications, collections, and data: over 4,000 ethnographic objects from Pacific islands and surrounding continents, 50,000 horticultural specimens, over 2,000 birds ready for mounting, 134 mammals, almost 600 fish species, over 1,000 insects (both dead and alive), and finally, Dana's vast collection of fossils, coral, and crustacean.[11] The collections alone constituted enough material to establish a natural history museum, which it did with the creation of the Smithsonian Institution. In terms of printed material, the expedition produced twenty-three published volumes of narrative and scientific reports, plus enough maps, survey charts, and illustrations to fill a modest library.[12] Add to these official productions the ongoing scientific investigations based on data and experiences derived from the US Ex. Ex. voyage, and the intellectual throw weight of the expedition appears staggering. Despite these accomplishments, controversies and recriminations so marred the expedition's return that many observers deemed it a failure. The expedition's commander, Charles Wilkes, faced a handful of court-martial charges and received one conviction. Short of a discovery on the scale of the Northwest Passage or a mountain laden with gold—such as California's Sierra—it was doubtful the scientific findings could long sustain the nation's interest.

Leaving the Norfolk, Virginia, shipyards in August 1838, the forty-year-old Lieutenant Wilkes commanded a fleet of six sailing vessels with the object of discovering (and thereafter charting) the Southern continent of Antarctica, surveying specific Pacific islands and ports to assist American shipping, and scientific discovery.[13] Wilkes—narcissistic, domineering, and increasingly insecure to the point of paranoia—clearly viewed the voyage as his manifest route to professional fame and personal fortune. Thus, before the fleet even reached the Pacific Ocean, Wilkes had elevated himself to the military rank of captain, an honor denied him by the naval command prior to the voyage.[14] The message could not have been clearer to officers, enlisted sailors, and scientists: Wilkes would rashly take what he believed was his due, and more rash acts would soon follow.

The expedition's greatest achievements included the charting of a fifteen hundred-mile section section of Antarctica still known as Wilkes Land, even if discovery rights likely go to the British and American sailors who glimpsed the Southern continent in the early 1820s. Aside from this exploration feat, the US Ex. Ex. boldly went where many others had gone before, because by the 1840s the Pacific held few major geographic mysteries left to discover. After the first Antarctic exploration south of Tierra del Fuego in early 1839, the fleet (now reduced to five ships; the *Sea Gull* and crew were lost at sea) sailed along the Pacific coast of South America to Callao, and then crossed the Pacific by way of Tahiti, Samoa, and the Marshall Islands. By late November the US Ex. Ex. had reconnoitered in Sydney, Australia, in order to launch its second approach on Antarctica. Four of the remaining five ships sailed for Antarctica on December 26, 1839, and Midshipman William Reynolds made the historic sighting of that continent from high atop the *Peacock*'s rigging on January 16, 1840. After charting the Antarctic coastline, the US Ex. Ex. spent much of the year surveying South Pacific islands en route to Hawai'i and then the Northwest American coastline. Dana's ship, the *Peacock*, spent the first half of 1841 resurveying islands in the South Pacific before heading to the Columbia River, where it struck the bar at the river's mouth and was crushed by breakers. All hands survived, but Dana and several others continued their travels to San Francisco overland. By late 1841, the long way home entailed an entire circumnavigation of the globe: Hawai'i, Manila, Singapore, through the Indian Ocean to Cape Town, Saint Helena, and finally New York City.

The US Ex. Ex. spent over four years at sea, mostly following the paths of previous voyages dating back to the 1770s. And yet the US Ex. Ex. left a legacy of its own that paralleled the nation's westward course of empire: instances of extreme violence directed against indigenous populations as well as its own crew. Midshipman Reynolds appeared particularly troubled by this fact. "It seems to me," Reynolds wrote in his private journal three years into the voyage, "that our path through the Pacific is to be marked in blood."[15] Reynolds referred in this instance to the slaughter of as many as twenty inhabitants of Tabiteuea, an island in the Kiribati group, on May 1, 1841. William Hudson, commander of the *Peacock*, ordered the attack on the village after a sailor disappeared the previous day. While Wilkes and Hudson justified this attack as retaliation, Reynolds saw violent behavior engulfing the expedition as a whole. The violence emanated in part from Wilkes's fiery and irrational temper (Reynolds likened him to "the Devil") and took form on board ship with excessive punishment of sailors for minor infractions—crimes for which a military court convicted Wilkes upon his return.[16]

The expedition's brutality against natives climaxed in July 1840 on Fiji with the burning of a village called Solevu, followed two weeks later by the torching of Malolo that left almost one hundred villagers dead. Wilkes justified this assault because villagers had killed two crewmembers the previous day, including his nephew, Wilkes Henry.[17] In the midst of this violence, Wilkes took a Fijian chief named Ro-Veidovi as prisoner to stand trial once the expedition returned to the United States. Ro-Veidovi died of an illness the day after arriving in New York. Navy surgeons quickly decapitated the chief and pickled his head, a gruesome end to the expedition's aggressive diplomacy among Pacific peoples.[18]

Dana in the Vast Ocean

The voyage's "Scientifics" (as Wilkes dubbed them) remained fairly removed from such acts of violence; for them, the Pacific voyage was an unparalleled opportunity for fieldwork separated by long periods at sea for theorizing and writing. This was especially true in the case of James Dwight Dana. Within seven years of Dana's return from the voyage, he had published groundbreaking theories on volcanoes, the origins of continents, islands and coral reefs, and the earth's cooling process. In the coming decades Dana's scholarship earned him a privileged place among the nation's leading scientists. The Pacific Basin had deeply affected his scientific practice—his observational abilities, specific geological theories, and the Pacific's relationship to the world as a whole. Like Charles Darwin before him, Dana's study of specific places and phenomena led him to develop broader scientific theories regarding nature's interconnections. In this way, the Pacific's sheer immensity and its geological mysteries helped fashion his Humboldtian mind. Dana viewed the Pacific Ocean and the neighboring landmasses as an immense jigsaw puzzle of interrelated parts: islands, continents, earth crust, ocean, and mountains. As a geologist, Dana recognized the three-dimensionality of the puzzle (above and below the earth's crust) and how the parts related to one another, revealing earth-forming processes in action.

Such fervent scientific philosophizing (before Dana had even turned thirty) may seem out of step with his equally devout Christianity. In fact, the two belief systems appeared to reinforce one another. Born in 1813 into a nominally religious Utica family—his father owned a small store—Dana's early years were steeped in a mixture of education and market commercialism that defined the rising sectors of New York's "Burned-Over District."[19] Dana scavenged for flora, rocks, and minerals during his youth and developed an interest in natural history at Utica High School, a private boarding school with strengths in the natural sciences (Asa Gray taught there in the decade before accepting Harvard University's Fisher Professorship in Natural History). Dana continued his studies in the natural sciences at Yale College under the tutelage of the eminent scientist Benjamin Silliman, and upon graduation in 1833, Dana received Silliman's endorsement to teach math and science aboard the US naval ship *Delaware* in the Mediterranean Sea. Dana corresponded with Silliman throughout the voyage, and his account of Vesuvius just prior to its eruption found publication in Silliman's *American Journal of Science and Arts*, the nation's leading scientific journal.[20]

Dana's career gained momentum upon his return from the Mediterranean. In quick succession, Dana secured a position under Silliman as research and editorial assistant in 1835, published *A System of Mineralogy* in 1837 (which went through six editions in his lifetime and remains in print today), and received Asa Gray's recommendation to join the US Exploring Expedition as geologist. In the midst of this professional ascent, Dana underwent a personal conversion that ultimately emboldened the young scientist. "I have never supposed myself a Christian," Dana wrote to his father in 1835, distinguishing his weekly church attendance from the personal conversion required by evangelical Protestantism.[21] And yet three years later, facing a dangerous voyage and hearing news of his siblings' conversions during a Utica revival, Dana decided "now or never" he would determine his "destiny for an eternity."[22] Dana scribed a three-page statement in his journal:

> This day do I, with the utmost solemnity, surrender myself to thee. I renounce all former bonds that have had dominion over me; and I consecrate to thee all that I am, and all that I have; the faculties of my mind, the members of my body, my worldly possessions, my time, and my influence over others to be all used entirely for thy glory, and resolutely employed in obedience to thy commands.[23]

Dana's "surrender" hardly impeded his science. To the contrary, it seemed to focus his intellectual pursuits and spark his scientific inquiry. The two belief systems—"geology and Genesis," as historian of geology Martin J. Rudwick called it—operated compatibly in his mind.[24] At the very least, religious faith comforted Dana during the often harrowing four-year voyage.

Dana's private faith may have also given him the confidence to grapple with very large concepts, such as the "Origin of the Grand Outline Features of the Earth," which he published in the *American Journal of Science and Arts* upon his return from the Pacific.[25] Like many of Dana's publications in this journal, "Origin of the Grand Outline Features of the Earth" was somewhat speculative and brief, a set of theories offered to gauge the reaction of the larger scientific community. The global "system" proposed by Dana concerned the organization of landforms: continental coastlines *parallel* one another; groups of islands ("submerged mountain ranges") *trend* in corresponding directions; the earth's dominant features are curvature; and where those curved features intersect, they do so at right angles.[26] To the extent Dana could adequately support these points, he drew upon numerous examples from his observation of Pacific islands, coastlines, and mountain ranges. Dana also attempted to synthesize and rebut the work of leading geologists and naturalists, including Otto von Buch, Louis Albert Necker, and Charles Darwin. At heart, Dana offered his readers a grand overview of the earth's geological structure—part creation story, part evidence of the jigsaw puzzle he hoped to unveil. His ideas on the earth's grand features resulted from his experience in the Pacific, which began with his first sighting of a Pacific island.

Coral Reefs and "Myriads of Tiny Architects"

Islands provided the initial key to Dana's geological thinking about the Pacific. Dana, as much as anyone else on the US Ex. Ex. or any previous naturalist, loved Pacific islands. "These coral islands are truly fairy spots in the ocean," Dana wrote to his brother John from Tahiti in September 1839.

> They rise but a few feet above the water's surface, and are covered with a luxuriant tropical vegetation. On one of these, which was not inhabited, the birds were so tame that they permitted themselves to be taken from the bushes and trees, and flew about our heads so near us that we could almost take them with our hands. They did not know enough to fear.[27]

While other members of the expedition eagerly anticipated opportunities of the flesh, Dana longed for the scientific playground afforded by Pacific islands. Each one was entirely unique, and yet at the same time their relationships to one another hinted at patterns and systems for categorization. Dana knew some basic differences, such as the distinction between continental islands and oceanic islands. The former rest on a continental shelf generally not too distant from a continent, while the latter rise from the ocean floor through geological action and break through the waves "like a gasping whale," according to David Quammen.[28] The former include Bali, New Zealand, and California's coastal islands; the latter include just about every Pacific island in between. Continental islands certainly interested Dana, but oceanic islands truly fascinated him. Oceanic islands showed the geological process of creation itself, which in Dana's mind revealed divine inspiration. They also had coral reefs and volcanoes, both of which Dana found sublime.

Dana's first scientific breakthrough on the voyage involved coral reefs and island atolls. From this discovery derived so much that followed. The American Philosophical Society had asked the secretary of the navy to instruct the expedition's scientists to study coral islands:

The circular figure and deep water of the Coral Islands having given rise
to the conjecture that these fabrics of the Zoophytes are based upon the
craters of submarine volcanoes, the collection of any facts calculated to
throw light upon this subject will form one of the interesting duties of
the Geologists.[29]

Dana assumed this "duty" when the US Ex. Ex. first crossed the Pacific in 1839,
visiting the coral-rich Tuamotus, Society, and Samoan groups en route to Australia. During the next two years Dana examined more coral islands and zoophytes (such as coral, an invertebrate animal) than any previous scientist. His
official report for the US Ex. Ex., *Zoophytes* (1846), exceeded seven hundred
pages and included meticulous illustrations, many hand drawn by Dana. But his
study of coral islands also benefited from Charles Darwin's work on the subject,
which began circulating in print just as the US Ex. Ex. entered the Pacific. Darwin had studied a few coral reefs and atolls when the *Beagle* crossed the Pacific in
1835, and he first presented his findings to the Geological Society of London in
1837. Charles Lyell offered a brief account of Darwin's findings in *Principles
of Geology*, published in 1838. Dana carried this book with him on the voyage,
and he received a copy of Lyell's *Elements of Geology* during the stopover in
Valparaiso.[30] Dana may have also chanced across a newspaper summary of
Darwin's island "subsidence theory" once the US Ex. Ex. reached Australia. "The
[newspaper] paragraph threw a flood of light over the subject and called forth
feelings of peculiar satisfaction, and of gratefulness to Mr. Darwin," Dana wrote
three decades later in his book *Corals and Coral Islands*.[31] Reaching Dana through
one channel or another, Darwin's ideas offered crucial assistance for Dana's more
extensive investigations.

Darwin solved most of the "classic geological problem" regarding the origin
of coral islands and atolls.[32] Islands, he postulated, are subject to subsidence into
the ocean, while reefs grow upward due to the steady work of zoophytes. The
rising coral reef creates either a bay open to the ocean or a completely closed off
lagoon, depending on external factors influencing the reef's growth. Eventually
the island disappears altogether and leaves behind a barrier reef, fringing reef, or
circular atoll. Darwin's subsidence theory therefore explained much about the
origin of coral reefs and oceanic islands, but it was also about as far as Darwin
could go with the subject given his meager chances for observations while
aboard the *Beagle*. Darwin had sighted a number of atolls in the Tuamotus, but
only from the *Beagle*'s deck. Tahiti offered the next opportunity to observe reefs,
yet he wrote little about them during his monthlong stay.[33] Finally, Darwin outlined some ideas in his journal once he examined the reefs at Cocos-Keeling
Atoll in the Indian Ocean: "We see certain Isds in the Pacifick, such as Tahiti &
Eimeo, mentioned in this journal, which are encircled by a Coral reef separated

from the shore by channels & basins of still water. Various causes tend to check the growth of the most efficient kinds of Corals in these situations." He pondered such factors as island subsidence, ocean currents, and the creation of island lagoons. "Under this view," Darwin concluded with his characteristic eye for beauty in the minuscule, "we must look at a Lagoon Isd as a monument raised by myriads of tiny architects, to mark the spot where a former land lies buried in the depths of the ocean."[34]

Darwin thought it perfectly logical that ocean currents and wave action affected coral growth and the resulting reefs. But Darwin's guesswork faltered here, while Dana had his first important contribution to the science of corals and reefs. Dana's thoughts turned to *erosion* as the mechanism that shaped most landforms. This idea—which ultimately made him one of the first fluvial geomorphologists—came directly from the grunt work of a field geologist: hiking up and down mountains, looking at dirt and rocks.[35] Mountain uplift fascinated both Darwin and Dana, and yet Dana spent more time than Darwin thinking about all the debris sliding and tumbling down a mountain. Erosion as a geological agent piqued Dana's interest even before the US Ex. Ex. entered the Pacific. Dana described in one correspondence how the "most striking peculiarity of the mountain scenery [near Rio de Janeiro] consists in the jagged outline of the ridges ... and the deep precipitous gorges which cut through the highest mountains almost to their bases."[36] By what process had these "precipitous gorges" formed? He knew the answer—erosion—by the time he witnessed the affect of a torrential downpour during his ascent of Tahiti's Mount Aorai, 6,770 feet above sea level.[37]

Erosion occurs when a trickle of water moves a particle of dirt. Erosion also results when a rainstorm uproots trees, dislodges large boulders, and liquefies topsoil, sending everything downhill in a raging fury. In this way, erosion carves out valleys; on islands, those valleys become bays or lagoons when subsidence gradually lowers the island itself. A raging fluvial mess can also open gaps in reefs, which partially accounts for the shape of island reefs. "If we remember," Dana wrote in *Geology*, "that these mountain streams at times increase their violence a million fold when the rains swell the waters to a flood, all incredulity on this point must be removed."[38] Dana was offering a geological explanation to the romantic depictions of dramatic Pacific peaks and valleys going back to Captain James Cook's first voyage. Three generations of Pacific explorers had pondered the natural forces creating those iconic Pacific landscapes, to which Dana answered simply: "erosion."

Darwin and Dana exchanged letters and criticism during the three decades following their respective publications on corals and island atolls. These exchanges were generally amicable and supportive, and despite their theological differences, the two men maintained a guarded respect for one another. "[Dana] strikes me as a very clever fellow," Darwin wrote to Charles Lyell in 1849 after reading Dana's *Geology*, "[but] I wish he was not quite so great a generaliser."[39] Dana *did* generalize with astonishing insight about Pacific geology and its meaning for global processes, and his theories show the machinations of an imaginative mind captivated by daily observations. For instance, he marveled at the sight of an island peak, "alive with waterfalls, gliding, leaping, or plunging, on their way down from the giddy heights"—and only *then* did Dana's mind ponder the meaning of this sight in scientific terms.[40] And like Darwin's own generalizations, which posited an evolutionary timescale, Dana's sense of nature's inner workings traversed the temporal ground from human time to geological time. Throughout the voyage he sought geological evidence for what Alexander von Humboldt famously termed "the chain of connection, by which all natural forces are linked together and made mutually dependent on each other."[41]

Islands, Volcanoes, and Hot Spots

In thinking about the origins of Pacific islands, James Dwight Dana may have consulted the Polynesian demigod Maui. Maui lived—and in mythological terms, continues to live—a very busy life. He captured the sun with his fishing net in order to slow the sun's progression across the sky, thereby bringing daily warmth to mortals on earth. He tamed man-eating plants and animals in order for people to practice agriculture and animal husbandry. Always attentive to human needs, Maui stole the secret of fire from the fire deity so people could cook food and warm themselves, although he almost ignited the entire world in the process. Like most tricksters, Maui often acted in haste and faced the consequences for his actions, but he always attempted to order the universe for the best interests of those on earth.

Maui also created the Hawaiian Islands. While only a child demigod, Maui went fishing one day with his brothers. They paddled out to a fishing ground called Poʻo, and Maui dropped a large fishhook fashioned from his grandmother's bones.[42] They hooked many great fish from deep down near the ocean floor and began the long process of bringing their catch to the surface. This feat took two days. As they pulled the fish toward their canoe, the catch was transformed into a group of islands that scattered apart on the ocean's surface, thus explaining the current alignment of the Hawaiian Island chain.[43]

This Maui story predated and eventually mirrored western scientific ideas of the nineteenth century, particularly in regard to geology. Oceanic islands rose from the sea as part of the geological processes shaping the entire globe; the Maui legends explained this process of island uplift as clearly as western science—and arguably, to a much larger audience. Islanders' cosmology merged entertainment and science: through Maui and other characters they learned about mountains rising from the ocean, volcanoes as agents of cataclysmic change, and the gradual subsidence of land back into the sea. Maui spoke to the primary concerns of a people who inhabited a small landmass surrounded by a very large ocean: how did the islands originate, and how did they relate to earth-forming processes as a whole?

These questions raise geological, cosmogonic, and spiritual issues—three levels of inquiry that may be treated separately or understood as intrinsically connected. The Maui legends reveal the intrinsic connections. Maui uplifted islands from the ocean floor and established their place in the ocean (geology). The half-man, half-god manipulated basic life elements of fire, water, and sustenance, thereby creating a universe in which people could comfortably live (cosmogony). Maui's work did not result in a perfect garden with no need for gods, but instead continued on through mythological and historical time as people required the explanatory power of creation stories and the intervention of their gods (spirituality). In these ways, Maui's life answers basic questions of science, humanity, and religion.

James Dwight Dana did not mention Maui in *Geology*, his massive report on the Pacific Basin's geology for the United States Exploring Expedition. If he heard these stories during the US Ex. Ex.'s four-year Pacific voyage—an inquisitive observer and listener, it is hard to believe he did not—they most likely captivated him. Dana would have recognized the basic process of island uplift described in Maui's fishing episode, and he would have heartily agreed with the divine origin of geological events. The Maui character may have struck the evangelical Dana as "native superstition" and "heathenish," terms he frequently used in correspondence to portray indigenous religious systems.[44] Dana proposed a different, highly technical set of causes for the Hawaiian Islands' creation. His *Geology* intricately described "the operation of igneous causes in modifying the earth's surface," citing numerous "examples of denudation and disruption, commensurate with the magnitude of the mountain elevations."[45] Most inhabitants of Hawai'i, Tahiti, New Zealand, and the United States would have found these explanations utterly unintelligible, but Dana wrote *Geology* for a Western scientific audience rather than for popular appeal.

How are rock structures assembled? Whether coral reefs or pyramids, most things are assembled piece by piece, suggesting a structural quality as well as a temporal progression. The time progression mattered a great deal to Dana because he viewed geology as the earth's grand historical record. Dana saw history—whether in human time or geological time—as a movement from one epoch to another; it moved forward according to "a plan or system of development" guided by "the Infinite Creator."[46] Indigenous islanders and mainlanders also share an appreciation for history, although most islanders and mainlanders would have viewed Dana's reliance on linear time as simplistic and unaccommodating. Instead, most islanders believed that cyclical time best explained the workings of the earth as well as the lived experiences of humans. The past was not only alive with present meaning, in some respects, the past was not even past. For instance, the volcano goddess Pele journeyed to the Hawaiian Islands sometime in the past and eventually settled her family in the Kilauea crater on the island of Hawaiʻi.[47] But she, like the demigod Maui, remains an active presence in the lives and stories of many native Hawaiians today, embodying the natural forces that connect humanity to the cosmos.

Dana experienced those natural forces at Kilauea in November 1840, and perhaps uncharacteristically given his evangelical Christianity, Dana's account of the volcano suggests a high level of respect for Pele as a Hawaiian deity. Hiking to the rim 4,190 feet above sea level, Dana and his small party camped adjacent to the crater and noted "surprise at the stillness of the scene. The incessant motion in the blood-red pools was like that of a cauldron in constant ebullition." The volcano held an ominous silence by day, Dana wrote, and at night "Pele's pit" revealed a scene "of indescribable sublimity."

> We were encamped on the edge of the crater, with the fires full in view. The large cauldron, in place of its bloody glare, now glowed with intense brilliancy, and the surface sparked with shifting points of dazzling light, occasioned by the jets in constant play. . . . Two other pools in another part of the pit tossed up their molten rock much like the larger cauldron, and occasionally burst out with jets forty or fifty feet in height. . . . And over this scene of restless fires and fiery vapours the heavens by contrast seemed unnaturally black, with only here and there a star like a dim point of light. . . . Pele was in one of her sober moods. Yet we have reason to believe that this is her usual state, and assuredly there is a terrible grandeur even in her quiet.[48]

Even this "sober mood" involved constant motion and lava flows; Kilauea was (and still is) one of the world's most active volcanoes.

Dana likely knew of the Pele legend from available sources and therefore his references to the goddess were not surprising.[49] More surprising is Dana's use of Pele as a narrative device for his report on Kilauea, a scientific study brimming with fieldwork data and theories. Dana repeatedly invokes the goddess (he peers into "the depths of Pele" and refers to himself as "the explorer of Pele's pit") in recounting his terror of standing on the crater's rim. "Long continued rumbling sounds from the falling walls twice broke the deep silence of the pit, while I was upon the verge of the precipice," wrote Dana.[50] Comparing Kilauea to Vesuvius—the first volcano Dana studied, in 1834—Dana remarked: "Thus simple and quiet was the action of Lua Pele. And this repose is, perhaps, more fearfully sublime than the fitful heavings of a Vesuvius."[51]

Dana's evocative descriptions of Kilauea suggest the personal significance he attached to the experience—he was clearly moved "to the brink of fear," as Ralph Waldo Emerson expressed in *Nature*, published four years earlier—as well as the scientific importance he attached to the volcano itself. For instance, he concluded his remarks with the statement that "Lua Pele's" repose was "more fearfully sublime than the fitful heavings of a Vesuvius." Dana used the word "sublime" here and elsewhere with specific connotations: not only to evoke the grandeur and beauty of the scene, but also to express a barely repressed terror and the presence of divine forces at work.[52] Dana certainly experienced great fear on Kilauea's rim; that much is apparent from his narration of the event. The terror, furthermore, connected Dana's religious beliefs to his geology: he felt a divine presence that was in some way responsible for creating the volcano he stood atop. Such brief encounters with powerful natural forces deeply infused his thinking, inspired his science, and sustained him during the tedious months at sea.

Before the US Ex. Ex. entered the Pacific, Dana observed volcanoes in Madeira, the Cape Verde Islands, and years earlier, Vesuvius. But Dana hit volcanic pay dirt in the Pacific Basin, where he studied volcanoes in Tahiti, Fiji, the Pacific Northwest, California, and Hawaiʻi. The Pacific afforded him the chance to see more volcanoes than any previous naturalist, and these observations led him to theorize their significance. "A grand volcanic border" surrounded the Pacific Ocean, Dana would write upon his return to the United States, clarifying an idea he had outlined in letters written during the voyage.[53] What geologists today call the "Ring of Fire" stretches in an arc from New Zealand to the eastern edge of Asia, across the Aleutian Islands and southward along the coast of North and South America. The edges of the "ring" contain approximately 75 percent of the earth's active and dormant volcanoes, due in large part to the Pacific Plate colliding with and sliding beneath (subducting) the surrounding six plates. The subduction zones produce enormous volcanic and seismic energy, turning rock into magma, which rises to the surface in the form of lava, creating volcanoes.[54]

While Dana could not begin to imagine subduction zones, he did reason that volcanic action unified the disparate landforms of the Pacific Basin. "It is a fact of no little interest that the Pacific Ocean should thus be nearly encircled with volcanoes, active or extinct, as well as by high mountains, while the sides of the narrow Atlantic and Indian Oceans have comparatively few traces of such fires, and it tends to confirm the opinion thrown out as to the agency by which the deep ruptures and elevated ranges of the globe have been produced."[55] Here Dana rebutted the work of Leopold von Buch, a leading German geologist (and close associate of Humboldt) who proposed a U-shaped volcanic band linking

Sumatra, Java, and the Philippines. Leopold von Buch never actually observed this band because he had never strayed far from Europe.[56] But Dana could rebut the aristocratic German with an authority born of experience: The volcanic band described by von Buch was merely one section of the volcanic ring encircling the entire Pacific.

In the middle of this fiery perimeter lay the volcanic Hawaiian chain. Dana believed this chain held "the key to Polynesian Geology" because it demonstrated how islands emerged from the sea, the arrangement of island chains, the destruction of islands by volcanic eruption and subsidence, and the geological difference between the Pacific Ocean's floor and the surrounding continents.[57] Despite the great importance he placed on the Hawaiian chain, Dana only spent three months among the islands, much of it aboard the *Peacock*. He spent a mere five days on the volcanically active island of Hawai'i, at which point Captain Wilkes ordered the *Peacock* (Dana's ship) to complete island surveys in the South Pacific. Five days provided Dana enough time to walk from Kealakekua to Hilo, stopping along the way to observe Mauna Loa from a distance and view Kilauea from the crater's rim. While Dana would have relished the opportunity to collect extensive data at both volcanoes (and participate in Wilkes's ascent of the 13,679-foot summit of Mauna Loa to establish the volcano's first observatory), he was later able to draw upon the observations and measurements collected by Charles Pickering, Joseph Drayton, and Charles Wilkes. Furthermore, Dana's science at this point was more about ideas than data collection, and those ideas took definite form during the following months at sea, return to the states, and subsequent period of frenzied writing.

Dana's ideas on volcanoes intersected with his observations of Pacific coral reefs and islands. Like the age progression of coral islands—the island slowly subsides into the ocean; the reef gradually grows up from the waterline—volcanic islands reveal an age progression from the young and active to the dormant and subsiding volcanic island. The active agent of change for reefs—erosion, according to Dana—also shaped the volcanic islands of the Pacific Basin. These parallels struck Dana as simple intuition, given that coral reefs were in fact the surviving offspring of volcanic islands (of course, over *geological* time). To the extent that Dana originated these theories in the Western scientific community, Pacific islanders had already grasped some of the elements. According to two leading volcanologists, "the distinctive northwest-southeast alignment of the Hawaiian chain was known to the early Hawaiians. Their legends clearly reveal that they recognized that the islands are progressively younger from the northwest to the southeast."[58] The goddess Pele, for instance, initially landed in a pit on the island of Kaua'i, but the goddess of water (Na-maka-o-kaha'i) kept flooding Pele's pit, making it inactive and severely eroded. Pele then moved through the Hawaiian Islands until she found the youngest, most volcanically active island

and settled into Mauna Loa and Kilauea.[59] Ancient Hawaiians understood volcano and island age progression to such an extent that these concepts had become entrenched in their cosmology.

Dana reasoned that erosion levels alongside other factors testified to the age progression of volcanoes in the Hawaiian chain. Mauna Loa showed few signs of serious erosion and therefore represented the youngest active volcano in the chain.[60] Dana estimated the subaerial portion took four hundred thousand years to build; modern radiometric studies show this guess to be remarkably accurate. Kilauea came next in age, due to its constant state of eruption and inward collapse of the rim, leading to Dana's novel theory of "eruption-collapse" for "shield" volcanoes.[61] (Again, modern studies basically agree with Dana's "eruption-collapse" theory.) From Kilauea, the volcano age progression continued in a northwest line across the islands: Haleakala, Mauna Kea, Koolau, Maui, Waianae, and finally, Kaua'i.[62]

Observable volcanic islands are difficult to miss in the middle of an ocean, given a viewer's close proximity. Detecting subsurface volcanic peaks—those submerged by the ocean—requires more imagination, and in Dana's case, also a sense for geological process throughout the entire Pacific Basin. Dana guessed that Pacific islands were basically oceanic mountain chains, and he surmised only the tallest peaks broke the ocean's surface. But how extensive was this Hawaiian chain? "We might say," Dana wrote, "that these [existing islands] are all out of a number [of] unknown [peaks], which stretched along for fifteen hundred miles, the length of the whole range. This appears to be a correct view of the Hawaiian Islands."[63]

Dana's guess (without the help of modern sonar equipment) was an eerily accurate depiction of the Hawaiian chain. The Hawaiian chain runs 1,860 miles northwest of Kilauea, at which point it abruptly turns to the north and merges into the Emperor Seamounts, ending just southwest of the Aleutian Islands.[64] The Hawaiian-Emperor chain, in conjunction with the more southerly Line Islands and Tuamotu Archipelago (ending near Pitcairn Island), forms a line essentially dividing the Pacific's extensive floor in two. The result is a defining feature of the Pacific floor: subsurface mountains, trenches, and islands fill the ocean floor west of this line, while parallel fracture zones stretch east to the American coastlines. The contiguous line of peaks along the chain remains highly volcanic, especially Alaska's Aleutian Islands, where the Pacific plate slides beneath the North American plate. The Hawaiian Islands reside at the center of this complex ocean floor. As Dana's "key to Polynesian geology," these islands opened his mind to the features and forces uniting one-third of the earth's surface.

Hawai'i was the "key" to another mystery that, at best, Dana could only begin to theorize. The Pacific Ocean contains eight (approximately one-third) of the earth's prominent "hot spots"—extremely hot regions below the earth's plates that produce magma. The magma rises up through the plate in "thermal plumes" and releases lava through the resulting volcanic mountains. Canadian geophysicist John Tuzo Wilson originated hot spot theory in 1963 with an article titled "A Possible Origin of the Hawaiian Islands," which numerous international journals rejected before publication in the *Canadian Journal of Physics*.[65] Wilson did not use the term "hot spot" in this initial publication; instead, he posited—like Dana's theorizing, in fairly speculative terms—that the Hawaiian chain's linear shape resulted from the Pacific Plate moving over a "system of convection currents in the earth." Those currents "might break the crust and rift it apart where they rise under mid-ocean ridges, exposing fresh surfaces of the mantle to hydration and alteration," thus providing a "continuing supply of heat" such that "each volcano has gone through the same life cycle." Wilson believed the heat source was stationary under the Pacific Plate (subsequent work would confirm the hot spot has been there for forty million years), but he was even more concerned with the ongoing scientific debate over whether plates and continents (the lithosphere) drifted on the earth's inner layer, the asthenosphere. Continents moved, Wilson argued. "The Earth is indeed mobile."[66]

Dana knew nothing about the existence of hot spots, but Wilson's theory referenced many of the factors that led Dana to view Hawai'i as a geological "key" to Polynesia and the Pacific Ocean. Wilson echoed Dana (as well as the Pele legend) on the age progression of Pacific volcanoes, and while Wilson could utilize radioactive carbon dating to establish the age of a volcanic island, he also fell back on Dana's most cherished concept of erosion levels to illustrate island age differences.[67] Wilson wrote (in a near paraphrase of Dana): "Each volcanic island in turn went through a similar cycle of volcanism and erosion, one after the other."[68] Unlike Wilson, however, Dana only speculated in the broadest terms about the source of energy that rose through the earth and ignited volcanism (he referred to "internal fires within the globe").[69] Moving well beyond his own contemporaries, Dana correctly viewed that energy source as global rather than local in origin, and he believed that a volcano's "lava conduits" ultimately connected to a "common source" or "central conduit" deep in the earth's mantle (Wilson's "rising convection current").[70]

None of Dana's thinking led directly to Wilson's hot spot theory. Instead, Dana offered some remarkably prescient ideas on volcanoes that derived from his prolonged study of the Pacific Ocean, a region displaying many of the earth's formative geological processes. That attempt to identify global processes placed Dana outside the geological mainstream, a mainstream defined by European scientists studying European rock formations and volcanoes such as Aetna and Vesuvius. The Pacific Basin offered Dana completely different geological circumstances—the Pacific was "a grand anomaly" in geological terms, and it forced him to scrap textbook knowledge and develop his own questions about the earth.[71] The four-year-long voyage, furthermore, presented Dana with seemingly countless days and nights aboard ship with little to do but ponder those questions.

In this way his journey (both physical and intellectual) followed those of previous scientific explorers who found themselves awakened by new environments: Johann and George Forster on Cook's second Pacific voyage, Alfred Russel Wallace's Indonesian studies in the 1850s, Darwin's *Beagle* voyage to South America and the Pacific, and even John Wesley Powell's surveys of the Grand Canyon and Great Basin.[72] Each of these explorations resembled, to a greater or lesser extent, an effort at holistic science. The boundaries of scientific disciplines grew porous. The encounters with exotic places gave rise to novel theories. Nature itself seemed to pose questions in the guise of land formations, species, or phenotype. Indeed, the very geography through which these journeys took place seemed open to interpretation: new continents appeared (Antarctica), subtle zoogeographical divisions arose (Wallace's Line), and ocean basins assumed greater spatial coherence (the Pacific). Dana's voyage—like these others' travels—was the time of his life, and his head whirled with baffling questions.

The Pacific Context of Continental Geology

Dana studied coral reefs, island atolls, volcanoes, and "convection currents" as distinct entities *and* as constituent parts of a larger Pacific Ocean. Until 1841, he studied these geological features primarily inside the Pacific Ocean, rather than along its continental rim. When his ship, the *Peacock*, was wrecked at the mouth of the Columbia River in 1841, Dana found himself on a North American continent he only knew from its eastern edge. In the coming decades American geologists (including Josiah Whitney, William Brewer, and Dana's student Clarence King) would survey this geography as the western terminus of the North American continent. Closer to Dana's time, John Charles Frémont traversed the Oregon Territory and central California during his second western expedition in 1843–1844, and some of his *Report*'s geological notes were provided by Dana. Frémont and Wilkes may have shared a vision of conquest and commerce for the Far West; specifically, that the nation would soon stretch to the Pacific and commerce with Asia would enrich the United States.[73] But Dana appeared little interested by such expansionist matters during his brief exploration of Oregon and California in 1841. He read the terrain in geological rather than geopolitical terms, and viewed the "Pacific Slope" of Oregon and California through its connection to the ocean more so than its connection with the continent.

In fact, Dana may have been the only geologist before US conquest to closely examine the Oregon Territory and Alta California, and he did so specifically in the context of Pacific geology. Following the loss of the *Peacock*, Charles Wilkes ordered his group of Scientifics to trek overland from the Columbia River south to San Francisco Bay.[74] What Dana described as a 750-mile "land tour" took the party through the Willamette Valley, past Mount Shasta to the upper Sacramento River, and down the river to San Francisco Bay. Glancing east to the towering Sierra range, Dana may have sighted the 13,061-foot-high Yosemite peak that would bear his name two decades later. This trek, according to geologist Daniel Appleman, threw Dana "into the midst of some of the most complicated geology in the world."[75] The Scientifics traversed the North American portion of the Pacific's Ring of Fire—including the volcanically active Cascade Range— mountains resulting from 200 million years of collision between the Pacific and North American plates. Dana also identified the extinct California volcano now known as Sutter Buttes, allowing him to once again reflect on volcano age progression and his favorite geological force, erosion.

Despite the fact this "land tour" took place on North American soil, Dana's frame of reference remained the Pacific Basin throughout his sixty-seven-page report. Perhaps this should be no surprise, given his previous three years in the Pacific Ocean. But many things had changed between the time of his "land tour"(1841), his initial chapter draft for *Geology* (1845–1846), and the book's publication (1849)—including the hasty work of US consolidation over California and the Oregon Territory. Dana alluded to these circumstances only once in his report, referring to California and Oregon as "that portion belonging to the territory of the United States."[76] Quite likely he inserted this phrase just prior to publication, but unfortunate for a geologist, also prior to the announcement of California's massive goldfields (which Dana somehow failed to notice).

Dana's report placed this complex geological region squarely within a Pacific Basin context. The Sierra and Rocky mountain ranges revealed a "vast shed" bordering the eastern Pacific that reappeared in Mexico (Dana cited Humboldt) and the South American Andes (Dana cited the French naturalist Alcide d'Orbigny). These mountains, looming above the Cascade and Coastal ranges, formed "great parallel lines of elevation" with a "probable connexion [to] the depressing of the Pacific Ocean." The river plains leading into the ocean exhibited clear signs of erosion, he wrote, just like "the valleys of the [island] Pacific and those of Australia." The Northwest Coast's "narrow channels which cut into the coast to a great depth, like artificial canals" reminded Dana of "similar passages" in Lower Patagonia and the Tierra del Fuego as well as the Bering Strait. As to the causes of these deep bays and passageways, Dana directed readers to his previous chapters on Tahiti and the Gambier Islands.[77]

It made good sense that Dana would view coastal North American geology as part of the Pacific, because, more so than Darwin or any previous naturalist, Dana was attempting to assemble the geological components of the earth's largest ocean basin. The North American coastline was a vital piece of the puzzle. Therefore, he saw the coastal North American mountains, volcanoes, rivers, and eroded valleys as inextricably connected to the Pacific Basin—not simply parts on the margins, but parts that made the whole. Dana did not discount the fact that his "land tour" took place on a continent possessing its own geological history; in fact, he hoped "at some future period" to give "the Continent a general survey." Such a survey, he wrote in 1849, "must throw new light on the great geological changes that have been in progress throughout the globe."[78] Unfortunately, that global context was all but forgotten when he finally penned a continental survey of North America seven years later.

Patriotic Geology

Dana returned to New Haven in June 1842, and he spent the next decade in a furious pace of writing and publishing.[79] His three scientific reports for the US Exploring Expedition (*Zoophytes*, *Geology*, and *Crustacea*) exceeded three thousand pages of carefully crafted text, and he complemented these volumes with dozens of journal articles, two new editions of *A System of Mineralogy*, and the initial work on his hugely successful *Manual of Geology*.[80] Much of this scholarly output derived from his pathbreaking research in the Pacific, written with the energetic zeal of a triumphant naturalist-explorer. It approached geology (as one facet of the natural world) with a mix of Humboldtian scale and Emersonian awe, surveying tiny zoophytes and immense mountains alike, marveling at cataclysmic volcanic eruptions as well as the quiet workings of erosion in a secluded river valley. His writings proposed holistic theories (one of his first post-voyage articles was titled "Origin of the Grand Outline Features of the Earth") and novel, even whimsical, comparisons (such as "The Volcanoes of the Moon"). In sum, Dana's work during the late 1840s and early 1850s revealed the inspiration of scientific discovery brought forth by years of Pacific meanderings.

Then something happened that marked a real departure from his work on the Pacific. Dana became an *American* geologist. Elected president of the American Association for the Advancement of Science in 1854, Dana presented a paper titled "On American Geological History" as his presidential address in 1855. Echoing the nationalistic and providential drumbeat so pervasive across nineteenth-century American life and letters, Dana declared the independence of North American geology—its geologists, their ideas, and the very rocks themselves—from European science. According to Dana, God had endowed the American continent with a simplicity and completeness of form that per-fectly expressed the earth's geological principles. North America, sequentially created from the Appalachian Mountains westward to the Pacific coastline, rep-resented the land of freedom by virtue of its geological foundation. The ideas Dana used to consecrate American rocks harkened back to the origins of Amer-ican exceptionalism and forward to the nineteenth-century nationalistic cur-rent running from Jefferson to Emerson to Frederick Jackson Turner. Dana was far from alone in his discipline or other branches of science in declaring the uniqueness of American nature. But Dana's address did show how far he had traveled from the Pacific world of intellectual inquiry and holistic science to this ideological anthem of national geology.

Dana's address relied upon the recent researches of his American colleagues. "Each continent has its own periods and epochs," Dana contended, and Ameri-can geologists "have wisely recognized this fact, disregarding European *stages* or subdivisions."[81] At the outset, Dana argued, "we are struck with the comparative simplicity of the North American continent, both in form and structure. In *out-line*, it is a triangle, the simplest of mathematical figures; in *surface*, it is only a vast plain lying between two mountain ranges . . . and on its *contour* it has water, east, west, north, and south." By contrast, he wrote, Europe "is a world of complex-ities. It is but one corner of the Oriental Continent—which includes Europe, Asia, and Africa—and while the ocean bounds it on the north and west, conti-nental lands inclose it on the south and east." Europe's geology was excessively messy while America's was neat and unblemished; Europe was inconveniently connected to darker continents while North America stood virtually alone like a geological beacon to illuminate the world.[82]

To what end was Dana headed? Could continental geology support ideolo-gies of a political, social, and religious nature? Surely it could. Geological "rev-olutions" and "devastations" marked the transitions from one period to the next. As the continent appeared from east to west "like a single unfolding flower in its systems of evolutions," Dana proclaimed "the fact that there has been a plan or system of development in [this] history" initiated by "the Infi-nite Creator."[83] For Dana, "God of the universe" not only "filled all nature with harmonies" but also created an "ordered evolution of a human being" (such theological science led many scientists to question his ideas).[84] The over-arching argument almost perfectly mirrored mid-nineteenth-century ideolo-gies of nationalism and expansionism: "revolutions" had created a harmonious land stretching westward, endowed by God for the proper evolution of human society. The nation had finally reached its western terminus through wars of conquest. While some Americans (most notably the expansionist senator Thomas Hart Benton) viewed the Pacific shore not as a terminus but instead as a crucial step on the longer "North American road to India," Dana was not so inclined.[85] He was content to dwell on the majesty of the continental empire as a unitary whole.

Does this reading of Dana's report on American geology distort his intent? His conclusion suggests otherwise:

> The diversified features and productions of the Old World conspired to adapt it for the childhood and development of the race; and that, when beyond his pupilage, having accomplished his rescue from himself and the tyranny of forces around him, and broken the elements into his service, he needed to emerge from the trammels of the school-house in order to enjoy his fullest freedom of thought and action, and social union. Professor Guyot observes further, that America, ever free, was the appointed land for this freedom and union,—of which its open plains, and oneness of structure, were a fit emblem; and that, although long without signs of progress or hope in its future, this land is to be the centre of hope and light to the world.[86]

Dana's conclusion contained little originality. To the contrary, it encapsulated the mantra of American exceptionalism: the Old World developed "the race," while the New World would nurture natural freedoms and thereby bring light to the world. Dana supported this ideology with the very geological structure of North America. His history of the continent combined geological determinism with patriotic fervor, a complete system set in motion by the essay's final words: "His will." Dana had recently come to support this systematic thinking through association with Arnold Guyot, a Swiss scientist and founding professor of geology and geography at Princeton University.[87] Guyot's *The Earth and Man* (1853) described the "simplicity" and "unity" of North America's structure, "its fruitful plains" and "oceanic position" as geographical signs of its "magnificent theatre." North America, Guyot argued, "is made, not to give birth and growth to a new civilization, but to receive one ready-made" from Europe, to furnish "the life-giving principle of modern times—the principle of free association."[88] Dana borrowed these words from Guyot almost to the letter.

Dana's patriotic geology was hardly outside the norm for the natural sciences at midcentury. "All nineteenth-century science, including Humboldt's, was tinged with imperialism," historian Aaron Sachs has argued.[89] But Americans had special conditions upon which to think and act, according to William Goetzmann: "the necessity for a great scientific inventory of the natural and human resources of the new [continental] domain."[90] Both impulses—imperialism and resource accounting—had influenced the "geopolitics" of the US Exploring Expedition, and now, in the mid-1850s, those impulses went into overdrive for the celebrated geological surveys of the American West conducted by Josiah Whitney, Clarence King, Ferdinand Hayden, John Wesley Powell, and others.[91] None of these explorer-geologists developed an appreciation for the geological and spatial relationship between the American Far West and the Pacific Ocean.[92]

Conclusion

American geologists' turn toward local and national surveys reflected a broader shift in the field. National surveys thrived in Europe and North America during the 1870s and 1880s, as synthesis and theory lost ground to the study of more localized settings. Swiss geologist Eduard Suess's textbook *The Face of the Earth* (1883) was a remarkable work of synthesis that drew upon decades of localized geological research (including Dana's), but, despite its title, its true focus never strayed too far from European geology. When *The Face of the Earth* mentioned the Pacific, Suess turned to Dana's work as authoritative. The important theorists of the late nineteenth and early twentieth centuries, including Suess, Marcel Bertrand, and T. C. Chamberlin among others, drew upon some of Dana's theories that he had first pondered in the Pacific Ocean. But no geologist until the mid-twentieth century even considered a study of the Pacific Ocean in the context of global geology, similar to Dana's. The use of sonar to chart the ocean's floor would revolutionize Pacific geology after World War II, with Lawrence Chubb and H. W. Menard leading the way in the 1950s.[93]

Something was certainly lost in the late nineteenth-century trend of American geologists focusing almost exclusively on the nation's landforms. The Pacific Ocean—its rim abutting the western Americas, its volcanic and tectonic interconnectedness, its islands and floor—literally fell off the map in terms of geological study. Geology remained one field of study in which Americans *could* (and arguably, *should*) understand their nation in extra-continental terms, but this required ambitions beyond the practical uses and material gains of the field. Given the rapidly growing concentration of scientists and engineers in the American West (and California especially), it would have made good sense for western geologists in particular to launch comparative studies around the Pacific. Others had begun to ponder these possibilities in a variety of fields, including marine biology (William Ritter helped establish Scripps Institution of Oceanography), history (Herbert Eugene Bolton's work on Spanish borderlands contained a Pacific perspective), and ecology (George Perkins Marsh gave attention to Pacific forests). But for most Americans and its geologists, the vast ocean that lay west of the nation's continent held little direct relationship to the continental nation.

Few people actually read Dana's report on Pacific Basin geology. The US government printed only a limited number of copies beyond those it sent to foreign heads of state and preeminent libraries, and in 1849 (the year *Geology* appeared), worldwide attention on the Pacific was drawn to the one geological component entirely missed by Dana: gold. For those who did read it—primarily American and European scientists—Dana's *Geology* had an influence far beyond its geographical subject matter. It combined keen observation with innovative geological theory. It examined specific geological structures as part of the Pacific Basin and indeed the entire globe. It derived new conclusions about the formation of coral islands, the nature of volcanoes, the age progression of Pacific islands, the existence of ocean basin mountain chains, and the possible existence of stationary hot spots. For a young scientist with marginal training in geology, Dana's assembling of the Pacific was a singular achievement. The nineteenth century's greatest naturalist, Alexander von Humboldt, considered Dana's work "the most splendid contribution to science of the present day."[94]

Despite the pathbreaking nature of Dana's *Geology*, the US government may have printed only one hundred copies of the report, including those it sent to foreign heads of state and preeminent libraries.[95] "It is most shameful," Dana wrote, "that I have not received from [the] government even one single copy of my own work."[96] The government *did* send one copy across the Pacific Ocean for the library of China's emperor. The governor general of Canton received it, but he could not present it to the emperor because of the chaos involved in the Taiping Rebellion. A friend of Dana's, Dr. Wells Williams, discovered this book in a Canton shop during the mid-1850s. Williams purchased it and sent it back across the Pacific Ocean. Dana received this well-traveled copy of *Geology* in 1858, and perhaps because it had twice traversed the oceanic geology it attempted to comprehend, he kept it for his private library.[97]

Conclusion

When East Became West

News of phenomenally rich gold deposits in the "valley of the Sacramento" spread rapidly around the Pacific Ocean in early 1848. Whalers in Magdalena Bay heard the rumors within a few months via the latest vessel from Honolulu, where reports of the discovery swiftly circulated with the arrival of every ship from California. By the summer of 1848, able-bodied workers were fleeing ports from Acapulco to Callao, and "gold fever" spread from the Northwest Coast to Australia.[1] Merchants in Canton received the same reports with the first inbound vessel from California in mid-1848. As these rumors gained credibility, Canton merchants such as John Heard, of Augustine Heard & Company, had to ponder a proper course of action. A cautious and conservative trader, Heard carefully assembled a cargo of goods for the *Eveline* and sent it east across the Great Ocean in early 1849. The *Eveline* returned several months later with the information that anything and everything was selling at exorbitant prices in California. Heard quickly loaded a second ship, the *Frolic*, and wished a safe passage to the vessel's captain, Edward Horatio Faucon.

Faucon had sound experience in the Pacific trade.[2] He had run opium from India to Canton aboard the *Frolic* for the previous four years, and he knew this 209-ton ship as only a captain who had lived on the vessel since its construction would. Faucon also possessed great knowledge of California—or, at least, the former Alta California, where during the 1830s he captained ships for Bryant & Sturgis, the most successful company in the hide and tallow trade.[3] Faucon was a seasoned captain of the Pacific in every way but one: he had yet to navigate a ship eastward across the ocean from China to California's treacherous and typically fog-bound northern coast. Before seeing the *Frolic* off, John Heard purchased the only map of the North American coast he could find in Canton, which included only a rudimentary outline of northern California derived from George Vancouver's 1792–1793 chart of the North Pacific. The map lacked many details, and more resembled a rough sketch rather than a functional guide.

The *Frolic* departed Hong Kong on June 10, 1850, carrying a large load of silks and "$15,000 in Chowchow"—China trade jargon for miscellaneous goods. This "Chowchow" included porcelain, beer, furniture, paintings, swords, and a prefabricated house. Two American-born officers served under Faucon's command. The crew included twenty-three men: Lascar, Malay, and Chinese sailors carried over from the *Frolic*'s latest opium run. The vessel made it across the ocean in good time, and toward the end of the forty-sixth day Captain Faucon saw "the faint outline of highland" far in the distance. By his estimate the *Frolic* was one hundred miles north of San Francisco Bay. Unfortunately, the "highland" he sighted was a ridge well inland, while the rocky coast itself—unseen in the fading daylight—was much closer. The sound of nearby breakers just before midnight gave the only warning of imminent disaster.

Minutes later the *Frolic* crashed into North America. The ship struck a towering rock directly north of Point Cabrillo. Most hands scrambled into the *Frolic*'s two boats and safely made it to shore several miles south of the wreck, but six crewmen unaccountably chose to stay on the sinking vessel. The next morning Captain Faucon gave orders for the crew to return to the wreck site, and then the three officers began a long walk to San Francisco. Faucon reported these and other details in a letter to Augustine Heard & Company immediately upon his arrival in San Francisco ten days later.[4] He would never learn what happened to the crewmen who remained on the *Frolic*, which fortunately drifted into the shallow bay. Nor would he learn the fate of the crewmen who waded out to the *Frolic*, salvaged as much cargo as they could carry, and then disappeared in the direction of the gold country. Nor did he know that Mitom Pomo Indians had watched this entire event unfold from shore, patiently waiting their turn to recover goods from the ship before it settled on the floor of the coast. Those salvaged items would turn a profitable trade for the Pomo and their Indian neighbors, all of whom presently lived in relative safety well north of the early gold rush settlements.

Captain Faucon hardly recognized the California he entered in 1850, despite the many years he had spent on the coast during the 1830s. The San Francisco waterfront looked like a bobbing forest of trees with its multitude of ships lashed together, their naked masts jutting skyward from the bay. A bustle of constant activity vibrated through the commercial district, and Faucon heard a garble of different languages spoken by gold rush migrants who arrived from all points around the globe. Despite such diversity, Faucon could not fail but notice that California was now decidedly American territory. US flags dangled from businesses and residences. California's hurried 1850 admission to the Union was all the talk in saloons and land offices. An American citizen by birth, Captain Faucon nonetheless felt strangely out of place in this US port that he remembered as part of a very different maritime world.

While the gold strike utterly transformed California, it also sent shock waves around the Pacific. The rush to California altered patterns and volumes of maritime commerce, a result of the state's burgeoning population, markets, and newfound investment capital.[5] It simultaneously inspired new migration flows from Asia, Latin America, the United States, Pacific islands, and Europe. The United States had claimed California through the spoils of war with Mexico, but it was the explosive event of the gold rush that would ultimately ensure imperial consolidation of a much longer stretch of coastline all the way north to Alaska, and, in the coming decades, the annexation of Hawai'i. This vast stretch of eastern Pacific coastline—previously oriented around the ocean's maritime commerce—now became the American Far West, part of a "bordered" and continental empire long predicted by US traders going back to William Shaler of the *Lelia Byrd*.[6] Meanwhile, the few remaining coastal areas with autonomous indigenous communities faced shocking changes in the 1850s. By 1857, the Mitom Pomo villagers who salvaged goods from the *Frolic* were "scattered" and forcibly relocated to two Indian reservations, a government-sanctioned removal that mirrored the conquest of Native Americans across the territory and history of the United States.[7]

But this was not a complete break from the past. These economic, demographic, and cultural transformations were also the culmination of events circulating throughout the Pacific since the late eighteenth century. Maritime trade had gradually increased over the preceding decades, bringing material wealth to some, ruin to others, and deadly pathogens to many indigenous communities along the way. International and heterogeneous maritime worlds formed during these decades—polyglot communities of foreigners and natives on ships and in shoreline areas. No single empire, nation, or group could exert total control in the eastern Pacific. Power, in this sense, was essentially circumstantial and local—the power to kill, or harness someone else's labor, or safely navigate the ocean and return home with a profitable cargo. The eastern Pacific contained maritime worlds defined in part by commodities, trade patterns, social entanglements, and interconnected ports. For outsiders, the eastern Pacific's spatial coherence was a function of their own gathered knowledge as well as the familiar transits across the ocean's vast distances—they had to fathom the Great Ocean in its entirety in order to survive the long voyages.

The eventual ascendance of the United States in the Pacific was hardly a foregone conclusion prior to the war with Mexico. Instead, the nation's presence appeared gradually, even individually, on voyages of speculative trade. Indigenous groups on the Northwest Coast first recognized American persistence in the fur trade just before 1800, while alarmed officials of the British East Indian Company also noted their mounting role in the China trade. American traders established merchant houses in the Hawaiian Islands during the 1820s, followed in the next decade by a sporadic coastal trade from Alta California to Peru for cattle hides, tallow, and finished products. In the 1830s and 1840s, Americans slaughtered whales throughout the Pacific for the growing demands of an upstart industrial economy—and this whaling fleet represented the largest number of Americans in the Pacific to date. Americans were neither exceptional nor constantly successful in their maritime activities. The potential for tragedy and failure accompanied each venture, ranging from Captain John Paty's delivery of smallpox to the Tahitians, to young John Perkins's demise by the tail of a whale.

Despite the mounting presence of US traders, whalers, and exploratory voyages—best symbolized by the US Exploring Expedition—the Pacific should not be construed as an American frontier during this period. Americans had voyaged into the Pacific for decades and accumulated great knowledge and wealth from it. But these ventures had not intentionally advanced an American territorial agenda to match the individual economic ambitions of the voyagers themselves. Prior to the 1840s, few leaders or citizens of the young republic bordering the Atlantic Ocean could even begin to imagine how that *other* ocean, the Pacific, could relate geographically to their national domain. They viewed the Great Ocean as a place distinct and apart from their known world. James Dwight Dana considered the ocean basin a discrete geological space unto itself, rather than a watery backside to the western Americas. This scientific rendering of its difference also implied its proximate connection to all surrounding continents, not simply North America. Some astute observers, such as Adelbert von Chamisso, readily recognized the tremendous variety of this oceanic space—a multifaceted intersection of cultures and intimate relations that seemed like no other part of the world. In all these ways, American traders were only one of many groups operating in the Pacific.

Those people who vied for advantage in the eastern Pacific—including indigenous communities, Europeans, and Americans—repeatedly encountered unexpected pathways and outcomes to their actions. In charting their routes from place to place, they entered waterscapes and littoral borderlands that defied the imagination.[8] John Kendrick, whose 1787 voyage into the Pacific opened this book, quite likely lost his mental bearings as his ship cut a circuitous path around the ocean for the next six years. Two decades later, the Russian serf-turned-expedition-leader Timofei Tarakanov entered a bafflingly complex indigenous world of rivalries and temporary alliances on the Northwest Coast, and the diversity of that coastal borderland mirrored other heterogeneous regions around the Great Ocean. Little more than a generation after Tarakanov's disastrous voyage, Edward Horatio Faucon set off from China on the *Frolic*. His route from the coast of Asia to North America followed a course established centuries earlier by Spanish galleons, and sailed more recently by innumerable ships that sought to reach the eastern Pacific. In 1850, the *Frolic* was wrecked on the coast of an indigenous territory that, for a few more years, still resembled the native country of past centuries. Throughout these decades—from the time of John Kendrick to the gold rush voyage of the *Frolic*—the eastern Pacific remained an intricate set of overlapping borderlands linked by some very treacherous seas.

As the *Frolic* approached its fate on the rocky coast of North America in 1850, major transformations around the Pacific signaled the advent of a new era. Commodore Matthew Perry of the US Navy was busily reading up on Tokugawa Japan in preparation for his first unsolicited visit to that island nation in 1853, which initiated the gunboat diplomacy ending Japan's long-declared isolation from the world. In the North Pacific, Alaska was fast becoming the "lost colony" of the Russian Empire due to wide-ranging reforms enacted by the imperial government as well as the anachronistic nature of the Russian-American Company itself. Meanwhile, in Hawai'i, the Māhale land division of 1848 had privatized the communal lands of native Hawaiians. This "quiet revolution" largely benefited the foreign interests who reaped great profits from their land tenure. Independent nations elsewhere in the Pacific garnered wealth from foreign trade. By the early 1850s, Peru had climbed its way out of staggering debt through guano sales to British merchants who now increasingly employed the revolutionary technology of steam, rather than wind and sail, to power their ships. While the *Frolic* settled on the floor of the bay near Point Cabrillo, the first steam-powered US mail ship made its way up the northern California coastline, marking a new phase of maritime technology for this west coast of the United States.[9]

These striking midcentury transformations in Japan, Alaska, Hawai'i, Peru, California, and many other places around the Great Ocean forecast further changes in the coming decades. Yet they also culminated from the interplay of global trends and local contingencies born during the previous seven decades: the demands by free traders for open markets, the destabilizing and depopulation of indigenous communities, the near-extermination of certain natural species, the decline and rise of various imperial powers, and the worldwide circulation of knowledge regarding the Pacific. Disparate regions of the Pacific had become increasingly connected through oceanic transits as well as the often brutal relations between outsiders and indigenous groups. By the 1850s, the ocean's people, markets, and natural resources were thoroughly entwined with the surrounding world. Herman Melville's omniscient narrator Ishmael recognized this phenomenon; then he went one step further and echoed the timeless belief of indigenous people from the Great Ocean: "Thus this mysterious, divine Pacific zones the world's whole bulk about; makes all coasts one bay to it; seems the tide-beating heart of earth. Lifted by those eternal swells, you needs must own the seductive god, bowing your head to Pan."[10]

NOTES

Introduction

1. Scott Ridley makes a convincing case that Kendrick's death was not accidental, but instead a result of simmering tensions with British traders, especially Captain William Brown in command of the *Jackall*. Accounts vary as to whether the *Lady Washington* fired a salute before the *Jackall*. For his stirring biography and celebratory account of Kendrick's voyages, see Scott Ridley, *Morning of Fire: John Kendrick's Daring American Odyssey in the Pacific* (New York: William Morrow, 2010). On these two ships and the Northwest fur trade, see *Voyages of the "Columbia" to the Northwest Coast, 1787–1790 and 1790–1793*, ed. Frederic W. Howay (Boston: Massachusetts Historical Society, 1941); and *Fur Traders from New England: The Boston Men in the North Pacific, 1787–1800*, ed. Briton C. Busch and Barry M. Gough (Spokane, WA: Arthur H. Clark, 1997).
2. John Kendrick to Joseph Barrell, March 28, 1792; in Howay, *Voyages of the "Columbia,"* 473.
3. On the complexity of Pacific geography and the Northwest Coast in particular, see Paul W. Mapp, *The Elusive West and the Contest for Empire, 1713–1763* (Chapel Hill: University of North Carolina Press, 2011).
4. Pedro Fagés to Lt. José Darío Argüello, May 13, 1789, C-A I: 53, Bancroft Library, University of California, Berkeley.
5. The tensions between Kendrick and other traders are described throughout Ridley, *Morning of Fire*. For Delano's view on Kendrick, see Amasa Delano, *A Narrative of Voyages and Travels, in the Northern and Southern Hemispheres: Comprising Three Voyages round the World* (Boston: E. G. House, 1817), 400.
6. For two examples of indigenous worldviews as constructed through creation stories, see *The Kumulipo: A Hawaiian Creation Chant*, ed. Martha Beckwith (Honolulu: University of Hawai'i Press, 1951); and *California's Chumash Indians: A Project of the Santa Barbara Museum of Natural History Education Center*, ed. Lynne McCall and Rosalind Perry (Santa Barbara: John Daniel, 1986).
7. Epeli Hau'ofa, "Our Sea of Islands," *Contemporary Pacific* 6 (Spring 1994): 153. For an excellent introduction to indigenous studies of the island Pacific, see Vicente M. Diaz and J. Kehaulani Kauanui, "Native Pacific Cultural Studies on the Edge," *Contemporary Pacific* 13 (Fall 2001): 315–341.
8. Jon M. Erlandson, Madonna L. Moss, and Matthew Des Lauriers, "Life on the Edge: Early Maritime Cultures of the Pacific Coast of North America," *Quaternary Science Reviews* 27 (2008): 2232–2245.
9. *Seascapes: Maritime Histories, Littoral Cultures, and Transoceanic Exchanges*, ed. Jerry H. Bentley, Renate Bridenthal, and Kären Wigen (Honolulu: University of Hawai'i Press, 2007), 1. For recent interventions in ocean history, see Rainer F. Buschmann, *Oceans in World History* (New York: McGraw-Hill, 2007); Helen M. Rozwadowski, "Ocean's Depths,"

Environmental History 15 (July 2010): 520–525; Jerry H. Bentley, "Sea and Ocean Basins as Frameworks of Historical Analysis," *Geographical Review* 89 (April 1999): 215–224; W. Jeffrey Bolster, "Putting the Ocean in Atlantic History: Maritime Communities and Marine Ecology in the Northwest Atlantic, 1500-1800," *American Historical Review* 113 (February 2008): 19–47; and Michael N. Pearson, "Littoral Society: The Concept and the Problems," *Journal of World History* 17 (December 2006): 353–373.

10. Lilikalā Kameʻeleihiwa, *Native Land and Foreign Desires: Pehea Lā E Pono Ai? How Shall We Live in Harmony?* (Honolulu: Bishop Museum Press, 1992), 1; Greg Dening, "Encompassing the Sea of Islands," *Common-place* 5 (January 2005); Patrick Kirch and Roger Green, *Hawaiki, Ancestral Polynesia: An Essay in Historical Anthropology* (Cambridge: Cambridge University Press, 2001); Patrick Vinton Kirch, A *Shark Going Inland Is My Chief: The Island Civilization of Ancient Hawaiʻi* (Berkeley: University of California Press, 2012); and Geoffrey Irwin, *The Prehistoric Exploration and Colonisation of the Pacific* (Cambridge: Cambridge University Press, 1992).

11. Dennis O. Flynn and Arturo Giraldez, "Spanish Profitability in the Pacific: The Philippines in the Sixteenth and Seventeenth Centuries," in *Pacific Centuries: Pacific and Pacific Rim History since the Sixteenth Century*, ed. Dennis O. Flynn, Lionel Frost, and A.J.H. Latham (London: Routledge, 1999), 23–37; Flynn and Giraldez, "Cycles of Silver: Global Economic Unity through the Mid-Eighteenth Century," *Journal of World History* 13 (Fall 2002), 391–427; O.H.K. Spate, *Monopolists and Freebooters* (Minneapolis: University of Minnesota Press, 1983); K. N. Chaudhuri, *The Trading World of Asia and the English East India Company* (Cambridge: Cambridge University Press, 1985); Yen-pʼing Hao, *The Commercial Revolution in Nineteenth-Century China: The Rise of Sino-Western Mercantile Capitalism* (Berkeley: University of California Press, 1986); Kenneth Pomeranz and Steven Topik, *The World That Trade Created: Society, Culture, and the World Economy, 1400 to the Present* (Armonk, NY: M. E. Sharpe, 1999); and Tonio Andrade, *How Taiwan Became Chinese: Dutch, Spanish, and Han Colonization in the Seventeenth Century* (New York: Columbia University Press, 2007).

12. On this point, see Kornel Chang, *Pacific Connections: The Making of the U.S.-Canadian Borderlands* (Berkeley: University of California Press, 2012), 6–11.

13. While this study draws on numerous accounts left by missionaries around the Pacific, their activities and the larger topic of religion are not covered in this book. For a fascinating reappraisal of missionary-indigenous relations in one part of the Pacific, see Vicente Diaz, *Repositioning the Missionary: Rewriting the Histories of Colonialism, Native Catholicism, and Indigeneity in Guam* (Honolulu: University of Hawaiʻi Press, 2010). On religious and scientific missions, see Sujit Sivasundaram, *Nature and the Godly Empire: Science and Evangelical Mission in the Pacific, 1795-1850* (Cambridge: Cambridge University Press, 2005).

14. This argument echoes the frontier/borderland framework developed by Jeremy Adelman and Stephen Aron: "As colonial borderlands gave way to national borders, fluid and 'inclusive' intercultural frontiers yielded to hardened and more 'exclusive' hierarchies." See Jeremy Adelman and Stephen Aron, "From Borderlands to Borders: Empires, Nation-States, and the Peoples in between in North American History," *American Historical Review* 104 (June 1999): 816. For a recent assessment of Borderlands scholarship, see Pekka Hämäläinen and Samuel Truett, "On Borderlands," *Journal of American History* 98 (September 2011): 338–361.

15. For a recent endorsement of the Pacific World concept, see Katrina Gulliver, "Finding the Pacific World," *Journal of World History* 22 (March 2011): 83–100. For more nuanced approaches to different histories *in* the Pacific, see Matt K. Matsuda, "AHR Forum: The Pacific," *American Historical Review* 111 (June 2006): 758–780; Greg Dening, "History 'in' the Pacific," in *Voyaging through the Contemporary Pacific*, ed. David Hanlon and Geoffrey M. White (Lanham, MD: Rowman and Littlefield, 2000), 135–140; and Ryan Tucker Jones, "A 'Havoc Made among Them': Animals, Empire, and Extinction in the Russian North Pacific, 1741-1810," *Environmental History* 16 (September 2011): 585–609.

16. On Atlantic World scholarship, see Joyce E. Chaplin, "Expansion and Exceptionalism in Early American History," *Journal of American History* 89 (March 2003): 1431–1455; Nicholas Canny, "Writing Atlantic History; or, Reconfiguring the History of Colonial

British America," *Journal of American History* 86 (December 1999): 1093–1114; Peter A. Coclanis, "*Drang Nach Osten*: Bernard Bailyn, the World-Island, and the Idea of Atlantic History," *Journal of World History* 13 (Spring 2002), 169–182; Robin D. G. Kelley, "How the West Was One: The African Diaspora and the Re-Mapping of U.S. History," in *Rethinking American History in a Global Age*, ed. Thomas Bender (Berkeley: University of California Press, 2002), 123–147; *The Atlantic World and Virginia*, ed. Peter Mancall (Chapel Hill: University of North Carolina Press, 2007); and Alison Games, "Atlantic History: Definitions, Challenges, and Opportunities," *American Historical Review* 111 (June 2006): 741–757.

17. For an excellent statement on the interconnectedness of ocean basins, see Rainer F. Buschmann, "Oceans of World History: Delineating Aquacentric Notions in the Global Past," *History Compass* 2 (January 2004): 1–5.

18. Fernand Braudel, *The Mediterranean and the Mediterranean World in the Age of Philip II*, trans. Siân Reynolds (New York: Harper and Row, 1972–1973 [1949]), vol. 1: 224.

19. Matsuda, "AHR Forum: The Pacific," 758, 759. For a more complete explication of this concept, see Matt K. Matsuda, *Pacific Worlds: A History of Seas, Peoples, and Cultures* (Cambridge: Cambridge University Press, 2012).

20. *The Cambridge History of the Pacific Islanders*, ed. Donald Denoon (Cambridge: Cambridge University Press, 1997); Greg Dening, *Islands and Beaches: Discourse on a Silent Land: Marquesas 1774–1880* (Honolulu: University of Hawai'i Press, 1980); and David A. Chappell, "Active Agents versus Passive Victims: Decolonized Historiography or Problematic Paradigm?" *Contemporary Pacific* 7 (Spring 1995): 303–326.

21. On the coherence of the Mediterranean world, Fernand Braudel conceded: "The Mediterranean has no unity but that created by the movements of men, the relationships they imply, and the routes they follow." We may disagree with Braudel on many levels (perhaps beginning with his elision of women from the Mediterranean world), but his sense of people in motion and the resulting connections or "routes" between disparate lands was a clear starting place for discussions of oceanic worlds. Braudel, *The Mediterranean and the Mediterranean World in the Age of Philip II*, vol. 1: 267. For a recent Mediterranean history centered on the sea itself, see David Abulafia, *The Great Sea: A Human History of the Mediterranean* (New York: Oxford University Press, 2011).

22. For discussion of historical "scales," see Richard White, "The Nationalization of Nature," *Journal of American History* 86 (December 1999): 976–986; and Tonio Andrade, "A Chinese Farmer, Two African Boys, and a Warlord: Toward a Global Microhistory," *Journal of World History* 21 (December 2010): 573–591. My thoughts on historical scales have also been greatly influenced by the work of Anne Salmond; see Salmond, *The Trial of the Cannibal Dog: The Remarkable Story of Captain Cook's Encounters in the South Seas* (New Haven, CT: Yale University Press, 2003).

23. Ann Laura Stoler, "Preface to the 2010 Edition: Zones of the Intimate in Imperial Formation," *Carnal Knowledge and Imperial Power: Race and the Intimate in Colonial Rule* (Berkeley: University of California Press, 2010), xx.

24. Patrick Vinton Kirch, *How Chiefs Became Kings: Divine Kingship and the Rise of Archaic States in Ancient Hawai'i* (Berkeley: University of California Press, 2010).

25. On Chief Maquinna, see Anya Zilberstein, "Objects of Distant Exchange: The Northwest Coast, Early America, and the Global Imagination," *William and Mary Quarterly* 64 (July 2007): 589–618. For an example of local dynamics that connect with a much broader context, see Coll Thrush, *Native Seattle: Histories from the Crossing-Over Place* (Seattle: University of Washington Press, 2007).

26. Alejandro Malaspina, *The Malaspina Expedition, 1789–1794: Journal of the Voyage by Alejandro Malaspina*, ed. Andrew David et al. (London: Hakluyt Society, 2001–2004).

27. Ken Pomeranz will have to excuse this take-off on the title of his superb study, *The Great Divergence: China, Europe, and the Making of the Modern World Economy* (Princeton, NJ: Princeton University Press, 2000). For a more contemporary perspective, see *China in Oceania: Reshaping the Future?* ed. Terence Wesley Smith and Edgar A. Porter (New York: Berghahn Books, 2010).

28. John Kendrick to Joseph Barrell, March 28, 1792, in Howay, *Voyages of the "Columbia,"* 473.

Chapter 1

1. T. T. Waterman, *Yurok Geography* (Berkeley: University of California Press, 1920); and Alfred L. Kroeber, *Yurok Myths* (Berkeley: University of California Press, 1976).

2. William Shaler, *Journal of a Voyage between China and the North-Western Coast of America, Made in 1804* (Philadelphia, 1808), 140. Also see the account by Shaler's business partner, Richard Jeffry Cleveland, *Voyages and Commercial Enterprises, of the Sons of New England* (New York: Burt Franklin, 1857), 404–407.

3. Shaler, *Journal of a Voyage*, 145.

4. Ibid., 160.

5. Ibid., 161.

6. Ibid., 171.

7. John T. Hudson, "Journal and Logbook of John T. Hudson, 1805–1807," Huntington Library; and Adele Ogden, *The California Sea Otter Trade, 1784–1848* (Berkeley: University of California Press, 1941), 42–43.

8. For recent work on Borderlands history, especially as it incorporates oceanic space, see Pekka Hämäläinen and Samuel Truett, "On Borderlands," *Journal of American History* 98 (September 2011): 338–361. See also Jeremy Adelman and Stephen Aron, "From Borderlands to Borders: Empires, Nation-States, and the Peoples in Between in North American History," *American Historical Review* 104 (June 1999): 816.

9. Waterman, *Yurok Geography*, 220–221.

10. Jeanne E. Arnold, "The Chumash in World and Regional Perspectives," in *The Origins of a Pacific Coast Chiefdom: The Chumash of the Channel Islands*, ed. Jeanne E. Arnold (Salt Lake City: University of Utah Press, 2001), 1–19.

11. Jeanne E. Arnold, Aimee M. Preziosi, and Paul Shattuck, "Flaked Stone Craft Production and Exchange in Island Chumash Territory," in Arnold, *Origins of a Pacific Coast Chiefdom*, 113–131.

12. Gwenn A. Miller, *Kodiak Kreol: Communities of Empire in Early Russian America* (Ithaca, NY: Cornell University Press, 2010) 1–48; *Looking Both Ways: Heritage and Identity of the Alutiiq People*, ed. Aron L. Crowell, Amy F. Steffian, and Gordon L. Pullar (Fairbanks: University of Alaska Press, 2001); John R. Bockstoce, *The Opening of the Maritime Fur Trade at Bering Strait* (Philadelphia: American Antiquarian Society, 2005), 18–21; and Ogden, *California Sea Otter Trade*, 11–14.

13. Theodore Morgan, *Hawai'i: A Century of Economic Change, 1778–1876* (Cambridge, MA: Harvard University Press, 1948), 47–49; and William Ellis, *A Journal of a Tour around Hawai'i* (Boston: Crocker and Brewster, 1825), 30–31.

14. The classic study of the Kula Ring is Bronislaw Malinowski, *Argonauts of the Western Pacific: An Account of Native Enterprise and Adventure in the Archipelagoes of Melanesian New Guinea* (New York: Dutton, 1922). See also Jerry W. Leach and Edmund Ronald Leach, *The Kula: New Perspectives on Massim Exchange* (Cambridge: Cambridge University Press, 1983).

15. Marshall I. Weisler and Patrick V. Kirch, "Interisland and Interarchipelago Transfer of Stone Tools in Prehistoric Polynesia," *Proceedings of the National Academy of Science* 93 (February 1996): 1381–1385.

16. Robert Marks, "Maritime Trade and the Agro-Ecology of South China,1685–1850," in *Pacific Centuries: Pacific Rim Economic History Since the Sixteenth Century*, ed. Dennis O. Flynn, A.J.H. Latham, and Lionel Frost (London: Routledge, 1998), 87.

17. Ibid., 91.

18. Dennis O. Flynn, Arturo Giraldez, and James Sobredo, *European Entry into the Pacific: Spain and the Acapulco-Manila Galleons* (Aldershot, UK: Ashgate, 2001); see especially "Introduction," xiii–xxxviii; C. R. Boxer, "*Plata es Sangre*: Sidelights on the Drain of Spanish-American Silver in the Far East, 1550–1700," 165–186; and Maria Lourdes Diaz-Trechuelo, "Eighteenth Century Philippine Economy: Commerce," 281–308. For a recent critique of the "Spanish Lake" concept, see Ryan Crewe, "Sailing for the 'Chinese Indies': Charting the Asian-Latin American Rim, Conduits, and Barriers of the Early Modern Pacific World," paper presented at the 18th Annual Conference of the Omohundro Institute of Early American History and Culture, June 16, 2012.

19. Hugh Golway, "The Cruise of the Lelia Byrd," *Journal of the West* 8 (July 1969): 396–398; and Richard F. Pourade, *Time of the Bells* (San Diego: Union-Tribune Publishing, 1961), 96–101.

20. Richard Henry Dana, quoted in Richard Jeffry Cleveland, *Voyages of a Merchant Navigator of the Days That Are Past* (New York: Harper, 1886), 95.

21. Steven W. Hackel, "Land, Labor, and Production: The Colonial Economy of Spanish and Mexican California," in *Contested Eden: California Before the Gold Rush*, ed. Ramón A. Gutiérrez and Richard Orsi (Berkeley: University of California Press, 1998), 118–129.

22. Shaler and Cleveland had exchanged their cargo of pelts and furs for a large quantity of silks and tea in Canton; the silk traveled to New York with Cleveland aboard the American ship *Alert* and Shaler took the tea to California and Hawai'i. Cleveland apparently amassed $70,000 from these dealings. Cleveland, *Voyages of a Merchant Navigator*, 100.

23. Shaler, *Journal of a Voyage*, 144.

24. Ogden, *California Sea Otter Trade*, 42–43.

25. Shaler, *Journal of a Voyage*, 148; and Ogden, *California Sea Otter Trade*, 43.

26. Shaler, *Journal of a Voyage*, 153. Emphasis added.

27. William Shaler to R. J. Cleveland, n.d. in Cleveland, *Voyages and Commercial Enterprises*, 406.

28. See the manuscript collection "Trading Vessels on the California Coast, 1786–1847," Adele Ogden Collection, Bancroft Library, University of California, Berkeley.

29. Fray José Señán to José de la Guerra, July 24, 1822, Bancroft Library; Hackel, "Land, Labor, and Production," 128–130; and David J. Weber, *The Mexican Frontier, 1821–1846: The American Southwest under Mexico* (Albuquerque: University of New Mexico Press, 1982), 151–153.

30. Argüello quoted in Steven W. Hackel, *Children of Coyote, Missionaries of Saint Francis: Indian-Spanish Relations in Colonial California, 1769–1850* (Chapel Hill: University of North Carolina Press, 2005), 371.

31. F. W. Howay, *A List of Trading Vessels in the Maritime Fur Trade, 1785–1825* (Kingston, ON: Limestone Press, 1973); J. S. Cumpston, *Shipping Arrivals and Departures: Sydney, 1788–1825*, 3 vols. (Canberra: A.C.T.: Roebuck Society, 1963); Bernice Judd, *Voyages to Hawai'i before 1860* (Honolulu: University of Hawai'i Press, 1974); Rhys Richards, *Honolulu: Centre of Trans-Pacific Trade: Shipping Arrivals and Departures, 1820–1840* (Honolulu: Hawaiian Historical Society, 2000); and Rhys Richards, "United States Trade with China, 1784–1814," *American Neptune* 54 (1994): 5–76.

32. David Igler, "Database of California Shipping" (unpublished). This database is compiled from the records of Adele Ogden, "Trading Vessels on the California Coast, 1786–1847," Bancroft Library. Ogden's sources for each vessel include the original shipping logs, travel accounts, Mexican and Spanish archival collections, and an extensive survey of secondary literature. I entered each record into a spreadsheet with forty-four possible entry fields (including ownership, flag, types of cargo, and destinations) and used Stata to analyze the data. While Odgen's records may not be entirely complete, they represent by far the most comprehensive (and unexamined) compilation of California shipping prior to the gold rush.

33. Igler, "Database of California Shipping." While all the vessels in this database entered California's coastal waters, they did not all enter a California port. This important distinction sheds light on the nature of Spanish rule in California prior to 1821. Vessels involved in the sea otter trade often avoided Spanish ports in California and Mexico for fear of having their cargoes (and sometimes ships) impounded. Therefore, many ships remained offshore and dropped anchor near the coastal islands, where the majority of sea otter hunting was conducted. See Ogden, *California Sea Otter Trade*, 32–45.

34. The surge in trade also coincided with general improvements in transoceanic sailing vessels, the sandalwood and bêche-de-mer (dried sea slugs) trade between Pacific islands and China, and the entrance of the American whaling fleet into Pacific waters during the 1820s. Whaling vessels comprised 26 percent of ships in California during the 1820s, and much larger numbers of whalers docked in Honolulu than in California.

35. This point is significant for Pacific commerce as a whole, but it holds a particular resonance for California—a place generally periodized through clear-cut stages from Indian to Spanish to Mexican to American rule, with few other groups involved. Instead, California's littoral zone suggests a different story and set of actors with a distinct international character.

36. Adele Odgen's complete list of vessel ownership by nation/region included Spain, England, Peru, Russia, Mexico, United States (Boston, New York, Hartford, Baltimore, Philadelphia), France, Hawai'i, California, Bengal, Canton, Columbia, Hudson's Bay Company, Germany, Hamburg, Sardinia, Mauritius, Ecuador, Chile, Sweden, Canada, Central America, and Denmark.

37. Karen Ordahl Kupperman, "International at the Creation: Early Modern American History," in *Rethinking American History in a Global Age*, ed. Thomas Bender (Berkeley: University of California Press, 2002), 105.

38. Igler, "Database of California Shipping."

39. Jennifer Newell, *Trading Nature: Tahitians, Europeans, and Ecological Exchange* (Honolulu: University of Hawai'i Press, 2010).

40. Gary Okihiro, *Island World: A History of Hawai'i and the United States* (Berkeley: University of California Press, 2008).

41. Judd, *Voyages to Hawai'i before 1860*, 1–17. Judd's figures include some ships that arrive twice during the same year, meaning that ship would account for two arrivals rather than one distinct ship arriving in Hawai'i. This accounts for some of the discrepancy between her figures and a second source, which lists only 94 ships arriving in Hawai'i before 1819. See "Ships to Hawai'i before 1819," http://www.hawaiian-roots.com/shipsB1880.htm, accessed July 2002. By comparison, 188 ships entered California waters between 1786 and 1819, but 102 of these voyages were Spanish ships that only sailed between San Blas, California, and the Northwest. Thus, California and Hawai'i received approximately the same number of transoceanic voyages (overwhelmingly British and American).

42. These data come from historian and economist Theodore Morgan, who admits to "varying degrees of doubt" regarding their accuracy. Morgan writes: "From all these data a certain subtraction is necessary in order to get the number of *ships* [from] all those which touched more than once. In the case of whalers, this deduction is estimated to be about one-third." Morgan, *Hawai'i*, 225–226. Comparative data on whalers comes from Rhys Richards, who counts 1,565 whaling vessels docking in Honolulu between 1820 and 1840. His figures do not include the port of Lahaina nor do they account for the rising number of ships in the 1840s; overall Richards's counting is approximately one-third lower than Morgan's. Richards, *Honolulu*, 12.

43. Patrick Kirch, *Feathered Gods and Fishhooks: An Introduction to Hawaiian Archaeology and Prehistory* (Honolulu: University of Hawai'i Press, 1985), 27–30, 65–67, 215–231.

44. Marshall Sahlins argues that Hawaiian chiefs "appropriated Western commodities to their own hegemonic projects—which is also to say, to traditional conceptions of their own divinity. . . . The specific effects of the global-material forces depend on the various ways they are mediated in local cultural schemes." Marshall Sahlins, "Cosmologies of Capitalism: The Trans-Pacific Sector of 'The World System,'" in *Culture/Power/History: A Reader in Contemporary Social Theory*, ed. Nicholas B. Dirks, Geoff Eley, and Sherry B. Ortner (Princeton, NJ: Princeton University Press, 1994), 414. On Hawai'i as an "archaic state" and its emerging political economy, see Patrick Vinton Kirch, *How Chiefs Became Kings: Divine Kingship and the Rise of Archaic States in Ancient Hawai'i* (Berkeley: University of California Press, 2010), especially 114–123.

45. Charles Pierre Claret Fleurieu, *Voyage autour du monde: pendant les annees 1790, 1791 et 1792* (Paris: De l'Imprimerie de la République, 1798–1800), vol. 1: 410.

46. Peter Corney, *Early Voyages in the North Pacific* (Fairfield, WA: Ye Galleon Press, 1965 [1836]).

47. Ibid., 127. On Hawaiian workers in the Pacific Northwest, see Jean Barman and Bruce McIntyre Watson, *Leaving Paradise: Indigenous Hawaiians in the Pacific Northwest, 1787–1898* (Honolulu: University of Hawai'i Press, 2006).

48. Robert Crichton Wyllie, "Analytic view of the goods imported for consumption at . . . Honolulu . . . and of the goods transshipped . . . during the year 1843," *The Friend, of Temperance and Seamen* (June 1, 1844): 56–59.

49. Adele Ogden assembled thousands of these letters from various merchant collections held by the Bancroft Library, the Harvard Business School, and Harvard's Houghton Library. See Ogden, "Mexican California: Topics Found in Maritime MS Materials," Bancroft Library, University of California, Berkeley.

50. O. A. Bushnell, *The Gifts of Civilization: Germs and Genocide in Hawai'i* (Honolulu: University of Hawai'i Press, 1983), 215–264.

51. Marks, "Maritime Trade and the Agro-Ecology of South China, 1685–1850," 97, 100. Marks further notes that China won out in the overall balance of trade with foreigners until large imports of opium by British and American traders in the 1830s.

52. Howay, *List of Trading Vessels in the Maritime Fur Trade*.

53. Paul A. Van Dyke, *The Canton Trade: Life and Enterprise on the China Coast, 1700–1845* (Hong Kong: Hong Kong University Press, 2005), 5–18.

54. Lord George Macartney to Erasmus Gower, July 27, 1793, "China Embassy Letters Received," box G/12/92, East India Company Collection, British Library.

55. C. H. Philips, *The East India Company, 1784–1834* (Manchester, UK: Manchester University Press, 1940), 302; and John Keay, *The Honourable Company: A History of the English East India Company* (New York: Macmillan, 1994), 430.

56. Van Dyke, *Canton Trade*, 117–142. On piracy, see Robert J. Antony, "Sea Bandits of the Canton Delta, 1780–1839," *International Journal of Maritime History* 17 (December 2005): 1–29.

57. William Dane Phelps to Joseph B. Eaton, November 17, 1868, William Dane Phelps Collection, Widener Memorial Library, Harvard University.

58. This assessment of the *Eagle's* trade comes from the California merchant John Meeks. See William Heath Davis, *Sixty Years in California* (San Francisco: A. J. Leary, 1889), 299.

59. "List of American Vessels at the Port of Canton, Season 1820, 1821," in "Canton Diary for Season 1820/1821," East India Company Collection, British Library.

60. N.H.C. Plowden to Joseph Dart, Secret Committee/Department, June 27, 1821, "Secret Letters Received from China, June 27, 1821 to February 6, 1823," box G/12/284, East India Company Collection, British Library.

61. "List of American Vessels at the Port of Canton, Season 1821, 1822" and "Estimate of the Import Trade on American Vessels at the Port of Canton, Season 1821, 1822," in "Canton Diary for Season 1821/1822," East India Company Collection, British Library.

62. Plowden to Dart, June 27, 1821.

63. On market activity in Canton and Guangdong province during this period, see Robert Marks, *Tigers, Rice, Silk, and Silt: Environment and Economy in Late Imperial South China* (Cambridge: Cambridge University Press, 1998), 163–194.

64. Jacques M. Downs, *The Golden Ghetto: The American Commercial Community in Canton and the Shaping of American China Policy, 1784–1844* (Bethlehem, PA: Lehigh University Press, 1997), 44.

65. Keay, *Honourable Company*, 454–456; and Downs, *Golden Ghetto*, 46.

66. See letters between the Select Committee and Secret Committee, March 19 and April 18, 1822, box G/12/284; "Statement of Opium imported into China Season 1821,1822," box G/12/225, East India Company Collection, British Library.

67. Howay, *Trading Vessels in the Maritime Fur Trade*. This number represents annual visits, with some ships stopping more than one time on the same voyage. I am grateful to Marion Gee for entering Howay's information into a database.

68. Howay's records show British ships accounted for 14 percent of the overall traffic while American vessels made up 75 percent of the trade. Howay, *Trading Vessels in the Maritime Fur Trade*, 2.

69. Camille de Roquefeuil, *Journal d'un voyage autour du monde: Pendant les années 1816, 1817, 1818, et 1819* (Paris: Ponthieu, 1823), vol. 1: 191. Adelbert von Chamisso, aboard the Russian vessel *Rurik*, noted this ship, the *Chirik*, and its captain, "Mr. Binzemann," who had a wooden right leg. See Chamisso, *A Voyage around the World with the Romanzov Expedition in the Years 1815–1818* (Honolulu: University of Hawai'i Press, 1986), 95.

70. James R. Gibson, *Otter Skins, Boston Ships, and China Goods: The Maritime Fur Trade of the Pacific Northwest, 1785–1841* (Seattle: University of Washington Press, 1992), 38.

71. Howay, *Trading Vessels in the Maritime Fur Trade*.

72. Robin Fisher, *Contact and Conflict: Indian-European Relations in British Columbia, 1774–1890* (Vancouver: University of British Columbia Press, 1977), 1–48; and Daniel

W. Clayton, *Islands of Truth: The Imperial Fashioning of Vancouver Island* (Vancouver: University of British Columbia Press, 2000), 78.

73. John Meares, *Voyages Made in the Years 1788 and 1789, From China to the North West Coast of America* (London: Logographic Press, 1790), 141–142.

74. James Cook, *The Journals of Captain Cook*, ed. Philip Edwards (London: Penguin Books, 1999), 545–546.

75. Howay's "List of Trading Vessels" includes numerous incidences of violence between Indians and traders, although only some of these involved concerted attempts to take over ships. See also Robin Fisher, "Arms and Men on the Northwest Coast, 1774–1825," *BC Studies* 29 (1976): 3–18.

76. Dorothy Burne Goebel, "British Trade to the Spanish Colonies, 1796–1823," *American Historical Review* 43 (January 1938): 318.

77. Ibid., 319.

78. Charles Darwin, *The Voyage of the Beagle*, ed. Leonard Engel (New York: Natural History Library, 1962), 365–368; W. M. Mathew, "The Imperialism of Free Trade: Peru, 1820–70," *Economic History Review* 21 (December 1968): 562–579; and Mathew, "Peru and the British Guano Market, 1840–1870," *Economic History Review* 23 (April 1970): 112–128.

79. Edward Inskeep, "San Blas, Nayarit: An Historical and Geographic Study," *Journal of the West* 2 (1963): 133–144; and Warren L. Cook, *Flood Tide of Empire: Spain and the Pacific Northwest, 1543–1819* (New Haven, CT: Yale University Press, 1973), 48–51.

80. Ogden, *California Sea Otter Trade*, 45–65; Ivan Veniaminov, *Notes on the Islands of the Unalaska District*, ed. Lydia T. Black and R. H. Geoghegan (Fairbanks, AK: Limestone Press, 1984 [1804]), 248–258; and Miller, *Kodiak Kreol*, 44, 71–72. On the Russian-American Company, see Ilya Vinkovetsky, *Russian America: An Overseas Colony of a Continental Empire, 1804–1867* (New York: Oxford University Press, 2011); and Ryan Tucker Jones, "A 'Havoc Made among Them': Animals, Empire, and Extinction in the Russian North Pacific, 1741–1810," *Environmental History* 16 (September 2011): 585–609.

81. Morrell not only dedicated the narrative to her "fellow countrywomen," but also to those who were "single by choice" and "married by consent." Abby Jane Morrell, *Narrative of a Voyage to the Ethiopic and South Atlantic Ocean, Indian Ocean, Chinese Sea, North and South Pacific Ocean, in the years 1829, 1830, 1831* (New York: J. and J. Harper, 1833), 2. Also see Benjamin Morrell, *A Narrative of Four Voyages: To the South Sea, North and South Pacific Ocean, Ethiopic and Southern Atlantic Ocean, Indian and Antarctic Ocean, from the year 1822 to 1831* (New York: J. and J. Harper, 1832). Both narratives were heavily revised by ghostwriters hired by the publisher. See Eugene Exman, *The Brothers Harper: A Unique Publishing Partnership and Its Impact upon the Cultural Life of America from 1817 to 1853* (New York: Harper and Row, 1965), 29–30. I am grateful to Michael Block for bringing this fact to my attention.

82. On the bêche-de-mer trade, see R. Gerald Ward, "The Pacific *Bêche-de-mer* Trade with Special Reference to Fiji," in *Man in the Pacific Islands: Essays on Geographical Change in the Pacific Islands* (Oxford: Clarendon Press, 1972), 91–123.

83. Morrell, *Narrative of a Voyage*, 57.

84. Ibid., 59, 67; and Morrell, *Narrative of Four Voyages*, 450.

85. Morrell, *Narrative of a Voyage*, 68.

86. Ibid., 70, 143.

87. Morrell wrote: "I hope to live to see the islands in this ocean inhabited by my countrymen, under the protection of my country. There is no obstacle in the way of this." Ibid., 224.

88. John Turnbull, *A Voyage round the World, in the Years 1800, 1801, 1802, 1803, and 1804* (Richard Phillips: London 1805), vol. 2: 13–14.

89. Captain [Alexander] M'Konochie, *A Summary View of the Statistics and Existing Commerce of the Principal Shores of the Pacific Ocean* (London: J. M. Richardson, 1818), ix, 98.

90. Ibid., 98.

91. Ibid., ix.

92. Ibid., 100.

93. Ibid., 225. Emphasis added.

94. Ibid., 98.

95. Shaler, *Journal of a Voyage,* 166, 168.
96. Robert C. Schmitt, "The Okuu—Hawai'i's Greatest Epidemic," *Hawai'i Medical Journal* 29 (May–June 1970): 359–364.
97. The most direct account was given by the Russian Captain Urey Lisiansky, who was on Kaua'i and Hawai'i in 1804. See Urey Lisiansky, *A Voyage round the World in the Years 1803, 1804, 1805, and 1806* (London: John Booth, 1814), 111–113.
98. Lorrin Andrews, *A Dictionary of the Hawaiian Language* (Honolulu: Henry M. Whitney, 1865), 97.
99. Golway, "The Cruise of the Lelia Byrd," 399.

Chapter 2

1. *The Journals of Captain James Cook on His Voyages of Discovery,* J. C. Beaglehole, ed. (Cambridge: Hakluyt Society, 1955–1974), vol. 3, pt. 1: 540, 699, 700.
2. Clerke to Banks, August 10, 1779; in Beaglehole, *Journals,* vol. 3, pt. 2: 1542–1543. Most historians note Clerke's stay in another debtors' prison, the Fleet. In either case, Clerke served time because his brother had sailed for India to avoid his creditors.
3. Anne Salmond, *The Trial of the Cannibal Dog: The Remarkable Story of Captain Cook's Encounters in the South Seas* (New Haven, CT: Yale University Press, 2003), 309; Clerke to Admiralty Secretary, August 1, 1776; Clerke to Banks, August 1, 1776; Clerke to Banks, November 23, 1776; in Beaglehole, *Journals,* vol. 3, pt. 2: 1513, 1514, 1518.
4. Beaglehole, *Journals,* vol. 3, pt. 1: 259. According to Lieutenant James Burney, Clerke and Anderson contemplated taking leave of the ships in Huahine in order to repair their health. See Burney, *A Chronological History of North-Eastern Voyages of Discovery* (London: Paine and Foss, 1819), 233–234.
5. Beaglehole, *Journals,* vol. 3, pt. 1: 406.
6. Sir James Watt, "Medical Aspects and Consequences of Cook's Voyages," in *Captain James Cook and His Times,* ed. Robin Fisher and Hugh Johnston (Seattle: University of Washington Press, 1979), 149.
7. Ibid., 134–149.
8. The literature on disease in the Americas is vast, including Alfred W. Crosby, *The Columbian Exchange: Biological and Cultural Consequences of 1492* (Westport, CT: Greenwood Publishers, 1972); Henry Dobyns, *Their Numbers Become Thinned: Native American Population Dynamics in Eastern North America* (Knoxville: University of Tennessee Press, 1983); Ann F. Ramenofsky, *Vectors of Death: The Archaeology of European Contact* (Albuquerque: University of New Mexico Press, 1987); Suzanne Alchon, *A Pest in the Land: New World Epidemics in a Global Perspective* (Albuquerque: University of New Mexico Press, 2003); and Robert Boyd, *The Coming of the Spirit of Pestilence: Introduced Infectious Diseases and Population Decline among Northwest Coast Indians, 1774–1874* (Seattle: University of Washington Press, 1999).
9. Emmanuel Le Roy Ladurie, *The Mind and Method of the Historian,* trans. Siân Reynolds and Ben Reynolds (Chicago: University of Chicago Press, 1981), 12.
10. On disease and depopulation in the Pacific islands, see *The Growth and Collapse of Pacific Island Societies: Archaeological and Demographic Perspectives,* ed. Patrick V. Kirch and Jean-Louis Rallu (Honolulu: University of Hawai'i Press, 2007); A. D. Cliff, P. Haggett, and M. R. Smallman-Raynor, *Island Epidemics* (New York: Oxford University Press, 1998); David E. Stannard, "Disease, Human Migration, and History," in *The Cambridge World History of Human Disease,* ed. K. F. Kiple (Cambridge: Cambridge University Press, 1993), 35–43; John Miles, *Infectious Diseases: Colonising the Pacific?* (Dunedin, NZ: University of Otago Press, 1997); David E. Stannard, *Before the Horror: The Population of Hawai'i on the Eve of Western Contact* (Honolulu: University of Hawai'i Press, 1989); O. A. Bushnell, *The Gifts of Civilization: Germs and Genocide in Hawai'i* (Honolulu: University of Hawai'i Press, 1983); and Alan Moorehead, *The Fatal Impact: An Account of the Invasion of the South Pacific* (New York: Harper and Row, 1966). Pacific "islander-oriented" scholars who comment on the effects of population decline include K. R. Howe, *The Loyalty Islands: A History of Culture Contact, 1840–1900* (Honolulu: University of Hawai'i Press, 1977); Howe, "The Fate

of the 'Savage' in Pacific Historiography," *New Zealand Journal of History* 11 (1977): 137–154; David Hanlon, *Upon a Stone Altar: A History of the Island of Pohnpei to 1890* (Honolulu: University of Hawai'i Press, 1988); and Lilikalā Kame'eleihiwa, *Native Land and Foreign Desires: Pehea Lā E Pono Ai? How Shall We Live in Harmony?* (Honolulu: Bishop Museum Press, 1992).

11. David S. Jones, "Virgin Soils Revisited," *William and Mary Quarterly* 60 (October 2003): 703–742.

12. The environment constitutes one of three components in "disease ecology," according to geographer Linda Newson. She writes: "Human diseases emerge from interactions between parasites, hosts, and their environments: no understanding of their origins, spread, and impact can be achieved if any of these three elements is excluded." See Linda A. Newson, "A Historical-Ecological Perspective on Epidemic Disease," in *Advances in Historical Ecology*, ed. William Balee (New York: Columbia University Press, 1998), 42.

13. On pre-contact health conditions, see Ramenofsky, *Vectors of Death*; O. A. Bushnell, "Hygiene and Sanitation Among the Ancient Hawaiians," *Hawai'i Historical Review* 2 (1966): 316–336; and Patrick Kirch, *On the Road of the Winds: An Archaeological History of the Pacific Islands* (Berkeley: University of California Press, 2000), 56–57. On different disease types and categories, see Leslie B. Marshall, "Disease Ecologies of Australia and Oceania"; and Stannard, "Disease, Human Migration, and History," 482–496, 35–43.

14. Mary Kawena Pukui, ed. *'Ōlelo No'eau: Hawaiian Proverbs and Poetical Sayings* (Honolulu: Bishop Museum Press, 1983), 211; and Joseph Keawe'aimoku Kaholokula, "Colonialism, Acculturation, and Depression among Kānaka Maoli of Hawai'i," in *Penina uliuli: Contemporary Challenges in Mental Health for Pacific Peoples*, ed. Philip Culbertson and Margaret Nelson Agee (Honolulu: University of Hawai'i Press, 2007), 181.

15. The British missionary John Williams, describing a disease introduced on the island of Rarotonga in the late 1820s, left one of the best examples of this thinking: "The natives said that the pestilence was brought to their island by a vessel which visited them just before it commenced its ravages. It is certainly a fact, which cannot be controverted, that most of the diseases which have raged in the islands during my residence there, have been introduced by ships; and what renders this fact remarkable is, that there might be no appearance of disease among the crew of the ship that conveyed this destructive importation, and that the infection was not communicated by any criminal conduct on the part of the crew, but by the common contact of ordinary intercourse." John Williams, *A Narrative of Missionary Enterprises in the South Sea Islands* (London: J. Snow, 1837), 281–282.

16. The missionary William Wyatt Gill further translates this phrase to "I am suffering from sickness brought by some ship." See Gill, *Life in the Southern Isles: or, Scenes and Incidents in the South Pacific and New Guinea* (London: Religious Tract Society, 1876), 106.

17. Boyd, *Coming of the Spirit of Pestilence*, 54.

18. Samuel M. Kamakau, *Ka Po'e Kahiko: The People of Old* (Honolulu: University of Hawai'i Press, 1964), 109.

19. August Hirsch, *Handbook of Historical and Geographical Pathology*, 3 vols. (London: New Sydenham Society, 1883 [1864]). On the development of nineteenth-century medical history, see Linda Nash, *Inescapable Ecologies: A History of Environment, Disease, and Knowledge* (Berkeley: University of California Press, 2006), 28–30; and Nicolaas A. Rupke, "Humboldtian Medicine," *Medical History* 40 (July 1996): 293–310.

20. Hirsch, *Handbook of Historical and Geographical Pathology*, vol. 2: 74.

21. These "gifts" were not limited to diseases, but also included transfers of flora and fauna as well as material economies. See Bushnell, *Gifts of Civilization*, 1–23; and Alfred W. Crosby, *Ecological Imperialism: The Biological Expansion of Europe, 900–1900* (New York: Cambridge University Press, 1986), 217–268. For a nuanced approach to colonial medicine in New Zealand, see Toeolesulusulu Damon Salesa, "'The Power of the Physician': Doctors and the 'Dying Maori' in Early Colonial New Zealand," *Health and History* 3 (2001): 13–40.

22. Elizabeth A. Fenn, *Pox Americana: The Great Smallpox Epidemic of 1775–82* (New York: Hill and Wang, 2001); and Boyd, *Coming of the Spirit of Pestilence*.

23. On smallpox and the Northwest Coast, see Cole Harris, "Voices of Disaster: Smallpox around the Strait of Georgia in 1782," *Ethnohistory* 41 (Fall 1994): 591–626; Christon I. Archer, "Whose Scourge? Smallpox Epidemics on the Northwest Coast," in *Pacific Empires: Essays in Honour of Glyndwr Williams*, ed. Alan Frost and Jane Samson (Vancouver: University of British Columbia Press, 1999), 165–191; and Boyd, *Coming of the Spirit of Pestilence*, 21–60.
24. William Charley, "The First White Man among the Klikitats," cited in Boyd, *Coming of the Spirit of Pestilence*, 115.
25. William Shaler, *Journal of a Voyage between China and the North-Western Coast of America, Made in 1804* (Philadelphia, 1808), 152. For a parallel account on disease and starvation in Russian Alaska, see Ivan Veniaminov, *Notes on the Islands of the Unalashka District*, trans. Lydia T. Black and R. H. Geoghegan, ed. Richard A. Pierce (Kingston, ON: Limestone Press, 1984 [1840]), 257–258.
26. Clerke to Banks, August 1, 1776, *Journals*, vol. 3, pt. 2: 1514. On his departure from prison, see Richard Hough, *Captain James Cook* (New York: W. W. Norton, 1994), 286.
27. Hough, *Captain James Cook*, 275.
28. Anonymous, August 26, 1805, "Supercargo's Log of the Brig *Lydia*, 1804–1807," Western Americana Collection, Beinecke Rare Book and Manuscript Library, Yale University. I am grateful to Jennifer Staver for bringing this source to my attention.
29. William Reynolds, *The Private Journal of William Reynolds, United States Exploring Expedition, 1838–1842*, ed. Nathaniel Philbrick and Thomas Philbrick (New York: Penguin Books, 2004), 119.
30. On the *taupou* system and the broader anthropological debate over Samoan sexual mores, see Paul Shankman, "The History of Samoan Sexual Conduct and the Mead-Freeman Controversy," *American Anthropologist* 98 (September 1996): 555–567; and Jeanette Marie Mageo, *Theorizing Self in Samoa: Emotions, Genders, and Sexualities* (Ann Arbor: University of Michigan Press, 1998).
31. Reynolds, *Private Journal*, 119. Emphasis in original.
32. Ibid.
33. David A. Chappell, "Shipboard Relations between Pacific Island Women and Euroamerican Men, 1767–1887," *Journal of Pacific History* 27 (December 1992): 131–149.
34. Shaler, *Journal of a Voyage*, 171.
35. David Samwell, *Some Account of a Voyage to South Seas in 1776–1778*; in Beaglehole, *Journals*, vol. 3, pt. 2: 1083.
36. William Ellis, *Authentic Narrative of a Voyage Performed by Captain Cook and Captain Clerke, 1776–1780* (London: G. Robinson, 1783), 152.
37. Edmond Le Netrel, *Voyage of the Héros: Around the World with Duhaut-Cilly in the Years 1826, 1827, 1828 & 1829*, trans. Blanche Collet Wagner (Los Angeles: Glen Dawson, 1951), 172.
38. *News from New Cythera: A Report of Bougainville's Voyage 1766–1769*, ed. L. Davis Hammond (Minneapolis: University of Minnesota Press, 1970), 44.
39. J[ean]. F[rançois]. G[alaup]. La Pérouse, *A Voyage round the World in the Years 1785, 1786, 1787, and 1788* (London: J. Johnson, 1798), vol. 2: 18, emphasis added.
40. Nicholas Thomas, *Cook: The Extraordinary Voyages of Captain James Cook* (New York: Walker, 2003), 159.
41. Bougainville, quoted in Salmond, *Trial of the Cannibal Dog*, 52.
42. Marshall Sahlins, *Islands of History* (Chicago: University of Chicago Press, 1985), 26.
43. Caroline Ralston, "Changes in the Lives of Ordinary Women in Early Post-Contact Hawai'i," in *Family and Gender in the Pacific: Domestic Contradictions and the Colonial Impact*, ed. Margaret Jolly and Martha Macintyre (Cambridge: Cambridge University Press, 1989), 64.
44. Ibid., 64. Jocelyn Linnekin has a similar analysis: "In their early liaisons with foreigners Hawaiian women aggressively used their sexual favors in hopes of acquiring higher status for their children and a secure future for themselves." Linnekin, *Sacred Queens and Women of Consequence: Rank, Gender, and Colonialism in the Hawaiian Islands* (Ann Arbor: University of Michigan Press, 1990), 55.
45. Reynolds, *Private Journal of William Reynolds*, 110.

46. On prostitution in Hawai'i, see Jennifer Fish Kashay, "Competing Imperialisms and Hawaiian Authority: The Cannonading of Lāhainā in 1827," *Pacific Historical Review* 77 (August 2008): 369–390.

47. Kirsten Fischer makes a similar point about interracial sex in her study of colonial North Carolina. See Fischer, *Suspect Relations: Sex, Race, and Resistance in Colonial North Carolina* (Ithaca, NY: Cornell University Press, 2002), 56–57. On sexual relations in colonial settings, see Ann Laura Stoler, *Race and the Education of Desire: Foucault's History of Sexuality and the Colonial Order of Things* (Durham: University of North Carolina Press, 1995).

48. Hammond, *News from New Cythera*, 43–44.

49. George Forster, *Observations Made during a Voyage round the World*, ed. Nicholas Thomas, Harriet Guest, and Michael Dettelbach (Honolulu: University of Hawai'i Press, 1996), 260. William Wales rejected Forster's account of these relations; see Wales, *Remarks on Mr. Forster's Account of Captain Cook's Last Voyage round the World* (London: J. Nourse, 1778).

50. Winston L. Sarafian, "Smallpox Strikes the Aleuts," *Alaska Journal* 7 (Winter 1977): 46–49; Jackson, "Epidemic Disease and Population Decline in the Baja California Missions," 308–346; and Warren L. Cook, *Flood Tide of Empire: Spain and the Pacific Northwest, 1543–1819* (New Haven, CT: Yale University Press, 1973), 309–310.

51. For slavery on the Northwest Coast, see Leland Donald, *Aboriginal Slavery on the Northwest Coast of North America* (Berkeley: University of California Press, 1997); and Boyd, *Coming of the Spirit of Pestilence*, 65–66.

52. José Mariano Moziño, *Noticias de Nutka, An Account of Nootka Sound in 1792*, ed. Iris Higbie Wilson (Seattle: University of Washington Press, 1970), 43.

53. Daniel W. Clayton, *Islands of Truth: The Imperial Fashioning of Vancouver Island* (Vancouver: University of British Columbia Press, 2000), 111.

54. Shaler, *Journal of a Voyage*, 42.

55. Caroline Ralston, "Polyandry, 'Pollution', 'Prostitution': The Problems of Eurocentrism and Androcentrism in Polynesian Studies," in *Crossing Boundaries: Feminisms and the Critique of Knowledges*, ed. Barbara Caine, E. A. Grosz, and Marie de Lepervanche (Sydney: Allen and Unwin, 1988), 79.

56. The similarities of these diseases caused some European voyagers to initially believe syphilis preexisted in the region—at least until they witnessed the impact of the real disease on natives. On the significance of yaws in the Hawaiian Islands, see Seth Archer, "A Hawaiian Shatter Zone," paper presented at the 18th Annual Conference of the Omohundro Institute of Early American History and Culture, June 16, 2012.

57. The above discussion is drawn from epidemiological and medical history sources, including *The Myth of Syphilis: The Natural History of Treponematosis in North America*, ed. Mary Lucas Powell and Della Collins Cook (Gainesville: University of Florida Press, 2005), 9–53; Miles, *Infectious Diseases*, 53–62; Deborah Hayden, *Pox: Genius, Madness, and the Mysteries of Syphilis* (New York: Basic Books, 2003), 28–42; Claude Quétel, *The History of Syphilis*, trans. Judith Braddock and Brian Pike (Baltimore: Johns Hopkins University Press, 1992); Boyd, *Coming of the Spirit of Pestilence*, 61–83; Stannard, *Before the Horror*, 69–77; and Alfred Crosby, "The Early History of Syphilis: A Reappraisal," *American Anthropologist* 71 (April 1969): 218–227.

58. On treatments, see Hayden, *Pox*, 43–50; and Quetel, *History of Syphilis*, 90–93.

59. On pre- and post-contact herbal medicine in Polynesia, see Paul Alan Cox, "Polynesian Herbal Medicine," in *Islands, Plants, and Polynesians: An Introduction to Polynesian Ethnobotany*, ed. Paul Alan Cox and Sandra A. Banack (Portland, OR: Dioscorides Press, 1991), 147–168. On indigenous medicine in California, see S. F. Cook, "Disease of the Indians of Lower California in the Eighteenth Century," *California and Western Medicine* 43 (December 1935): 432–434.

60. On the three main theories for the origins of syphilis and doubt about the Columbian theory, see Powell and Cook, *Myth of Syphilis*, 31–39; C. Meyer et al., "Syphilis 2001: A Palaeopathological Reappraisal," *HOMO* 53 (2002): 41–42; and Brenda J. Baker and George J. Armelagos, "The Origin and Antiquity of Syphilis," *Current Anthropology* 29 (December 1988): 703–720. For an assessment of the "Unitarian theory" and how non-venereal yaws could have transformed to venereal syphilis, see S. J. Watts, *Epidemics and*

History: Disease, Power, and Imperialism (New Haven, CT: Yale University Press, 1997), 126–127. According to one recent study, a fourth "alternative theory" holds that syphilis may have originated in tropical Africa and was carried back to Africa by European traders. See Frank B. Livingstone, "On the Origins of Syphilis: An Alternative Approach," *Current Anthropology* 32 (December 1991): 587–590.

61. Desiderius Erasmus, quoted in Alfred Crosby, "The Early History of Syphilis: A Reappraisal," *American Anthropologist* 71 (April 1969): 218. For one assessment of its worldwide spread, see Watts, *Epidemics and History*, 122–165.

62. Crosby, "Early History of Syphilis," 218.

63. M. Rollin, MD, "Dissertation on the Inhabitants of Easter Island and the Island of Mowee," quoted in David E. Stannard, "Disease and Infertility: A New Look at the Demographic Collapse of Native Populations in the Wake of Western Contact," *Journal of American Studies* 24 (December 1990): 329–330.

64. *A Voyage to the North West Side of America: The Journals of James Colnett, 1786–89*, ed. Robert Galois (Vancouver: UBC Press, 2004), 186.

65. Ibid., 200.

66. Clerke to Banks, November 23, 1776; in Beaglehole, *Journals*, vol. 3, pt. 2: 1518.

67. On eighteenth-century treatments, see Hayden, *Pox*, 43–50; and Quétel, *History of Syphilis*, 90–93.

68. William Bayly, in Beaglehole, *Journals*, vol. 3, pt. 1: 233.

69. Stannard, *Before the Horror*, 70; and Norma McArthur, *Island Populations of the Pacific* (Canberra: Australian National University Press, 1967), 244. Cook blamed the outbreak of venereal disorders among his sailors on Tahitian women and presumed those women received the disease during the previous year from French sailors under the command of Louis Antoine de Bougainville. The French ultimately blamed either Cook's crew or that of the British ship *Dolphin*, which arrived in Tahiti just prior to Bougainville.

70. Beaglehole, *Journals*, vol. 3, pt. 1: 265, 276. For a detailed discussion of these events, see O. Bushnell, *Gifts of Civilization*, 135–141. Cook gave one known syphilitic, William Bradeley, two dozen lashes for sleeping with Hawaiian women.

71. Beaglehole, *Journals*, vol. 3, pt. 1: 474. William Ellis, the *Discovery* surgeon's second mate, also confirmed the spread across the islands. See William Ellis, *An Authentic Narrative of a Voyage* (London, 1783), 73–74.

72. Beaglehole, *Journals*, vol. 3, pt. 1: 474.

73. "Log of Edward Riou," quoted in Beaglehole, *Journals*, vol. 3, pt. 1: 474–475.

74. Beaglehole, *Journals*, vol. 3, pt. 1: 474, 576.

75. Stannard, "Disease and Infertility," 330. Stannard cites specific accounts by George Vancouver, Ivan Krusenstern, and Isaac Iselin for the period between 1788 and 1806.

76. David M.K.I. Liu, "Eao luau a hualima: Writing and Rewriting the Body and the Nation," *Californian Journal of Health Promotion* (December 2005): 73–75; and Kameʻeleihiwa, *Native Land and Foreign Desires*, 25–33.

77. For an example of an elite Hawaiian visiting a traditional healer in the 1870s, see Alfons L. Korn and Mary Kawena Pukui, "News from Molokai: The Letters of Peter Young Kaeo (Kekuakalani) to Queen Emma, 1873–1876," *Pacific Historical Review* 32 (February 1963): 20–23.

78. David Malo, "On the Decrease of Population on the Hawaiian Islands," *Hawaiian Spectator* 2 (April 1839): 128, 130.

79. On Hawaiian missionary physicians, see Seth Archer, "Remedial Agents: Missionary Physicians and the Depopulation of Hawaiʻi," *Pacific Historical Review* 79 (November 2010): 513–544. For the very low rates of infant mortality in the pre-contact period, see Stannard, *Before the Horror*, 64.

80. Artemas Bishop, "An Inquiry into the Causes of Decrease of the Population of the Sandwich Islands," *Hawaiian Spectator* 1 (1838): 61.

81. For a survey of mission census records, see Stannard, "Disease and Infertility," 331–333. Also see Robert C. Schmitt, *The Missionary Censuses of Hawaiʻi* (Honolulu: Bishop Museum, 1973).

82. Linnekin, *Sacred Queens and Women of Consequence*, 210.

83. Patrick Kirch's demographic study of the Kahikinui district of Maui, south of where Cook landed on his second visit, shows steep population declines by the early 1800s alongside a very low child to adult population ratio. Kirch estimates that between one-sixth and one-eighth of the contact population still remained by the 1830s, although he notes that outmigration, drought, and other conditions affected the population decline. He writes: "This is indeed a veritable population collapse, even if short of a true decimation in the literal sense." Patrick V. Kirch, "Paleodemography in Kahikinui, Maui: An Archaeological Approach," in Kirch and Rallu, *Growth and Collapse of Pacific Island Societies*, 105.

84. Jean-Louis Rallu, "Pre- and Post-Contact Population in Island Polynesia," in Kirch and Rallu, *Growth and Collapse of Pacific Island Societies*, 15–34.

85. Greg Dening, *Islands and Beaches: Discourse on a Silent Land: Marquesas 1774–1880* (Honolulu: University of Hawai'i Press, 1980), 184; and Rallu, "Pre- and Post-Contact Population in Island Polynesia," 30–31.

86. Linda A. Newson, "Conquest, Pestilence, and Demographic Collapse in the Early Spanish Philippines," *Journal of Historical Geography* 32 (January 2006): 3–20.

87. Veniaminov, "Notes on the Islands of the Unalaska District," 258.

88. The possible candidates are bejels, yaws, and pinta. The most likely disease was bejels (or something "identical" to the bejels found elsewhere in the world). See J. El Molto, Bruce M. Rothschild, Robert Woods, and Christine Rothschild, "Unique Aspects of West Coast Treponematosis," *Chungara* 32 (July 2000), http://www.scielo.cl/scielo.php?pid=S0717-73562000000200004&;script=sci_arttext accessed November 10, 2009.

89. Phillip L. Walker, Patricia M. Lambert, Michael Schultz, and Jon M. Erlandson, "The Evolution of Treponemal Disease in the Santa Barbara Channel Area of Southern California," in Powell and Cook, *Myth of Syphilis*, 281–305.

90. Ibid., 296.

91. Lynn Gamble suggests this as one possibility, noting that Chumash social disruption and violence observed by Juan Crespí in 1769 could have resulted from disease spread. See Gamble, *The Chumash World at European Contact: Power, Trade, and Feasting Among Complex Hunter-Gatherers* (Berkeley: University of California Press, 2008), 272–273.

92. Ibid., 267–269.

93. On the encounters with explorers prior to Spanish colonization, see Kent G. Lightfoot and William S. Simmons, "Culture Contact in Protohistoric California: Social Contexts of Native and European Encounters," *Journal of California and Great Basin Anthropology* 20 (1998): 138–169. On the possibility of disease introductions prior to Spanish settlement, see Preston, "Portents of Plague from California's Protohistoric Period," *Ethnohistory* 49 (Winter 2002): 69–121; and Jon M. Erlandson et al., "Dates, Demography, and Disease: Cultural Contacts and Possible Evidence for Old World Epidemics among the Protohistoric Island Chumash," *Pacific Coast Archaeological Society Quarterly* 37 (Summer 2001): 11–26.

94. Jean-Baptiste Chappe D'Auterouche, *A Voyage to California* (London: Edward and Charles Dilly, 1778), 70; and Iris Engstrand, *Royal Officer in Baja California, 1768–1770, Joaquín Velázquez de León* (Los Angeles: Dawson's Book Shop, 1976), 81. On population estimates, see Sherburne Cook, "Extent and Significance of Disease among the Indians of Baja California from 1697 to 1773," *Ibero-Americana* 2 (1937): 25–30; Steven W. Hackel, *Children of Coyote, Missionaries of Saint Francis: Indian-Spanish Relations in Colonial California, 1769–1850* (Chapel Hill: University of North Carolina Press, 2005), 40; and Jackson, "Epidemic Disease and Population Decline," 330–336.

95. For one accounting of baptisms and burials during the 1790s, see Jackson, "Epidemic Disease and Population Decline," 332.

96. In addition to sources on disease introduction cited above, see Homer Aschmann, *The Central Desert of Baja California: Demography and Ecology* (Berkeley: University of California Press, 1959), 181–268.

97. Cook, "Extent and Significance of Disease among the Indians of Baja California," 23.

98. Ibid., 29. Soldiers from Sinaloa brought in to quell the revolt may have contributed to the spread of syphilis.

99. Engstrand, *Royal Officer in Baja California*, 51–52.

100. Pedro Fages, "Informe del Estado de las Misiones," (1786), quoted in Fr. Zephyrin Engelhardt, O.F.M., *The Missions and Missionaries of California* (San Francisco: James H. Barry, 1908), vol. 1: 530. Fages appeared to show little sympathy for the Indians' plight. He wrote: "All the Indians of [Baja] California are alike lazy, incapable, and stupid. Their only aspiration is to rove about the country" (529).

101. Moziño, *Noticias de Nutka*, 44.

102. For an excellent account of Spanish observations and the effects of venereal syphilis and gonorrhea, see James Sandos, *Converting California: Indians and Franciscans in the Missions* (New Haven, CT: Yale University Press, 2004), 111–127. Sandos credits Sherburne F. Cook with dating the introduction of venereal disease to the Gaspar de Portolá expedition of 1769. See Cook's classic work, *The Conflict between the California Indians and White Civilization* (Berkeley: University of California Press, 1943).

103. On the possibility of some Franciscans carrying venereal disease, see Sandos, *Converting California*, 122–124.

104. José Longinos Martínez, *Journal of José Longinos Martínez: Notes and Observations of the Naturalist of the Botanical Expedition in Old and New California and the South Coast, 1791–1792*, ed. Lesley Byrd Simpson (San Francisco: John Howell Books, 1961), 44.

105. On the "dual revolutions," see Hackel, *Children of Coyote, Missionaries of Saint Francis*, 65–123.

106. Ibid., 123.

107. These infant mortality rates, according to Hackel, were generally consistent with the "most unhealthful communities in Europe through the seventeenth and eighteenth centuries." And yet the childhood mortality rate was nearly four times the rate of England in the period. Ibid., 103–107.

108. George Peard, *To the Pacific and Arctic with Beechey: The Journal of Lieutenant George Peard of H.M.S. "Blossom" 1825–1828*, ed. Barry M. Gough (Cambridge, UK: Hakluyt Society, 1973), 178. Peard held a dim view of the Spanish missionaries, whom he viewed in general as "ignorant and bigoted" (179).

109. Steven Hackel, "Beyond Virgin Soil: Impaired Fertility in the Indian Population of Spanish California," paper presented at Social Science History Association meeting, Long Beach, 2009. Hackel is careful to point out that these figures account for adult sterility as well as the death of one parent after marriage.

110. Nataly Zappia, "The Interior World: Trading and Raiding in Native California," PhD dissertation, University of California, Santa Cruz, 2008.

111. Shaler, *Journal of a Voyage*, 42; and Richard A. Gould, "Tolowa," in *Handbook of North American Indians*, ed. Robert F. Heizer (Washington, DC: Smithsonian Institution, 1978), vol. 8: 128–135.

112. Kent G. Lightfoot, *Indians, Missionaries, and Merchants: The Legacy of Colonial Encounters on the California Frontiers* (Berkeley: University of California Press, 2005), 158.

113. William Bauer Jr., "Native Californians in the Nineteenth Century," in *A Companion to California History*, ed. William Deverell and David Igler (Oxford, UK: Wiley-Blackwell, 2008), 196.

114. Charles Wilkes, *Narrative of the United States Exploring Expedition during the Years 1838, 1839, 1840, 1841, 1842* (Philadelphia: Lea and Blanchard, 1845), vol. 1: 325. Also see Reynolds, *Private Journal of William Reynolds*, 85–86.

115. Andrew Cheyne, *The Trading Voyages of Andrew Cheyne, 1841–1844*, ed. Dorothy Shineberg (Honolulu: University of Hawai'i Press, 1971), 257, 271–272.

116. Cliff et al., *Island Epidemics*, 176; and Robert C. Schmitt and Eleanor C. Nordyke, "Death in Hawai'i: The Epidemics of 1848–49," *Hawaiian Journal of History* 35 (Winter 2001): 2.

117. On the Pacific's western rim, Chinese medical texts establish smallpox outbreaks more than three thousand years ago, but the Americas and the eastern Pacific rim had to await the sixteenth-century arrival of Europeans and their viral agents. Smallpox raged through the Aztec and Inca empires during the 1520s. Peru, stretching two thousand miles along the Pacific shoreline, received repeated introductions from the 1520s onward and these outbreaks nearly decimated the coastal and Andean populations. On the general history of smallpox and its specific role in the Americas, see Donald R. Hopkins, *The Greatest Killer:*

Smallpox in History (Chicago: University of Chicago Press, 2002); Watts, *Epidemics and History*, 84–93; and Fenn, *Pox Americana*.

118. Vaccination was employed by Spanish and Russian physicians on some indigenous groups within a decade of Edward Jenner's 1796 discovery of the vaccination process. Knowledge of this new medical intervention traveled fast. For example, a Spanish medical expedition headed by Francisco Xavier de Balmis circumnavigated the globe between 1803 and 1806, vaccinating more than one hundred thousand people around the Spanish empire. Balmis kept the vaccine alive throughout the three-year journey by using a succession of young boys as carriers. On the Balmis expedition, see J. Antonio Aldrete, "Smallpox Vaccination in the Early 19th Century Using Live Carriers: The Travels of Francisco Xavier de Balmis," *Southern Medical Journal* 97 (April 2004): 375–378; and Rosemary Keupper Valle, "Prevention of Smallpox in Alta California during the Franciscan Mission Period (1769–1833)," *California Medicine* 119 (July 1973): 73–77.

119. Robert T. Boyd's comprehensive study of this outbreak suggests three possible introduction routes: a Russian origin through Kamchatka, where smallpox was prevalent in the late 1760s; a Spanish origin through trading vessels between 1774 and 1776; and a Great Plains–Columbia River route in the late 1770s. Elizabeth Fenn's work on smallpox during the 1770s and 1780s favors the Great Plains–Columbia River route. See Boyd, *Coming of the Spirit of Pestilence*, 21–45; and Fenn, *Pox Americana*, 226–232.

120. The British trader Nathaniel Portlock described the results for a coastal Tlingit village in 1787:

> On the beach was a large boat, and three of a smaller size; the large boat capable of holding thirty persons, and the others about ten people each. From this circumstance I expected to have seen a numerous tribe, and was quite surprised when I found that it consisted only of three men, three women, the same number of girls, two boys about twelve years old, and two infants. . . . I observed the oldest of the men to be very much marked with the small-pox, as was a girl who appeared to be about fourteen years old. The old man . . . told me that the distemper carried off great numbers of the inhabitants, and that he himself had lost ten children by it; he had ten strokes tattooed on one of his arms, which I understood were marks for the number of children he had lost. I did not observe any of the children under ten or twelve years of age that were marked; therefore I have great reason to suppose that the disorder raged a little more than that number of years ago.

Particularly interesting in Portlock's account is the relationship he drew between diseased bodies, the passing of time, and mourning. He read the pock-marked bodies as calendars of the disease's outbreak, and similarly, the "old man" had tattooed his own arm in memory and mourning of his ten lost children. See Nathaniel Portlock, *A Voyage round the World; But More Particularly to the North-West Coast of America: Performed in the Years 1785, 1786, 1787, and 1788* (London: John Stockdale, 1789), 270–271.

121. For Paty's abridged journal, see John Paty, "Journal of Captain John Paty, 1807–1868," *California Historical Society Quarterly* 14 (December 1935): 291–346.

122. Ibid., 322.

123. William Heath Davis, *Sixty Years in California: A History of Events and Life in California* (San Francisco: A. J. Leary, 1889), 373.

124. Paty, "Journal of Captain John Paty," 323.

125. Charles Wilson to George Bennet, November 9, 1841; in *South Sea Letters*, London Missionary Society, Mitchell Library, Sydney, Australia.

126. Cliff et al., *Island Epidemics*, 140–141.

127. Especially in the early 1800s, a ship's captain would have been entirely responsible for seeking out vaccination material for sailors. The American captain Amasa Delano, for instance, sailed from Hawai'i to Canton in 1801 with five Hawaiians on board the *Perseverance*. "When I arrived at Canton my first concern for these people was to have them inoculated for the smallpox. I had in my previous voyages seen many of these poor creatures die with that loathsome and fatal disorder in that place," he wrote. See Amasa Delano, *A Narrative of Voyages and Travels in the Northern and Southern Hemispheres: Comprising Three Voyages round the World; Together with a Voyage of Survey and Discovery, in the Pacific Ocean and Oriental Islands* (Boston: E. G. House, 1818), 393.

128. David A. Chappell, *Double Ghosts: Oceanian Voyagers on Euroamerican Ships* (Armonk, NY: M. E. Sharpe, 1997), 161. Chappell's sample group included 250 of the "best documented" indigenous shipboard workers. For examples of Hawaiian crewmembers succumbing to smallpox, see Mary Brewster, *"She Was a Sister Sailor": The Whaling Journals of Mary Brewster, 1845–1851,* ed. Joan Druett. (Mystic, CT: Mystic Seaport Museum, 1992), 350; and "Edward Vischer's First Visit to California," edited and translated by Erwin Gustav Gudde, *California Historical Society Quarterly* 19 (September 1940): 195.

129. Robert Boyd discusses the use of this term by Yakutat Tlingits in his book *The Coming of the Spirit of Pestilence,* 54.

130. Ibid., 93.

131. This description comes from William Charley, a Klikitat storyteller, in "The First White Man among the Klickitats," Lucullus McWhorter Collection, Holland Library, Washington State University, Pullman; cited in Boyd, *Coming of the Spirit of Pestilence,* 114.

132. The *Owyhee,* owned by the Boston partnership Marshall & Wildes, was a constant presence in the Pacific during the 1820s. It first appeared in Alta California in 1822 and traded along the Northwest Coast at least once prior to this voyage. It took sea otter pelts to Canton in 1826. See Adele Ogden, "California Trading Vessels, 1786–1847," Bancroft Library, University of California, Berkeley.

133. On Captain John Dominis and the activities of the *Owyhee* drawn from the ship's log book, see F. W. Howay, "The Brig Owhyhee in the Columbia, 1829–30," *Oregon Historical Society Quarterly* 35 (March 1934): 12.

134. Boyd, *Coming of the Spirit of Pestilence,* appendix 2, 289–293.

135. Ibid., 86.

136. David Douglas, "Second Journey to the Northwestern Parts of the Continent of North America during the Years 1829–'30–'31–'32–'33," *Oregon Historical Society Quarterly* 6 (September 1905): 292. Italics in original.

137. Ogden's and McKay's statements are both cited in Boyd, *Coming of the Spirit of Pestilence,* 86–87.

138. Douglas, "Second Journey to the Northwestern Parts," 303, 306–307, 308.

139. Boyd, *Coming of the Spirit of Pestilence,* 84.

140. Some traditional practices proved especially risky. Boyd describes how Indian women would gather wapato bulbs (a root vegetable) in the swampy areas of the lower Columbia, especially near the initial epicenter of Sauvie Island. Indians also camped during the summer months in the open air by rivers or lakes, precisely where the mosquitoes bred. See Boyd, *Coming of the Spirit of Pestilence,* 108–109.

141. Ibid., 90.

142. "Big-Tail," in John R. Swanton, *Haida Texts and Myths* (Washington, DC: Smithsonian Institution, Bureau of American Ethnology, 1905), 299; cited in Boyd, *Coming of the Spirit of Pestilence,* 54.

143. William Charley's oral history is quoted at length in Boyd, *Coming of the Spirit of Pestilence,* 114–115.

144. William Tolmie, *The Journals of William Fraser Tolmie: Physician and Fur Trader* (Vancouver, BC: Mitchell Press, 1963), 238.

145. Jason Lee, quoted in Boyd, *Coming of the Spirit of Pestilence,* 113.

146. Boyd, *Coming of the Spirit of Pestilence,* 46, 112–113.

147. Le Roy Ladurie, *Mind and Method of the Historian,* 13.

148. Epeli Hau'ofa, "Our Sea of Islands," *Contemporary Pacific* (Spring 1994): 155.

Chapter 3

1. For Timofei Tarakanov's narrative of these events, see *The Wreck of the Sv. Nikolai,* ed. Kenneth Owens (Lincoln: University of Nebraska Press, 2001), 41, 42–43. For a more complete treatment of Tarakanov, see Kenneth Owens, "Frontiersman for the Tsar: Timofei Tarakanov and the Expansion of Russian America," *Montana* 56 (Autumn 2006): 3–21. Aleksandr A. Baranov of the Russian-American Company dispatched the *Sv. Nikolai* to search for hunting grounds and study the possibility of establishing a Russian trading fort

in present-day Oregon. For Baranov's intentions, see "Instructions from Aleksandr A. Baranov to his Assistant, Ivan A. Kuskov, Regarding the Dispatch of a Hunting Party to the Coast of Spanish California," October 14, 1808, in *The Russian American Colonies: To Siberia and Russian America, Three Centuries of Russian Eastward Expansion, 1798–1867*, ed. Basil Dmytryshyn, E.A.P. Crownhart-Vaughan, and Thomas Vaughan (Portland: Oregon Historical Society, 1989), vol. 3: 165–174. On the *Tamana*, see "Journal and Logbook of John T. Hudson, 1805–1807," Huntington Library, San Marino.

2. Owens, *Wreck of the Sv. Nikolai*, 44.

3. Ibid. Tarakanov's account derives from two sources: a rough diary he kept during the two-year-long ordeal, and the later reassemblage of those events by Tarakanov and the famous Russian naval captain Vasilii M. Golovnin. From these sources derived the 1822 serial "Krushenie sudna Sv. Nikolai" ("The Wreck of the *Sv. Nikolai*"). On the publication history of the narrative, see Owens, *Wreck of the Sv. Nikolai*, 13–14.

4. Ibid., 44, 45.

5. According to I. C. Campbell, "The moments when different cultures first came into contact were occasions of wonder and uncertainty, full of dramatic potential." In fact, he argues, such moments "elicited forms of behavior that might reasonably be described as not being part of the normal cultural expressions of the parties involved." See I. C. Campbell, "The Culture of Culture Contact: Refractions from Polynesia," *Journal of World History* 14 (March 2003): 63, 64, 66. These moments of "encounter" also continued on well after first meetings, writes Greg Dening: "Encounters, according to the prejudice of our established histories of them, are short, sudden, and violent. In fact, encounters are slow, drawn out. They belong to the *longue durée* of living." Greg Dening, "Deep Times, Deep Spaces: Civilizing the Sea," in *Sea Changes: Historicizing the Ocean*, ed. Bernhard Klein and Gesa Mackenthus (New York: Routledge, 2004), 27. See also Malama Meleisea and Penelope Schoeffel, "Discovering Outsiders," in *The Cambridge History of the Pacific Islanders*, ed. Donald Denoon (Cambridge: Cambridge University Press, 1997), 120.

6. For various treatments of captivity, see Linda Colley, *Captives: Britain, Empire, and the World, 1600–1850* (New York: Anchor Books, 2002); June Namias, *White Captives: Gender and Ethnicity on the American Frontier* (Chapel Hill: University of North Carolina Press, 1995); Leland Donald, *Aboriginal Slavery on the Northwest Coast of North America* (Berkeley: University of California Press, 1997); Robert H. Ruby and John A. Brown, *Indian Slavery in the Pacific Northwest* (Spokane, WA: Arthur H. Clark, 1993); and John Demos, *The Unredeemed Captive: A Family Story from Early America* (New York: Vintage, 1995). For indigenous practices of captivity in the Southwest borderlands, see James F. Brooks, *Captives and Cousins: Slavery, Kinship, and Community in the Southwest Borderlands* (Chapel Hill: University of North Carolina Press, 2002); and Ned Blackhawk, *Violence over the Land: Indians and Empires in the Early American West* (Cambridge, MA: Harvard University Press, 2006).

7. For the Russian practice of captivity, see Ilya Vinkovetsky, *Russian America: An Overseas Colony of a Continental Empire, 1804–1867* (New York: Oxford University Press, 2011), 121–126; and Gwenn A. Miller, *Kodiak Kreol: Communities of Empire in Early Russian America* (Ithaca, NY: Cornell University Press, 2010), 39–48. The first Japanese person to visit Europe was a man named Dembei, taken captive by native Kamchatka fishermen in the late 1600s and subsequently brought by the Cossack explorer Vladimir Atlasov to meet Peter the Great in 1701. See Walter A. McDougall, *Let the Sea Make a Noise: A History of the North Pacific from Magellan to MacArthur* (New York: Basic Books, 1993), 57.

8. In this context, "imperial" may indicate the formal representatives of European empires, or merely those who sailed under a particular flag but, as Ann Laura Stoler contends, "might have refused *imperial* or *colonial* as applicable adjectives" for their intended business. See Stoler, *Carnal Knowledge and Imperial Power: Race and the Intimate in Colonial Rule*, 2nd ed. (Berkeley: University of California Press, 2010), xx. Emphasis in original.

9. *Voyages of the "Columbia" to the Northwest Coast, 1787–1790 and 1790–1793*, ed. Frederic W. Howay (New York: Da Capo Press, 1969).

10. John Hoskins, "The Narrative of a Voyage, etc.," in ibid., 186.

11. Ibid., 185.

12. On Chief Wickaninish and power relations among Nuu-chah-nulth chiefs, see Daniel W. Clayton, *Islands of Truth: The Imperial Fashioning of Vancouver Island* (Vancouver: University of British Columbia Press, 2000), 154–156; and Yvonne Marshall, "A Political History of the Nuu-chah-nulth: A Case Study of the Mowachaht and Muchalaht tribes," PhD dissertation, Department of Archaeology, Simon Fraser University, 1993.

13. Hoskins, "Narrative of a Voyage, etc.," 186–187.

14. Clayton, *Islands of Truth*, 129.

15. In November 1790, the British *Argonaut*'s Captain James Colnett (who had sailed with Cook's second voyage and found himself briefly taken captive by the Spanish at Nootka Sound in 1789) made hostages of Tootiscoosettle and another lesser chief, demanding the return of the bodies of six sailors whose launch had crashed on a ledge of rocks. Without the bodies, Colnett threatened, he "would kill those two Chiefs and every native he could find." Hoskins, "Narrative of a Voyage, etc.," 188.

16. John Boit, "Remarks on the Ship Columbia's Voyage from Boston," in Howay, *Voyages of the "Columbia" to the Northwest Coast*, 370.

17. Hoskins, "Narrative of a Voyage, etc.," 186.

18. David A. Chappell, *Double Ghosts: Oceanian Voyagers on Euroamerican Ships* (Armonk, NY: M. E. Sharpe, 1997), 101.

19. Howay, *Voyages of the "Columbia,"* x–xiii. On Atu, see Howay, "Early Relations with the Pacific Northwest," in *The Hawaiian Islands*, ed. Albert P. Taylor (Ann Arbor: University of Michigan Press, 2005), 14–17.

20. Howay, "Early Relations with the Pacific Northwest," 14.

21. "Officers and Crew of the Columbia," in Howay, *Voyages of the "Columbia,"* 447.

22. Hoskins, "Narrative of a Voyage, etc.," 185.

23. *Joseph Ingraham's Journal of the Brigantine Hope on a Voyage to the Northwest Coast of North America, 1790–92*, ed. Mark D. Kaplanoff (Barre, MA: Imprint Society, 1971), 76.

24. Kaplanoff, *Joseph Ingraham's Journal*, 233.

25. Howay, "Early Relations with the Pacific Northwest," 16.

26. F. W. Howay, *A List of Trading Vessels in the Maritime Fur Trade, 1785–1825* (Kingston, ON: Limestone Press, 1973), 13–18.

27. *A New Vancouver Journal on the Discovery of Puget Sound*, ed. Edmond S. Meany (Seattle: n.p., 1915), 33. On this journal's provenance and likelihood of James Bell as author, see ii–iii.

28. George Vancouver, *A Voyage of Discovery to the North Pacific Ocean and around the World, 1791–1795*, ed. W. Kaye Lamb (London: Hakluyt Society, 1984 [1798]), vol. 3: 894–895, 893.

29. Vancouver's extremely lengthy account of returning the young women to Hawai'i appears to be a response to US reports that the British were selling Hawaiian captives on the Northwest Coast. See ibid., vol. 3: 839.

30. Kaplanoff, *Joseph Ingraham's Journal*, 109–110, 207.

31. "The Voyage of Juan Rodriquez Cabrillo up the Pacific Coast," in *New American World: A Documentary History of North America to 1612*, ed. David B. Quinn (New York: Arno Press, 1979), vol. 1: 453, 455, 460. On other Spanish expeditions to California and hostage-taking, see Kent Lightfoot and William Simmons, "Culture Contact in Protohistoric California: Social Contexts of Native and European Encounters," *Journal of California and Great Basin Anthropology* 20 (1998): 138–169.

32. Joyce Chaplin argues that captives were most frequently utilized as pilots because of their supposed knowledge of ports or coastlines unknown to Europeans. See Chaplin, "Atlantic Antislavery and Pacific Navigation," paper presented at The New Maritime History: A Conference in Honor of Robert C. Ritchie, Huntington Library, San Marino, November 11, 2011.

33. The following examples are drawn from Cook's journals as well as two recent studies of his voyages: Anne Salmond, *The Trial of the Cannibal Dog: The Remarkable Story of Captain Cook's Encounters in the South Seas* (New Haven, CT: Yale University Press, 2003); and Nicholas Thomas, *Cook: The Extraordinary Voyages of Captain James Cook* (New York: Walker, 2003).

34. Greg Dening, "The Hegemony of Laughter: Purea's Theatre," in *Pacific Empires: Essays in Honour of Glyndwr Williams*, ed. Alan Frost and Jane Samson (Vancouver: University of British Columbia Press, 1999), 143.

35. James Cook, *The Journals of Captain James Cook on His Voyages of Discovery*, ed. J. C. Beaglehole (London: Hakluyt Society, 1955–1974), vol. 3, pt 1: 530. Emphasis added.

36. Anne Salmond, *Two Worlds: First Meetings Between Maori and Europeans, 1642–1772* (Honolulu: University of Hawai'i Press, 1996), 87.

37. Ibid., 88.

38. Ibid.

39. Charles Ryskamp, *Boswell: The Ominous Years* (New York: McGraw-Hill, 1963), 341.

40. Anya Zilberstein, "Objects of Distant Exchange: The Northwest Coast, Early America, and the Global Imagination," *William and Mary Quarterly*, 3rd series, 64 (July 2007): 589–618.

41. The least mediated version of Jewitt's captivity is John Jewitt, *A Journal, Kept at Nootka Sound by John Rodgers Jewitt, One of the Surviving Crew of the Ship Boston, John Salter, Commander, Who Was Massacred on the 22d of March, 1803; Interspersed with Some Account of the Natives, Their Manners and Customs* (Boston: n.p., 1807). Both subsequent "narratives" were highly embellished by their editors and should be used with caution. See John Jewitt, *A Narrative of the Adventures and Sufferings of John R. Jewitt*, ed. Richard Alsop (Middletown, CT: S. Richards, 1815); and John Jewitt, *The Captive of Nootka: Or the Adventures of John R. Jewitt*, ed. Samuel Griswold Goodrich (New York: J. P. Peaslee, 1835). I appreciate Anya Zilberstein's advice on these various publications.

42. Jewitt, *Journal*, 3.

43. Ibid., 4.

44. Ibid., 23.

45. Ibid., 30–31. One apparent witness to the marriage later told an early white settler of Jewitt "courting" and "finally abducting the charming daughter of the Ahousaht chief," though Jewitt maintained he was forced into the union by Maquinna. See Gilbert Malcolm Sproat, *Scenes and Studies of Savage Life* (London: Smith, Elder, 1868), 6.

46. According to Jewitt, Maquinna "gave me liberty to dispense with the girl that he had forced me to take for a partner, which I did with great satisfaction." Jewitt, *Journal*, 40.

47. Jewitt, *Narrative*, 120–124.

48. Jewitt, *Journal*, 29; and Jewitt, *Narrative*, 124.

49. Jewitt, *Journal*, 47–48.

50. Cole Harris, "Social Power and Cultural Change in Pre-Colonial British Columbia," *BC Studies* 115/116 (Autumn/Winter 1997/1998): 73. Also see Zilberstein, "Objects of Distant Exchange."

51. Clayton, *Islands of Truth*, 154–155.

52. Jewitt, *Journal*, 20. The best evaluation of these tensions as an ecological crisis is Zilberstein, "Objects of Distant Exchange," 606–608.

53. Jewitt, *Narrative*, 24–25. Jewitt's *Journal* confirms the outline of this story, but the *Narrative* provides better detail, especially as it relates to Maquinna's reaction.

54. Clayton, *Island of Truth*, 23.

55. Owens, "Frontiersman for the Tsar," 3–8.

56. Owens, *Wreck of the Sv. Nikolai*, 45.

57. Ben Hobucket, "The Narrative of Ben Hobucket," in ibid., 69. Sometime between 1905 and 1909 Hobucket had this story transcribed by the Indian agent and ethnologist Albert Reagan. Hobucket at the time was gravely ill with tuberculosis, a disease that had killed his ancestors for at least three generations. See Owens, *Wreck of the Sv. Nikolai*, 15–17.

58. "Narrative of Ben Hobucket," 70. On the Quileute, see George A. Pettitt, *The Quileute of La Push, 1775–1945* (Berkeley: University of California Press, 1950).

59. "Narrative of Ben Hobucket," 72–73.

60. For example, some Maori referred to European voyagers as "shallow-rooting shellfish" in contrast to their own people as "the shellfish of deep waters." Shallow-rooting shellfish moved with the tide and lacked a sense of place. The Maori chiefs may have also meant simply shallow or unsubstantial. Some terms for outsiders evoked the varying degrees of alarm sparked by the foreigners' alien appearance and sudden arrival. Samoans and Tongans,

according to one source, called the newcomers *papālagi* or "sky bursters," in order to account for the ships that appeared on the horizon as if they had burst through the sky. For these terms, see Anne Salmond, "Kidnapped: Tuki and Huri's Involuntary Visit to Norfolk Island in 1793," in *From Maps to Metaphors: The Pacific World of George Vancouver*, ed. Robin Fisher and Hugh Johnston (Vancouver: University of British Columbia Press, 1993), 192; and Meleisea and Schoeffel, "Discovering Outsiders," 119.

61. "Narrative of Ben Hobucket," 73.
62. Namias, *White Captives*, especially 84–115.
63. Owens, *Wreck of the Sv. Nikolai*, 53.
64. Ibid., 59.
65. Ibid.
66. On this expression in a Pacific context, see I. C. Campbell, *Gone Native in Polynesia: Captivity Narratives and Experiences from the South Pacific* (Westport, CT: Greenwood Press, 1998).
67. Richard Pierce, *Russian America: A Biographical Dictionary* (Kingston, ON: Limestone Press, 1990), 24; and Owens, *Wreck of the Sv. Nikolai*, v.
68. On McKay (or MacKay), see Warren L. Cook, *Flood Tide of Empire: Spain and the Pacific Northwest, 1543–1819* (New Haven, CT: Yale University Press, 1973), 102–103; and Owens, *Wreck of the Sv. Nikolai*, 24.
69. Jewitt, *Narrative*, 124.
70. Owens, *Wreck of the Sv. Nikolai*, 64.
71. Owens, "Frontiersman for the Tsar," 4.
72. Richard A. Pierce, *Russia's Hawaiian Adventure, 1815–1818* (Berkeley: University of California Press, 1965).
73. Owens, "Frontiersman for the Tsar," 17–20.
74. Hobucket, "Narrative of Ben Hobucket," 69.
75. Hobucket's narrative also indicates the wanderers' evil intent. "Some years later a large vessel anchored in Quillayute Bay with the avowed purpose of enticing Indians on board to capture them and take them as slaves," he said. But fortunately for the Quileute, a native woman on board the ship warned them off. According to Hobucket, that woman turned out to be the Aleut captive they had taken from the *Sv. Nikolai*. See ibid., 73.
76. In Alta California, for instance, a level of sexual violence marked the Spanish social relations with mission and non-mission Indian women. In 1772, Father Luís Jayme recorded "continuous outrages" committed by Spanish soldiers against Kumeyaay women attached to Mission San Diego, including at least two different incidences of gang rape. This incident was hardly out of the ordinary in Alta California, and it also speaks to the broader context of unfree indigenous populations in the Spanish Americas. See Albert L. Hurtado, *Intimate Frontiers: Sex, Gender, and Culture in Old California* (Albuquerque: University of New Mexico Press, 1999), 13. On sexual violence in Alta California, see Miroslava Chavez-Garcia, *Negotiating Conquest: Gender and Power in California, 1770–1880* (Tucson: University of Arizona Press, 2004); and James A. Sandos, *Converting California: Indians and Franciscans in the Missions* (New Haven, CT: Yale University Press, 2004).
77. According to historian Robin Fisher, "Prostitution for economic gain was something that the Indians learned from the European." Robin Fisher, *Contact and Conflict: Indian-European Relations in British Columbia, 1774–1890* (Vancouver: University of British Columbia Press, 1977), 19. On indigenous slavery, see William Christie MacLeod, "Economic Aspects of Indigenous American Slavery," *American Anthropologist* 30 (October 1928): 632–650. On Northwest Coast slavery, see Ruby and Brown, *Indian Slavery on the Northwest Coast*; and Donald, *Aboriginal Slavery on the Northwest Coast*.
78. David Samwell, in Cook, *Journals of Captain James Cook*, vol. 4, 1094–1095.
79. Robert Boyd examines these different accounts in *The Coming of the Spirit of Pestilence: Introduced Infectious Diseases and Population Decline among Northwest Coast Indians, 1774–1874* (Seattle: University of Washington Press, 1999), 65.
80. Alejandro Malaspina, *The Malaspina Expedition, 1789–1794: Journal of the Voyage by Alejandro Malaspina*, ed. Andrew David et al. (London: Hakluyt Society, 2001–2004), vol. 2: 110.

81. Ibid.
82. Alejandro Malaspina, *Viaje político-científico alrededor del mundo por las Corbetas Descubi-erta y Atrevida, al mando de los capitanes de navio D. Alejandro Malaspina y D. José Bustamante y Guerra desde 1789 a 1794*, ed. Pedro Novo y Colson (Madrid: Impr. de la viuda é hijos de Abienzo, 1885), 347.
83. Malaspina, *Malaspina Expedition*, vol. 2: 114.
84. Ibid., 105–106.

Chapter 4

1. Mary Brewster, *"She Was a Sister Sailor": The Whaling Journals of Mary Brewster, 1845–1851*, ed. Joan Druett (Mystic, CT: Mystic Seaport Museum, 1992), 317; hereafter cited as Brewster, *Journals*. I am indebted to Joan Druett's deeply researched and richly annotated edition of Mary Brewster's journals, which in addition to Druett's other works, go well beyond spotlighting the mere presence of "sister sailors" on nineteenth-century Pacific voyages. See also Druett, *Hen Frigates: The Wives of Merchant Captains under Sail* (New York: Simon and Schuster, 1998); Druett, *Petticoat Whalers: Whaling Wives at Sea, 1820–1920* (Auckland: Collins, 1991); and Druett, *Rough Medicine: Surgeons at Sea in the Age of Sail* (New York: Routledge, 2001). Mary Brewster's original journals are kept at the G. W. Blunt White Library, Mystic Seaport Museum, Connecticut.
2. John T. Perkins, *John T. Perkins' Journal at Sea, 1845* (Mystic, CT: Marine Historical Association, 1943), 142. For another example of crewmen's superstitions about a captain's wife being on board a whaleship, see Charles Goodall, "Log of a Whaler's Voyage from New Bedford into the Pacific and Back, 1843–1846," December 27, 1844, unpublished journal, Huntington Library, San Marino.
3. October 6, 1846, *Whalemen's Shipping List* (New Bedford, MA).
4. Perkins, *Journal at Sea*, 145, 146, 149.
5. Brewster, *Journals*, 90–91. Emphasis in original.
6. Ibid., 116; Prentice Mulford, *Prentice Mulford's Story: Life by Land and Sea* (New York: F. J. Needham, 1889), 73.
7. Mark Twain, *Roughing It* (Hartford, CT: American Publishing, 1872): 448; and Brewster, *Journals*, 163.
8. Barnard L. Colby, *Whaling Captains of New London County, Connecticut: For Oil and Buggy Whips* (Mystic, CT: Mystic Seaport Museum, 1990), 45, 47; see also Brewster, *Journals*, 177.
9. Brewster, *Journals*, 177.
10. The secondary literature on different components of the marine mammals hunt is vast. For a global perspective on the fur trade as part of early modern resource exploitation, see John F. Richards, *The Unending Frontier: An Environmental History of the Early Modern World* (Berkeley: University of California Press, 2003), 463–616. On the indigenous and Russian hunters of Alaska and the Arctic, see John R. Bockstoce, *Furs and Frontiers in the Far North: The Contest among Native and Foreign Nations for the Bering Strait Fur Trade* (New Haven, CT: Yale University Press, 2009); and Ryan Jones, "Empire of Extinction: Nature and Natural History in the Russian North Pacific, 1739–1799," PhD dissertation, Columbia University, 2008. On sea otters and seals, see Briton Cooper Busch, *The War against the Seals: A History of the North American Seal Industry* (Kingston, ON: McGill-Queen's University Press, 1985); and Jim Hardee, "Soft Gold: Animal Skins and the Early Economy of California," in *Studies in Pacific History: Economics, Politics, and Migration*, ed. Dennis O. Flynn, Arturo Giráldez, and James Sobredo (Aldershop, UK: Ashgate, 2002), 23–39. For whaling and the gray whale in particular, see Margaret S. Creighton, *Rites and Passages: The Experience of American Whaling, 1830–1870* (Cambridge: Cambridge University Press, 1995); David A. Henderson, *Men & Whales at Scammon's Lagoon* (Los Angeles: Dawson's Book Shop, 1972); and Lance E. Davis, Robert E. Gallman, and Karin Gleiter, *In Pursuit of Leviathan: Technology, Institutions, Productivity, and Profits in American Whaling, 1816–1906* (Chicago: University of Chicago Press, 1997). The most useful published primary sources on whaling remains Charles R. Scammon, *The Marine Mammals of the Northwest Coast of*

North America (San Francisco: John H. Carmany, 1874); and Alexander Starbuck, *History of the American Whale Fishery from its Earliest Inception to 1876* (Waltham, MA: n.p., 1878).

11. In terms of whaling, the Makah of the Northwest Coast may have been the most notable hunters, although other groups also pursued whales. The Makah primarily caught "se-whow" (gray whales) from their long dugout canoes. According to historian Josh Reid, "a [Makah] whaler harpooned his prey several times, bleeding it to death with a lance amidst 'great fountains of crimson spray.' In extreme cases, whalers leapt onto harpooned whales who took too long to die. They held onto the lines connecting the whale to the canoe while stabbing the leviathan to dispatch it." Northwest indigenous whaling communities might capture up to a dozen whales in any given year, sufficient for their subsistence and trade economies but holding no discernible impact for the Pacific's whale population. See Joshua Leonard Reid, "'The Sea Is My Country': The Maritime World of the Makah: An Indigenous Borderlands People," PhD dissertation, University of California, Davis, 2009, 219.

12. William Cronon, *Nature's Metropolis: Chicago and the Great West* (New York: W. W. Norton, 1991), 340.

13. Lewis Coolidge, *Lewis Coolidge and the Voyage of the Amethyst, 1806–1811*, ed. Evabeth Miller Kienast and John Phillip Felt (Columbia: University of South Carolina Press, 2009), 19.

14. Georg Steller, "Journal of His Sea Voyage," in F. A. Golder, *Bering's Voyages: An Account of the Efforts of the Russians to Determine the Relations of Asia and America* (New York: American Geographical Society, 1925), vol. 2: 220.

15. For the first British description of this trade at Kiakhta and Mai-mai-ch'eng, see William Coxe, *Account of the Russian Discoveries between Asia and America* (London: J. Nichols, 1780), 211–243; see also Bockstoce, *Furs and Frontiers*, 104–110. For estimates of sea otters taken prior to 1800, see Ryan Jones, "Sea Otters and Savages in the Russian Empire: The Billings Expedition, 1785–1793," *Journal of Maritime Research* (December 2006), www.jmr.nmm.ac.uk/server/show/ConJmrArticle.217, accessed April 28, 2010; Karl W. Kenyon, *The Sea Otter in the Eastern Pacific Ocean* (Washington, DC: US Bureau of Sport Fisheries and Wildlife, 1969), 136; and Busch, *War against the Seals*, 6–7. On the western Pacific origins of the otter trade, see Richard Ravalli, "Soft Gold and the Pacific Frontier: Geopolitics and Environment in the Sea Otter Trade," PhD dissertation, University of California, Merced, 2009.

16. P. A. Tikhmenev, *A History of the Russian American Company*, trans. Richard A. Pierce and Alton S. Donnelly (Seattle: University of Washington Press, 1978 [1861–1863]), 201–204.

17. Ryan Tucker Jones, "A 'Havoc Made among Them': Animals, Empire, and Extinction in the Russian North Pacific, 1741–1810," *Environmental History* 16 (September 2011): 585–609; and Martin Sauer, *An Account of a Geographical and Astronomical Expedition to the Northern Parts of Russia* (London: T. Cadell, 1802), 161, 166.

18. On sea otter ecology and behavior, see Kenyon, *Sea Otter in the Eastern Pacific Ocean*; M. L. Reidman and J. A. Estes, *The Sea Otter* (Enhydra lutris): *Behavior, Ecology, and Natural History* (Washington, DC: Fish and Wildlife Service, 1990); and Scammon, *Marine Mammals*, 168–175.

19. Kenyon, *Sea Otter in the Eastern Pacific Ocean*, 216.

20. William Sturgis, "The Northwest Fur Trade," *Hunt's Merchants' Magazine* 14 (1846): 534; reprinted in *Fur Traders from New England: The Boston Men in the North Pacific, 1787–1800*, ed. Briton C. Busch and Barry Gough (Spokane, WA: Arthur C. Clark, 1996).

21. Sauer, *Account*, 267; cited in Jones, "A 'Havoc Made among Them,'" 596. For a useful review of Russian-language literature on Russian America, see Andrei V. Grinëv, "A Brief Survey of the Russian Historiography of Russian America of Recent Years," trans. Richard L. Bland, *Pacific Historical Review* 79 (May 2010): 265–278.

22. J[ean]. F[rançois]. G[alaup]. La Pérouse, *A Voyage round the World in the Years 1785, 1786, 1787, and 1788* (London: J. Johnson, 1798), vol. 1: 189–190; and G. T. Emmons, "Native Account of the Meeting between La Perouse and the Tlingit," *American Anthropologist* 13 (April–June 1911): 294–298.

23. La Pérouse, *Voyage round the World*, vol. 1: 190. On Vicente Vasadre y Vega and the Philippine Company, see Adele Ogden, *The California Sea Otter Trade, 1784–1848* (Berkeley: University of California Press, 1941), 15–21.

24. Odgen, *California Sea Otter Trade*, 18–31. William S. Laughlin estimates an 80 percent decline of Aleuts by the 1790s. See Laughlin, *Aleuts: Survivors of the Bering Land Bridge* (New York: Holt, Rinehart, and Winston, 1980), 21.

25. American traders averaged approximately 50 percent of the voyages to the Northwest Coast during the 1790s. In 1800 and thereafter, Americans constituted over 90 percent of the fur trading voyages. See F. W. Howay, *A List of Trading Vessels in the Maritime Fur Trade, 1785–1825* (Kingston, ON: Limestone Press, 1973).

26. "A Report by Imperial Russian Navy Lieutenant Nikolai A. Khvostov concerning the Condition of the Ships of the Russian American Company," June 1804, in *The Russian American Colonies: To Siberia and Russian America, Three Centuries of Russian Eastward Expansion, 1798–1867*, ed. Basil Dmytryshyn, E.A.P. Crownhart-Vaughan, and Thomas Vaughan (Portland: Oregon Historical Society, 1989), vol. 3: 47.

27. "Secret Instructions from the Main Administration of the Russian American Company in Irkutsk to Chief Administrator in America," April 18, 1802, in *Russian American Colonies*, vol. 3: 27.

28. Lydia T. Black, "The Nature of Evil: Of Whales and Sea Otters," in *Indians, Animals, and the Fur Trade: A Critique of Keepers of the Game*, ed. Shepard Krech III (Athens: University of Georgia Press, 1981), 109–147; Jones, "A 'Havoc Made among Them.'"

29. Black, "The Nature of Evil," 120. On the new labor requirements for Aleuts demanded by the RAC, see also Lydia T. Black, *Russians in Alaska, 1732–1867* (Fairbanks: University of Alaska Press, 2004), 127–132. Kenneth Owens suggests that Aleuts and Kodiak islanders (also called *Alutiiq*) had their own system of servants, war captives, and conscripted workers. These indentured or enslaved people were variously called "kalgas" or "kaiurs." Personal correspondence with Kenneth Owens, July 1, 2010. For similar circumstances in Siberian and North American hunters, see Yuri Slezkine, *Arctic Mirrors: Russia and the Small Peoples of the North* (Ithaca, NY: Cornell University Press, 1994); and Arthur Ray, *Indians and the Fur Trade: Their Role as Trappers, Hunters, and Middlemen in the Lands Southwest of Hudson Bay* (Toronto: University of Toronto Press, 1974), 117–136.

30. Ivan Veniaminov, *Notes on the Islands of the Unalaska District*, trans. L. T. Black and R. H. Geoghegan, ed. R. A. Pierce (Kingston, ON: Limestone Press, 1984), 192.

31. Jonathan Winship, quoted in Thomas Vaughan, *Soft Gold: The Fur Trade & Cultural Exchange on the Northwest Coast of America* (Portland: Oregon Historical Society, 1982), 22.

32. José Joaquín Arrillaga to José de Iturrigaray, March 2, 1804, Arrillaga Correspondence, 1794–1814, Bancroft Library, University of California, Berkeley.

33. William Dane Phelps, "Solid Men of Boston in the Northwest," in Busch and Gough, *Fur Traders from New England*, 45, 46, 47.

34. Georg Heinrich von Langsdorff, *Voyages and Travels in Various Parts of the World, during the Years, 1803, 1804, 1805, 1806, and 1807* (London: H. Colburn, 1813–1814), vol. 2: 180.

35. These figures come from Adele Odgen's comprehensive survey of numerous Russian and American sources. See Ogden, *California Sea Otter Trade*, 50.

36. Captain William Heath Davis was the father of William Heath Davis Jr., noted author of *Sixty Years in California* (1889). Only scattered references exist regarding Captain Davis's activities on the coast. See "Miscellaneous Papers" in the William Heath Davis Papers, 1840–1905, Bancroft Library, University of California, Berkeley.

37. Phelps, "Solid Men of Boston in the Northwest," 50–51.

38. George Nidever, *The Life and Adventures of George Nidever*, ed. William Henry Ellison (Berkeley: University of California Press, 1937), 45. This narrative was originally dictated in 1878 by Nidever to Edward F. Murray, one of Hubert Howe Bancroft's assistants. The original dictation is in the Bancroft Library.

39. Kenyon, *Sea Otter in the Eastern Pacific Ocean*, 41.

40. Ilya Vinkovetsky, "The Russian-American Company as a Colonial Contractor for the Russian Empire," in *Imperial Rule*, ed. Alexei Miller and Alfred J. Rieber (Budapest: Central European University Press, 2004), 171.

41. Vasiliĭ Nikolaevich Berkh, *A Chronological History of the Discovery of the Aleutian Islands, or, The Exploits of Russian Merchants: With A Supplement of Historical Data on the Fur Trade*, ed. Richard A. Pierce, trans. Dmitri Krenov (Kingston, ON: Limestone Press, 1974 [1823]), 93.

42. For estimates, see Jones, "Sea Otters and Savages in the Russian Empire"; Kenyon, *Sea Otter in the Eastern Pacific Ocean*, 136; and Busch, *War against the Seals*, 6–7.

43. Amasa Delano, *A Narrative of Voyages and Travels, in the Northern and Southern Hemispheres: Comprising Three Voyages round the World* (Boston: E. G. House, 1817), 306.

44. This number is an approximation. Busch estimates 5.2 million fur seals were killed in the southern parts of the Pacific Ocean, almost 60 percent taken on the Juan Fernández Islands. In the North Pacific, nearly as many fur seals were killed with the largest numbers taken on the Pribilof Islands. See Busch, *War against the Seals*, 36, 111; and Berkh, *Chronological History of the Discovery of the Aleutian Islands*, 93.

45. John Meares, *Voyages Made in the Years 1788 and 1789, from China to the North West Coast of America* (London: Logographic Press, 1790): 203; and Scammon, *Marine Mammals*, 119. For the many uses of seal byproducts by Makah Indians, see Reid, "'The Sea Is My Country,'" 220.

46. Aleksandr F. Kashevarov, "A Description of Hunting and Conservation in the Russian American Colonies," March 9, 1862, in Dmytryshyn, *Russian American Colonies*, 519.

47. Jones, "A 'Havoc Made among Them,'" 594.

48. William Dampier, *A New Voyage round the World: The Journal of an English Buccaneer* (London: Hummingbird Press, 1998 [1697]), 54.

49. In addition to Más Afuera and Más a Tierra (known today as Alejandro Selkirk and Robinson Crusoe, respectively), the two other islands are San Felix and San Ambrosio.

50. Busch, *War against the Seals*, 10–11.

51. Edmund Fanning, *Voyages and Discoveries in the South Seas, 1792–1832* (Salem, MA: Marine Research Society, 1924 [1833]), 79.

52. "Log of the *Minerva*," cited in Busch, *War against the Seals*, 16.

53. Busch, *War against the Seals*, 16.

54. Lewis Coolidge, "Journal of a Voyage Perform'd on the Ship *Amethyst*," in *Lewis Coolidge and the Voyage of the* Amethyst, ed. Evabeth Miller Kienast and John Phillip Felt (Columbia, SC: University of South Carolina Press, 2009), 7. Hereafter cited as Coolidge, "Journal." For additional material on the *Amethyst*, see "Typescript log of ship *Amethyst*, 1806–1811," Phillips Library, Peabody Museum, Salem.

55. Coolidge, "Journal," 1–2.

56. Coolidge's journal lists the names of forty crewmembers whom he remembered shipping out of Boston; seventeen of those forty he lists as "died" during the four-year voyage. See ibid., 62–63. The thirty-five thousand skins sold in Canton include those carried by a sister ship, the *Triumph*, of New Haven.

57. Ibid., 3.

58. Coolidge's journal is filled with recitations of poetry and references to landscape painters, reflecting a high level of education in his hometown of Boston. The editors of his journal, Evabeth Miller Kienast and John Phillip Felt, carefully tracked down his many references and misattributions. For instance, this line of poetry, which Coolidge attributes to Thomas Chatterton, was actually written by the Scottish poet James Beattie (1735–1803), in his 1774 poem, "The Minstrel; Or, The Progress of Genius—Book II."

59. One possible explanation would be the nutritional deficiency causing scurvy most affected those with preexisting conditions, such as venereal disease. The sailor Tim Connor offers a potential example.

60. Coolidge, "Journal," 21.

61. Ibid., 18. The owners sold their cargo as well as the *Amethyst* itself in Canton, and Coolidge returned to New York on the *Brum*.

62. Foster Rhea Dulles, *The Old China Trade* (Boston: Houghton Mifflin, 1930), 106, 210.

63. On recovery and endangered status, see: http://www.nmfs.noaa.gov/pr/species/mammals/pinnipeds/guadalupefurseal.htm, accessed June 9, 2010.

64. Coolidge, "Journal," 11. This line of verse comes from Ann Ward Radcliffe's *The Mysteries of Udolpho* (London: G. G. and J. Robinson, 1794).

65. Reuben Delano, *Wanderings and Adventures of Reuben Delano: Being a Narrative of Twelve Years Life in a Whale Ship!* (Boston: Redding, 1846); quoted in Brewster, *Journals*, 177, fn. 26.

66. John Adams to Secretary [John] Jay, August 25, 1785, *Works of John Adams, Second President of the United States*, ed. Charles Francis Adams (Boston: Little, Brown, 1853), vol. 8, 308–309.

67. Davis et al., *In Pursuit of Leviathan*, 364.

68. The best source on these industrial trends is ibid., 344–358.

69. Ibid., 18–19; Scammon, *Marine Mammals*, 212–215; and Starbuck, *History of the American Whale Fishery*, 700–702.

70. Davis et al., *In Pursuit of Leviathan*, 323.

71. Whaleships generally carried four boats (with often two more as replacements) labeled according to the position from which they were lowered into the water. The four boats were known as the Starboard boat (SB), Larboard boat (LB), Waist boat (WB), and Bow boat (BB). For an excellent source of information on all whaling terms, ship types, and equipment, see http://www.whalecraft.net/, accessed July 8, 2010.

72. Brewster, *Journals*, 179.

73. Ibid., 185–186. Druett's superb editing of Brewster's diary includes numerous incidences, such as this death, which are cross-referenced to contemporary periodicals. Wilkinson's death was reported in the *Friend* (Honolulu, HI) on April 1, 1847.

74. Brewster, *Journals*, 189.

75. *Friend* (Honolulu, HI), April 1, 1847.

76. Brewster, *Journals*, 187.

77. *Friend*, April 2, 1849.

78. Henderson, *Men & Whales*, 88; Mulford, *Prentice Mulford's Story*, 70; and J. Ross Browne, "Explorations in Lower California," *Harper's New Monthly Magazine* 37 (October 1868): 10. The French frigate *La Venus* and the British ship HMS *Sulphur* each surveyed Magdalena Bay in 1839. During the late 1830s some whalers also used Magdalena Bay as a safe haven to carry out repairs to their ships. See Henderson, *Whales & Men*, 82.

79. David S. Wilcove, *No Way Home: The Decline of the World's Great Animal Migrations* (Washington, DC: Island Press, 2008): 144; see also *The Gray Whale: Eschrichtius robustus*, ed. Mary Lou Jones, Steven L. Swartz, and Stephen Leatherwood (Orlando, FL: Academic Press, 1984).

80. Grays were also derisively called "scrag" whales for the "scragged" bumps receding down their back in place of a dorsal fin. The gray whale was a bottom-feeder, a "Mussel-digger" that reappeared on the ocean's surface covered in "dark ooze" from the ocean floor, which complemented the barnacle-like parasites and orange-colored lice covering their bodies— altogether a rather messy-looking creature, as whales go. Their blubber came off easily (hence another gruesome nickname, "Rip-sack"). In addition to these less attractive characteristics, the gray whales contained no baleen ("whalebone") worth putting in women's "rib-compressing" corsets. Whalebone was used for both its strength and flexibility in such items as umbrellas, whips, and the stays in women's corsets. One narrator said baleen was "bone to manufacture death-dealing, rib-compressing, liver-squeezing corsets from." See Mulford, *Prentice Mulford's Story*, 76.

81. Ibid., 75.

82. *Polynesian* (Honolulu), March 21, 1846; and *Whalemen's Shipping List*, June 16, 1846.

83. "Diary of Benjamin Boodry, *Arnolda*," cited in Creighton, *Rites and Passages*, 75.

84. L. H. Vermilyea, "Whaling Adventure in the Pacific," *California Nautical Magazine* 1 (1862–1863): 229.

85. Scammon, *Marine Mammals*, 29.

86. Ibid., 26–27, 268.

87. Dennis Wood, "Abstracts of Whaling Voyages" (5-volume manuscript, 1831–73), New Bedford Free Public Library, New Bedford, MA, vol. 2: 280, 652; *Whalemen's Shipping List*, June 16, 1846; and Brewster, *Journals*, 189.

88. Brewster, *Journals*, 186. Joan Druett states that Mary Brewster hereafter shunned Captain Hussey of the *J. E. Donnell*, suggesting he may have been the one delivering the woman to another boat.

89. Ibid., 181. Emphasis added.

90. Ibid., 179.

91. The son of the prominent American missionary Artemas Bishop, young Sereno Edwards Bishop took passage on the *William Lee* from Hawai'i to his boarding school in Rhode Island. Sereno Edwards Bishop, "Journal Kept in Passage from Sandwich Islands to Newport in ship William Lee, 1839–1840," Papers of Sereno Edwards Bishop, Huntington Library, San Marino.

92. Bishop, "Journal," February 1, 1840.

93. Mulford, *Prentice Mulford's Story*, 77.

94. Bishop, "Journal," February 6, 1840.

95. Brewster, *Journals*, 93–94.

96. Thomas Atkinson, "Journal and Memoirs of Thomas Atkinson, 1845–1882," unpublished manuscript, Huntington Library, San Marino, 28.

97. Couper, *Sailors and Traders*, 121; reported in the *Mercury* (Hobart, Tasmania), December 2, 1880.

98. Sailors' wages, called "lays," were a fixed percentage of the value of oil collected. See Davis et al., *In Pursuit of Leviathan*, 364.

99. Brewster, *Journals*, 188, 195.

100. Scammon, *Marine Mammals*, 266. The *Friend* (March 1, 1848) listed more than twenty ships at "Margarita Bay" (and many not counted) in early 1848.

101. *Friend*, March 1, 1848. During this season the whaleship *Hope* struck a rock and sank in the bay. No lives were lost and the ship's owners recovered $30,000 in insurance money. See *Whalemen's Shipping List*, May 2, 1848.

102. According to the *Whalemen's Shipping List* (June 27, 1848), these seven deserters only made it forty miles up the coastline, "where they were attacked and two of them killed." The *WSL* offered no further details.

103. *Whalemen's Shipping List*, March 12, 1850. On gold rush desertions from ships around the Pacific, see Davis et al., *In Pursuit of Leviathan*, 192–194; and Brewster, *Journals*, 169.

104. Brewster, *Journals*, 165. This report of war news arrived with Captain Samuel Jeffrey of the whaleship *Brookline*, which had just arrived from La Paz.

105. Ibid., 270.

106. Bruce Cumings, *Dominion from Sea to Sea: Pacific Ascendency and American Power* (New Haven, CT: Yale University Press, 2009), 74–78.

107. On Webster's anti-expansionist politics and support for economic imperialism, see his speeches "The Mexican War, March 1, 1847" and "Objects of the Mexican War, March 23, 1848," in *The Papers of Daniel Webster: Speeches and Formal Writings*, ed. Charles M. Wiltse (Hanover, NH: Published for Dartmouth College by the University Press of New England, 1988), 2: 435–476; and Robert V. Remini, *Daniel Webster: The Man and His Time* (New York: W. W. Norton, 1997), 574–580.

108. Daniel Webster to James K. Polk, May 14, 1846; Papers of John A. Rockwell, Huntington Library, San Marino. Four other New England congressmen cosigned this letter.

109. George McDuffie, quoted in John W. Foster, *A Century of American Diplomacy* (Boston: Houghton, Mifflin, 1901), 312.

110. On whaling as a stimulant to the entire economy, see Howard Kushner, "Hellships: Yankee Whaling along the Coast of Russian-America, 1835–1852," *New England Quarterly* 45 (March 1972): 81–95.

111. Herman Melville, *Moby-Dick; or, The Whale* (New York: Harper and Brothers, 1851), 306.

112. Davis et al., *In Pursuit of Leviathan*, 359.

113. Brewster, *Journals*, 337.

114. Davis et al., *In Pursuit of Leviathan*, 357–362; Scammon, *Marine Mammals*, 242–243; and Creighton, *Rites and Passages*, 35–37.

115. Jones et al., *Gray Whale*, 166–175; Henderson, *Men & Whales*, 175–179; and Wilcove, *No Way Home*, 145–147.

116. Scammon, *Marine Mammals*, 33.

117. Henderson, *Men & Whales*, 230. On whaling in the twentieth century, see J. N. Tonnessen and A. O. Johnsen, *A History of Modern Whaling*, trans. R. I. Christophersen (Berkeley: University of California Press, 1982).

Chapter 5

1. On the Marshall Islands and Kadu's background, see Julianne M. Walsh, "Imagining the Marshalls: Chiefs, Tradition, and the State on the Fringes of United States Empire," PhD dissertation, University of Hawai'i, 2003, 128–146.

2. Adelbert von Chamisso, *A Voyage around the World with the Romanzov Exploring Expedition in the Years 1815–1818 in the Brig Rurik, Captain Otto von Kotzebue,* trans. and ed. Henry Kratz (Honolulu: University of Hawai'i Press, 1986 [1836]), 159.

3. Ibid., 186.

4. Ibid., 69; Adelbert von Chamisso, "Remarks and Opinions, of the Naturalist of the Expedition," in Otto von Kotzebue, *A Voyage of Discovery: into the South Sea and Beering's Straits for the Purpose of Exploring a North-East Passage, Undertaken in the Years 1815–1818* (London, 1821), vol. 3: 168.

5. Anne Salmond, *Two Worlds: First Meetings between Maori and Europeans, 1642–1772* (Honolulu: University of Hawai'i Press, 1991), 87.

6. Naturalists, like the officers and crewmembers of European voyages, were overwhelmingly male. For brief accounts of women (often disguised as men) involved in scientific exploration, see Honore Forster, "Voyaging through Strange Seas: Four Women Travellers in the Pacific," *National Library of Australia News* (January 2000): 3–6; and Londa Schiebinger, *Plants and Empire: Colonial Bioprospecting in the Atlantic World* (Cambridge, MA: Harvard University Press, 2004), 46–51.

7. William Reynolds, *The Private Journal of William Reynolds, United States Exploring Expedition, 1838–1842,* ed. Nathaniel Philbrick and Thomas Philbrick (New York: Penguin Books, 2004), 13, 8. Italics in the original. Charles Wilkes, the commander of the US Exploring Expedition, used the term "Scientifics."

8. For a general introduction to European and American naturalists in the Pacific, see Jacques Brosse, *Great Voyages of Discovery: Circumnavigators and Scientists, 1764–1843,* trans. Stanley Hochman (New York: Facts on File Publications, 1983). On the role of scientific patrons, see Harry Liebersohn, *The Travelers' World: Europe to the Pacific* (Cambridge, MA: Harvard University Press, 2006); and David Mackay, *In the Wake of Cook: Exploration, Science and Empire* (London: Croom Helm, 1985). Two important volumes of collected essays on scientific exploration are *Darwin's Laboratory: Evolutionary Theory and Natural History in the Pacific,* ed. Roy MacLeod and Philip F. Rehbock (Honolulu: University of Hawai'i Press, 1994); and *Visions of Empire: Voyages, Botany, and Representations of Nature,* ed. David P. Miller and Peter H. Reill (Cambridge: Cambridge University Press, 1996). On the connection between imperial ventures and the development of environmental concerns, see Richard Grove, *Green Imperialism: Colonial Expansion, Tropical Island Edens, and the Origins of Environmentalism, 1600–1860* (Cambridge: Cambridge University Press, 1995); John F. Richards, *The Unending Frontier: An Environmental History of the Early Modern World* (Berkeley: University of California Press, 2003); and Aaron Sachs, *The Humboldt Current: Nineteenth-Century Exploration and the Roots of American Environmentalism* (New York: Viking, 2006). On natural history and the emergence of "ecology," see Donald Worster, *Nature's Economy: A History of Ecological Ideas* (New York: Cambridge University Press, 1994).

9. On the Seven Years' War and the global contest for power, see Paul W. Mapp's superb study, *The Elusive West and the Contest for Empire, 1713–1763* (Chapel Hill: University of North Carolina Press, 2011); and Fred Anderson, *Crucible of War: The Seven Years' War and the Fate of Empire in British North America* (New York: Vintage, 2001).

10. See the splendid works by Helen Rozwadowski for the interface of ocean science and cultural approaches to the seas; especially Rozwadowski, *Fathoming the Ocean: The Discovery and Exploration of the Deep Sea* (Cambridge, MA: Harvard University Press, 2005).

11. Mackay suggests the economic motivation gained speed with Cook's voyages: "By putting remote parts of the world within reach, Cook had facilitated the sort of imperial economic unity which these scientists almost by instinct envisaged." Mackay, *In the Wake of Cook,* 194.

12. Ryan Jones, "A 'Havoc Made among Them': Animals, Empire, and Extinction in the Russian North Pacific, 1741–1810." *Environmental History* 16 (September 2011): 587.

13. Anonymous [William Ellis], *An Authentic Narrative of a Voyage Performed by Captain Cook and Captain Clerke, in His Majesty's Ships Resolution and Discovery, during the Years 1776, 1777, 1778, 1779, and 1780* (Altenburg: Gottlob Emanuel Richter, 1788): 138–167.

14. Mackay, *In the Wake of Cook*, 41.

15. On the search for the Northwest Passage, see Glyn Williams, *Voyages of Delusion: The Quest for the Northwest Passage* (New Haven, CT: Yale University Press, 2002); and Peter Mancall, *Fatal Journey: The Final Expedition of Henry Hudson—A Tale of Mutiny and Murder in the Arctic* (New York: Basic Books, 2009).

16. Count Rumiantsev was frequently referred to as Romanzov. Lieutenant Kotzebue was the son of a famous German playwright, August von Kotzebue. On these two, see Kratz "Introduction" in Chamisso, *A Voyage Around the World*, xi–xii. On this expedition in the context of previous Russian maritime ventures, see Glynn Barratt, *Russia in Pacific Waters, 1715–1825* (Vancouver: University of British Columbia Press, 1981), 176–185.

17. Kotzebue, *Voyage of Discovery*, 10–11. For Kotzebue's assessment of the post–Napoleonic War political context, see pp. 7–9.

18. On artistic renderings of the Pacific as reflections of European civilization, see Harriet Guest, *Empire, Barbarism, and Civilisation: Captain Cook, William Hodges, and the Return to the Pacific* (Cambridge: Cambridge University Press, 2007).

19. On Eschscholtz's collections, see Richard G. Beidleman, *California's Frontier Naturalists* (Berkeley: University of California Press, 2006), 48–55.

20. On Chamisso, see Kratz, "Introduction," in Chamisso, *Voyage around the World*, xi–xxiv.

21. Chamisso, "Remarks and Opinions," in Kotzebue, *Voyage of Discovery*, vol. 2: 353, 354, 384, 398.

22. Ibid., vol. 3: 265.

23. Ibid., vol. 2: 404–405.

24. Ibid., vol. 3: 21, 24, 22. Chamisso continued: "History has decided on the revolution to which the United States of America owe their existence, their prosperity, their rapidly increasing population and power" (22).

25. Ibid., vol. 3: 42, 47, 43.

26. Ibid., vol. 3: 314–315. On the claims of earlier naturalists, see Ryan Tucker Jones, "Sea Otters and Savages in the Russian Empire: The Billings Expedition, 1785–1793," *Journal of Maritime Research* (December 2006): 106–121.

27. Barratt, *Russia in Pacific Waters*, 176–186.

28. Chamisso, *A Voyage around the World*, 198.

29. Ibid., 79. Kotzebue was also extremely ill at this time, spitting up blood and breathing erratically due to the cold.

30. Kotzebue, *Voyage of Discovery*, 7–11. On explorations for the Northwest and Northeast Passage, see Williams, *Voyages of Delusion*, 241–242, 276–278; and William J. Mills, *Exploring Polar Frontiers: A Historical Encyclopedia* (Santa Barbara, CA: ABC-CLIO, 2003), vol. 1: 366–368.

31. Brosse, *Great Voyages of Discovery*, 124–167.

32. According to Chamisso, Kotzebue's official account "did not conform to my expectations." Chamisso, *Voyage around the World*, 7.

33. Walsh, "Imagining the Marshalls," 129–130.

34. Chamisso, *Voyage around the World*, 136, 139, 129.

35. Chamisso continued this comment with the opinion that Kadu "understood . . . the connection [between] this unlimited intellectual curiosity [and] the knowledge upon which our superiority rested." Ibid., 161.

36. Ibid., 80–81, 161. Chamisso donated the skulls to the Berlin Anatomical Museum. On Kadu's possible fear that he had joined a voyage of cannibals, see p. 160.

37. Ibid., 119–120.

38. Ibid., 168, 352, 268.

39. Ibid., 102; Chamisso, "Remarks and Opinions," v. 3, 45; 47.

40. Publications in France from the *Héros*'s voyage include Auguste Bernard Duhaut-Cilly, *Voyage autour du monde, principalement à la Californie et aux Iles Sandwich, pendant les années 1826, 1827, 1828, et 1829*, 2 vols. (Paris, 1834–1835); Paul-Emile Botta, "Observations sur

les habitants des Iles Sandwich. Observations sur les habitans de la Californie. Observations diverses faites en mer," *Nouvelles annales des voyages* 22 (1831): 129–176; and Edmond Le Netrel, "Voyage autour du monde pendant les années 1826, 1827, 1828, 1829, par M. Duhautcilly commandant le navire *Le Héros*. Extraits du journal de M. Edmond Le Netrel, lieutenant à bord ce vaisseau," *Nouvelles annales des voyages* 15 (1830): 129–182. I have relied upon the three most recent English translations: Auguste Duhaut-Cilly, *A Voyage to California, the Sandwich Islands, and around the World in the Years 1826–1829*, trans. August Frugé and Neal Harlow (Berkeley: University of California Press, 1999); Paulo Emilio Botta, *Observations on the Inhabitants of California, 1827–1828*, trans. John Francis Bricca (Los Angeles: Glen Dawson, 1952); and Lt. Edmond Le Netrel, *Voyage of the Héros: Around the World with Duhaut-Cilly in the Years 1826, 1827, 1828, and 1829*, trans. Blanche Collet Wagner (Los Angeles: Glen Dawson, 1951).

41. On Rives and the circumstances of the voyage, see Alfons L. Korn, "Shadows of Destiny: A French Navigator's View of the Hawaiian Kingdom and Its Government in 1828," *Hawaiian Journal of History* 17 (1983): 1–39; and Edgar C. Knowlton Jr. "Paul-Emile Botta, Visitor to Hawai'i in 1828," *Hawaiian Journal of History* 18 (1984): 13–38.

42. Duhaut-Cilly, *Voyage*, 3; 79.

43. "Orders for the *Héros* expedition," quoted in Beidleman, *California's Frontier Naturalists*, 83.

44. In 1828 Rives left the voyage with orders by Duhaut-Cilly to bring a load of goods to the Northwest Coast and Sitka on the chartered brig *Waverly*. Rives instead directed the brig south to Mazatlan, where Mexican officials impounded the goods. Rives appears to have drifted into the interior and soon thereafter died of cholera. Relations between Rives and the other officers had turned sour almost immediately, certainly by the time Rives's servant attempted suicide on the ship in fear of punishment at Rives's hand for a minor offence. See Duhaut-Cilly, *Voyage*, 14–15.

45. Ibid., 49.

46. Ibid., 51, 61.

47. Botta, *Observations*, 16–17.

48. Duhaut-Cilly, *Voyage*, 65.

49. Le Netrel, *Voyage*, 24, 38.

50. Duhaut-Cilly, *Voyage*, 101.

51. Ibid., 101–102. This is certainly one of the earliest descriptions of a Native American "rabbit drive." On the widespread practice of rabbit drives in the late nineteenth-century American West, see William Deverell and David Igler, "The Abattoir of the Prairie," *Rethinking History* 4 (Fall 1999): 321–323.

52. Duhaut-Cilly, *Voyage*, 133; and Le Netrel, *Voyage*, 26.

53. Duhaut-Cilly, *Voyage*, 186, 128.

54. For a comparative colonial setting in which natural "abundance" was consistently noted, see William Cronon, *Changes in the Land: Indians, Colonists, and the Ecology of New England* (New York: Hill and Wang, 1983), 19–33.

55. Le Netrel, *Voyage*, 26.

56. Recent works by historians and anthropologists have developed this argument, countering previous portrayals of California Indians as unsophisticated managers of the land. See Kent Lightfoot and Otis Parrish, *California Indians and Their Environments: An Introduction* (Berkeley: University of California Press, 2009); and M. Kat Anderson, *Tending the Wild: Native American Knowledge and the Management of California's Natural Resources* (Berkeley: University of California Press, 2006).

57. Duhaut-Cilly, *Voyage*, 85, 153; and Le Netrel, *Voyage*, 46–47.

58. Le Netrel, *Voyage*, 36, 24, 44.

59. Duhaut-Cilly, *Voyage*, 153, 31.

60. Ibid., 153, 85, 80–82, 55.

61. Ibid., 168, 167.

62. Ibid., 168, 161, 137, 93–95, 79.

63. Frederick Stenn, "Paul Emile Botta—Assyriologist, Physician," *Journal of the American Medical Association* 174 (November 1969): 1651.

64. Botta, *Observations*, 3–7.

65. Ibid., 3.
66. Duhaut-Cilly, *Voyage*, 153.
67. See George Forster, *A Voyage round the World*, ed. Nicholas Thomas and Oliver Berghof, 2 vols. (Honolulu: University of Hawai'i Press, 2000); and Ryan Jones, "Sea Otters and Savages in the Enlightened Empire: The Billings Expedition, 1785–1793," *Journal for Maritime Research* (November 2006) at http://www.jmr.nmm.ac.uk/.
68. William Fraser Tolmie, *Diary*, March 28, 1833; William Fraser Tolmie Records, 1830–1883, British Columbia Archives, Victoria, Canada.
69. A. G. Harvey, "Meredith Gairdner: Doctor of Medicine," *British Columbia Historical Quarterly* 9 (April 1945): 91–92.
70. Meredith Gairdner, "Observations during a Voyage from England to Fort Vancouver, on the North-West Coast of America," *Edinburgh New Philosophical Journal* 16 (April 1834): 290, 299. The following year he published a second article on Hawai'i, "Physico-Geognostic Sketch of the Island of Oahu, One of the Sandwich Group," *Edinburgh New Philosophical Journal* 19 (1835): 1–14.
71. Tolmie, *Diary*, May 1, 1833; and Gairdner, "Observations," 302.
72. Gairdner to William Hooker, November 7, 1834; cited in Harvey, "Meredith Gairdner," 100.
73. Robert Boyd, *The Coming of the Spirit of Pestilence: Introduced Infectious Diseases and Population Decline among Northwest Coast Indians, 1774–1874* (Seattle: University of Washington Press, 1999), 84–115.
74. Gairdner, "Notes on the Geography of the Columbia River," *Journal of the Royal Geographical Society of London* 11 (1841): 250–257. The journal came to his mother following his death in 1837 and a colleague likely edited it for publication.
75. Ibid., 252–253.
76. Ibid., 253.
77. Ibid., 256.
78. Although no birth date records exist for Concomly, most scholars believe he was born in the 1760s. Some observers wrote his name as "Comcomly."
79. For William Clark's brief mention of Concomly, see *Original Journals of the Lewis and Clark Expedition, 1804–1806*, ed. Reuben Gold Thwaites (New York: Dodd, Mead, 1905), vol. 3: 238. Raven married Duncan McDougall around 1812, who left the Northwest Coast in 1817. She married Archibald McDonald in 1823 and died in childbirth two years later.
80. Gairdner to John Richardson, November 21, 1835; cited in A. G. Harvey, "Chief Concomly's Skull," *Oregon Historical Quarterly* 40 (June 1939): 166. On head-flattening and craniology, see Ann Fabian's marvelous study *The Skull Collectors: Race, Science, and America's Unburied Dead* (Chicago: University of Chicago Press, 2010), 47–76.
81. Gairdner to Hooker, November 19, 1835; cited in Harvey, "Meredith Gairdner," 102.
82. Gairdner to John Richardson, November 21, 1835; cited in Harvey, "Meredith Gairdner," 166.
83. Harvey, "Chief Concomly's Skull," 166–167. One of Gairdner's predecessors, Dr. John Scouler, narrowly escaped with his life after being caught by the Chinook with three skulls from a burial ground. Immediately following Gairdner's incident, the American John Townsend was discovered by HBC officials with a wrapped Chinook body. They forced him to return it to the grieving brother. See Fabian, *Skull Collectors*, 67–68.
84. Fabian, *Skull Collectors*, 46.
85. Gairdner to John Richardson, November 21, 1835; cited in Harvey, "Meredith Gairdner," 166.
86. Gairdner, "Observations during a Voyage," 302.

Chapter 6

1. William Reynolds, *The Private Journal of William Reynolds: United States Exploring Expedition, 1838–1842*, ed. Nathaniel Philbrick and Thomas Philbrick (New York: Penguin Books, 2004), 11.
2. Ibid., 259.

3. Ibid., 309.
4. Ibid., 316.
5. James D. Dana, *Geology* (New York: Geo. P. Putnam, 1849), 10. The digitized version of Dana's *Geology*, as well as the entire collection of US Ex. Ex. publications, can be viewed at http://www.sil.si.edu/digitalcollections/usexex/.
6. Ibid., 13. Dana made this statement in specific reference to linear island groups, but it applies to his geological theories in general.
7. On this theme of national expansion and the place of the Pacific and Asia, see Henry Nash Smith, *Virgin Land: The American West as Symbol and Myth* (Cambridge, MA: Harvard University Press, 1950), 19–34.
8. On the history of the United States Exploring Expedition, see Nathaniel Philbrick, *Sea of Glory: America's Voyage of Discovery, The U.S. Exploring Expedition, 1838–1842* (New York: Viking, 2003); William Stanton, *The Great United States Exploring Expedition* (Berkeley: University of California Press, 1975); Herman J. Viola and Carolyn Margolis, eds., *Magnificent Voyagers: The U.S. Exploring Expedition, 1838–1842* (Washington, DC: Smithsonian Institution Press, 1985); and Barry Alan Joyce, *The Shaping of American Ethnography: The Wilkes Exploring Expedition, 1838–1842* (Lincoln: University of Nebraska Press, 2001).
9. Also included among the scientific corps were the artists Alfred T. Agate and Joseph Drayton.
10. On scientific voyages in general and US employment of them in the mid-nineteenth century, see Helen M. Rozwadowski, *Fathoming the Ocean: The Discovery and Exploration of the Deep Sea* (Cambridge, MA: Harvard University Press, 2005), 46–62; and Michael L. Smith, *Pacific Visions: California Scientists and the Environment, 1850–1915* (New Haven, CT: Yale University Press, 1990), 12–16.
11. Philbrick, *Sea of Glory*, 331–333.
12. For all this material, see http://www.sil.si.edu/digitalcollections/usexex/index.htm.
13. These vessels included the flagship *Vincennes* (war sloop; 700 tons), *Peacock* (war sloop; 559 tons), *Porpoise* (brig; 224 tons), *Relief* (storeship; 468 tons), *Sea Gull* (tender; 110 tons), and *Flying Fish* (tender; 96 tons). Wilkes purchased the *Oregon* (brig, 250 tons) while at Astoria to replace the shipwrecked *Peacock*.
14. On Wilkes, see Philbrick, *Sea of Glory*; and Joye Leonhart, "Charles Wilkes: A Biography" and E. Jeffrey Stann, "Charles Wilkes as Diplomat," in Herman and Margolis, *Magnificent Voyagers*, 189–204, 205–226.
15. Reynolds, *Private Journal of William Reynolds*, 237.
16. On the court-martial charges, see Philbrick, *Sea of Glory*, 303–330.
17. The best account of these incidences is Reynolds, *Private Journal of William Reynolds*, 182–199.
18. Ro-Veidovi's (called Vendovi by the American press) supposed crimes were unrelated to these incidences. He was charged with organizing a deadly assault on sailors from the American ship *Charles Dagget* in 1834. The sailors were curing bêche-de-mer on a Fijian beach at the time of the assault. I appreciate Ann Fabian's guidance on this incident and her excellent essay, "One Man's Skull: A Tale from the Sea-Slug Trade," *Common-place* 8 (January 2008). See also *New York Herald*, June 11 and 26, 1842; and T. D. Stewart, "The Skull of Vendovi: A Contribution of the Wilkes Expedition to the Physical Anthropology of Fiji," *Archaeology and Physical Anthropology in Oceania* 13 (1978): 204–214.
19. On the area of Dana's birth, see Mary Ryan, *Cradle of the Middle Class: The Family in Oneida County, New York, 1790–1865* (Cambridge: Cambridge University Press, 1981). For biographical information on Dana, see Daniel C. Gilman, *The Life of James Dwight Dana: Scientific Explorer, Mineralogist, Geologist, Zoologist, Professor in Yale University* (New York: Harper and Brothers, 1899), 3–20; M. L. Prendergast, "James Dwight Dana: Problems in American Geology," PhD dissertation, University of California, Los Angeles, 1978; Daniel E. Appleman, "James Dwight Dana and Pacific Geology," in Herman and Margolis, *Magnificent Voyagers*, 89–90; and James H. Natland, "James Dwight Dana and the Beginnings of Planetary Volcanology," *American Journal of Science* 297 (March 1997): 317–319.
20. James Dwight Dana, "On the Conditions of Vesuvius in July, 1834," *American Journal of Science and Arts* 27 (1835): 281–288.

21. James Dwight Dana to James Dana, April 13, 1835; Dana Family Papers, Yale University Library, New Haven, Connecticut.

22. James Dwight Dana to Harriet Dana, May 17, 1838; Dana Family Papers.

23. Dana, "Dedication," April 29, 1838; and Prendergast, "James Dwight Dana," 147–148. Dana joined New Haven's First Church in July 1838.

24. On the conflict between "geology and Genesis," see the many works of Martin J. S. Rudwick, especially *Bursting the Limits of Time: The Reconstruction of Geohistory in the Age of Revolution* (Chicago: University of Chicago Press, 2005), 115–118; and Rudwick, *Worlds before Adam: The Reconstruction of Geohistory in the Age of Reform* (Chicago: University of Chicago Press, 2008), 563–565.

25. James Dwight Dana, "Origin of the Grand Outline Features of the Earth," *American Journal of Science and Arts* 3 (May 1847): 381–398.

26. Ibid., 382–388.

27. James Dwight Dana to John Dana, September 16, 1839; Dana Family Papers.

28. David Quammen, *The Song of the Dodo: Island Biogeography in an Age of Extinctions* (New York: Simon and Schuster, 1996), 53.

29. David R. Stoddart, "'This Coral Episode': Darwin, Dana, and the Coral Reefs of the Pacific," in *Darwin's Laboratory: Evolutionary Theory and Natural History in the Pacific*, ed. Roy MacLeod and Philip F. Rehbock (Honolulu: University of Hawai'i Press, 1994), 24. Charles Wilkes failed to believe that tiny zoophytes could construct reefs and atolls. He wrote: "It seems almost absurd to suppose that these immense reefs should have been raised by the exertions of a minute animal." See Charles Wilkes, *Narrative of the United States Exploring Expedition during the Years 1838, 1839, 1840, 1841* (Philadelphia: Lea and Blanchard, 1845), vol. 4: 270.

30. On this chain of events, see Stoddart, "'This Coral Episode,'" 22–26; and Prendergast, "James Dwight Dana," 165.

31. James Dwight Dana, *Corals and Coral Islands* (New York: Dodd and Mead, 1872), 7. According to Stoddart, "This statement by Dana is referred to by all who have subsequently commented on his reef work though it is curious that there appears to be no reference to Darwin's theory in any Sydney newspaper, either while Dana himself was in Australia or for the twelve months preceding his arrival." Stoddart, "'This Coral Episode,'" 26.

32. Appleman, "James Dwight Dana and Pacific Geology," 91.

33. Stoddart, "'This Coral Episode,'" 22.

34. Charles Darwin, *Charles Darwin's "Beagle" Diary*, ed. Richard Darwin Keynes (Cambridge: Cambridge University Press, 1988), 418.

35. Regarding the work of a field geologist, Dana wrote: "Geology is eminently an out-door science; for strata, rivers, oceans, mountains, valleys, volcanoes cannot be taken into a recitation-room. Sketches and sections serve a good purpose in illustrating the objects which the science treats, but they do not set aside the necessity of seeing the objects themselves." James Dwight Dana, *The Geological Story Briefly Told: An Introduction to Geology for the General Reader and for Beginners in the Science* (New York: Ivison, Blakeman, 1875), iii.

36. James Dwight Dana to Edward C. Herrick, November 22, 1838; Dana Family Papers.

37. Dana did not entirely discount the significance of oceanic forces on island shorelines. See *Geology*, 379–393.

38. Ibid., 388–389.

39. Charles Darwin, *The Correspondence of Charles Darwin*, ed. Frederick Burkhardt and Sydney Smith (Cambridge: Cambridge University Press, 1985–1994), vol. 4: 290.

40. Gilman, *Life of James Dwight Dana*, 93.

41. Aaron Sachs, *The Humboldt Current: Nineteenth-Century Exploration and the Roots of American Environmentalism* (New York: Viking, 2006), 12.

42. The Maori version recalls the origin of New Zealand's two main islands—their literal emergence from the ocean by supernatural acts as well as the islands' discovery by Maori ancestors. In some accounts Maui's great fish hook comes not from his grandmother's bones but is generally referred to as Manai-a-ka-lani (Come from heaven). Such is the case with Maui's appearance in the *Kumulipo*, an ancient and lengthy Hawaiian creation chant that

Captain James Cook and his officers may have heard after anchoring in Kealakekua Bay in January 1779. See *The Kumulipo: A Hawaiian Creation Chant*, ed. and trans. Martha Beckwith (Honolulu: University of Hawai'i Press, 1951), 128–136; and *Voyages and Beaches: Pacific Encounters, 1769–1840*, ed. Alex Calder, Jonathan Lamb, and Bridget Orr (Honolulu: University of Hawai'i Press, 1999), 46.

43. The scattering of the islands, according to some sources, also explained the political divisions and conflicts between the island communities prior to the 1800s. On the Maui stories, see Martha Beckwith, *Hawaiian Mythology* (Honolulu: University of Hawai'i Press, 1970), 226–237; and Katherine Luomala, *Voices on the Wind: Polynesian Myths and Chants* (Honolulu: Bishop Museum Press, 1986), 85–98. On the place of "myths" and "legends" in indigenous history and thought, see Jocelyn Linnekin, "Contending Approaches," in *The Cambridge History of Pacific Islanders*, ed. Donald Denoon (Cambridge: Cambridge University Press, 1997), 3–36.

44. For Dana's depiction of Pacific islanders' religion and conversion attempts by missionaries, see Dana to Harriet Dana, December 1, 1839, and May 27, 1841; Dana Family Papers; Dana, "The Ways of the Feejees Half a Century Ago," in Gilman, *Life of James Dwight Dana*, 131–139.

45. Dana, *Geology*, 10.

46. Dana, "On American Geological History," *American Journal of Science and Arts* 22 (November 1856): 329–330.

47. Beckwith, *Hawaiian Mythology*, 168–179.

48. Dana, *Geology*, 172–173.

49. William Ellis, *Polynesian Researches: During a Residence of Nearly Six Years in the South Sea Islands* (London: Fisher, Son, and Jackson, 1829).

50. Dana, *Geology*, 175–176.

51. Ibid., 176.

52. "Sublime," by definition, contained another meaning for Dana the geologist: "to subject [a substance] to the action of heat in a vessel so as to convert it into vapor, which is carried off and on cooling is deposited in a solid form." Dana witnessed this chemical process while looking into the volcano. See the *Oxford English Dictionary*.

53. Dana, "Origin of the Grand Outline Features of the Earth," 398. During the voyage his correspondence contains specific reference to volcanic and tectonic action throughout the Pacific. See Dana to Benjamin Silliman, September 12, 1839; and Dana to Edward C. Herrick, November 30, 1840; Dana Family Papers.

54. On the "Ring of Fire," see Philip Kearey and Frederck J. Vine, *Global Tectonics* (Oxford: Blackwell Scientific Publications, 1990); and http://vulcan.wr.usgs.gov/Glossary/Plate-Tectonics/.

55. Dana, "Origin of the Grand Outline Features of the Earth," 398.

56. *Dictionary of Scientific Biography*, ed. Charles Coulston Gillispie (New York: Charles Scribner's Sons, 1973), vol. 2: 552–557.

57. Dana, *Geology*, 156.

58. G. R. Foulger and Don L. Anderson, "The Emperor and Hawaiian Volcanic Chains: How Well Do They Fit the Plume Hypothesis?" See www.MantlePlumes.org.

59. Beckwith, *Hawaiian Mythology*, 167–180.

60. Mauna Loa is over five and a half miles high if measured from the sea floor, higher than Mount Everest. Its base below the sea floor adds another five miles to the total height. See Philbrick, *Sea of Glory*, 243.

61. Shield volcanoes usually erupt nonexplosively; instead, they pour out large amounts of liquid lava during a slow process of eruption. The term "shield" derives from the shape of the mountain, which resembles the rounded design of a warrior's shield. Dana described the unique appearance of Hawaiian volcanoes, writing: "The idea of a volcano is so generally connected with the figure of a cone that the mind at once conceives of a lofty sugar-loaf ejecting fire, red-hot stones, and flowing lavas. But in place of slender walls around a deep crater, which the shaking of an eruption may tumble in, the summit of the Hawaiian volcano is nearly a plane, in which the crater, though several miles in circuit, is like a small quarry hole." Dana, *Geology*, 168.

62. Daniel E. Appleman, "James D. Dana and the Origins of Hawaiian Volcanology: The U.S. Exploring Expedition in Hawai'i, 1840–41," in *Volcanism in Hawai'i*, ed. Robert W. Decker, Thomas L. Wright, and Peter H. Stauffer (Washington, DC: USGPO, 1987), vol. 2: 1615–1617.

63. Dana, *Geology*, 280.

64. David A. Clague and G. Brent Dalrymple, "The Hawaiian-Emperor Volcanic Chain," in Decker et al., *Volcanism in Hawai'i*, 5–13.

65. J. Tuzo Wilson, "A Possible Origin of the Hawaiian Islands," *Canadian Journal of Physics* 41 (1963): 863–870.

66. Wilson, "Possible Origin of the Hawaiian Islands," 867, 869, 863; and Clague and Dalrymple, "Hawaiian-Emperor Volcanic Chain," 5. Dana, like all nineteenth-century geologists, believed the continents "were to a great extent fixed in the earliest periods of the condition and nature of the earth's crust." Dana, *Geology*, 436.

67. Wilson, "Possible Origin of the Hawaiian Islands," 866, 867. Dana did not realize that the age of volcano extinction also related to the age of island formation. In fact, he rejected this idea proposed by his colleague J. P. Couthouy. See Appleman, "James Dwight Dana and Pacific Geology," 112.

68. Wilson, "Possible Origin of the Hawaiian Islands," 867.

69. Dana, "On the Volcanoes of the Moon," *American Journal of Science and Arts* 2 (May 1846): 343.

70. Ibid., 349; Appleman, "James D. Dana and the Origins of Hawaiian Volcanology," 1611.

71. Natland, "At Vulcan's Shoulder," 324. The best testament to this geological mainstream in the late eighteenth century and early nineteenth centuries is Rudwick, *Bursting the Limits of Time*, and Rudwick, *Worlds before Adam*.

72. See George Forster, *A Voyage round the World*, ed. Nicholas Thomas and Oliver Berghof (Honolulu: University of Hawai'i Press, 2000); Martin Fichman, *An Elusive Victorian: The Evolution of Alfred Russel Wallace* (Chicago: University of Chicago Press, 2004); Donald Worster, *A River Running West: The Life of John Wesley Powell* (New York: Oxford University Press, 2001); and Stephen J. Pyne, *How the Canyon Became Grand: A Short History* (New York: Viking, 1998).

73. Tom Chaffin, *Pathfinder: John Charles Frémont and the Course of American Empire* (New York: Hill and Wang, 2002), 246–247.

74. Led by Lieutenant George Emmons, this group included Dana, William Rich, William Brackenridge, Titian Peale, Alfred Agate, Henry Eld, and Harold Colvocoresses.

75. Appleman, "James Dwight Dana and Pacific Geology," 114.

76. Dana, *Geology*, 613.

77. Ibid., 613, 612–613, 669, 673, 675, 676, 678.

78. Ibid., 674.

79. Within four weeks of his return, Dana was engaged to Henrietta Silliman, the daughter of his Yale mentor, Benjamin Silliman.

80. He also assumed editorial duties for the *American Journal of Science and Arts* in 1846 and became Yale's Silliman Professor of Natural History and Geology in 1850.

81. Dana, "On American Geological History," 307.

82. Ibid., 311.

83. Ibid., 320, 329–330.

84. Ibid., 330. The place of religion in Dana's work received mixed reactions from some of the world's leading scientists. T. H. Huxley, one of Darwin's staunchest defenders, observed that "Dana wrote with one eye on fact and the other on Genesis." Alexander von Humboldt found it difficult to understand the increasing role of religion in American science. Humboldt considered Dana's work on the Pacific "the most splendid contribution to science of the present day," but he also feared the appearance of a theocratic-based geology in the United States. Humboldt reportedly stated "that it was not safe for a man to pursue geology in the United States, for fear of falling within the ban of the Church." Dana, for his own part, never feared falling within the ban of church, state, or institutional science, and he maintained cordial correspondence throughout the years with many of his presumed critics across the Atlantic, including Charles Darwin. Robert H. Dott, "James Dwight Dana's Old

Tectonics: Global Contraction under Divine Direction," *American Journal of Science* 297 (March 1997): 307; S.F.B. Morse to James Dwight Dana, August 25, 1856, Dana Family Papers; and Gilman, *Life of James Dwight Dana*, 185.

85. Smith, *Virgin Land*, 23.
86. Dana, "On American Geological History," 334.
87. As a sign of respect for Guyot, Dana named his third son Arnold Guyot Dana. For Dana's correspondence with Guyot, see Gilman, *Life of James Dwight Dana*, 325–332.
88. Arnold Guyot, *The Earth and Man: Lectures on Comparative Physical Geography* (London: R. Bentley, 1850), 297–298.
89. Sachs, *Humboldt Current*, 20.
90. William Goetzmann, *Exploration and Empire: The Explorer and the Scientist in the Winning of the American West* (New York: Knopf, 1966), 232.
91. Smith, *Pacific Visions*, 14.
92. Dana never returned to the Pacific as a researcher. He suffered a mental breakdown shortly after the publication of "On American Geological History," likely a result of his frenetic scholarly pace during the previous decade. He continued teaching and writing for three more decades, though the pace of his scholarship slowed and its geographic frame became more local and continental, with brief interludes of writing about religion and science.
93. Natland, "At Vulcan's Shoulder," 336–337.
94. S.F.B. Morse to James Dwight Dana, August 25, 1856; Dana Family Papers. Samuel Morse (the inventor of Morse Code) had met with Humboldt, and their discussion evidently included this praise from the German naturalist.
95. Dana paid for the printing of an additional twenty-five copies, many of which he gave to friends and colleagues.
96. Gilman, *Life of James Dwight Dana*, 145.
97. For the inscription containing this information, see ibid., 143.

Conclusion

1. Thomas N. Layton, *The Voyage of the "Frolic": New England Merchants and the Opium Trade* (Stanford: Stanford University Press, 1997), 116. I am deeply indebted to Thomas Layton's superb history of the *Frolic* because it was one of the first studies to spark my interest in new approaches to maritime history and anthropology. Much of the account that follows is based on his work. For the spread of gold rush news around the Pacific, see James P. Delgado, *To California by Sea: A Maritime History of the California Gold Rush* (Columbia, SC: University of South Carolina Press, 1990). On the term "gold fever," see Angela Hawk, "Madness, Mining, and Migration in the Pacific World, 1848-1900," PhD dissertation, University of California, Irvine, 2011.
2. Layton, *Voyage of the "Frolic,"* 59–90.
3. Louise Pubols, *The Father of All: The de la Guerra Family, Power, and Patriarchy in Mexican California* (Berkeley: University of California Press, 2009).
4. Layton, *Voyage of the "Frolic,"* 141.
5. Richard Walker, "California's Golden Road to Riches: Natural Resources and Regional Capitalism, 1848-1940," *Annals of the Association of American Geographers* 91 (March 2001): 167–199.
6. Jeremy Adelman and Stephen Aron, "From Borderlands to Borders: Empires, Nation-States, and the Peoples in between in North American History," *American Historical Review* 104 (June 1999): 814–841.
7. Layton, *Voyage of the "Frolic,"* 6.
8. Pekka Hämäläinen and Samuel Truett, "On Borderlands," *Journal of American History* 98 (September 2011): 338–361.
9. On these various transformations, see Marius B. Jansen, *The Making of Modern Japan* (Cambridge, MA: Harvard University Press, 2002); Ilya Vinkovetsky, *Russian America: An Overseas Colony of a Continental Empire, 1804–1867* (New York: Oxford University Press, 2011); Lilikalā Kameʻeleihiwa, *Native Land and Foreign Desires: Pehea Lā E Pono Ai? How*

Shall We Live in Harmony? (Honolulu: Bishop Museum Press, 1992); J. Kēhaulani Kauanui, *Hawaiian Blood: Colonialism and the Politics of Sovereignty and Indigeneity* (Durham, NC: Duke University Press, 2008), 74–80; W. M. Mathew, "Peru and the British Guano Market, 1840–1870," *Economic History Review* 23 (April 1970): 112–128; and Karen Jenks, "The Pacific Mail Steamship Company, 1830–1860," PhD dissertation, University of California, Irvine, 2012.

10. Herman Melville, *Moby-Dick; or The Whale* (New York: Charles Scribner's Sons, 1902 [1851]), 416.

BIBLIOGRAPHY

Manuscript Collections

BANCROFT LIBRARY, UNIVERSITY OF CALIFORNIA, BERKELEY
Adele Ogden Collection
De la Guerra Family Archives
José Joaquín de Arrillaga Correspondence
William Heath Davis Papers

HUNTINGTON LIBRARY, SAN MARINO
Atkinson, Thomas. "Journal and Memoirs of Thomas Atkinson, 1845–1882."
Goodall, Charles. "Log of a Whaler's Voyage from New Bedford into the Pacific and Back, 1843–1846."
Hudson, John T. "Journal and Logbook of John T. Hudson, 1805–1807."
John A. Rockwell Papers
John Haskell Kemble Collection
Sereno Edwards Bishop Papers

BRITISH LIBRARY, LONDON
East India Company Collection

WIDENER MEMORIAL LIBRARY, HARVARD UNIVERSITY
William Dane Phelps Collection

MITCHELL LIBRARY, SYDNEY, AUSTRALIA
South Sea Letters, London Missionary Society

G. W. BLUNT WHITE LIBRARY, MYSTIC SEAPORT MUSEUM, CONNECTICUT
Logbook, 1845–1848, *Tiger* (ship)

PHILLIPS LIBRARY, PEABODY MUSEUM, SALEM, MASSACHUSETTS
Typescript log of ship *Amethyst*, 1806–1811

BRITISH COLUMBIA ARCHIVES, VICTORIA, CANADA
William Fraser Tolmie Records, 1830–1883

NEW BEDFORD FREE PUBLIC LIBRARY,
NEW BEDFORD, MASSACHUSETTS
Dennis Wood, "Abstracts of Whaling Voyages"

YALE UNIVERSITY LIBRARY, NEW HAVEN, CONNECTICUT
Anonymous, "Supercargo's Log of the Brig Lydia, 1804–1807." Western Americana Collection,
  Beinecke Rare Book and Manuscript Library.
Dana Family Papers

Newspapers

Friend (Honolulu, HI)
Hawaiian Spectator (Honolulu, HI)
The Mercury (Hobart, Tasmania)
New York Herald
The Polynesian (Honolulu, HI)
Whalemen's Shipping List (New Bedford, MA)

Published Primary Sources

Adams, John. *The Works of John Adams*. 10 vols. Edited by Charles Francis Adams. Boston: Little,
  Brown, 1850–1856.
Anonymous [William Ellis]. *An Authentic Narrative of a Voyage Performed by Captain Cook and
  Captain Clerke, in His Majesty's Ships Resolution and Discovery, during the Years 1776, 1777,
  1778, 1779, and 1780*. Altenburg: Gottlob Emanuel Richter, 1788.
Beaglehole, J. C., ed. *The Journals of Captain James Cook on His Voyages of Discovery*. 4 vols. Cam-
  bridge: Hakluyt Society, 1955–1974.
Beckwith, Martha, ed. *The Kumulipo: A Hawaiian Creation Chant*. Honolulu: University of Hawai'i
  Press, 1951.
Berkh, Vasiliĭ Nikolaevich. *A Chronological History of the Discovery of the Aleutian Islands, or, The
  Exploits of Russian Merchants: With a Supplement of Historical Data on the Fur Trade*. Edited
  by Richard A. Pierce. Translated by Dmitri Krenov. Kingston, ON: Limestone Press, 1974
  [1823].
Bishop, Artemas. "An Inquiry into the Causes of Decrease of the Population of the Sandwich
  Islands." *Hawaiian Spectator* 1 (1838).
Botta, Paulo Emilio. "Observations sur les habitants des Iles Sandwich. Observations sur les
  habitans de la Californie. Observations diverses faites en mer." *Nouvelles annales des voyages*
  22 (1831): 129–176.
———. *Observations on the Inhabitants of California, 1827–1828*. Translated by John Francis
  Bricca. Los Angeles: Glen Dawson, 1952.
Brewster, Mary. *"She Was a Sister Sailor": The Whaling Journals of Mary Brewster, 1845–1851*. Edited
  by Joan Druett. Mystic, CT: Mystic Seaport Museum, 1992.
Browne, J. Ross. "Explorations in Lower California." *Harper's New Monthly Magazine* 37 (October
  1868): 10.
Chamisso, Adelbert von. "Remarks and Opinions, of the Naturalist of the Expedition." In *A Voyage
  of Discovery: Into the South Sea and Beering's Straits for the Purpose of Exploring a North-East
  Passage, Undertaken in the Years 1815–1818*. By Otto von Kotzebue, vol. 3: 168. London, 1821.
———. *A Voyage around the World with the Romanzov Expedition in the Years 1815–1818 in the Brig
  Rurik, Captain Otto von Kotzebue*. Translated and edited by Henry Kratz. Honolulu: Univer-
  sity of Hawai'i Press, 1986 [1836].

Cheyne, Andrew. *The Trading Voyages of Andrew Cheyne, 1841–1844.* Edited by Dorothy Shineberg. Honolulu: University of Hawai'i Press, 1971.

Clark, William. *Original Journals of the Lewis and Clark Expedition, 1804–1806.* Edited by Reuben Gold Thwaites. New York: Dodd, Mead, 1905.

Cleveland, Richard Jeffry. *Voyages and Commercial Enterprises, of the Sons of New England.* New York: Burt Franklin, 1857.

———. *Voyages of a Merchant Navigator of the Days That Are Past.* New York: Harper, 1886.

Cook, James. *The Journals of Captain Cook.* Edited by Philip Edwards. London: Penguin Books, 1999.

Coolidge, Lewis. "Journal of a Voyage Perform'd on the Ship Amethyst." In *Lewis Coolidge and the Voyage of the Amethyst.* Edited by Evabeth Miller Kienast and John Phillip Felt. Columbia, SC: University of South Carolina Press, 2009.

Corney, Peter. *Early Voyages in the North Pacific.* Fairfield, WA: Ye Galleon Press, 1965 [1836].

Coxe, William. *Account of the Russian Discoveries between Asia and America.* London: J. Nichols, 1780.

Cumpston, J. S. *Shipping Arrivals and Departures: Sydney, 1788–1825.* 3 vols. Canberra: A.C.T.: Roebuck Society, 1963.

Dampier, William. *A New Voyage round the World: The Journal of an English Buccaneer.* London: Hummingbird Press, 1998 [1697].

Dana, James Dwight. "On the Conditions of Vesuvius in July, 1834." *American Journal of Science and Arts* 27 (1835): 281–288.

———. "On the Volcanoes of the Moon." *American Journal of Science and Arts* 2 (May 1846): 335–355.

———. "Origin of the Grand Outline Features of the Earth." *American Journal of Science and Arts* 3 (May 1847): 381–398.

———. *Geology.* New York: Geo. P. Putnam, 1849.

———. "On American Geological History." *American Journal of Science and Arts* 22 (November 1856): 305–334.

———. *Corals and Coral Islands.* New York: Dodd and Mead, 1872.

———. *The Geological Story Briefly Told: An Introduction to Geology for the General Reader and for Beginners in the Science.* New York: Ivison, Blakeman, 1875.

Darwin, Charles. *The Voyage of the Beagle.* Edited by Leonard Engel. New York: Natural History Library, 1962.

———. *The Correspondence of Charles Darwin.* Edited by Frederick Burkhardt and Sydney Smith. Cambridge: Cambridge University Press, 1985–1994.

———. *Charles Darwin's "Beagle" Diary.* Edited by Richard Darwin Keynes. Cambridge: Cambridge University Press, 1988.

D'Auterouche, Jean-Baptiste Chappe. *A Voyage to California.* London: Edward and Charles Dilly, 1778.

Delano, Amasa. *A Narrative of Voyages and Travels in the Northern and Southern Hemispheres: Comprising Three Voyages round the World; Together with a Voyage of Survey and Discovery, in the Pacific Ocean and Oriental Islands.* Boston: E. G. House, 1817.

Delano, Reuben. *Wanderings and Adventures of Reuben Delano: Being a Narrative of Twelve Years Life in a Whale Ship!* Boston: Redding, 1846.

Duhaut-Cilly, Auguste Bernard. *Voyage autour du monde, principalement à la Californie et aux Iles Sandwich, pendant les années 1826, 1827, 1828, et 1829.* 2 vols. Paris, 1834–1835.

———. *A Voyage to California, the Sandwich Islands, and around the World in the Years 1826–1829.* Translated by August Frugé and Neal Harlow. Berkeley: University of California Press, 1999.

Ellis, William. *An Authentic Narrative of a Voyage Performed by Captain Cook and Captain Clerke, 1776–1780.* London: G. Robinson, 1783.

———. *A Journal of a Tour around Hawai'i.* Boston: Crocker and Brewster, 1825.

———. *Polynesian Researches: During a Residence of Nearly Six Years in the South Sea Islands.* London: Fisher, Son, and Jackson, 1829.

Fanning, Edmund. *Voyages and Discoveries in the South Seas, 1792–1832.* Salem, MA: Marine Research Society, 1924 [1833].

Fleurieu, Charles Pierre Claret. *Voyage autour du monde: pendant les annees 1790, 1791 et 1792*. Vol. 1. Paris: De l'Imprimerie de la République, 1798–1800.

Forster, George. *Observations Made during a Voyage round the World*. Edited by Nicholas Thomas, Harriet Guest, and Michael Dettelbach. Honolulu: University of Hawai'i Press, 1996.

———. *A Voyage round the World*. Edited by Nicholas Thomas and Oliver Berghof, 2 vols. Honolulu: University of Hawai'i Press, 2000.

Galois, Robert, ed. *A Voyage to the North West Side of America: The Journals of James Colnett, 1786–89*. Vancouver: University of British Columbia Press, 2004.

Gairdner, Meredith. "Observations during a Voyage from England to Fort Vancouver, on the North-West Coast of America." *Edinburgh New Philosophical Journal* 16 (April 1834): 290–302.

———. "Physico-Geognostic Sketch of the Island of Oahu, One of the Sandwich Group." *Edinburgh New Philosophical Journal* 19 (1835): 1–14.

———. "Notes on the Geography of the Columbia River." *Journal of the Royal Geographical Society of London* 11 (1841): 250–257.

Gill, William Wyatt. *Life in the Southern Isles: or, Scenes and Incidents in the South Pacific and New Guinea*. London: Religious Tract Society, 1876.

Gudde, Erwin Gustav, ed., trans. "Edward Vischer's First Visit to California." *California Historical Society Quarterly* 19 (September 1940): 190–216.

Hammond, L. Davis, ed. *News from New Cythera: A Report of Bougainville's Voyage 1766–1769*. Minneapolis: University of Minnesota Press, 1970.

Hobucket, Ben. "The Narrative of Ben Hobucket." In *The Wreck of the Sv. Nikolai*. Edited by Kenneth Owens. Lincoln: University of Nebraska Press, 2001.

Howay, Frederic W., ed. *Voyages of the "Columbia" to the Northwest Coast, 1787–1790 and 1790–1793*. Boston: Massachusetts Historical Society, 1941.

———. *A List of Trading Vessels in the Maritime Fur Trade, 1785–1825*. Kingston, ON: Limestone Press, 1973.

Jewitt, John. *A Journal, Kept at Nootka Sound by John Rodgers Jewitt, One of the Surviving Crew of the Ship Boston, John Salter, Commander, Who Was Massacred on the 22d of March, 1803; Interspersed with Some Account of the Natives, Their Manners and Customs*. Boston: n.p., 1807.

———. *A Narrative of the Adventures and Sufferings of John R. Jewitt*. Edited by Richard Alsop. Middletown, CT: S. Richards, 1815.

———. *The Captive of Nootka: Or the Adventures of John R. Jewitt*. Edited by Samuel Griswold Goodrich. New York: J. P. Peaslee, 1835.

Kaplanoff, Mark D., ed. *Joseph Ingraham's Journal of the Brigantine Hope on a Voyage to the Northwest Coast of North America, 1790–92*. Barre, MA: Imprint Society, 1971.

Kotzebue, Otto von. *A Voyage of Discovery: Into the South Sea and Beering's Straits for the Purpose of Exploring a North-East Passage, Undertaken in the Years 1815–1818*. London, 1821.

Langsdorff, Georg Heinrich von. *Voyages and Travels in Various Parts of the World, during the Years, 1803, 1804, 1805, 1806, and 1807*. London: H. Colburn, 1813–1814.

La Pérouse, J[ean]. F[rançois]. G[alaup]. *A Voyage round the World in the Years 1785, 1786, 1787, and 1788*. London: J. Johnson, 1798.

Le Netrel, Edmond. "Voyage autour du monde pendant les années 1826, 1827, 1828, 1829, par M. Duhautcilly commandant le navire Le Héros. Extraits du journal de M. Edmond Le Netrel, lieutenant à bord ce vaisseau." *Nouvelles annales des voyages* 15 (1830): 129–182.

———. *Voyage of the Héros: Around the World with Duhaut-Cilly in the years 1826, 1827, 1828 & 1829*. Translated by Blanche Collet Wagner. Los Angeles: Glen Dawson, 1951.

Lisiansky, Urey. *A Voyage round the World in the Years 1803, 1804, 1805, and 1806*. London: John Booth, 1814.

Malaspina, Alejandro. *Viaje político-científico alrededor del mundo por las Corbetas Descubierta y Atrevida, al mando de los capitanes de navio D. Alejandro Malaspina y D. José Bustamante y Guerra desde 1789 a 1794*. Edited by Pedro Novo y Colson. Madrid: Impr. de la viuda é hijos de Abienzo, 1885.

————. *The Malaspina Expedition, 1789–1794: Journal of the Voyage by Alejandro Malaspina.* 3 vols. Edited by Andrew David et al. London: Hakluyt Society, 2001–2004.

Martínez, José Longinos. *Journal of José Longinos Martínez: Notes and Observations of the Naturalist of the Botanical Expedition in Old and New California and the South Coast, 1791–1792.* Edited by Lesley Byrd Simpson. San Francisco: John Howell Books, 1961.

Meany, Edmond S., ed. *A New Vancouver Journal on the Discovery of Puget Sound.* Seattle: n.p., 1915.

Meares, John. *Voyages Made in the Years 1788 and 1789, From China to the North West Coast of America.* London: Logographic Press, 1790.

Melville, Herman. *Moby-Dick; or, The Whale.* New York: Charles Scribner's Sons, 1902 [1851]).

M'Konochie, Captain [Alexander]. *A Summary View of the Statistics and Existing Commerce of the Principal Shores of the Pacific Ocean.* London: J. M. Richardson, 1818.

Morrell, Abby Jane. *Narrative of a Voyage to the Ethiopic and South Atlantic Ocean, Indian Ocean, Chinese Sea, North and South Pacific Ocean, in the years 1829, 1830, 1831.* New York: J. and J. Harper, 1833.

Morrell, Benjamin. *A Narrative of Four Voyages: To the South Sea, North and South Pacific Ocean, Chinese Sea, Ethiopic and Southern Atlantic Ocean, Indian and Antarctic Ocean, from the year 1822 to 1831.* New York: J. and J. Harper, 1832.

Moziño, José Mariano. *Noticias de Nutka, An Account of Nootka Sound in 1792.* Edited by Iris Higbie Wilson. Seattle: University of Washington Press, 1970.

Mulford, Prentice. *Prentice Mulford's Story: Life by Land and Sea.* New York: F. J. Needham, 1889.

Nidever, George. *The Life and Adventures of George Nidever.* Edited by William Henry Ellison. Berkeley: University of California Press, 1937.

Paty, John. "Journal of Captain John Paty, 1807–1868." *California Historical Society Quarterly* 14 (December 1935): 291–346.

Peard, George. *To the Pacific and Arctic with Beechey: The Journal of Lieutenant George Peard of H.M.S. "Blossom" 1825–1828.* Edited by Barry M. Gough. Cambridge, UK: Hakluyt Society, 1973.

Perkins, John T. *John T. Perkins' Journal at Sea, 1845.* Mystic, CT: Marine Historical Association, 1943.

Portlock, Nathaniel. *A Voyage round the World; But More Particularly to the North-West Coast of America: Performed in the Years 1785, 1786, 1787, and 1788.* London: John Stockdale, 1789.

Reynolds, William. *The Private Journal of William Reynolds, United States Exploring Expedition, 1838–1842.* Edited by Nathaniel Philbrick and Thomas Philbrick. New York: Penguin Books, 2004.

Roquefeuil, Camille de. *Journal d'un voyage autour du monde: Pendant les années 1816, 1817, 1818, et 1819.* Vol. 1. Paris: Ponthieu, 1823.

Samwell, David. "Some Account of a Voyage to South Sea's in 1776–1778." In *The Journals of Captain James Cook on His Voyages of Discovery.* Edited by J. C. Beaglehole. Cambridge: Hakluyt Society, 1955–1974.

Sauer, Martin. *An Account of a Geographical and Astronomical Expedition to the Northern Parts of Russia.* London: T. Cadell, 1802.

Scammon, Charles R. *The Marine Mammals of the Northwest Coast of North America.* San Francisco: John H. Carmany, 1874.

Shaler, William. *Journal of a Voyage between China and the North-Western Coast of America, Made in 1804.* Philadelphia, 1808.

Smithsonian Institution Libraries. "The United States Exploring Expedition, 1838–1842." http://www.sil.si.edu/digitalcollections/usexex/index.htm.

Sproat, Gilbert Malcolm. *Scenes and Studies of Savage Life.* London: Smith, Elder, 1868.

Starbuck, Alexander. *History of the American Whale Fishery from its Earliest Inception to 1876.* Waltham, MA: n.p., 1878.

Steller, Georg. "Journal of His Sea Voyage." In *Bering's Voyages: An Account of the Efforts of the Russians to Determine the Relations of Asia and America.* By F. A. Golder. New York: American Geographical Society, 1925.

Tarakanov, Timofei. *The Wreck of the Sv. Nikolai.* Edited by Kenneth Owens. Lincoln: University of Nebraska Press, 2001.

Tikhmenev, P. A. *A History of the Russian American Company*. Translated by Richard A. Pierce and Alton S. Donnelly. Seattle: University of Washington Press, 1978 [1861–1863].

Tolmie, William. *The Journals of William Fraser Tolmie: Physician and Fur Trader*. Vancouver, BC: Mitchell Press, 1963.

Turnbull, John. *A Voyage round the World, in the Years 1800, 1801, 1802, 1803, and 1804*. Vol. 2. London: Richard Phillips, 1805.

Twain, Mark. *Roughing It*. Hartford, CT: American Publishing, 1872.

Vancouver, George. *A Voyage of Discovery to the North Pacific Ocean and around the World, 1791–1795*. Edited by W. Kaye Lamb. London: Hakluyt Society, 1984 [1798].

Veniaminov, Ivan. *Notes on the Islands of the Unalaska District*. Edited by Lydia T. Black and R. H. Geoghegan. Fairbanks, AK: Limestone Press, 1984 [1804].

Vermilyea, L. H. "Whaling Adventure in the Pacific." *California Nautical Magazine* 1 (1862–1863): 229.

Wales, William. *Remarks on Mr. Forster's Account of Captain Cook's Last Voyage round the World*. London: J. Nourse, 1778.

Wallis, Mary. *Life in Feejee: Or, Five Years among the Cannibals*. Boston: W. Heath, 1851.

Webster, Daniel. *The Papers of Daniel Webster: Speeches and Formal Writings*. Edited by Charles M. Wiltse, vol. 2: 435–476. Hanover, NH: Published for Dartmouth College by the University Press of New England, 1988.

Wilkes, Charles. *Narrative of the United States Exploring Expedition during the Years 1838, 1839, 1840, 1841, 1842*. Philadelphia: Lea and Blanchard, 1845.

Williams, John. *A Narrative of Missionary Enterprises in the South Sea Islands*. London: J. Snow, 1837.

Secondary Sources

Abulafia, David. *The Great Sea: A Human History of the Mediterranean*. New York: Oxford University Press, 2011.

Adelman, Jeremy, and Stephen Aron. "From Borderlands to Borders: Empires, Nation-States, and the Peoples in between in North American History." *American Historical Review* 104 (June 1999): 814–841.

Alchon, Suzanne. *A Pest in the Land: New World Epidemics in a Global Perspective*. Albuquerque: University of New Mexico Press, 2003.

Aldrete, J. Antonio. "Smallpox Vaccination in the Early 19th Century Using Live Carriers: The Travels of Francisco Xavier de Balmis." *Southern Medical Journal* 97 (April 2004): 375–378.

Anderson, Fred. *Crucible of War: The Seven Years' War and the Fate of Empire in British North America*. New York: Vintage, 2001.

Anderson, M. Kat. *Tending the Wild: Native American Knowledge and the Management of California's Natural Resources*. Berkeley: University of California Press, 2006.

Andrade, Tonio. *How Taiwan Became Chinese: Dutch, Spanish, and Han Colonization in the Seventeenth Century*. New York: Columbia University Press, 2007.

———. "A Chinese Farmer, Two African Boys, and a Warlord: Toward a Global Microhistory." *Journal of World History* 21 (December 2010): 573–591.

Andrews, Lorrin. *A Dictionary of the Hawaiian Language*. Honolulu: Henry M. Whitney, 1865.

Antony, Robert J. "Sea Bandits of the Canton Delta, 1780–1839." *International Journal of Maritime History* 17 (December 2005): 1–29.

Appleman, Daniel E. "James Dwight Dana and Pacific Geology." In *Magnificent Voyagers: The U.S. Exploring Expedition, 1838–1842*. Edited by Herman J. Viola and Carolyn Margolis. Washington, DC: Smithsonian Institution Press, 1985.

———. "James D. Dana and the Origins of Hawaiian Volcanology: The U.S. Exploring Expedition in Hawai'i, 1840–41." In *Volcanism in Hawai'i*. Edited by Robert W. Decker, Thomas L. Wright, and Peter H. Stauffer, vol. 2. Washington, DC: USGPO, 1987.

Archer, Christon I. "Whose Scourge? Smallpox Epidemics on the Northwest Coast." In *Pacific Empires: Essays in Honour of Glyndwr Williams*. Edited by Alan Frost and Jane Samson. Vancouver: University of British Columbia Press, 1999.

Archer, Seth. "Remedial Agents: Missionary Physicians and the Depopulation of Hawai'i." *Pacific Historical Review* 79 (November 2010): 513–544.

———. "A Hawaiian Shatter Zone." Paper presented at the 18th Annual Conference of the Omohundro Institute of Early American History and Culture, June 16, 2012.

Arnold, Jeanne E., ed. "The Chumash in World and Regional Perspectives." In *The Origins of a Pacific Coast Chiefdom: The Chumash of the Channel Islands*. Edited by Jeanne E. Arnold. Salt Lake City: University of Utah Press, 2001.

Arnold, Jeanne E., Aimee M. Preziosi, and Paul Shattuck. "Flaked Stone Craft Production and Exchange in Island Chumash Territory." In *The Origins of a Pacific Coast Chiefdom: The Chumash and the Channel Islands*. Edited by Jeanne E. Arnold. Salt Lake City: University of Utah Press, 2001.

Aschmann, Homer. *The Central Desert of Baja California: Demography and Ecology*. Berkeley: University of California Press, 1959.

Baker, Brenda J., and George J. Armelagos. "The Origin and Antiquity of Syphilis." *Current Anthropology* 29 (December 1988): 703–720.

Barman, Jean, and Bruce McIntyre Watson. *Leaving Paradise: Indigenous Hawaiians in the Pacific Northwest, 1787–1898*. Honolulu: University of Hawai'i Press, 2006.

Barratt, Glynn. *Russia in Pacific Waters, 1715–1825*. Vancouver: University of British Columbia Press, 1981.

Bauer, William Jr. "Native Californians in the Nineteenth Century." In *A Companion to California History*. Edited by William Deverell and David Igler. Oxford, UK: Wiley-Blackwell, 2008.

Beckwith, Martha. *Hawaiian Mythology*. Honolulu: University of Hawai'i Press, 1970.

Beidleman, Richard G. *California's Frontier Naturalists*. Berkeley: University of California Press, 2006.

Bentley, Jerry H. "Sea and Ocean Basins as Frameworks of Historical Analysis." *Geographical Review* 89 (April 1999): 215–224.

Bentley, Jerry H., Renate Bridenthal, and Kären Wigen, eds. *Seascapes: Maritime Histories, Littoral Cultures, and Transoceanic Exchanges*. Honolulu: University of Hawai'i Press, 2007.

Black, Lydia T. "The Nature of Evil: Of Whales and Sea Otters." In *Indians, Animals, and the Fur Trade: A Critique of Keepers of the Game*. Edited by Shepard Krech III. Athens: University of Georgia Press, 1981.

———. *Russians in Alaska, 1732–1867*. Fairbanks: University of Alaska Press, 2004.

Blackhawk, Ned. *Violence over the Land: Indians and Empires in the Early American West*. Cambridge, MA: Harvard University Press, 2006.

Bockstoce, John R. *The Opening of the Maritime Fur Trade at Bering Strait*. Philadelphia: American Antiquarian Society, 2005.

———. *Furs and Frontiers in the Far North: The Contest among Native and Foreign Nations for the Bering Strait Fur Trade*. New Haven, CT: Yale University Press, 2009.

Bolster, W. Jeffrey. "Putting the Ocean in Atlantic History: Maritime Communities and Marine Ecology in the Northwest Atlantic, 1500–1800." *American Historical Review* 113 (February 2008): 19–47.

Boxer, C.R. "*Plata es Sangre*: Sidelights on the Drain of Spanish-American Silver in the Far East, 1550–1700." In *European Entry into the Pacific: Spain and the Acapulco-Manila Galleons*. Edited by Dennis O. Flynn, Arturo Giraldez, and James Sobredo. Aldershot, UK: Ashgate, 2001.

Boyd, Robert. *The Coming of the Spirit of Pestilence: Introduced Infectious Diseases and Population Decline among Northwest Coast Indians, 1774–1874*. Seattle: University of Washington Press, 1999.

Braudel, Fernand. *The Mediterranean and the Mediterranean World in the Age of Philip II*. Translated by Siân Reynolds. 2 vols. New York: Harper and Row, 1972–73 [1949].

Brooks, James F. *Captives and Cousins: Slavery, Kinship, and Community in the Southwest Border-lands*. Chapel Hill: University of North Carolina Press, 2002.

Brosse, Jacques. *Great Voyages of Discovery: Circumnavigators and Scientists, 1764–1843*. Translated by Stanley Hochman. New York: Facts on File Publications, 1983.

Burney, James. *A Chronological History of North-Eastern Voyages of Discovery*. London: Paine and Foss, 1819.

Busch, Briton C. *The War against the Seals: A History of the North American Seal Industry*. Kingston, ON: McGill-Queen's University Press, 1985.

Busch, Briton C., and Barry M. Gough, eds. *Fur Traders from New England: The Boston Men in the North Pacific, 1787–1800*. Spokane, WA: Arthur H. Clark Company, 1997.

Buschmann, Rainer F. "Oceans of World History: Delineating Aquacentric Notions in the Global Past." *History Compass* 2 (January 2004): 1–9.

———. *Oceans in World History*. New York: McGraw-Hill, 2007.

Bushnell, O. A. "Hygiene and Sanitation Among the Ancient Hawaiians." *Hawai'i Historical Review* 2 (1966): 316–336.

———. *The Gifts of Civilization: Germs and Genocide in Hawai'i*. Honolulu: University of Hawai'i Press, 1983.

Calder, Alex, Jonathan Lamb, and Bridget Orr, eds. *Voyages and Beaches: Pacific Encounters, 1769–1840*. Honolulu: University of Hawai'i Press, 1999.

Campbell, I. C. *Gone Native in Polynesia: Captivity Narratives and Experiences from the South Pacific*. Westport, CT: Greenwood Press, 1998.

———. "The Culture of Culture Contact: Refractions from Polynesia." *Journal of World History* 14 (March 2003): 63, 64, 66.

Canny, Nicholas. "Writing Atlantic History; or, Reconfiguring the History of Colonial British America." *Journal of American History* 86 (December 1999): 1093–1114.

Chaffin, Tom. *Pathfinder: John Charles Frémont and the Course of American Empire*. New York: Hill and Wang, 2002.

Chang, David A. "Borderlands in a World at Sea: Concow Indians, Native Hawaiians, and South Chinese in Indigenous, Global, and National Spaces." *Journal of American History* 98 (September 2001): 384–403.

Chang, Kornel. *Pacific Connections: The Making of the U.S.-Canadian Borderlands*. Berkeley: University of California Press, 2012.

Chaplin, Joyce E. "Expansion and Exceptionalism in Early American History." *Journal of American History* 89 (March 2003): 1431–1455.

———. "Atlantic Antislavery and Pacific Navigation." Paper presented at "The New Maritime History: A Conference in Honor of Robert C. Ritchie," Huntington Library, San Marino, November 11, 2011.

Chappell, David A. "Shipboard Relations between Pacific Island Women and Euroamerican Men, 1767–1887." *Journal of Pacific History* 27 (December 1992): 131–149.

———. "Active Agents versus Passive Victims: Decolonized Historiography or Problematic Paradigm?" *Contemporary Pacific* 7 (Spring 1995): 303–326.

———. *Double Ghosts: Oceanian Voyagers on Euroamerican Ships*. Armonk, NY: M. E. Sharpe, 1997.

Chaudhuri, K. N. *The Trading World of Asia and the English East India Company*. Cambridge: Cambridge University Press, 1985.

Chavez-Garcia, Miroslava. *Negotiating Conquest: Gender and Power in California, 1770–1880*. Tucson: University of Arizona Press, 2004.

Clague, David A., and G. Brent Dalrymple. "The Hawaiian-Emperor Volcanic Chain." In *Volcanism in Hawai'i*. Edited by Robert W. Decker, Thomas L. Wright, and Peter H. Stauffer. Washington, DC: USGPO, 1987.

Clayton, Daniel W. *Islands of Truth: The Imperial Fashioning of Vancouver Island*. Vancouver: University of British Columbia Press, 2000.

Cliff, A. D., P. Haggett, and M. R. Smallman-Raynor. *Island Epidemics*. New York: Oxford University Press, 1998.

Coclanis, Peter A. "*Drang Nach Osten*: Bernard Bailyn, the World-Island, and the Idea of Atlantic History." *Journal of World History* 13 (Spring 2002): 169–182.

Colby, Barnard L. *Whaling Captains of New London County, Connecticut: For Oil and Buggy Whips*. Mystic, CT: Mystic Seaport Museum, 1990.

Colley, Linda. *Captives: Britain, Empire, and the World, 1600–1850*. New York: Anchor Books, 2002.

Cook, Sherburne F. "Disease of the Indians of Lower California in the Eighteenth Century." *California and Western Medicine* 43 (December 1935): 432–434.

———. "Extent and Significance of Disease among the Indians of Baja California from 1697 to 1773." *Ibero-Americana* 2 (1937): 2–48.

———. *The Conflict between the California Indians and White Civilization*. Berkeley: University of California Press, 1943.

Cook, Warren L. *Flood Tide of Empire: Spain and the Pacific Northwest, 1543–1819*. New Haven, CT: Yale University Press, 1973.

Cox, Paul Alan. "Polynesian Herbal Medicine." In *Islands, Plants, and Polynesians: An Introduction to Polynesian Ethnobotany*. Edited by Paul Alan Cox and Sandra A. Banack. Portland, OR: Dioscorides Press, 1991.

Creighton, Margaret S. *Rites and Passages: The Experience of American Whaling, 1830–1870*. Cambridge: Cambridge University Press, 1995.

Crewe, Ryan. "Sailing for the 'Chinese Indies': Charting the Asian-Latin American Rim, Conduits, and Barriers of the Early Modern Pacific World." Paper presented at the 18th Annual Conference of the Omohundro Institute of Early American History and Culture, June 16, 2012.

Cronon, William. *Changes in the Land: Indians, Settlers, and the Ecology of New England*. New York: Hill and Wang, 1983.

———. *Nature's Metropolis: Chicago and the Great West*. New York: W. W. Norton, 1991.

Crosby, Alfred W. "The Early History of Syphilis: A Reappraisal." *American Anthropologist* 71 (April 1969): 218–227.

———. *The Columbian Exchange: Biological and Cultural Consequences of 1492*. Westport, CT: Greenwood Publishers, 1972.

Crowell, Aron L., Amy F. Steffian, and Gordon L. Pullar, eds. *Looking Both Ways: Heritage and Identity of the Alutiiq People*. Fairbanks: University of Alaska Press, 2001.

Cumings, Bruce. *Dominion from Sea to Sea: Pacific Ascendency and American Power*. New Haven, CT: Yale University Press, 2009.

Davis, Lance E., Robert E. Gallman, and Karin Gleiter. *In Pursuit of Leviathan: Technology, Institutions, Productivity, and Profits in American Whaling, 1816–1906*. Chicago: University of Chicago Press, 1997.

Davis, William Heath. *Sixty Years in California: A History of Events and Life in California*. San Francisco: A. J. Leary, 1889.

Delgado, James P. *To California by Sea: A Maritime History of the California Gold Rush*. Columbia: University of South Carolina Press, 1990.

Demos, John. *The Unredeemed Captive: A Family Story from Early America*. New York: Vintage, 1995.

Dening, Greg. *Islands and Beaches: Discourse on the Silent Land: Marquesas, 1774–1880*. Honolulu: University of Hawai'i Press, 1980.

———. "The Hegemony of Laughter: Purea's Theatre." In *Pacific Empires: Essays in Honour of Glyndwr Williams*. Edited by Alan Frost and Jane Samson. Vancouver: University of British Columbia Press, 1999.

———. "History 'in' the Pacific." In *Voyaging through the Contemporary Pacific*. Edited by David Hanlon and Geoffrey M. White. Lanham, MD: Rowman and Littlefield, 2000.

———. "Deep Times, Deep Spaces: Civilizing the Sea." In *Sea Changes: Historicizing the Ocean*. Edited by Bernhard Klein and Gesa Mackenthus. New York: Routledge, 2004.

———. "Encompassing the Sea of Islands." *Common-place* 5 (January 2005).

Denoon, Donald, ed. *The Cambridge History of the Pacific Islanders*. Cambridge: Cambridge University Press, 1997.

Deverell, William, and David Igler. "The Abattoir of the Prairie." *Rethinking History* 4 (Fall 1999): 321–323.

Diaz, Vicente. *Repositioning the Missionary: Rewriting the Histories of Colonialism, Native Catholicism, and Indigeneity in Guam.* Honolulu: University of Hawai'i Press, 2010.

Diaz, Vicente, and J. Kehaulani Kauanui, "Native Pacific Cultural Studies on the Edge." *Contemporary Pacific* 13 (Fall 2001): 315–341.

Diaz-Trechuelo, Maria Lourdes. "Eighteenth Century Philippine Economy: Commerce." In *European Entry into the Pacific: Spain and the Acapulco-Manila Galleons.* Edited by Dennis O. Flynn, Arturo Giraldez, and James Sobredo. Aldershot, UK: Ashgate, 2001.

Dmytryshyn, Basil, E.A.P. Crownhart-Vaughan, and Thomas Vaughan, eds. "Instructions from Aleksandr A. Baranov to His Assistant, Ivan A. Kuskov, Regarding the Dispatch of a Hunting Party to the Coast of Spanish California," October 14, 1808. In *The Russian American Colonies: To Siberia and Russian America, Three Centuries of Russian Eastward Expansion, 1798–1867.* Portland: Oregon Historical Society, 1989.

Dobyns, Henry. *Their Numbers Become Thinned: Native American Population Dynamics in Eastern North America.* Knoxville: University of Tennessee Press, 1983.

Donald, Leland. *Aboriginal Slavery on the Northwest Coast of North America.* Berkeley: University of California Press, 1997.

Dott, Robert H. "James Dwight Dana's Old Tectonics: Global Contraction under Divine Direction." *American Journal of Science* 297 (March 1997): 283–311.

Douglas, David. "Second Journey to the Northwestern Parts of the Continent of North America during the Years 1829–'30–'31–'32–'33." *Oregon Historical Society Quarterly* 6 (September 1905): 292.

Downs, Jacques M. *The Golden Ghetto: The American Commercial Community in Canton and the Shaping of American China Policy, 1784–1844.* Bethlehem, PA: Lehigh University Press, 1997.

Druett, Joan. *Petticoat Whalers: Whaling Wives at Sea, 1820–1920.* Auckland: Collins, 1991.

———. *"She Was a Sister Sailor": The Whaling Journals of Mary Brewster, 1845–1851.* Mystic, CT: Mystic Seaport Museum, 1992.

———. *Hen Frigates: The Wives of Merchant Captains under Sail.* New York: Simon and Schuster, 1998.

———. *Rough Medicine: Surgeons at Sea in the Age of Sail.* New York: Routledge, 2001.

Dulles, Foster Rhea. *The Old China Trade.* Boston: Houghton Mifflin, 1930.

El Molto, J., Bruce M. Rothschild, Robert Woods, and Christine Rothschild. "Unique Aspects of West Coast Treponematosis." *Chungara* 32 (July 2000).

Emmons, G. T. "Native Account of the Meeting Between La Perouse and the Tlingit." *American Anthropologist* 13 (April–June 1911): 294–298.

Engelhardt, Fr. Zephyrin O.F.M. *The Missions and Missionaries of California.* Vol. 1. San Francisco: James H. Barry, 1908.

Engstrand, Iris. *Royal Officer in Baja California, 1768–1770, Joaquín Velázquez de Léon.* Los Angeles: Dawson's Book Shop, 1976.

Erlandson, Jon M., Madonna L. Moss, and Matthew Des Lauriers. "Life on the Edge: Early Maritime Cultures of the Pacific Coast of North America." *Quaternary Science Reviews* 27 (2008): 2232–2245.

Erlandson, Jon M., Torben C. Rick, Douglas J. Kennett, and Philip L. Walker. "Dates, Demography, and Disease: Cultural Contacts and Possible Evidence for Old World Epidemics among the Protohistoric Island Chumash." *Pacific Coast Archaeological Society Quarterly* 37 (Summer 2001): 11–26.

Exman, Eugene. *The Brothers Harper: A Unique Publishing Partnership and Its Impact upon the Cultural Life of America from 1817 to 1853.* New York: Harper and Row, 1965.

Fabian, Ann. "One Man's Skull: A Tale from the Sea-Slug Trade." *Common-place* 8 (January 2008).

———. *The Skull Collectors: Race, Science, and America's Unburied Dead.* Chicago: University of Chicago Press, 2010.

Fenn, Elizabeth A. *Pox Americana: The Great Smallpox Epidemic of 1775–82*. New York: Hill and Wang, 2001.

Fichman, Martin. *An Elusive Victorian: The Evolution of Alfred Russel Wallace*. Chicago: University of Chicago Press, 2004.

Fischer, Kirsten. *Suspect Relations: Sex, Race, and Resistance in Colonial North Carolina*. Ithaca, NY: Cornell University Press, 2002.

Fisher, Robin. "Arms and Men on the Northwest Coast, 1774–1825." *BC Studies* 29 (1976): 3–18.

———. *Contact and Conflict: Indian-European Relations in British Columbia, 1774–1890*. Vancouver: University of British Columbia Press, 1977.

Flynn, Dennis O., and Arturo Giraldez. "Spanish Profitability in the Pacific: The Philippines in the Sixteenth and Seventeenth Centuries." In *Pacific Centuries: Pacific and Pacific Rim History since the Sixteenth Century*. Edited by Dennis O. Flynn, Lionel Frost, and A.J.H. Latham. London: Routledge, 1999.

———. "Cycles of Silver: Global Economic Unity through the Mid-Eighteenth Century." *Journal of World History* 13 (Fall 2002): 391–427.

Flynn, Dennis O., Arturo Giraldez, and James Sobredo, eds. *European Entry into the Pacific: Spain and the Acapulco-Manila Galleons*. Aldershot, UK: Ashgate, 2001.

Forster, Honore. "Voyaging through Strange Seas: Four Women Travellers in the Pacific." *National Library of Australia News* (January 2000): 3–6.

Foster, John W. *A Century of American Diplomacy*. Boston: Houghton Mifflin, 1901.

Foulger, G. R., and Don L. Anderson. "The Emperor and Hawaiian Volcanic Chains: How Well Do They Fit the Plume Hypothesis?" www.MantlePlumes.org.

Gamble, Lynn. *The Chumash World at European Contact: Power, Trade, and Feasting Among Complex Hunter-Gatherers*. Berkeley: University of California Press, 2008.

Games, Alison. *Migration and the Origins of the English Atlantic World*. Cambridge, MA: Harvard University Press, 1999.

———. "Atlantic History: Definitions, Challenges, and Opportunities." *American Historical Review* 111 (June 2006): 741–757.

Gibson, James R. *Otter Skins, Boston Ships, and China Goods: The Maritime Fur Trade of the Pacific Northwest, 1785–1841*. Seattle: University of Washington Press, 1992.

Gillispie, Charles Coulston, ed. *Dictionary of Scientific Biography*. Vol. 2. New York: Charles Scribner's Sons, 1973.

Gilman, Daniel C. *The Life of James Dwight Dana: Scientific Explorer, Mineralogist, Geologist, Zoologist, Professor in Yale University*. New York: Harper and Brothers, 1899.

Goebel, Dorothy Burne. "British Trade to the Spanish Colonies, 1796–1823." *American Historical Review* 43 (January 1938): 288–320.

Goetzmann, William. *Exploration and Empire: The Explorer and the Scientist in the Winning of the American West*. New York: Knopf, 1966.

Golway, Hugh. "The Cruise of the Lelia Byrd." *Journal of the West* 8 (July 1969): 396–398.

Gould, Richard A. "Tolowa." In *Handbook of North American Indians*. Vol. 8. Edited by Robert F. Heizer. Washington, DC: Smithsonian Institution, 1978.

Grinëv, Andrei V. "A Brief Survey of the Russian Historiography of Russian America of Recent Years." Translated by Richard L. Bland. *Pacific Historical Review* 79 (May 2010): 265–278.

Grove, Richard. *Green Imperialism: Colonial Expansion, Tropical Island Edens, and the Origins of Environmentalism, 1600–1860*. Cambridge: Cambridge University Press, 1995.

Guest, Harriet. *Empire, Barbarism, and Civilisation: Captain Cook, William Hodges, and the Return to the Pacific*. Cambridge: Cambridge University Press, 2007.

Gulliver, Katrina. "Finding the Pacific World." *Journal of World History* 22 (March 2011): 83–100.

Guyot, Arnold. *The Earth and Man: Lectures on Comparative Physical Geography*. London: R. Bentley, 1850.

Hackel, Steven W. "Land, Labor, and Production: The Colonial Economy of Spanish and Mexican California." In *Contested Eden: California Before the Gold Rush.* Edited by Ramón A. Gutiérrez and Richard Orsi. Berkeley: University of California Press, 1998.

———. *Children of Coyote, Missionaries of Saint Francis: Indian-Spanish Relations in Colonial California, 1769–1850.* Chapel Hill: University of North Carolina Press, 2005.

———. "Beyond Virgin Soil: Impaired Fertility in the Indian Population of Spanish California." Paper presented at Social Science History Association meeting, Long Beach, 2009.

Hämäläinen, Pekka, and Samuel Truett. "On Borderlands." *Journal of American History* 98 (September 2011): 338–361.

Hanlon, David. *Upon a Stone Altar: A History of the Island of Pohnpei to 1890.* Honolulu: University of Hawai'i Press, 1988.

Hao, Yen-p'ing. *The Commercial Revolution in Nineteenth-Century China: The Rise of Sino-Western Mercantile Capitalism.* Berkeley: University of California Press, 1986.

Hardee, Jim. "Soft Gold: Animal Skins and the Early Economy of California." In *Studies in Pacific History: Economics, Politics, and Migration.* Edited by Dennis O. Flynn, Arturo Giráldez, and James Sobredo. Aldershop, UK: Ashgate, 2002.

Harris, Cole. "Voices of Disaster: Smallpox around the Strait of Georgia in 1782." *Ethnohistory* 41 (Fall 1994): 591–626.

———. "Social Power and Cultural Change in Pre-Colonial British Columbia." *BC Studies* 115/116 (Autumn/Winter 1997/1998): 73.

Harvey, A. G. "Chief Concomly's Skull." *Oregon Historical Quarterly* 40 (June 1939): 161–167.

———. "Meredith Gairdner: Doctor of Medicine." *British Columbia Historical Quarterly* 9 (April 1945): 89–111.

Hau'ofa, Epeli. "Our Sea of Islands." *Contemporary Pacific* 6 (Spring 1994): 153.

Hawaiian Roots: Genealogy for Hawaiians. "Ships to Hawai'i before 1819." July 2002. http://www.hawaiian-roots.com/shipsB1880.htm.

Hawk, Angela. "Madness, Mining, and Migration in the Pacific World, 1848–1900." PhD dissertation, University of California, Irvine, 2011.

Hayden, Deborah. *Pox: Genius, Madness, and the Mysteries of Syphilis.* New York: Basic Books, 2003.

Henderson, David A. *Men & Whales at Scammon's Lagoon.* Los Angeles: Dawson's Book Shop, 1972.

Hirsch, August. *Handbook of Historical and Geographical Pathology.* 3 vols. London: The New Sydenham Society, 1883 [1864].

Hopkins, Donald R. *The Greatest Killer: Smallpox in History.* Chicago: University of Chicago Press, 2002.

Hough, Richard. *Captain James Cook.* New York: W. W. Norton, 1994.

Howay, F. W. "Early Relations with the Pacific Northwest." In *The Hawaiian Islands.* Edited by Albert P. Taylor. Ann Arbor: University of Michigan Press, 2005 [1930].

———. "The Brig Owyhee in the Columbia, 1829–30." *Oregon Historical Society Quarterly* 35 (March 1934): 10–21.

———. *Voyages of the "Columbia" to the Northwest Coast, 1787–1790 and 1790–1793.* New York: Da Capo Press, 1969.

———. *A List of Trading Vessels in the Maritime Fur Trade, 1785–1825.* Kingston, ON: Limestone Press, 1973.

Howe, K. R. "The Fate of the 'Savage' in Pacific Historiography." *New Zealand Journal of History* 11 (1977): 137–154.

———. *The Loyalty Islands: A History of Culture Contact, 1840–1900.* Honolulu: University of Hawai'i Press, 1977.

Hurtado, Albert L. *Intimate Frontiers: Sex, Gender, and Culture in Old California.* Albuquerque: University of New Mexico Press, 1999.

Igler, David. "Diseased Goods: Global Exchanges in the Eastern Pacific Basin, 1770–1850." *American Historical Review* 109 (June 2004): 692–719.

Inskeep, Edward. "San Blas, Nayarit: An Historical and Geographic Study." *Journal of the West* 2 (1963): 133–144.

Irwin, Geoffrey. *The Prehistoric Exploration and Colonisation of the Pacific*. Cambridge: Cambridge University Press, 1992.

Jackson, Robert H. "Epidemic Disease and Population Decline in the Baja California Missions." *Southern California Quarterly* 63 (Winter 1982): 308–346.

Jansen, Marius B. *The Making of Modern Japan*. Cambridge, MA: Harvard University Press, 2002.

Jenks, Karen. "The Pacific Mail Steamship Company, 1830–1860." PhD dissertation, University of California, Irvine, 2012.

Jones, David S. "Virgin Soils Revisited." *William and Mary Quarterly* 60 (October 2003): 703–742.

Jones, Mary Lou, Steven L. Swartz, and Stephen Leatherwood, eds. *The Gray Whale: Eschrichtius robustus*. Orlando, FL: Academic Press, 1984.

Jones, Ryan Tucker. "Sea Otters and Savages in the Russian Empire: The Billings Expedition, 1785–1793." *Journal of Maritime Research* (December 2006): 106–121. www.jmr.nmm.ac.uk/server/show/ConJmrArticle.217. Accessed April 28, 2010.

———. "Empire of Extinction: Nature and Natural History in the Russian North Pacific, 1739–1799." PhD dissertation, Columbia University, 2008.

———. "A 'Havoc Made among Them': Animals, Empire, and Extinction in the Russian North Pacific, 1741–1810." *Environmental History* 16 (September 2011): 585–609.

Joyce, Barry Alan. *The Shaping of American Ethnography: The Wilkes Exploring Expedition, 1838–1842*. Lincoln: University of Nebraska Press, 2001.

Judd, Bernice. *Voyages to Hawai'i before 1860*. Honolulu: University of Hawai'i Press, 1974.

Kaholokula, Joseph Keawe'aimoku. "Colonialism, Acculturation, and Depression among Kānaka Maoli of Hawai'i." In *Penina uliuli: Contemporary Challenges in Mental Health for Pacific Peoples*. Edited by Philip Culbertson and Margaret Nelson Agee. Honolulu: University of Hawai'i Press, 2007.

Kamakau, Samuel M. *Ka Po'e Kahiko: The People of Old*. Honolulu: University of Hawai'i Press, 1964.

Kame'eleihiwa, Lilikalā. *Native Land and Foreign Desires: Pehea Lā E Pono Ai? How Shall We Live in Harmony?* Honolulu: Bishop Museum Press, 1992.

Kashay, Jennifer Fish. "Competing Imperialisms and Hawaiian Authority: The Cannonading of Lāhainā in 1827." *Pacific Historical Review* 77 (August 2008): 369–390.

Kauanui, J. Kēhaulani. *Hawaiian Blood: Colonialism and the Politics of Sovereignty and Indigeneity*. Durham, NC: Duke University Press, 2008.

Kearey, Philip, and Frederck J. Vine. *Global Tectonics*. Oxford: Blackwell Scientific Publications, 1990.

Keay, John. *The Honourable Company: A History of the English East India Company*. New York: Macmillan, 1994.

Kelley, Robin D. G. "How the West Was One: The African Diaspora and the Re-Mapping of U.S. History." In *Rethinking American History in a Global Age*. Edited by Thomas Bender. Berkeley: University of California Press, 2002.

Kenyon, Karl W. *The Sea Otter in the Eastern Pacific Ocean*. Washington, DC: US Bureau of Sport Fisheries and Wildlife, 1969.

Kirch, Patrick. *Feathered Gods and Fishhooks: An Introduction to Hawaiian Archaeology and Prehistory*. Honolulu: University of Hawai'i Press, 1985.

———. *On the Road of the Winds: An Archaeological History of the Pacific Islands*. Berkeley: University of California Press, 2000.

———. "Paleodemography in Kahikinui, Maui: An Archaeological Approach." In *Growth and Collapse of Pacific Island Societies: Archaeological and Demographic Perspectives*. Edited by Patrick V. Kirch and Jean-Louis Rallu. Honolulu: University of Hawai'i Press, 2007.

———. *How Chiefs Became Kings: Divine Kingship and the Rise of Archaic States in Ancient Hawai'i*. Berkeley: University of California Press, 2010.

———. *A Shark Going Inland Is My Chief: The Island Civilization of Ancient Hawai'i*. Berkeley: University of California Press, 2012.

Kirch, Patrick, and Roger Green. *Hawaiki, Ancestral Polynesia: An Essay in Historical Anthropology.* Cambridge: Cambridge University Press, 2001.

Kirch, Patrick V., and Jean-Louis Rallu, eds. *The Growth and Collapse of Pacific Island Societies: Archaeological and Demographic Perspectives.* Honolulu: University of Hawaiʻi Press, 2007.

Knowlton, Edgar C. Jr. "Paul-Emile Botta, Visitor to Hawaiʻi in 1828." *Hawaiian Journal of History* 18 (1984): 13–38.

Korn, Alfons L. "Shadows of Destiny: A French Navigator's View of the Hawaiian Kingdom and Its Government in 1828." *Hawaiian Journal of History* 17 (1983): 1–39.

Korn, Alfons L., and Mary Kawena Pukui. "News from Molokai: The Letters of Peter Young Kaeo (Kekuakalani) to Queen Emma, 1873–1876." *Pacific Historical Review* 32 (February 1963): 20–23.

Kratz, Henry. "Introduction." In *A Voyage Around the World with the Romanzov Expedition in The Years 1815–1818.* By Adelbert von Chamisso. Honolulu: University of Hawaiʻi Press, 1986.

Kroeber, Alfred L. *Yurok Myths.* Berkeley: University of California Press, 1976.

Kupperman, Karen Ordahl. "International at the Creation: Early Modern American History." In *Rethinking American History in a Global Age.* Edited by Thomas Bender. Berkeley: University of California Press, 2002.

Kushner, Howard. "Hellships: Yankee Whaling along the Coast of Russian-America, 1835–1852." *New England Quarterly* 45 (March 1972): 81–95.

Ladurie, Emmanuel Le Roy. *The Mind and Method of the Historian.* Translated by Siân Reynolds and Ben Reynolds. Chicago: University of Chicago Press, 1981.

Laughlin, William S. *Aleuts: Survivors of the Bering Land Bridge.* New York: Holt, Rinehart, and Winston, 1980.

Layton, Thomas N. *The Voyage of the "Frolic": New England Merchants and the Opium Trade.* Stanford, CA: Stanford University Press, 1997.

Leach, Jerry W., and Edmund Ronald Leach. *The Kula: New Perspectives on Massim Exchange.* Cambridge: Cambridge University Press, 1983.

Leland, Donald. *Aboriginal Slavery on the Northwest Coast of North America.* Berkeley: University of California Press, 1997.

Liebersohn, Harry. *The Travelers' World: Europe to the Pacific.* Cambridge, MA: Harvard University Press, 2006.

Leonhart, Joye. "Charles Wilkes: A Biography." In *Magnificent Voyagers: The U.S. Exploring Expedition, 1838–1842.* Edited by Herman J. Viola and Carolyn Margolis. Washington, DC: Smithsonian Institution Press, 1985.

Lightfoot, Kent G. *Indians, Missionaries, and Merchants: The Legacy of Colonial Encounters on the California Frontiers.* Berkeley: University of California Press, 2006.

Lightfoot, Kent, and Otis Parrish. *California Indians and Their Environments: An Introduction.* Berkeley: University of California Press, 2009.

Lightfoot, Kent G., and William S. Simmons. "Culture Contact in Protohistoric California: Social Contexts of Native and European Encounters." *Journal of California and Great Basin Anthropology* 20 (1998): 138–169.

Linnekin, Jocelyn. *Sacred Queens and Women of Consequence: Rank, Gender, and Colonialism in the Hawaiian Islands.* Ann Arbor: University of Michigan Press, 1990.

———. "Contending Approaches." In *The Cambridge History of Pacific Islanders.* Edited by Donald Denoon. Cambridge: Cambridge University Press, 1997.

Liu, David M.K.I. "Eao luau a hualima: Writing and Rewriting the Body and the Nation." *Californian Journal of Health Promotion* (December 2005): 73–75.

Livingstone, Frank B. "On the Origins of Syphilis: An Alternative Approach." *Current Anthropology* 32 (December 1991): 587–590.

Luomala, Katherine. *Voices on the Wind: Polynesian Myths and Chants.* Honolulu: Bishop Museum Press, 1986.

Mackay, David. *In the Wake of Cook: Exploration, Science and Empire.* London: Croom Helm, 1985.

MacLeod, William Christie. "Economic Aspects of Indigenous American Slavery." *American Anthropologist* 30 (October 1928): 632–650.

MacLeod, Roy, and Philip F. Rehbock, eds. *Darwin's Laboratory: Evolutionary Theory and Natural History in the Pacific*. Honolulu: University of Hawai'i Press, 1994.

Mageo, Jeanette Marie. *Theorizing Self in Samoa: Emotions, Genders, and Sexualities*. Ann Arbor: University of Michigan Press, 1998.

Malinowski, Bronislaw. *Argonauts of the Western Pacific: An Account of Native Enterprise and Adventure in the Archipelagoes of Melanesian New Guinea*. New York: Dutton, 1922.

Malo, David. "On the Decrease of Population on the Hawaiian Islands." *Hawaiian Spectator* 2 (April 1839): 127–131.

Mancall, Peter, ed. *The Atlantic World and Virginia*. Chapel Hill: University of North Carolina Press, 2007.

———. *Fatal Journey: The Final Expedition of Henry Hudson—A Tale of Mutiny and Murder in the Arctic*. New York: Basic Books, 2009.

Mapp, Paul W. *The Elusive West and the Contest for Empire, 1713–1763*. Chapel Hill: University of North Carolina Press, 2011.

Marks, Robert. *Tigers, Rice, Silk, and Silt: Environment and Economy in Late Imperial South China*. Cambridge: Cambridge University Press, 1998.

———. "Maritime Trade and the Agro-Ecology of South China, 1685–1850." In *Pacific Centuries: Pacific Rim Economic History since the Sixteenth Century*. Edited by Dennis O. Flynn, A.J.H. Latham, and Lionel Frost. London: Routledge, 1999.

Marshall, Leslie B. "Disease Ecologies of Australia and Oceania." In *The Cambridge World History of Human Disease*. Edited by K. F. Kiple. Cambridge: Cambridge University Press, 1993.

Marshall, Yvonne. "A Political History of the Nuu-chah-nulth: A Case Study of the Mowachaht and Muchalaht Tribes." PhD dissertation, Simon Fraser University, 1993.

Mathew, W. M. "The Imperialism of Free Trade: Peru, 1820–70." *Economic History Review* 21 (December 1968): 562–579.

———. "Peru and the British Guano Market, 1840–1870." *Economic History Review* 23 (April 1970): 112–128.

Matsuda, Matt K. "AHR Forum: The Pacific." *American Historical Review* 111 (June 2006): 758–780.

———. *Pacific Worlds: A History of Seas, Peoples, and Cultures*. Cambridge: Cambridge University Press, 2012.

McArthur, Norma. *Island Populations of the Pacific*. Canberra: Australian National University Press, 1967.

McCall, Lynne, and Rosalind Perry, eds. *California's Chumash Indians: A Project of the Santa Barbara Museum of Natural History Education Center*. Santa Barbara: John Daniel, 1986.

McDougall, Walter A. *Let the Sea Make a Noise: A History of the North Pacific from Magellan to MacArthur*. New York: Basic Books, 1993.

Meleisea, Malama, and Penelope Schoeffel. "Discovering Outsiders." In *The Cambridge History of the Pacific Islanders*. Edited by Donald Denoon. Cambridge: Cambridge University Press, 1997.

Meyer, C., et al. "Syphilis 2001: A Palaeopathological Reappraisal." *HOMO* 53 (2002): 39–58.

Miles, John. *Infectious Diseases: Colonising the Pacific?* Dunedin, NZ: University of Otago Press, 1997.

Miller, David P., and Peter H. Reill, eds. *Visions of Empire: Voyages, Botany, and Representations of Nature*. Cambridge: Cambridge University Press, 1996.

Miller, Gwenn A. *Kodiak Kreol: Communities of Empire in Early Russian America*. Ithaca, NY: Cornell University Press, 2010.

Mills, William J. *Exploring Polar Frontiers: A Historical Encyclopedia*. Vol. 1. Santa Barbara, CA: ABC-CLIO, 2003.

Moorehead, Alan. *The Fatal Impact: An Account of the Invasion of the South Pacific*. New York: Harper and Row, 1966.

Morgan, Theodore. *Hawai'i: A Century of Economic Change, 1778–1876*. Cambridge, MA: Harvard University Press, 1948.

Namias, June. *White Captives: Gender and Ethnicity on the American Frontier*. Chapel Hill: University of North Carolina Press, 1995.

Nash, Linda. *Inescapable Ecologies: A History of Environment, Disease, and Knowledge*. Berkeley: University of California Press, 2006.

Natland, James H. "James Dwight Dana and the Beginnings of Planetary Volcanology." *American Journal of Science* 297 (March 1997): 317–319.

Newell, Jennifer. *Trading Nature: Tahitians, Europeans, and Ecological Exchange*. Honolulu: University of Hawai'i Press, 2010.

Newson, Linda A. "A Historical-Ecological Perspective on Epidemic Disease." In *Advances in Historical Ecology*. Edited by William Balee. New York: Columbia University Press, 1998.

———. "Conquest, Pestilence, and Demographic Collapse in the Early Spanish Philippines." *Journal of Historical Geography* 32 (January 2006): 3–20.

Ogden, Adele. *The California Sea Otter Trade, 1784–1848*. Berkeley: University of California Press, 1941.

Okihiro, Gary. *Island World: A History of Hawai'i and the United States*. Berkeley: University of California Press, 2008.

Owens, Kenneth. *The Wreck of the Sv. Nikolai*. Lincoln: University of Nebraska Press, 2001.

———. "Frontiersman for the Tsar: Timofei Tarakanov and the Expansion of Russian America." *Montana* 56 (Autumn 2006): 3–21.

Pearson, Michael N. "Littoral Society: The Concept and the Problems." *Journal of World History* 17 (December 2006): 353–373.

Pettitt, George A. *The Quileute of La Push, 1775–1945*. Berkeley: University of California Press, 1950.

Pierce, Richard A. *Russia's Hawaiian Adventure, 1815–1818*. Berkeley: University of California Press, 1965.

———. *Russian America: A Biographical Dictionary*. Kingston, ON: Limestone Press, 1990.

Phelps, William Dane. "Solid Men of Boston in the Northwest." In *Fur Traders from New England: The Boston Men in the North Pacific, 1787–1800*. Edited by Briton C. Busch and Barry M. Gough. Spokane, WA: Arthur H. Clark, 1997.

Philbrick, Nathaniel. *Sea of Glory: America's Voyage of Discovery, The U.S. Exploring Expedition, 1838–1842*. New York: Viking, 2003.

Philips, C. H. *The East India Company, 1784–1834*. Manchester, UK: Manchester University Press, 1940.

Pomeranz, Kenneth. *The Great Divergence: China, Europe, and the Making of the Modern World Economy*. Princeton, NJ: Princeton University Press, 2000.

Pomeranz, Kenneth, and Steven Topik. *The World That Trade Created: Society, Culture, and the World Economy, 1400 to the Present*. Armonk, NY: M. E. Sharpe, 1999.

Pourade, Richard F. *Time of the Bells*. San Diego: Union-Tribune Publishing, 1961.

Powell, Mary Lucas, and Della Collins Cook, eds. *The Myth of Syphilis: The Natural History of Treponematosis in North America*. Gainesville: University of Florida Press, 2005.

Prendergast, M. L. "James Dwight Dana: Problems in American Geology." PhD dissertation, University of California, Los Angeles, 1978.

Preston, William. "Portents of Plague from California's Protohistoric Period." *Ethnohistory* 49 (Winter 2002): 69–121.

Pubols, Louise. *The Father of All: The de la Guerra Family, Power, and Patriarchy in Mexican California*. Berkeley: University of California Press, 2009.

Pukui, Mary Kawena, ed. *'Ōlelo No'eau: Hawaiian Proverbs and Poetical Sayings*. Honolulu: Bishop Museum Press, 1983.

Pyne, Stephen J. *How the Canyon Became Grand: A Short History*. New York: Viking, 1998.

Quammen, David. *The Song of the Dodo: Island Biogeography in an Age of Extinctions*. New York: Simon and Schuster, 1996.

Quétel, Claude. *The History of Syphilis*. Translated by Judith Braddock and Brian Pike. Baltimore: Johns Hopkins University Press, 1992.

Quinn, David B., ed. "The Voyage of Juan Rodriquez Cabrillo up the Pacific Coast." In *New American World: A Documentary History of North America to 1612*. New York: Arno Press, 1979.

Radcliffe, Ann Ward. *The Mysteries of Udolpho*. London: G. G. and J. Robinson, 1794.

Rallu, Jean-Louis. "Pre- and Post-Contact Population in Island Polynesia." In *Growth and Collapse of Pacific Island Societies: Archaeological and Demographic Perspectives*. Edited by Patrick V. Kirch and Jean-Louis Rallu. Honolulu: University of Hawai'i Press, 2007.

Ralston, Caroline. "Polyandry, 'Pollution', 'Prostitution': The Problems of Eurocentrism and Androcentrism in Polynesian Studies." In *Crossing Boundaries: Feminisms and the Critique of Knowledges*. Edited by Barbara Caine, E. A. Grosz, and Marie de Lepervanche. Sydney: Allen and Unwin, 1988.

———. "Changes in the Lives of Ordinary Women in Early Post-Contact Hawai'i." In *Family and Gender in the Pacific: Domestic Contradictions and the Colonial Impact*. Edited by Margaret Jolly and Martha Macintyre. Cambridge: Cambridge University Press, 1989.

Ramenofsky, Ann F. *Vectors of Death: The Archaeology of European Contact*. Albuquerque: University of New Mexico Press, 1987.

Ravalli, Richard. "Soft Gold and the Pacific Frontier: Geopolitics and Environment in the Sea Otter Trade." PhD dissertation, University of California, Merced, 2009.

Ray, Arthur. *Indians and the Fur Trade: Their Role as Trappers, Hunters, and Middlemen in the Lands Southwest of Hudson Bay*. Toronto: University of Toronto Press, 1974.

Reid, Joshua Leonard. "'The Sea Is My Country': The Maritime World of the Makah: An Indigenous Borderlands People." PhD dissertation, University of California, Davis, 2009.

Reidman, M. L., and J. A. Estes. *The Sea Otter* (Enhydra lutris): *Behavior, Ecology, and Natural History*. Washington, DC: Fish and Wildlife Service, 1990.

Remini, Robert V. *Daniel Webster: The Man and His Time*. New York: W. W. Norton, 1997.

Richards, John F. *The Unending Frontier: An Environmental History of the Early Modern World*. Berkeley: University of California Press, 2003.

Richards, Rhys. "United States Trade with China, 1784–1814." *American Neptune* 54 (1994): 5–76.

———. *Honolulu: Centre of Trans-Pacific Trade: Shipping Arrivals and Departures, 1820–1840*. Honolulu: Hawaiian Historical Society, 2000.

Ridley, Scott. *Morning of Fire: John Kendrick's Daring American Odyssey in the Pacific*. New York: William Morrow, 2010.

Rozwadowski, Helen M. *Fathoming the Ocean: The Discovery and Exploration of the Deep Sea*. Cambridge, MA: Harvard University Press, 2005.

———. "Ocean's Depths." *Environmental History* 15 (July 2010): 520–525.

Ruby, Robert H., and John A. Brown. *Indian Slavery in the Pacific Northwest*. Spokane, WA: Arthur H. Clark Company, 1993.

Rudwick, Martin J. S. *Bursting the Limits of Time: The Reconstruction of Geohistory in the Age of Revolution*. Chicago: University of Chicago Press, 2005.

———. *Worlds Before Adam: The Reconstruction of Geohistory in the Age of Reform*. Chicago: University of Chicago Press, 2008.

Rupke, Nicolaas A. "Humboldtian Medicine." *Medical History* 40 (July 1996): 293–310.

Ryan, Mary. *Cradle of the Middle Class: The Family in Oneida County, New York, 1790–1865*. Cambridge: Cambridge University Press, 1981.

Ryskamp, Charles. *Boswell: The Ominous Years*. New York: McGraw-Hill, 1963.

Sachs, Aaron. *The Humboldt Current: Nineteenth-Century Exploration and the Roots of American Environmentalism*. New York: Viking, 2006.

Sahlins, Marshall. *Islands of History*. Chicago, University of Chicago Press, 1985.

———. "Cosmologies of Capitalism: The Trans-Pacific Sector of 'The World System.'" In *Culture/Power/History: A Reader in Contemporary Social Theory*. Edited by Nicholas B. Dirks, Geoff Eley, and Sherry B. Ortner. Princeton, NJ: Princeton University Press, 1994.

Salesa, Toelesulusulu Damon. "'The Power of the Physician': Doctors and the 'Dying Maori' in Early Colonial New Zealand." *Health and History* 3 (2001): 13–40.

———. *Racial Crossings: Race, Intermarriage, and the Victorian British Empire*. New York: Oxford University Press, 2011.

Salmond, Anne. *Two Worlds: First Meetings Between Maori and Europeans, 1642–1772*. Honolulu: University of Hawai'i Press, 1991.

———. "Kidnapped: Tuki and Huri's Involuntary Visit to Norfolk Island in 1793." In *From Maps to Metaphors: The Pacific World of George Vancouver*. Edited by Robin Fisher and Hugh Johnston. Vancouver: University of British Columbia Press, 1993.

———. *The Trial of the Cannibal Dog: The Remarkable Story of Captain Cook's Encounters in the South Seas*. New Haven, CT: Yale University Press, 2003.

Sandos, James. *Converting California: Indians and Franciscans in the Missions*. New Haven, CT: Yale University Press, 2004.

Sarafian, Winston L. "Smallpox Strikes the Aleuts." *Alaska Journal* 7 (Winter 1977): 46–49.

Schiebinger, Londa. *Plants and Empire: Colonial Bioprospecting in the Atlantic World*. Cambridge, MA: Harvard University Press, 2004.

Schmitt, Robert C. "The Okuu—Hawai'i's Greatest Epidemic." *Hawai'i Medical Journal* 29 (May–June 1970): 359–364.

———. *The Missionary Censuses of Hawai'i*. Honolulu: Bishop Museum, 1973.

Schmitt, Robert C., and Nordyke, Eleanor C. "Death in Hawai'i: The Epidemics of 1848–49." *Hawaiian Journal of History* 35 (Winter 2001): 1–13.

Shankman, Paul. "The History of Samoan Sexual Conduct and the Mead-Freeman Controversy." *American Anthropologist* 98 (September 1996): 555–567.

Sivasundaram, Sujit. *Nature and the Godly Empire: Science and Evangelical Mission in the Pacific, 1795–1850*. Cambridge: Cambridge University Press, 2005.

Slezkine, Yuri. *Arctic Mirrors: Russia and the Small Peoples of the North*. Ithaca, NY: Cornell University Press, 1994.

Smith, Henry Nash. *Virgin Land: The American West as Symbol and Myth*. Cambridge, MA: Harvard University Press, 1950.

Smith, Michael L. *Pacific Visions: California Scientists and the Environment, 1850–1915*. New Haven, CT: Yale University Press, 1990.

Smith, Terrence Wesley, and Edgar A. Porter, eds. *China in Oceania: Reshaping the Future?* New York: Berghahn Books, 2010.

Spate, O.H.K. *Monopolists and Freebooters*. Minneapolis: University of Minnesota Press, 1983.

Stann, E. Jeffrey. "Charles Whiles as Diplomat." In *Magnificent Voyagers: The U.S. Exploring Expedition, 1838–1842*. Edited by Herman J. Viola and Carolyn Margolis. Washington, DC: Smithsonian Institution Press, 1985.

Stannard, David E. *Before the Horror: The Population of Hawai'i on the Eve of Western Contact*. Honolulu: University of Hawai'i Press, 1989.

———. "Disease and Infertility: A New Look at the Demographic Collapse of Native Populations in the Wake of Western Contact." *Journal of American Studies* 24 (December 1990): 325–350.

———. "Disease, Human Migration, and History." In *The Cambridge World History of Human Disease*. Edited by K. F. Kiple. Cambridge: Cambridge University Press, 1993.

Stanton, William. *The Great United States Exploring Expedition*. Berkeley: University of California Press, 1975.

Stenn, Frederick. "Paul Emile Botta—Assyriologist, Physician." *Journal of the American Medical Association* 174 (November 1969): 1651–1652.

Stewart, T. D. "The Skull of Vendovi: A Contribution of the Wilkes Expedition to the Physical Anthropology of Fiji." *Archaeology and Physical Anthropology in Oceania* 13 (1978): 204–214.

Stoddart, David R. "'This Coral Episode': Darwin, Dana, and the Coral Reefs of the Pacific." In *Darwin's Laboratory: Evolutionary Theory and Natural History in the Pacific*. Edited by Roy MacLeod and Philip F. Rehbock. Honolulu: University of Hawai'i Press, 1994.

Stoler, Ann Laura. *Race and the Education of Desire: Foucault's History of Sexuality and the Colonial Order of Things*. Durham: University of North Carolina Press, 1995.

———. "Preface to the 2010 Edition: Zones of the Intimate in Imperial Formation." In *Carnal Knowledge and Imperial Power: Race and the Intimate in Colonial Rule*. Berkeley: University of California Press, 2010.

Sturgis, William. "The Northwest Fur Trade." *Hunt's Merchants' Magazine* 14 (1846): 534. Reprinted in *Fur Traders from New England: The Boston Men in the North Pacific, 1787–1800*. Edited by Briton C. Busch and Barry Gough. Spokane, WA: Arthur C. Clark Company, 1996.

Swanton, John R. "Big-Tail." In *Haida Texts and Myths*. Washington, DC: Smithsonian Institution, Bureau of American Ethnology, 1905.

Thomas, Nicholas. *Cook: The Extraordinary Voyages of Captain James Cook*. New York: Walker, 2003.

Thrush, Coll. *Native Seattle: Histories from the Crossing-Over Place*. Seattle: University of Washington Press, 2007.

Tonnessen, J. N., and A. O. Johnsen. *A History of Modern Whaling*. Translated by R. I. Christophersen. Berkeley: University of California Press, 1982.

Valle, Rosemary Keupper. "Prevention of Smallpox in Alta California during the Franciscan Mission Period (1769–1833)." *California Medicine* 119 (July 1973): 73–77.

Van Dyke, Paul A. *The Canton Trade: Life and Enterprise on the China Coast, 1700–1845*. Hong Kong: Hong Kong University Press, 2005.

Vaughan, Thomas. *Soft Gold: The Fur Trade & Cultural Exchange on the Northwest Coast of America*. Portland: Oregon Historical Society, 1982.

Vinkovetsky, Ilya. "The Russian-American Company as a Colonial Contractor for the Russian Empire." In *Imperial Rule*. Edited by Alexei Miller and Alfred J. Rieber. Budapest: Central European University Press, 2004.

———. *Russian America: An Overseas Colony of a Continental Empire, 1804–1867*. New York: Oxford University Press, 2011.

Viola, Herman J., and Carolyn Margolis, eds., *Magnificent Voyagers: The U.S. Exploring Expedition, 1838–1842*. Washington, DC: Smithsonian Institution Press, 1985.

Walker, Phillip L., Patricia M. Lambert, Michael Schultz, and Jon M. Erlandson. "The Evolution of Treponemal Disease in the Santa Barbara Channel Area of Southern California." In *The Myth of Syphilis: The Natural History of Treponematosis in North America*. Edited by Mary Lucas Powell and Della Collins Cook. Gainesville: University of Florida Press, 2005.

Walker, Richard. "California's Golden Road to Riches: Natural Resources and Regional Capitalism, 1848–1940." *Annals of the Association of American Geographers* 91 (March 2001): 167–199.

Walsh, Julianne M. "Imagining the Marshalls: Chiefs, Tradition, and the State on the Fringes of United States Empire." PhD dissertation, University of Hawai'i, 2003.

Ward, R. Gerald. "The Pacific *Bêche-de-mer* Trade with Special Reference to Fiji." In *Man in the Pacific Islands: Essays on Geographical Change in the Pacific Islands*. Oxford: Clarendon Press, 1972.

Waterman, T. T. *Yurok Geography*. Berkeley: University of California Press, 1920.

Watt, Sir James. "Medical Aspects and Consequences of Cook's Voyages." In *Captain James Cook and His Times*. Edited by Robin Fisher and Hugh Johnston. Seattle: University of Washington Press, 1979.

Watts, S. J. *Epidemics and History: Disease, Power, and Imperialism*. New Haven, CT: Yale University Press, 1997.

Weber, David. *The Mexican Frontier, 1821–1846: The American Southwest Under Mexico*. Albuquerque: University of New Mexico Press, 1982.

Weisler, Marshall I., and Patrick V. Kirch. "Interisland and Interarchipelago Transfer of Stone Tools in Prehistoric Polynesia." *Proceedings of the National Academy of Science* 93 (February 1996): 1381–1385.

Whaley, Gray H. *Oregon and the Collapse of the Illahee: U.S. Empire and the Transformation of an Indigenous World, 1792–1859*. Chapel Hill: University of North Carolina Press, 2010.

White, Richard. "The Nationalization of Nature." *Journal of American History* 86 (December 1999): 976–986.

Wilcove, David S. *No Way Home: The Decline of the World's Great Animal Migrations.* Washington, DC: Island Press, 2008.

Williams, Glyn. *Voyages of Delusion: The Quest for the Northwest Passage.* New Haven, CT: Yale University Press, 2002.

Wilson, J. Tuzo. "A Possible Origin of the Hawaiian Islands." *Canadian Journal of Physics* 41 (1963): 863–870.

Worster, Donald. *Nature's Economy: A History of Ecological Ideas.* New York: Cambridge University Press, 1994.

———. *A River Running West: The Life of John Wesley Powell.* New York: Oxford University Press, 2001.

Zappia, Nataly. "The Interior World: Trading and Raiding in Native California." PhD dissertation, University of California, Santa Cruz, 2008.

Zilberstein, Anya. "Objects of Distant Exchange: The Northwest Coast, Early America, and the Global Imagination." *William and Mary Quarterly* 64 (July 2007): 589–618.

INDEX

Acapulco (Mexico), 20, 26, 37
Adams, John, 118
Ahab *(Moby-Dick)*, 126
Ahousaht, 87
Alaska
  captive taking in, 76, 210n29
  disease in, 37, 46, 63
  fur trade and, 10, 21, 34, 37, 66
  geology and, 171
  Great Hunt and, 105–108, 111–113
  indigenous people in, 21, 37, 51, 106–108
  Russian rule in, 10, 26, 76, 185
  sex and, 51
  trade and, 9, 10, 13, 20–21, 26, 29, 32, 34, 37, 66
Aleut
  Great Hunt and, 21, 106–111, 114, 128
  Russians and, 51, 73–74, 94
  sex and, 51
  Sv. Nikolai and, 73–74, 91
  trade and, 34, 37, 51
Aleut (whaling ship), 127–128
Aleutian Islands, 51, 59, 105, 171
Alta California. *See* California
American Fur Company, 33
Amethyst, 115–117
Anderson, William, 44
Anopheles mosquito, 66, 68
Antarctic, 38–39
Antarctica, 114, 159–160
Arctocephalus townsendi. See fur seal
Argüello, José Darío, 25
Arrillaga, José Joaquín, 110
Astor, John Jacob, 33–34
Atkinson, Thomas, 123
Atlantic World, 10
Atrevida, 96
Atu, 78–80, 82
Audubon, John James, 151

Australia
  disease in, 44, 58
  geology and, 174
  trade and, 25, 35
  US Exploring Expedition and, 160

Bahía Magdalena. *See* Magdalena Bay (Baja California)
Baja California. *See also* Mexico
  disease in, 14, 59–60
  Great Hunt and, 14, 101–103, 105, 116–119, 121–125, 127–128
  indigenous people and, 60
  missionaries in, 59–60
  trade and, 23–24
Baker, James, 80–82
Banks, Joseph, 43, 54–55, 130, 132–133, 154
Baranov, Aleksandr Andreevich, 108–110
Barrell, Joseph, 15
Bayly, William, 55
Beagle, 164, 173
bêche-de-mer, 30, 38–40, 135
Bell, James, 81
Bellona, 47
Benton, Thomas Hart, 176
Bering Strait, 21, 137–138, 174
Bering, Vitus, 8, 105, 135
Berkh, Vasilii Nikolaevich, 112–113
Bertrand, Marcel, 178
Bishop, Artemas, 58
Bishop, Sereno Edwards, 122–123
Blackfeet, 151
Boit, John, 78
Bolton, Herbert Eugene, 178
Boston, 86–89
Boswell, James, 85
Botta, Paulo Emilio, 144–146, 148–149
Bougainville, Louis Antoine de, 49–51
Bounty, 49

Boyd, Robert, 68
Brackenridge, William D., 158
Braudel, Fernand, 10, 189n21
Brewer, William, 173
Brewster, Mary
  Baja California and, 14, 101, 117–119
  on killing whales, 101–103, 122–123
  portrait of, 100
  U.S.-Mexican War and, 125
  on whaling crew deaths, 101, 119
  whaling voyages of, 9, 14, 99–102, 117–119,
    121–123, 126–128
  on women, 121–122
Brewster, William, 99, 103, 121
Brown, Thomas, 92–93
Buch, Otto von, 163, 169–170
Bulygin, Nikolai Isaakovich, 73–74, 89, 91–93
Burney, James, 43

Cabrillo, Juan Rodriguez, 59, 75, 82–83
California
  captive taking in, 76–77, 82–83
  disease in, 14, 46, 59–63, 67–68, 138
  geology of, 174
  gold rush in, 5, 10, 124, 174, 179, 181–183
  Great Hunt and, 25, 107–111, 117, 124
  indigenous people in, 17–21, 23–24, 51–52,
    59–63, 107–108, 141–143, 145–149, 154,
    182–183, 207n76
  Mexican rule of, 25, 145, 148–149
  missionaries in, 23–24, 60–61, 76–77, 111, 138,
    141–142, 147
  naturalists and, 132, 145–146, 148–149, 154
  Russian presence in, 62, 145–147
  sex and, 51–52, 207n76
  Spanish rule of, 4, 18, 22–25, 109–110, 138,
    141–143, 147, 191n33, 207n76
  trade and, 13, 17–18, 20–21, 23–26, 29–30, 32,
    35, 37, 62
  United States and, 26
Callao (Peru), 20, 24, 26, 30, 36
Callorhinus ursinus. *See* fur seals
Canton (China)
  American presence in, 32–33, 39–40, 117, 181
  British presence in, 4, 13, 30–33, 40–41
  Hong merchants in, 31, 33, 41
  trade and, 13, 19–20, 22, 24–26, 29–33, 35,
    39–42, 105, 107, 111, 117, 179, 181
captives
  Africans as, 76
  conscription and, 76–77, 79–80
  European and American men as, 73–76, 78,
    86–93, 97
  European and American women as, 90, 92, 94
  exchanges and, 8, 14, 78, 80–81, 92–93
  indigenous men as, 18, 76–80, 82–85, 91–92,
    97

  indigenous women as, 76, 80–82, 94–97
  Northwest Coast and, 14, 74–75, 77–82,
    85–97
  Pacific Ocean basin and, 14
  sex and, 81, 95–97
  slavery and, 74, 76, 86, 90, 97
  Sv. Nikolai sailors as, 74
Caroline Islands, 63
Carpenter, John, 87
Cascade Mountains, 174
Catalina Island, 21, 23–24
Catherine, 101, 119
Cayuse, 151
Chamberlin, T. C., 178
Chamisso, Adelbert von
  California and, 138, 141–143
  Chile and, 137
  Hawai'i and, 141
  Kadu and, 15, 129–130, 139–142, 154
  Marshall Islands and, 139–142
  naturalist expeditions and, 9, 11, 15, 129–132,
    149, 156, 184
  portrait of, 131
  Remarks of a Naturalist and, 3
  Rurik and, 136–141
  Russian-American Company and, 138
Chappell, David, 65
Charley, William, 47, 69
Cheyne, Andrew, 63
Chile
  disease in, 63–65
  Great Hunt and, 103, 113–114
  independence and, 132, 137
  naturalists and, 131–132, 135
  trade and, 9, 25, 34–35, 64
China. *See also* Canton (China)
  Opium Wars in, 13, 33
  Pearl River Delta and, 19, 32
  Southeast Asia and, 22
  trade and, 9, 13, 19–20, 22, 24–26, 29–33, 35,
    39–42, 105, 107, 111, 117, 179, 181–182
Chinook, 47, 63, 66–67, 152–153
Choris, Louis, 28, 136, 140–143
*Chronological History of the Discovery of the
  Aleutian Islands* (Berkh), 112–113
Chubb, Lawrence, 178
Chukchi Peninsula (Asia), 21, 138
Chumash, 20–21, 59, 148
cinchona bark, 66–68
Clackamas, 68
Clarion, 32
Clayoquot Sound, 35, 77–79, 85–86
Clerke, Charles
  reputation of, 47–48
  sex and, 54–57
  tuberculosis and death of, 13–14, 43–44,
    47–48

Cleveland, Richard, 24, 191n22
Cocos-Keeling Atoll, 164
Colnett, James, 54, 82, 205n15
Columbia, 29, 77–79, 82
Columbia Rediviva, 3
Columbia River basin. *See also* Northwest Coast
  disease and, 14, 47, 66–68, 70
  fur trade and, 33
  naturalists and, 151
Columbus, Christopher, 10, 75
Commander Islands, 114
Commerson, Philibert, 133
Concomly, 152–154
Convoy, 66, 68–69
Cook Islands, 21, 46
Cook, James
  captive taking and, 82–85, 95
  death of, 8, 14, 43
  disease and, 13–14, 44, 49, 54–58, 62,
    199n69
  Hawai'i and, 27, 47, 49, 54–58, 75
  indigenous people and, 5, 35, 49, 62,
    84–85
  journals of, 5
  New Zealand and, 84–85, 130
  Northwest Coast and, 35, 95
  Northwest Passage and, 135
  Pacific Ocean and, 8–9, 12
Coolidge, Lewis, 9, 115–117, 211n58
Copping, Edward, 123
coral islands
  Dana on, 163–165, 170, 173
  Darwin on, 164–165
  erosion and, 165
  origins of, 164–165
Corals and Coral Islands (Dana), 155, 164
Corney, Peter, 29
Couthouy, Joseph P., 158
Crustacea (Dana), 175
Cunneah, 35

d'Orbigny, Alcide, 174
Dampier, William, 114
Dana, James Dwight
  California and, 158, 174
  Christianity of, 161–162, 167–169, 175–176,
    221n84
  coral islands and, 163–165, 170, 173
  correspondence with Darwin and,
    165–166
  erosion and, 165, 171–172
  geology and, 9, 11–12, 15, 156–159, 161–179,
    184, 219n35
  Hawai'i and, 167–171
  Northwest Coast and, 158, 173–174
  portrait of, 157
  volcanoes and, 163, 168–173, 220n61

Dana, Richard Henry, 18, 23
*Dance of the Inhabitants of California at Mission
  San Francisco* (Choris), 141–142
Daniell, William, 31
Darwin, Charles
  correspondence with Dana and,
    165–166
  geology and, 163–165, 173, 175
  Peru and, 36
Davis, William Heath, 32, 111
Defoe, Daniel, 17
Delano, Amasa, 4–5, 113–114
Descrubita, 135
desertion, 49, 66, 76, 79, 81–83, 99–100,
  124
Discovery, 43–44, 48–49, 55–56, 79–81
disease. *See also individual diseases*
  Alaska and, 37, 46, 63
  Australia and, 44, 58
  Baja California and, 14, 59–60
  California and, 14, 46, 59–63, 67–68, 138
  Chile and, 63–65
  Columbia River basin and, 14, 47, 66–68, 70
  demographic consequences of, 44, 46–47, 52,
    58, 60–62, 70
  environmental conditions and, 45–46, 61, 63,
    66, 68, 196n12
  epidemiology and, 44–47, 56–57, 62–63,
    65–66, 68–69, 71
  European sailors and, 43–44, 71
  Great Hunt and, 115–116
  Hawai'i and, 14, 41–42, 44, 46–47, 53–58, 61,
    63
  indigenous people and, 13–14, 44–47, 52–53,
    58–61, 65, 67–71, 202n118, 202n120,
    203n140
  New Zealand and, 44, 58
  nineteenth-century research on, 46
  Northwest Coast and, 14, 44–47, 63, 66–70,
    149–153
  Pacific Ocean and, 13–14
  Peru, 63
  sex and, 45, 49–52
  Tahiti and, 14, 44, 46, 55, 58, 63–65, 184
  vaccination and, 202n118, 202n127
  "virgin soil epidemics" and, 45
"disease boats," 46, 65–66, 69–70
Dolphin, 43, 47
Dominis, John, 66, 69
Don Quixote, 64–65
Douglas, David, 66–68
Drayton, Joseph, 170
Dryocopus lineatus (Lineated Woodpecker), 151
Duhaut-Cilly, Auguste, California voyages of,
  144–149, 154
Dutch East India Company, 38
dysentry, 44, 60

Eagle, 32
Earth and Man (Guyot), 177
East India Company (EIC), 4, 13, 31–33,
    40–41
Easter Island. *See* Rapa Nui
Ellis, William, 49, 95, 135
Emmert, Paul, 28
Empress of China, 32
Endeavour, 83–84, 154
England. *See* Great Britain
environment. *See* disease; naturalists
erosion, 165, 171–172, 174–175
Eschscholtz, Johann Friedrich, 136, 139–140
ethnography. *See under* naturalists
Eu-stochee-exqua, 87
"European Factories, Canton" (Daniell), 31
Eveline, 181

Face of the Earth (Suess), 178
Fages, Pedro, 60
Fanning, Edmund, 115
Faucon, Edward Horatio, 181–182, 184
Ferrelo, Bartolomé, 82
Fiji
    indigenous people and, 38, 160–161
    naturalists and, 135
    trade and, 21, 30, 38–39
    volcanoes in, 169
Flathead, 63, 151
Forster, George Reinhold, 51, 133, 149, 173
Forster, Johann, 173
Fort Ross (California), 62, 145–147
Fort Simpson, 34, 150
Fort Vancouver, 34, 66–67, 149–150,
    152–154
France
    California and, 143–147
    Great Hunt and, 107, 115
    Hawai'i and, 144
    Tahiti and, 49–50
Franciscan missionaries, 24, 60–61, 138,
    141–142, 147–148
free trade, ideology of, 12, 23–25, 37–40
Frémont, John Charles, 26, 159, 173
Frolic, 181–185
fur seals, 14, 103, 112–117, 135
fur trade. *See also* Great Hunt
    Boston and, 34
    California and, 24, 27, 62
    indigenous people and, 35, 86
    international character of, 34
    Northwest Coast and, 29, 33–34

Gagemeister, Leontii, 112
Gairdner, Meredith
    biography of, 149
    Hawai'i and, 150

interest in human remains and, 15, 152–154
    Northwest Coast and, 149–154
    tuberculosis and, 149, 152–153
Galápagos Islands, 26, 35, 114
Ganymede, 149–150, 154
Gardenia taitensis, 53
geology
    American exceptionalism and, 175–177
    Dana on, 9, 11–12, 15, 156–159, 161–179, 184,
        219n35
    traditional Hawai'ian explanations and,
        166–167, 170–171
Geology (Dana), 156, 165–167, 174–175, 179
Golovnin, Vasily, 85, 91
gonorrhea
    demographic consequences of, 53, 70
    Hawai'i and, 58
    Tahiti and, 55
gray whales
    Baja California and, 14, 101–103, 105, 117–119,
        121–125, 128
    Great Hunt and, 14, 101–103, 117–124, 127,
        184
    names for, 212n80
Gray, Asa, 161–162
Gray, Robert, 3, 77–79, 82
Great Britain. *See also* Cook, James; East India
        Company
    California and, 24, 26
    China and, 13, 30–33, 40–41, 183
    Great Hunt and, 103, 111, 115
    Hawai'i and, 40
    Northwest Coast and, 18–19, 33–34, 107
    Peru and, 36, 185
Great Hunt
    Alaska and, 105–108, 111–113
    Aleuts and, 21, 106–111, 114, 128
    Americans and, 107–111, 113–118, 184
    attacks on boats and, 101, 119–121, 184
    baidarkas (kayaks), 108–111
    Baja California and, 14, 101–103, 105, 116–119,
        121–125, 127–128
    Boston merchants and, 107
    California and, 25, 107–111, 117, 124
    Chile and, 113–115, 117, 128
    disease and, 115–116
    France and, 115
    fur seals and, 14, 103, 112–117
    gray whales and, 14, 101–103, 117–124, 127,
        184
    Great Britain and, 103, 111, 115
    hunting methods and, 102–103, 109–111, 113,
        118, 120–123, 127, 209n11
    hunting weapons and, 104, 113–114, 119, 121
    indigenous people and, 88–89, 103, 106–111,
        114, 116, 119, 128
    industrialization and, 103, 118, 126

Kodiak and, 106, 108, 110
land-based mammals and, 112–113
Northwest Coast and, 88, 107, 109, 127
Russians and, 10, 37, 89, 105–109, 112, 114, 128
scope of, 8, 110, 112–114, 117, 127
sea otters and, 14, 25, 103, 105–113, 128
Spain and, 107, 109–110, 115
U.S. imperial expansion and, 103, 118, 124–126
women and, 121–122
Guyot, Arnold, 177
Gyzelaar, Henry, 32

Hackel, Steven, 61
Haida, 63, 69
Hale, Horatio, 158
Hassell, William Henry, 119
Hau'ofa, Epeli, 5, 70
Hawai'i
  agriculture in, 27
  captives and, 84
  disease in, 14, 41–42, 44, 46–47, 53–58, 61, 63
  elites (*ali'i*) in, 27, 29
  French interests in, 144
  geology and, 166–171
  indigenous people and, 27–28, 41–42, 57–58, 154
  infertility and, 200n83
  land privatization in, 185
  missionaries in, 9, 58
  naturalist exploration and, 9, 131, 135, 154
  okuu (typhoid) in, 41–42
  origin myth of, 166–167
  Polynesian settlement of, 8, 27
  sex and, 9, 27, 49–50, 54–58, 141
  trade and, 9, 13, 20–21, 24–27, 29–30, 32, 35, 40–41
  volcanoes and, 168–172, 220n61
Hayden, Ferdinand, 178
Heard, John, 181
Héros
  California and, 132, 143–147, 154
  Hawai'i and, 49
  naturalists and, 132, 143–144, 154
  sex and, 49
Hibernia, 101, 119–121
Hill, Samuel, 88
Hirsch, August, 46
ho'kwat (wanderers), 73, 90, 94
Hobucket, Ben, 73, 89–92, 94
Hoh, 75–76, 89–92, 97
Honolulu (Hawai'i)
  artistic representations of, 28
  trade and, 27–30, 41
Hope, 79–82

Hoskins, John Box, 78–79
hostages. *See* captives
"hot spots," 172, 179
Howard, Victoria, 68
Huahine, 44, 83
Hudson, Henry, 135
Hudson, John, 19
Hudson, William, 160
Hudson's Bay Company (HBC)
  California and, 24
  fur trade and, 34–35
  Hawai'i and, 29
  Northwest Coast and, 33–35, 63, 66–69, 149–153
Humboldt, Alexander von, 158, 166, 174, 177, 179, 221n84
Hupa, 20

indigenous people. *See also individual groups*
  Alaska and, 21, 37, 51, 106–108
  Baja California and, 60
  California and, 17–21, 23–24, 51–52, 59–63, 107–108, 141–143, 145–149, 154, 182–183, 207n76
  captivity and, 18, 76–85, 91–92, 94–97
  as crew members, 29, 44, 64–66, 73, 78–81, 116, 129, 205n32
  disease and, 13–14, 44–47, 52–53, 58–61, 65, 67–71, 202n118, 202n120, 203n140
  Fiji and, 38, 160–161
  Great Hunt and, 88–89, 103, 106–111, 114, 116, 119, 128
  Hawai'i and, 27–28, 41–42, 57–58, 154
  initial European encounters and, 75–76, 90
  naturalists and, 8, 15, 129–132, 139–141, 151–154
  Northwest Coast and, 35–36, 63, 75, 85–97, 151
  sex and, 13, 18, 44–45, 48–52, 55, 59–60, 81, 94–97
  Spanish Empire and, 82–83, 137–138, 141, 207n76
  trade and, 4, 9, 17–21, 34–35, 37, 41, 51, 78, 88, 94
  violence and, 35–36, 38, 77–78, 92, 160
influenza
  Alaska and, 37
  California and, 62
  Chile and, 46
  Northwest Coast, 68
  Pacific voyages and, 44
  Samoa and, 63
Ingraham, Joseph, 79–82
International Fur Seal Treaty (1911), 111
Ishmael (*Moby-Dick*), 185
Isla Cedros, 23, 111, 116, 128

Jackall, 3–4, 187n1
Jameson, Robert, 150–151
Japan, 185
Jenny, 80–82, 94
Jesuit missionaries, 59–60
Jewitt, John, captivity of, 86–89, 91, 93, 97
*Journal of a Voyage between China and the
    North-Western Coast of America*
    (Shaler), 19
Juan Fernández Islands, 103, 113, 115, 117, 128

Kadu
    Alaska and, 129, 140
    Chamisso and, 15, 129–130, 139–142, 154
    Hawai'i and, 129, 141
    portrait of, 130
kakai mei tahi ("people from the sea"), 5
Kalani'opu'u, 84
Kamakau, Samuel, 46
Kamāmalu, 144
Kamchatka Peninsula, 35, 37, 43, 59, 114
Kamehameha, 12, 19, 29, 41–42
Kamehameha II (Liholiho), 29, 41, 144
Kangxi emperor (China), 22
Karok, 20
Kaua'i (Hawai'i), 21, 55–56, 58, 170–171
Kendrick, John
    death of, 3–4, 77, 187n1
    indigenous people and, 4
    merchants and, 4, 15
    naval expeditions of, 3–5, 11, 15, 77,
        184–185
Kennedy, John Frederick, 150
Kiakhta, 105
Kilauea (Hawai'i), 168–171
King, Clarence, 173, 178
King, James, 43, 84
Klikitat, 69
Kodiak (Alutiiq)
    disease and, 37
    Great Hunt and, 21, 37, 106, 108, 110
    Sv. Nikolai and, 73–74
Kodiak Island, 108, 110
Kotzebue, Otto von, 130, 136–139
Kow, 35
Kupperman, Karen, 26

La Pérouse, Jean-François de Galaup de, 8, 49,
    85, 107, 135
Lady Washington, 3–4, 15, 36, 77
Lahaina (Hawai'i), 27
Le Bordelais, 34
Le Netrel, Edmond, 49, 144–148
Legaic, 35
Lelia Byrd
    California and, 17–20, 22–23, 27, 47
    Canton and, 42

    cargo of, 18–19
    Hawai'i and, 19, 27, 41–42, 49
    sex and, 49, 94
León, Joaquín Velázquez de, 60
Leonore, 127
Lewis, Meriwether, 152
Light, Allen, 111
Liholiho. *See* Kamehameha II
Lima (Peru), 36, 144
Lua Pele, 169
Lydia, 87, 89, 92–93
Lyell, Charles, 164, 166

M'Konochie, Alexander, 39–40
macana, 146–147
Macao, 32, 35
Macartney, Lord George, 31
Magdalena Bay (Baja California), gray whales
    and, 12, 101–103, 105, 117–121, 124–125,
    127–128, 181
Magellan, Ferdinand, 8
Mai-mai-ch'eng, 105
Makah, 87, 91–93, 209n11
malaria
    California and, 46, 68
    Mexico and, 36
    Northwest Coast and, 66–69, 150, 152
    origin of, 68
    Pacific voyages and, 44
    treatment for, 66–68
Malaspina, Alejandro, 12, 85, 95–96, 132, 135
Malo, David, 57–58
Manila (Philippines), 22, 38, 45
Manual of Geology (Dana), 175
Maori, 51, 83–85, 130, 206n60, 219n42
Maquinna (Chief of the Nuu-chah-nulth), 12, 35,
    78, 86–89
Marquesas Islands
    disease and, 58
    sex and, 49–50
    trade and, 26, 35
Marsh, George Perkins, 178
Marshall Islands, 129–130, 136, 160
Martinez, Don Ignacio, 32, 145
Martínez, José Longinos, 61
Más a Tierra Island (Chile), 114
Más Afuera Island (Chile), 113–115
Matavai Bay, 64, 83
Matsuda, Matt, 11
Maui (Hawai'i), 54–56, 58, 120–121, 171
Maui (Polynesian demigod), 166–167, 219n42
Mauna Loa, 150, 170–171
McDuffie, George, 126
McKay, William, 67, 93
McLoughlin, John, 67
Meares, John, 35
measles, 46, 60, 63, 65, 144

Melanesia, 21
Melville, Herman, 49, 126, 185
Menard, H. W., 178
Menzies, Archibald, 133
Mercury, 55, 110–111
Messenger of Peace, 63
Mexico. *See also* Baja California
    independence of, 41, 132
    trade and, 20, 22, 24, 26, 30, 36–37
    war with the United States and, 10, 12,
        124–126, 183
Minerva, 115
Mission San Francisco de Asís (California),
        141–142
Mission San Gabriel (California), 61
Mission San Luis Obispo (California), 23
Mission Santa Clara (California), 147
missionaries
    Baja California and, 59–60
    California and, 23–24, 60–61, 76–77, 111, 138,
        141–142, 147
    Franciscans and, 24, 60–61, 138, 141–142,
        147–148
    Jesuits and, 59–60
Mitom Pomo. *See* Pomo
Miwok, 62
Mo'orea, 64–65, 83
Moby-Dick (Melville), 126, 185
Monarch, 46, 63
Monkhouse, William, 83
Morgan, Theodore, 192n42
Morrell, Abby Jane, 38–40, 94
Morrell, Benjamin, 38–39
Mount Hood, 154
Mowachaht, 86–88
Moziño, José Mariano, 51, 60

Naiad, 63
Napoleonic Wars, 11, 25, 38, 132, 135, 138–139,
        155
Native Americans. *See* indigenous people
naturalists
    birds and, 145–146, 151
    California and, 132, 145–146, 148–149, 154
    Chile and, 131–132, 135
    ethnography and, 132, 134, 136, 138–144,
        147–149, 151, 154
    fish and, 146
    Hawai'i and, 9, 131, 135, 154
    Héros and, 132, 143–144, 154
    human remains and, 140, 152–154, 217n83
    imperialism and, 132, 134–135, 137–138
    indigenous people and, 8, 15, 129–132,
        139–141, 151–154
    Northwest Coast and, 150–154
    rabbits, 145–146
    Rurik and, 129, 132, 136–140

"Scientifics" and, 133–135
    specimen gathering and, 8, 67, 130, 133–135,
        140, 144–145, 149–151, 154
    trade and, 135
Necker, Louis Albert, 163
Neisseria gonorrhoeae. See gonorrhea
New Zealand
    captive taking and, 83–85
    disease and, 44, 58
    geology and, 163
    sex and, 51
    volcanoes and, 169
Newson, Linda, 196n12
Nez Perce, 63, 151
Ni'ihau (Hawai'i), 21, 55, 79
Nicholas (cook on *Discovery*), 82
Nichols, Mr., 120
Nidever, George, 111
Nootka Sound, 12, 34–35, 80–81, 85–89, 95
Northeast Passage, 139
Northwest Coast
    captives and, 14, 74–75, 77–82, 85–97
    disease and, 14, 44–47, 63, 66–70, 149–153
    fur trade and, 30, 33–35, 66, 77, 85–86
    geology of, 174
    Great Britain and, 18–19, 33–34, 107
    Great Hunt and, 88, 107, 109, 127
    indigenous people and, 35–36, 63, 75, 85–97,
        151
    naturalists and, 150–154
    Russians and, 33–34, 109
    sex and, 51, 95–96
    Spanish Empire and, 12, 33–34
    trade and, 13, 25, 30, 33–35, 66, 77, 85–86, 94
Northwest Passage, 83, 134–139, 159
Norway, 127
Nuu-chah-nulth (Nootka)
    captives and, 77–79, 82, 86–89
    sex and, 51
    subsistence crisis of, 12
    trade and, 4, 78

O'Cain, 22, 89, 109–111
O'Cain, Joseph, 89, 108–110
"Observations during a Voyage from England to
        Fort Vancouver" (Gairdner), 150
"Observations sur les habitans de la Californie"
        (Botta), 148
Ogden, Peter Skene, 66–67, 191n32
O'ahu (Hawai'i), 21, 29, 125
Okhotsk (Russia), 24, 105–106
"On American Geological History" (Dana),
        175–176
Opai, 79–82
opium, 13, 33, 42, 148, 181–182
Oregon, 34, 68, 82, 173–174. *See also* Northwest
        Coast

"Origin of the Grand Outline Features of the Earth" (Dana), 162, 175
Ortega, Don Juan, 23, 32
Owyhee, 66, 68–70, 203n132

Pacific Northwest. *See* Northwest Coast
Pacific Plate, 169, 171–172
Pacific Rim
  imperial rivalry and, 4–5, 11, 38
  trade and, 4–5, 8–9, 11–13, 19–22, 26, 37–40, 70, 76
Pacific World, concept of, 10–11
Paez, Juan, 82
Palouses, 151
Paty, Henry, 64
Paty, John, 64–65, 184
Paul I (Tsar of Russia), 37
Payeras, Mariano, 61
Peacock
  Great Hunt and, 110–111
  Hawai'i and, 170
  Northwest Coast and, 155, 173–174
  United States Exploration Expedition and, 160, 170, 173–174
Peale, Titian R., 158
Peard, George, 61
Pele, 168–172
Perkins, John, 99–101, 184
Perkins, Thomas, 125
Perry, Matthew, 185
Peru
  disease in, 63
  Great Britain and, 36, 185
  independence and, 41, 132
  naturalists and, 135
  trade and, 9, 13, 20, 25–26, 34–36, 45, 183–185
Petrovna, Anna, 73–74, 89, 91–94
Philippines
  disease and, 59
  geology and, 170
  trade and, 9, 22, 24, 26, 38, 45
phrenology, 152–154
Pickering, Charles, 133, 158, 170
Piegans, 151
pinta, 52
Plan of the English Commerce (Defoe), 17
Plasmodium parasite, 66
Plowden, N. H. C., 32
Point Ellice, 152
Point Loma (California), 145–146
Polk, James K., 125–126
Polynesia. *See also individual islands*
  disease in, 8
  geology and, 170–172
  sex and, 51
  trade and, 21

Pomo, 20, 62, 182–183
Porpoise, 156
Port Ellice, 152
Port Mulgrave, 96
Portlock, Nathaniel, 85, 202n120
Powell, John Wesley, 173, 178
Pribilof Islands, 114, 128
Purea, 83

Quileute, 75, 89–91, 94
quinine, 66–68

Ra'iatea, 83
Raheina, 80–82, 94, 97
Ralston, Caroline, 50
Rapa Nui (Easter Island), 8, 49–50
Ratak, 129–130, 138–142
Raven, 152
Reao, 63
"Remarks and Opinions of the Naturalist of the Expedition" (Chamisso), 137–138
Resolution, 43–44, 48–49, 55–56, 83
Reynolds, Sam, 156
Reynolds, William, 48–50, 133, 155–156, 160
Rich, William, 158
Richardson, John, 152–154
Ring of Fire, 169–170, 174
Riou, Edward, 56
Ripoll, Antonio, 148
Ritter, William, 178
Rives, Jean-Baptiste, 144, 216n44
Ro-Veidovi, 161, 218n18
Rocky Mountains, 174
Rodríguez, Manuel, 23
Rollin, Claude-Nicolas, 54
Roquefeuil, M. Camille de, 34
Royal Philippine Company, 38, 107
Rumiantsev, Nikolai Petrovich, 135–136, 138–139, 154
Rurik
  California and, 138, 141
  Hawai'i and, 141
  indigenous people and, 139–140
  Marshall Islands and, 129–130, 136, 139–140
  naturalists and, 129, 132, 136–140
  Northwest Passage and, 135–139
Russia
  Alaska and, 10, 26, 76, 185
  Aleuts and, 51, 73–74, 94
  California and, 62, 145–147
  fur trade and, 19, 37, 51
  Great Hunt and, 10, 37, 89, 105–109, 112, 114, 128
  Northwest Coast and, 33–34, 109

Russian-American Company (RAC)
  Alaska and, 37, 138, 185
  California and, 24
  captives and, 74
  Great Hunt and, 10, 37, 89, 107–109, 112
  Hawai'i and, 93

Sahlins, Marshall, 50, 192n44
Saint Lawrence Island, 138, 140
Salish, 63
Salter, John, 86, 88–89
Samoan Islands. *See also individual islands*
  captives and, 83
  disease and, 63
  sex and, 48
  trade and, 21
  US Exploring Expedition and, 160, 164
Samwell, David, 49, 55, 95
San Benito (Baja California), 116–117
San Blas (Mexico), 20, 26, 36–37, 66
San Carlos Mission (California), 61
San Diego (California), 19, 23, 61, 109–110
San Francisco (California), 110–111, 141–143, 182
San Ignacio (Baja California), 60, 127
San Quintín (Baja Caliofrnia), 23, 109–110
San Salvador, 83
Sandwich Islands. *See* Hawai'i
Santa Rosa Island, 59
Sauer, Martin, 107, 149
Sauvie Island, 67
Scammon, Charles, 102, 104, 121, 124, 127
scarlet fever, 46
scientific investigations. *See* naturalists
Scott, Winfield, 125
sea otters
  fur of, 106
  Great Hunt and, 14, 25, 103, 105–113, 128
  mating and, 106
  value of, 103, 105–106, 111, 128
Seven Years' War, 11, 47, 134
sex. *See also* gonorrhea; syphilis
  California and, 51–52, 207n76
  captives and, 81, 95–97
  coercion and, 45, 50–52
  disease and, 45, 49–52
  between indigenous people and Europeans, 13, 18, 44–45, 48–52, 55, 59–60, 81, 94–97
  Northwest Coast and, 51, 95–96
  prostitution and, 50–51, 95–96
  Spanish Empire and, 51, 58–61, 96–97, 207n76
  status and, 50
  Tahiti and, 44, 49–51, 55
  trade and, 50–52
Shaler, William
  California and, 17–20, 23–27, 47, 51–52
  China and, 9, 13, 17, 19, 27

Hawai'i and, 19, 27, 41–42
  indigenous people and, 17–18, 20, 23–24, 41–42, 47, 49, 51–52
  sex and, 49, 51–52
  trading methods of, 40
  voyages of, 17–18, 22, 41, 49, 191n22
Shasta, 20
Sierra Nevada Mountains, 159, 174
Silliman, Benjamin, 161–162
Sitka (Alaska)
  disease in, 46
  Great Hunt and, 37, 110–111
  Russians in, 92–93
  trade and, 20, 26, 29, 36–37
Skull Gulch, 59
Slobodchikov, Pavel, 19
smallpox
  Alaska and, 37
  Baja California and, 60
  California and, 62–63
  Chile and, 64
  Northwest Coast and, 46–47, 63
  Peru and, 201n117
  Tahiti and, 64–65, 184
Smith, James, 101, 119–121
Smith, Jedediah, 24, 66
Smith, Richard, 101
Smith, Seth, 116–117
Smithsonian Institution, 153, 159
Society islands, 35, 83, 164
Solander, Daniel, 130
South China Sea, 22
Southeast Asia, 9, 21–22. *See also* Philippines
Southworth, Eli, 64
Spanish Empire
  California and, 4, 18, 22–25, 109–110, 138, 141–143, 147, 191n33, 207n76
  disease and, 59–61, 70
  Great Hunt and, 107, 109–110, 115
  independence movements and, 10, 12, 40–41, 132, 137, 143
  indigenous people and, 82–83, 137–138, 141, 207n76
  Northwest Coast and, 12, 33–34
  sex and, 51, 58–61, 96–97, 207n76
  trade and, 9, 22, 36, 110
sperm oil, 118, 126–127
Steller, Georg, 105, 132–133, 135
Stevens, Joshua, 120
Stoler, Ann, 11
Sturgis, William, 106–107
Suess, Eduard, 178
Sv. Nikolai. See also Tamana
  Aleut and, 73–74, 91
  crew of, 73–76
  purchase of, 19
  shipwreck of, 74–76, 89–91, 93–94

syphilis
  Baja California and, 60
  California and, 59, 61
  demographic consequences of, 52–53, 57–58, 60, 70
  European outbreaks of, 53
  European sailors and, 13, 44, 53, 55
  Hawai'i and, 41, 54, 56–58
  indigenous people and, 13, 41, 46, 52–53, 58–61, 70
  origins of, 53, 56–57
  physical symptoms of, 52, 54
  treatment of, 53, 55, 56–57
  Treponema pallidum bacterium and, 52–53
System of Mineralogy (Dana), 162, 175

Tabiteuea, 160
Tahiti
  captives and, 82–83
  coral islands and, 164–165
  disease in, 14, 44, 46, 55, 58, 63–65, 184
  sex and, 44, 49–51, 55
  trade and, 26
  US Exploring Expedition, 160, 164–165, 169
  volcanoes in, 169
Tamana, 19, 73. *See also Sv. Nikolai*
Tarakanov, Timofei
  biography of, 93
  captivity narrative of, 9, 14, 74–75, 89–93, 97, 184
  Great Hunt and, 109–110
  Sv. Nikolai and, 73–74
Te Taniwha, Horeta, 84–85, 130
Thompson, John, 86–88
Tiger, whale hunting by. *See also* Brewster, Mary
  Baja California and, 14, 101–103, 105, 117–119, 121–125, 128
  crew deaths and, 100–101
  Hawai'i and, 99–100
  Northwest Coast and, 127
Tillamooks, 63
Tlingit, 46, 63, 95–96, 107, 202n120
Tolmie, William, 69, 150
Tolowa, 20
Tonga, 21, 83, 120
Tongva (Gabrielino), 21, 24
Tootiscoosettle, 77–78, 82, 97
trade
  Alaska and, 9, 10, 13, 20–21, 26, 29, 32, 34, 37, 66
  Baja California and, 23–24
  California and, 13, 17–18, 20–21, 23–26, 29–30, 32, 35, 37, 62
  China and, 9, 13, 19–20, 22, 24–26, 29–33, 35, 39–42, 105, 107, 111, 117, 179, 181–182
  Defoe on, 17
  Fiji and, 21, 30, 38–39

  Hawai'i and, 9, 13, 20–21, 24–27, 29–30, 32, 35, 40–41
  indigenous people and, 4, 9, 17–21, 35, 37, 41, 78, 88, 94
  Mexico and, 20, 22, 24, 26, 30, 36–37
  Northwest Coast and, 13, 25, 30, 33–35, 66, 77, 85–86, 94
  Pacific Rim and, 4–5, 8–9, 11–13, 19–22, 26, 37–40, 70, 76
  Peru and, 9, 13, 20, 25–26, 34–36, 45, 183–185
  Philippines and, 9, 22, 24, 26, 38, 45
  Spanish Empire and, 9, 22, 36, 110
Treponema pallidum. *See* syphilis
Trescott, 119
Trinidad Bay (California), 17–18, 110
Tsuräu. *See* Trinidad Bay
Tuamotus, 164, 171
tuberculosis
  Europeans and, 13–14, 43–44, 47–48, 149, 152–153
  Hawai'i and, 41, 47, 58
  Northwest Coast and, 149, 152–153
Turnbull, John, 39
Tutaha, 83
Tutuila ("Emma"), 48
Twain, Mark, 101
Tyler Doctrine, 125
Tymarow, 80–82, 94, 97
typhoid, 41–42, 46, 58
typhus, 60

Ulatilla, Machee ("Yutramaki"), 87, 92–93, 97
Unalaska (Alaska), 129, 137, 140
United States
  China and, 32–33, 39–40, 117, 181
  Great Hunt and, 107–111, 113–118, 184
  imperial expansion and, 8, 10, 12, 103, 158–159, 173, 176–178, 183
  war with Mexico and, 10, 12, 124–126, 183
United States (whaling ship), 101, 120–121
United States Exploring Expedition (US Ex. Ex.).
    See also Dana, James Dwight
  destinations of, 160
  ethnography and, 159
  Fiji and, 160–161
  indigenous people and, 62–63, 160–161
  Northwest Coast and, 155–156
  reports of, 101, 156, 159, 164, 174, 179
  scientists on, 158
  specimen collection and, 159
  Tahiti and, 164–165
  U.S. imperial expansion and, 158–159, 173, 177–178, 183
Upquesta, 87
US-Mexico War, 10, 12, 124–126, 183
Utica (New York), 161–162

Valparaiso (Chile), 63–65, 164
Vancouver Island, 4, 77, 82, 88, 105
Vancouver, George, 79–82, 85, 135, 181
Vasadre y Vega, Vicente, 107
venereal disease. *See* gonorrhea; sex; syphilis
Veniaminov, Ivan, 109
Vermilyea, L. H., 121
Vesuvius, 162, 168–169, 172
"View of Honolulu" (Emmert), 28
View of the Presidio San Francisco (Choris),
    142–143
Vincennes, 48, 133
volcanoes
    Dana on, 163, 168–174, 220n61
    Fiji and, 169
    Hawai'i and, 168–172, 220n61
    New Zealand and, 169
    Tahiti and, 169
von Krusenstern, Adam Johann, 135
von Langsdorff, Georg Heinrich, 111

Wailuku River (Hawai'i), 21
Walla-Walla, 151
Wallace, Alfred Russel, 173
Wallis, Samuel, 49, 75
Webster, Daniel, 125–126
whale oil, 14, 101, 103, 118, 126–127
whaling. *See* Great Hunt
Whitney, Josiah, 173, 178
whooping cough *(Bordetella pertussis)*, 63

Wickaninish, 35, 78–79, 82
Wilkes, Charles
    California and, 174
    court martial of, 156, 159–160
    Hawai'i and, 170
    naturalists and, 133, 161
    Tahiti and, 63
    US Exploring Expedition and, 85,
        101, 156, 159–161, 170,
        173–174
Wilkinson, Ledger, 119
Willamette River, 67
William Lee, 122
Williams, John, 73, 196n15
Williams, Wells, 179
Wilson, Charles, 65
Wilson, Henry, 66
Wilson, John Tuzo, 172
Winship, Jonathan, 109–110
Wintu, 20
Wiyot, 20
Work, John, 67
Wyllie, Robert C., 30

Yap, 63
yaws, 52, 198n56
Yurok, 17–20, 51–52, 110–111
Yutramaki. *See* Ulatilla, Machee

Zoophytes (Dana), 164, 175

CPSIA information can be obtained
at www.ICGtesting.com
Printed in the USA
BVOW08s1225221116

468622BV00004B/6/P